terra australis 54

Terra Australis reports the results of archaeological and related research within the south and east of Asia, though mainly Australia, New Guinea and island Melanesia — lands that remained terra australis incognita to generations of prehistorians. Its subject is the settlement of the diverse environments in this isolated quarter of the globe by peoples who have maintained their discrete and traditional ways of life into the recent recorded or remembered past and at times into the observable present.

List of volumes in Terra Australis

1. *Burrill Lake and Currarong: Coastal Sites in Southern New South Wales*. R.J. Lampert (1971)
2. *Ol Tumbuna: Archaeological Excavations in the Eastern Central Highlands, Papua New Guinea*. J.P. White (1972)
3. *New Guinea Stone Age Trade: The Geography and Ecology of Traffic in the Interior*. I. Hughes (1977)
4. *Recent Prehistory in Southeast Papua*. B. Egloff (1979)
5. *The Great Kartan Mystery*. R. Lampert (1981)
6. *Early Man in North Queensland: Art and Archaeology in the Laura Area*. A. Rosenfeld, D. Horton and J. Winter (1981)
7. *The Alligator Rivers: Prehistory and Ecology in Western Arnhem Land*. C. Schrire (1982)
8. *Hunter Hill, Hunter Island: Archaeological Investigations of a Prehistoric Tasmanian Site*. S. Bowdler (1984)
9. *Coastal South-West Tasmania: The Prehistory of Louisa Bay and Maatsuyker Island*. R. Vanderwal and D. Horton (1984)
10. *The Emergence of Mailu*. G. Irwin (1985)
11. *Archaeology in Eastern Timor, 1966–67*. I. Glover (1986)
12. *Early Tongan Prehistory: The Lapita Period on Tongatapu and its Relationships*. J. Poulsen (1987)
13. *Coobool Creek*. P. Brown (1989)
14. *30,000 Years of Aboriginal Occupation: Kimberley, North-West Australia*. S. O'Connor (1999)
15. *Lapita Interaction*. G. Summerhayes (2000)
16. *The Prehistory of Buka: A Stepping Stone Island in the Northern Solomons*. S. Wickler (2001)
17. *The Archaeology of Lapita Dispersal in Oceania*. G.R. Clark, A.J. Anderson and T. Vunidilo (2001)
18. *An Archaeology of West Polynesian Prehistory*. A. Smith (2002)
19. *Phytolith and Starch Research in the Australian-Pacific-Asian Regions: The State of the Art*. D. Hart and L. Wallis (2003)
20. *The Sea People: Late-Holocene Maritime Specialisation in the Whitsunday Islands, Central Queensland*. B. Barker (2004)
21. *What's Changing: Population Size or Land-Use Patterns? The Archaeology of Upper Mangrove Creek, Sydney Basin*. V. Attenbrow (2004)
22. *The Archaeology of the Aru Islands, Eastern Indonesia*. S. O'Connor, M. Spriggs and P. Veth (eds) (2005)
23. *Pieces of the Vanuatu Puzzle: Archaeology of the North, South and Centre*. S. Bedford (2006)
24. *Coastal Themes: An Archaeology of the Southern Curtis Coast, Queensland*. S. Ulm (2006)
25. *Lithics in the Land of the Lightning Brothers: The Archaeology of Wardaman Country, Northern Territory*. C. Clarkson (2007)
26. *Oceanic Explorations: Lapita and Western Pacific Settlement*. S. Bedford, C. Sand and S. P. Connaughton (eds) (2007)
27. *Dreamtime Superhighway: Sydney Basin Rock Art and Prehistoric Information Exchange*. J. McDonald (2008)
28. *New Directions in Archaeological Science*. A. Fairbairn, S. O'Connor and B. Marwick (eds) (2008)
29. *Islands of Inquiry: Colonisation, Seafaring and the Archaeology of Maritime Landscapes*. G. Clark, F. Leach and S. O'Connor (eds) (2008)
30. *Archaeological Science Under a Microscope: Studies in Residue and Ancient DNA Analysis in Honour of Thomas H. Loy*. M. Haslam, G. Robertson, A. Crowther, S. Nugent and L. Kirkwood (eds) (2009)
31. *The Early Prehistory of Fiji*. G. Clark and A. Anderson (eds) (2009)
32. *Altered Ecologies: Fire, Climate and Human Influence on Terrestrial Landscapes*. S. Haberle, J. Stevenson and M. Prebble (eds) (2010)
33. *Man Bac: The Excavation of a Neolithic Site in Northern Vietnam: The Biology*. M. Oxenham, H. Matsumura and N. Kim Dung (eds) (2011)
34. *Peopled Landscapes: Archaeological and Biogeographic Approaches to Landscapes*. S. Haberle and B. David (eds) (2012)
35. *Pacific Island Heritage: Archaeology, Identity & Community*. J. Liston, G. Clark and D. Alexander (eds) (2011)
36. *Transcending the Culture–Nature Divide in Cultural Heritage: Views from the Asia-Pacific region*. S. Brockwell, S. O'Connor and D. Byrne (eds) (2013)
37. *Taking the High Ground: The archaeology of Rapa, a fortified island in remote East Polynesia*. A. Anderson and D.J. Kennett (eds) (2012)
38. *Life on the Margins: An Archaeological Investigation of Late Holocene Economic Variability, Blue Mud Bay, Northern Australia*. P. Faulkner (2013)
39. *Prehistoric Marine Resource Use in the Indo-Pacific Regions*. R. Ono, A. Morrison and D. Addison (eds) (2013)
40. *4000 Years of Migration and Cultural Exchange: The Archaeology of the Batanes Islands, Northern Philippines*. P. Bellwood and E. Dizon (eds) (2013)
41. *Degei's Descendants: Spirits, Place and People in Pre-Cession Fiji*. Aubrey Parke. M. Spriggs and D. Scarr (eds) (2014)
42. *Contextualising the Neolithic Occupation of Southern Vietnam: The Role of Ceramics and Potters at An Son*. C. Sarjeant (2014)
43. *Journeys into the Rainforest: Archaeology of Culture Change and Continuity on the Evelyn Tableland, North Queensland*. Å. Ferrier (2015)
44. *An Archaeology of Early Christianity in Vanuatu: Kastom and Religious Change on Tanna and Erromango, 1839–1920*. J.L. Flexner (2016)
45. *New Perspectives in Southeast Asian and Pacific Prehistory*. P.J. Piper, H. Matsumura and D. Bulbeck (eds) (2017)
46. *Ten Thousand Years of Cultivation at Kuk Swamp in the Highlands of Papua New Guinea*. J. Golson, T. Denham, P. Hughes, P. Swadling and J. Muke (eds) (2017)
47. *The Archaeology of Rock Art in Western Arnhem Land, Australia*. B. David, P. Taçon, J-J. Delannoy, J-M. Geneste (eds) (2017)
48. *The Archaeology of Sulawesi: Current Research on the Pleistocene to the Historic Period*. S. O'Connor, D. Bulbeck and J. Meyer (eds) (2018)
49. *Drawing in the Land: Rock Art in the Upper Nepean, Sydney Basin, New South Wales*. J. Dibden (2019)
50. *The Spice Islands in Prehistory: Archaeology in the Northern Moluccas, Indonesia*, P. Bellwood (ed.) (2019)
51. *Archaeologies of Island Melanesia: Current approaches to landscapes, exchange and practice*, M. Leclerc and J. Flexner (eds) (2019)
52. *Debating Lapita: Distribution, Chronology, Society and Subsistence*, S. Bedford and M. Spriggs (eds) (2019)
53. *Forts and Fortification in Wallacea: Archaeological and Ethnohistoric Investigations*. S. O'Connor, A. McWilliam and S. Brockwell (eds) (2020)

terra australis 54

Archaeological Perspectives on Conflict and Warfare in Australia and the Pacific

Edited by Geoffrey Clark
and Mirani Litster

ANU PRESS

Published by ANU Press
The Australian National University
Canberra ACT 2600, Australia
Email: anupress@anu.edu.au

Available to download for free at press.anu.edu.au

ISBN (print): 9781760464882
ISBN (online): 9781760464899

WorldCat (print): 1298875799
WorldCat (online): 1298875749

DOI: 10.22459/TA54.2021

This title is published under a Creative Commons Attribution-NonCommercial-NoDerivatives 4.0 International (CC BY-NC-ND 4.0).

The full licence terms are available at creativecommons.org/licenses/by-nc-nd/4.0/legalcode

Terra Australis Editorial Board: Sue O'Connor, Sally Brockwell, Ursula Frederick, Tristen Jones, Ceri Shipton and Mathieu Leclerc
Series Editor: Sue O'Connor

Cover design and layout by ANU Press. Cover photograph: Marquesan war club (U'u), National Gallery of Australia, Canberra (Object: 2008.185). Reproduction Licence 14092021.

This book is published under the aegis of the Terra Australis Editorial Board of the ANU Press.

This edition © 2022 ANU Press

Contents

List of figures		vii
List of tables		xi
1.	Archaeological perspectives on conflict and warfare in Australia and the Pacific Geoffrey Clark and Mirani Litster	1
2.	War is their principal profession: On the frequency and causes of Maori warfare and migration, 1250–1850 CE Atholl Anderson	39
3.	Violence and warfare in Aboriginal Australia Colin Pardoe	63
4.	Warfare in Rapa Nui (Easter Island) Helene Martinsson-Wallin	69
5.	Traditional places in conflict and their historic context: Ritidian, Guam Boyd Dixon, Andrea Jalandoni and Maria Kottermair	89
6.	The *'enata* way of war: An ethnoarchaeological perspective on warfare dynamics in the Marquesas Islands Guillaume Molle and Vincent Marolleau	107
7.	Practical defensive features in Palau's earthwork landscape Jolie Liston	131
8.	High-resolution lidar analysis of the Fisi Tea defensive earthwork at Lapaha, Kingdom of Tonga Phillip Parton, Geoffrey Clark and Christian Reepmeyer	147
9.	Geospatial analysis of fortification locations on the island of Tongatapu, Tonga Christian Reepmeyer, Geoffrey Clark, Phillip Parton, Malia Melekiola and David Burley	171
10.	The fortified homestead of the Australian frontier Nic Grguric	191
11.	Archives, oral traditions and archaeology: Dissonant narratives concerning punitive expeditions on Malakula Island, Vanuatu Stuart Bedford	211
12.	Invisible women at war in the West: An archaeology of the Australian Women's Army Service camp, Walliabup (Bibra Lake), Western Australia, c. 1943–1945 Sven Ouzman, Jillian Barteaux, Christine Cooper and the UWA Archaeology Fieldschool Class of 2017	227
13.	Painting war: The end of contact rock art in Arnhem Land Daryl Wesley and Jessica Viney	251
Contributors		267

List of figures

Figure 1.1. Relative abundance of fortified/defensive sites in the Pacific.   18

Figure 2.1. Distribution of *pa* sites and approximate latitudinal spans of marginal cultivation at the fourteenth century (A) and sixteenth century (B).   44

Figure 2.2. Temporal distribution of traditional Maori migrations by groups originating on the east and west coasts of the North Island, and their canoe ancestors from East Polynesia.   48

Figure 2.3. Phase I and II migrations.   50

Figure 2.4. Phase III migrations. Oval area with diagonal lines shows approximate area of origin of most Phase III migrations.   52

Figure 4.1. Map of Rapa Nui with main locations mentioned in text.   70

Figure 4.2. Two *mata'a* showing tanged attachment and crescent-shaped cutting edge.   70

Figure 4.3. The statue *Paro* at Ahu Te Pito Kura.   75

Figure 5.1. Guam and Ritidian with the Northern Mariana Islands.   90

Figure 5.2. Selected traditional places in conflict across Micronesia.   91

Figure 5.3. First depiction of a Chamorro warrior, c. 1590–1591 CE.   93

Figure 5.4. Ritidian Point to the south-east from the Guam National Wildlife Refuge.   95

Figure 5.5. Limestone and volcanic sling stones and human bone spearpoints.   97

Figure 5.6. Reconstruction of a Spanish raid on a Chamorro Village, c. 1680 CE.   97

Figure 5.7. B-29 over Northwest Field, Guam c. 1945.   100

Figure 6.1. Map of the Marquesas Islands.   108

Figure 6.2. Mouina, chief warrior of the Tayehs (Teiʻi tribe, Nuku Hiva).   111

Figure 6.3. Marquesan trophy skull.   115

Figure 6.4. Map of observation posts on the Penau ridge, Ua Huka.   119

Figure 6.5. Map of the cut-ridge of Penau, Hane valley, Ua Huka.   120

Figure 6.6. Map of Hanaipa defensive system, Hiva Oa.   122

Figure 6.7. Photo of the western Makahi trench, Ua Huka island.   124

Figure 7.1. Aerial view of the Type II Ngermedangeb complex and the Ngermelkii crown and ditch in the Ngatpang (1969-6-2-53).   133

Figure 7.2. A ridge-cut impeding access to the Ngetilai crown, a Type IIIa complex in Ngardmau.   134

Figure 7.3. Infilled ring-ditch around base of the Oratelruul crown in Ngiwal.   134

Figure 7.4. A ditch bisecting a levelled ridge crest at Ked ra Ikerbeluu in Ngatpang (1976-4-217).   135

Figure 7.5. Aerial view of a lateral ditch (lower ditch in photo) that may be a trail or water control feature leading to a crown in Aimeliik (1976-6-2). 136

Figure 7.6. Section where the Compact Road has cut through east side of the Ngebars earthworks in Ngatpang. 137

Figure 7.7. Profile of road cut through the Ngebars earthwork complex. 138

Figure 7.8. A Type III earthwork complex in Ngardmau. 139

Figure 7.9. Ngerkelalk, a Type IIIb complex with ridge-cuts and high step-terraces leading to a crown in Aimeliik. 140

Figure 7.10. Documented crowns and Type III complexes in the Ngaraard Earthwork District. 142

Figure 8.1. Map of Lapaha and hinterlands with location of Fisi Tea and other defensive earthworks highlighted. 149

Figure 8.2. Detail of Fisi Tea. 153

Figure 8.3. Pictorial overview of morphological attributes calculated at each elevation profile. 154

Figure 8.4. Plots of morphological variables. 156

Figure 8.5. Idealised rampart construction sequence. 159

Figure 8.6. Energetics calculation for construction of Fisi Tea. 161

Figure 8.7. Selected elevation profiles extracted from the length of Fisi Tea. 162

Figure 9.1. Topographic map (2 m isoclines) of Tongatapu with lidar digital elevation model (DEM) and site location of fortifications. 172

Figure 9.2. Map of Tongatapu with boundaries of 1500 m (solid black line) and 4500 m (dashed line) from the north shore showing area of intensive inhabitation and extent of intensive agriculture. 178

Figure 9.3. Density map of depressions indicating potential freshwater resources. 180

Figure 9.4. Map of Tongatapu with soil types based on the geospatial database from the Tongan Ministry Department for Land, Survey and Natural Resources. 181

Figure 9.5. Sightline analysis of fort locations 5 km in distance from each other. 183

Figure 9.6. Intervisibility analysis of fort location. 184

Figure 9.7. Ortho-image of Tongatapu showing modern settlements in relation to fort location. 186

Figure 10.1. Attack on a settler's hut. 194

Figure 10.2. Rear view of the 'men's hut', once part of Central Outstation, a sheep run on the western Eyre Peninsula of South Australia. 198

Figure 10.3. Plan view of the 'men's hut' at Central Outstation, with collapsed portions reconstructed based on physical evidence and a historical photograph. 198

Figure 10.4. Exterior of extant embrasure in the 'men's hut' at Central Outstation, subsequently blocked up. 199

Figure 10.5. Interior of extant embrasure in the 'men's hut' at Central Outstation, subsequently blocked up. 199

Figure 10.6. Door from 'Avenue Range' (later 'Keilira') pastoral station. 200

Figure 10.7. Eastern aspect of the 'coach-house' at the site of Lizard Lodge, once a semi-remote farm, now in suburban Adelaide. 201

Figure 10.8. Plan of the 'coach-house' at the site of Lizard Lodge showing the position of the internally splayed embrasures in relation to the fireplace and conventional casement window. 201

Figure 10.9. Western elevation of 'the Old Fort' store building at the former site of Springvale Station, near Katherine, Northern Territory. 202

Figure 10.10. Interior (left) and exterior (right) of the circular embrasures either side of the rear door of Springvale homestead. 204

Figure 11.1. A. Southwest Pacific and Vanuatu inset; B. Northern Malakula showing locations of 1. Bridges Store, Tautu; 2. Sanwer beach, landing location; 3. Bartanar village; 4. Mae village. 212

Figure 11.2. Australian troops who had been engaged in the Malakula campaign of 1916. 217

Figure 11.3. Memorial plaque to eight native policemen who had fallen for France on Malakula since 1914. The plaque was bulldozed during roadworks in south Malakula, Vanuatu Cultural Centre, 2015. 218

Figure 11.4. Remnant standing stones, Bartanar nasara, north Malakula, 2016. 220

Figure 11.5. Large impression said to be due to the result of naval shelling. Massing Tamendal (far left) and Chief Liten (second from right), 2016. 221

Figure 11.6. A. Fragment of 4-inch naval shell (inscribed on the nose: 1.05.No4.M.83 164.7.158.6£); B. Same shell fragment held by André Ralle, Peterpu village, north Malakula, 2015. 221

Figure 12.1. Location of World War II sites mentioned in text including Walliabup (Bibra Lake). 229

Figure 12.2. *Sunday Times* auction notice 'Lot 7, Searchlight Station 10', 16 September 1945. 232

Figure 12.3. Area surveyed and excavated by 2017 UWA Archaeology Fieldschool. 233

Figure 12.4. Site map of excavated areas, pathways (indicated by black lines) and compacted areas (grey ovals). 234

Figure 12.5. Selected finds from excavations at Walliabup (Bibra Lake). 236

Figure 12.6. General aspect, plan and section of BLA 002 (pathway) excavation. 237

Figure 12.7. General aspect, plan and section of BLA 007 (toilet block) excavation. Blue tarpaulin protecting large grass tree (*Xanthorrhoea* sp.). 238

Figure 12.8. General aspect and plan of BLA 040 (?laundry) clearance. 239

Figure 12.9. BLA 041 (septic tank) and finds. 240

Figure 12.10. Concrete pad, inset wooden supports and borehole. 241

Figure 12.11. Photographs of AWAS personnel at distinctive jarrah tree, Walliabup (Bibra Lake), 1 January 1944. 243

Figure 12.12. Photographs of AWAS personnel, Walliabup (Bibra Lake). 244

Figure 12.13. Community poster of 2017 AWAS archaeology fieldschool. 246

Figure 13.1. Location of the study area. 252

Figure 13.2. Rock art panel from Djulirri, Arnhem Land, illustrating the maritime imagery recorded by Indigenous artists. 252

Figure 13.3. Line drawing and photograph of Djulirri ship. 255

Figure 13.4. HMAS *Moresby* c. 1933, Bowen Queensland. 256

Figure 13.5. HMAS *Moresby* shooting party on Melville Island. 257

Figure 13.6. Rock art motif and D-stretch image of the aircraft from Maliwawa. 258

Figure 13.7. RAAF Avro Anson circa 1940 in flight. 259

List of tables

Table 3.1. Change in occurrence of violence from the Early to Late Holocene in what is now traditional Barapa territory, as measured by cranial trauma of the vault. 65

Table 6.1. List of Marquesan defensive sites identified as such in the archaeological literature. 117

Table 8.1. Root mean square (RMS) values calculated per vegetation type used in error analysis. 151

Table 8.2. Error matrix and accuracy assessment of vegetation classification for determination of digital elevation model (DEM) error zones. 151

Table 8.3. Fisi Tea radiocarbon ages from FT–2 and FT–11 excavations. 160

Table 9.1. Site names/locations for fortified sites on Tongatapu with basic geographic data for elevation, slope, distance to coast, distance to water sources and soil types. 175

Table 10.1. Textual references to the use of defensive architecture on the Australian frontier. 194

Table 12.1. Summary artefact table from excavations at Walliabup (Bibra Lake). 235

1

Archaeological perspectives on conflict and warfare in Australia and the Pacific

Geoffrey Clark and Mirani Litster

Johnson … laughed much at Lord Kames's opinion that war was a good thing occasionally, as so much valour and virtue were exhibited in it. A fire, says Johnson, might as well be thought a good thing: there is the bravery and address of the firemen employed in extinguishing it; there is much humanity exerted in saving the lives and properties of the poor sufferers; yet, says, he, after all this who can say fire is a good thing? (Hill and Powell 1934:393 n2)

Introduction

The overarching aim in producing an edited volume about conflict and warfare is to better understand the place of coercion and force in the Australia and Pacific region, how the region's populations were transformed through violence associated with contact, colonialism and globalisation, and the manner in which the legacies of past conflict have been communicated and received. To be sure, violence and conflict are not the only problems human societies face, but they are notorious for their devastating impact on social formations, natural environments and economic systems, and frequently mark significant historical inflection points in the development of nation-states and global systems. For these reasons, major thinkers have long theorised on the causes and purposes of warfare, especially in relation to the state, and whether conflict is innate to human behaviour and society. Our region has the clear potential to contribute more significantly to scholarship concerning the development and role of violence in hunter-gatherer communities over millennia, the evolution of conflict in circumscribed and 'open' island societies, and links frequently drawn between violence and warfare, and culture contact and colonialism. The latter was accompanied by the European introduction of new diseases, technologies and weaponry that, along with intrusive ideologies, had profound impacts on indigenous populations. Responses to intrusion and invasion often involved counter-responses: resistance, violence and warfare. These conflicts are important to remember and study (e.g. Connor 2002; Reynolds 1981; Smith 2000), as the acknowledgement of such events plays an important role in community and national dialogues that underpin reconciliation and truth-telling. Given the often sensitive nature of past events involving death and violence, it is essential that researchers responsibly investigate the history of past conflict.

Remembrance of past violence has been constructive in informing public discourse recently in the 'Colonial frontier massacres in Australia, 1788–1930' project at the University of Newcastle, which brings together a large, dispersed set of historical records on conflicts and massacres in Australia since the establishment of a British colony in 1788 CE (see Ryan 2010). Other events include the 250th anniversary in 2020 CE of the *Endeavour*'s arrival in Australia and the Pacific, which has stimulated debate about the negative effects of colonialism, from contact-era violence on the 'beach' to the subsequent dispossession of indigenous peoples of their land and culture. The entangled and complicated history of colonial campaigns is illustrated by the New Zealand Wars (Prickett 2016), in which sections of a Maori tribe (*iwi*) sometimes fought with British and colonial forces against other tribal groups, and other Pacific colonial conflicts where indigenous people were pitted against other Pacific Islanders, as in Vanuatu and Fiji (Bedford this volume; Douglas 1980; Nicole 2010). Similarly, in Australia and New Guinea, indigenous people were employed in 'pacification' to extend settler (Ryan 2010) and colonial government control—as with the Native Mounted Police in Queensland and the New Guinea Police Force (Burke and Wallis 2019; Kituai 1988; Wallis et al. 2017).

Archaeological investigation of places marked by violence such as Ruapekapeka Pā in northern New Zealand, where both European and Maori combatants died during significant military operations, has contributed to a national day of remembrance (*Rā Maumahara*) to acknowledge that while colonial settlement played a significant role in modern nation-building, so did intrusion, conflict and trauma. Even the arrival of Christian missionaries could lead to conflict (Howard and Kjellgren 1994) and 'Holy Wars' between the converted and those who maintained traditional beliefs (Cummins 1977), particularly in the Marianas, where Spanish colonisation in 1668 CE, primarily for religious conversion, led to significant outbreaks of warfare and violence (Burney 1813:274–315; Dixon et al. this volume). These examples reinforce a view that colonial expansion involved coercion, violence and punishment to emplace new economic, religious and power structures on both indigenous people and marginalised groups such as indentured workers, convicts and non-European migrants (Daly 2012; Evans and Thorpe 1992; Gunson 1969; Schamberger 2017). It seems likely that many conflict sites associated with marginalised groups will benefit from archaeological study and become foci for community memory and national recollection (Bedford this volume; Gilchrist 2003; Ouzman et al. this volume).

Much of the material evidence for past violence and warfare, even in the historical period, is ambiguous in revealing the particular type of conflict, the identity of the participants and the motivation and impetus for aggression. Developing accurate long-term records of conflict—an area where archaeological data and interpretation has a crucial role—requires new techniques and consideration of a broad range of site types such as buffer zones, refuges and observation/lookouts (Grguric this volume, 2008; Smith 2000). Although inter-group aggression usually occurred on land, there are instances of marine conflict in the Pacific Islands, including the use of 'naval' vessels and large numbers of combatants. In Palau, the paramount chief of Koror in 1783 CE mobilised a war flotilla of more than 300 canoes (Keate 1788); a Tahitian fleet of 330 large and small war canoes was observed by James Cook; and the leader of the island of Hawai'i, Kalaniopu'u, in 1779 CE sailed with 150 large double canoes carrying more than 5000 men in a military expedition against the island of Maui (Clark 2017; Pang 2003:133). Aboriginal warriors used bark canoes (*nawi*) to launch raids to defend lands and waterways against British encroachment (Gapps 2018), as Edward Eyre (1984:153) recorded when moving cattle through the lands of the Yirawirung:

> from the moment there was the least streak of dawn the canoes kept plying across the lagoon loaded with men, and by the time it was daylight we had them all ranged opposite against to us again with arms in their hand.

Coasts and waterways are natural corridors for human movement and exploration and are locations where boundary maintenance and disputes over territory and resources are likely to occur (Pardoe 2014). Ocean and freshwater conflict locations will often be difficult to investigate archaeologically, although there are rare sites with evidence for indigenous conflict, including on Chuuk, in Micronesia, where large numbers of sling stones are recorded underwater (Brooks 1981:31). European ships were also sites of early violence, and the investigation of vessel remains and remains of shore camps hold substantial information about contact-era violence, as in Palau (*Antelope*, wrecked 1783 CE; Clark and de Biran 2010), Vanikoro (*Boussole* and *Astrolabe*, 1788 CE; Hitchcock 2017; Stanbury and Green 2004) and Tonga (*Port au Prince*, 1806 CE; Martin 1991). Religious and ceremonial sites are another under-studied source of information about the role of belief systems and ritual in conflict and warfare (Loeb 1926), and include war temples, shrines and elite burial structures (e.g. Kolb 2006; Sheppard et al. 2000).

In addition to consideration of a wider range of site types and a focus on conflict landscapes (e.g. Parton et al. 2018), research on violence in the past will benefit from ongoing critical analysis of traditional datasets such as textual and depictive records, human remains and studies of material culture connected with violence. In the Dynamic Figure rock art tradition of northern Australia, for example, there are scenes interpreted as showing fighting by small groups along with 'tumbling' figures perhaps indicative of trance and visions (Chippindale et al. 2000).

The problematic and equivocal identification of ancient conflict is particularly acute, not just in our region, but in the world (e.g. Cork 2005; Keeley et al. 2007; Kyle et al. 2009; Lipo et al. 2016; O'Driscoll 2017; Taçon and Chippindale 1994). In this regard, Australia and the Pacific are an important but still under-studied region for examining and refining records of conflict and warfare using archaeological approaches and allied disciplines (e.g. Litster and Wallis 2011). Although the two areas are usually held to be separate in archaeology, there were times when people, their genes and their cultural traits crossed traditional geographic enclaves. Dumont d'Urville's rightly maligned geocultural zone of 'Melanesia' (Tcherkézoff 2003), in particular, has been a sociocultural 'hinge zone' between Aboriginal Australia and the remote islands of Oceania, in addition, of course, to the peoples and cultures of island Asia (Ambrose 1988; Wesley et al. 2014; Wright et al. 2013). The latter area is the subject of a recent Terra Australis volume investigating the origins and purpose of forts in Wallacea that are likely to have developed, at least in part, in response to incipient globalisation heralded by economic and political expansions made by Chinese, Portuguese, Dutch and Muslim interests (O'Connor et al. 2020). In western New Guinea, fortified settlements (*kota/otem*) likely date to the seventeenth–nineteenth centuries CE and are similarly related to external trade and migration, although some may date older (Wright et al. 2013:56, 65).

An example of regional boundary crossing and cultural connections involving violence is the Waiat ritual in the Torres Strait, which has origins in west New Guinea and links to Cape York: it culminated in an annual inter-island ceremony that traditionally involved the sacrifice of captured people from New Guinea (Haddon 1928:135). Similarly, there were maritime voyages involving raiding and slavery from the Polynesian outlier of Taumako into Melanesia in the early seventeenth century (Amherst and Thomson 1901), along with traditional evidence for Tongan voyaging involving conflict and colony emplacement in several parts of Oceania (e.g. Ella 1899; Feinberg 1998; Gifford 1929).

Episodic and fluctuating connections—both terrestrial and maritime—that penetrated orthodox cultural regions were conduits through which knowledge about non-local people and societies moved, including the status of distant political systems, their cultural norms and information about trade items/valuables. The opportunity presented by these connections (e.g. Luders 1996; McBryde 1978; McNiven 1998; Mitchell 2000) for raiding, conflict and warfare among indigenous societies, sometimes over significant distances, is in some respects paralleled by the European exploration and contact phase in Australia and Oceania, when long-distance voyaging, culture contact and violence were virtually synonymous (Clark 2017; Orchiston and Horrocks 1975; Pearson 1970).

There are many types of contemporary violence, conflict and warfare (e.g. cyber, culture, drone, information, generational, chemical, psychological), and in antiquity there were several kinds of behaviour that materialised 'violence', from damage to statues and monuments that symbolised the political and belief systems of elites, to the destruction of material culture (Walter et al. 2004:150) and human remains (Barber 2012; McNiven 2018), and reverential and desecratory termination rituals (e.g. Pagliaro et al. 2003) that extended to cannibalism and human sacrifice (Dening 1978; Filihia 1999; Kyle et al. 2009; Sissons 2011). In a recent paper, Bedford et al. (2020) examined missionary 'battles' over spiritual objects central to indigenous beliefs on Aneityum that had to be weakened to support conversion to Christianity, as was noted on Mangaia by the missionary John Williams (Moyle 1984:25):

> A very large Portion of the Inhabitants remain heathen; but their Idols temples have all been destroyed together with the Idols, so that it is Probable the whole Population will soon become Christians.

In Australia, the destruction and exclusion of Indigenous food supplies after European settlement has long been considered a major cause of cultural destabilisation (e.g. Rowley 1970), and more broadly colonialism and capitalist enterprises can be categorised as 'war capitalism' (Morrison et al. 2019). Missionary activity also contributed to cultural alienation, seen in the recent burning of Aboriginal sacred objects in the Kimberley. The missionary involved was from Tonga (Parke 2019), where representations of the traditional gods were hanged by the neck and displayed to Christian congregations in the nineteenth century (Neich 2007).

There are also behaviours and actions that are now classed—when viewed through the lens of contemporary standards—as 'violence', as with 'environmental violence' to describe the unsustainable use of fauna, flora and land in the past (Salcedo 2015), or the unintentional, but certainly predictable, population 'violence' wrought by the introduction of deadly pathogens to the 'new' lands and people of Australia and the Pacific (Crosby 1986; Igler 2015). Definitions of conflict and warfare abound, with most authorities viewing the use of interpersonal violence as a tool to achieve change in the sociopolitical position of an individual or a group relative to others (Kissel and Kim 2018:Table 1). Ember and Ember (1992:248) define warfare as: 'socially organized armed combat between members of different territorial units', while for Webster (1998:313), warfare consists of planned confrontations between groups of people who conceive of themselves as members of separate communities (factions) who organise and sanction group violence that may result in deliberate killings. The latter description encompasses the many kinds of conflict (e.g. homicide, feud, raid, ambush, chance meeting, battle) that are documented within and between pre-industrial societies, states and empires.

It is clear that conflict in the past has always had many dimensions and not all are currently amenable to investigation. As is common in archaeology, we are missing material evidence for an unknowable fraction of past human behaviour, and in seeking to understand conflict through limited data and a necessary level of subjective interpretation we run the risk of either pacifying the past or giving violence a societal prominence it never had. With these cautions in mind, we begin by outlining the early chronological evidence or 'residues' of past conflict in the Australia and Pacific region before identifying three areas where archaeological investigations might contribute to a deeper and nuanced historical understanding of aggression and conflict. These are: (1) The cause of conflict, particularly the role of resource shortfalls; (2) A frequent association between culture contact and violence; and (3) Why archaeological (and historic) evidence for conflict frequently patterns as punctuated events.

As archaeologists we are mostly concerned with the deep past through to the beginnings of the twentieth century, and with conflict affecting indigenous peoples, a perspective that omits many of the significant sites and experiences of the world wars. World War II, in particular, stands out in the Australia and Pacific, not just due to the scale of the conflict and its victims (Price and Knecht 2012), but also in its transformation of the region's economies and cultures, their increasing global integration and the growing postwar movement towards independence that was often accompanied by protest and resistance (Campbell 2009; Chappell 1993). Incorporating the material evidence and cultural experiences from relatively recent global events such as World War II (Ouzman et al. this volume; Price and Knecht 2012) and local conflicts (Kwai 2017) into our island and continental records of conflict is a challenge for researchers seeking to bridge an artificial and unnecessary division between conflict research of the past and the present.

The chapters in this volume explore only some of the issues raised above, as the geographic range and time depth of the Australia and Pacific region necessarily results in gaps in coverage, notably in areas of Melanesia and Micronesia, where a number of researchers were unable to complete papers due to the social and economic impacts from COVID-19. It was also apparent when contacting potential contributors that the archaeological study of violence in Australia is seen as highly sensitive, in part because the results may be misunderstood or misrepresented in contemporary debates.

Residues of early conflict

Australia and Island Melanesia

In land area, the Australia and Pacific region is dominated by the Australian continent, which is characterised by significant environmental and climatic variation and has been inhabited by Aboriginal populations for c. 65 000 years (Clarkson et al. 2017; Williams et al. 2013). The oldest indications of past violence are depictions of 'warriors' in the Dynamic Figure rock art of Arnhem Land (Taçon and Chippindale 1994) that likely date to the late Pleistocene (Jones et al. 2017:86). Taçon and Chippindale (1994) have suggested that some Dynamic Figure designs depict one-on-one skirmishes between combatants armed with boomerangs and barbed composite spears. Later art in 'simple figure' and 'energetic' styles may show organised battles between large numbers of combatants using weapons such as clubs, spear-throwers, hafted stone axes and barbed, pronged and stone-tipped spears. Unambiguous evidence for violence includes stone spear barbs (backed microliths) found in the remains of Narrabeen Man, dated to c. 3600 years ago (Fullagar et al. 2009; McDonald et al. 2007), and cut-marked bone from the more recent individual known as 'Kaakutja' (Westaway et al. 2016, see also Webb 1991 and Knuckey 1992). Consistent patterns of osteological trauma in Aboriginal remains suggest some level of violence and warfare among groups in the Murray Valley region over the past 7000 years (Brown 1989:176; Pardoe 2014).

Proximity to Australia, particularly during times of lower sea level during glacial expansion and periods of global cooling (Yokoyama et al. 2018), facilitated the spread of early modern humans through the merged Australia–New Guinea landmass (Sahul) and nearby archipelagos of western Melanesia at least 40 000–50 000 years ago (Summerhayes et al. 2010). The likelihood of some Pleistocene voyaging along the east Asian coast through to Melanesia is suggested by cultural deposits on Okinawa dated to c. 35 000 years ago (Fujita et al. 2016), and Pleistocene-age sites on Manus Island and Buka suggesting that early humans could also have spread a further

1000 km into Oceania by island-hopping through the main Solomon Islands (Frederickson et al. 1993; Lilley 2010). Relatively little is known about early Melanesian populations in terms of their social organisation and propensity for conflict, despite the emergence of Neolithic settlements and interaction networks in island and mainland Papua New Guinea some 5000 years ago (Shaw et al. 2020; Torrence et al. 2013), a lifeway associated elsewhere with significant inter-group aggression (e.g. Bocquentin and Bar-Yosef 2004; Fibiger et al. 2013; Meyer et al. 2015).

Lapita expansion and colonisation of West Micronesia

The remote islands of Oceania, defined as those east of Makira (San Cristobal) in the Solomons, were settled much later than Australia–New Guinea, with dispersal from 3150 to 2850 years ago as indicated from ceramic-bearing sites of the Lapita culture that are found from southern New Guinea eastward to Tonga and Samoa. The c. 4500 km span of Lapita sites in the western Pacific over 200–300 years is consistent with the deployment of a new maritime technology (Anderson 2000). The introduction of better sailing vessels and enhanced nautical wayfinding in insular Asia is also implied by long-distance passages to western Micronesia (Palau, possibly Yap, and the Mariana Islands) at a similar time to the Lapita dispersal (Clark 2005; Petchey et al. 2018), which probably originated in east Indonesia or from migrant groups on the north coast of New Guinea (Montenegro et al. 2016; Winter et al. 2012).

Recent aDNA and obsidian sourcing results show that Lapita people had an ultimate origin in island Asia (Skoglund et al. 2016), and that after Lapita dispersal there were early and later secondary migrations of people from New Guinea–island Melanesia that resulted in population mixing between Lapita-derived populations and west Oceanic migrants (Hudjashov et al. 2018). Genetic analysis (mtDNA) of contemporary Chamorro people of the Marianas (Vilar et al. 2012) points to a founding population of island Asian derivation, with a second migration from the same region c. 1000 CE that brought new cultural traits, including *latte* architecture, rice cultivation and mortuary practice.

Whether the migrations that came after Lapita settlement and human arrival in western Micronesia were accompanied by conflict is unknown, but the question is worth considering as inter-group violence frequently attends or is intensified by culture contact, both indigenous and from the expansion of Western societies (e.g. Bamforth 1994; Blick 1988; Hutchinson 1996; Knauft 1990). The sparse evidence for early conflict in Oceania consists of shell and basalt sling stones from a Lapita site in the Reef–Santa Cruz islands (Green 1979:39, but see Kirch and Green 2001:190). These distinctive double-pointed ovoid projectiles, mainly made in shell and stone, were designed to inflict serious damage to the body of an opponent, but have not been securely identified in the Lapita assemblages of Fiji, Tonga and Samoa, nor in early contexts in New Caledonia and the Mariana Islands, where they are predominantly associated with late prehistoric deposits (Sand 2001:81; York and York 2014). In these areas, unmodified and rounded sling stones may have been used (as in Fiji, Cook Islands and Marquesas, see Suggs 1961:27); in some places these were used to hunt birds, fish and other animals, while pointed sling stones are particularly associated with human inter-group conflict in many parts of the Pacific. It is unclear whether shaped sling stones in Reef–Santa Cruz Lapita sites indicate conflict during Lapita colonisation; if so, they would be the oldest surviving weapons present in Oceania. Shaped stones used in conflict and thrown by hand rather than from a sling are recorded from Niue Island (Isaac and Isaac 2011), Rapa Nui/Easter Island (Métraux 1940:165) and Tanna in Vanuatu, where cylindrical *kawas* stones were hand-thrown in inter-group conflicts (Turner 1861:81–82).

In West Micronesia, the oldest Pre-Latte burials (3200–1000 years ago) in the Marianas are associated with a few sling stones dating to c. 500 BCE or later, with the number increasing in *latte* burials made after 1000 CE (Walth 2016). York and York (2014:23) report the unpublished archaeological discovery on Guam of a human skull with a bipointed sling stone embedded in it. However, trauma in the skeletal remains of 370 individuals excavated from Pre-Latte (42 per cent) and Latte (57 per cent) contexts at the Naton Beach site on Guam did not suggest warfare in pre-contact populations, although the presence of more young males than females could reflect male hazards such as warfare (Walth 2016:16).

The earliest secure evidence for inter-group aggression in the Pacific Islands are earthworks with defensive traits made in Palau at c. 2500–1100 years ago (Liston this volume; Liston and Miko 2011:19; Liston and Tuggle 2006) and modified human bone consistent with cannibalism in Fiji before 1000 CE, and possibly as early as 500–100 BCE (Best 1984:562, DeGusta 1999; Pietrusewsky et al. 2007; Worthy and Clark 2009:244). Human remains at the Teouma Lapita site in Vanuatu (900 BCE) and the Talasiu burial ground (700 BCE) in Tonga bear small amounts of bone damage and modification that might result from interpersonal violence, but some of this damage likely derives from the complicated mortuary practices and bone manipulation techniques used by early colonising groups (e.g. Valentin et al. 2020).

Reconstructed terms in Proto-Polynesian (PPN; Kirch and Green 2001) for 'war' (PPN **tau*), weapon (PPN **masafu*) and fortified/enclosed settlement (PPN **kolo*) indicate the existence of organised conflict in Fiji–Western Polynesia sometime after 500 BCE. Caves and natural topographic 'defences' were used in the Sigatoka Valley of Fiji 2000 years ago (Field 2004), but distinguishing the archaeological evidence for raiding, refuge and conflict in unmodified sites such as ridges and caves (e.g. Carson 2017; Kyle et al. 2009) is problematic in the absence of weapons and built defences (see also Kolb and Dixon 2002:518–519). In New Caledonia, there are substantial forts in the Loyalty Islands, including the impressive Hnakudotit structure on Maré, with stone walls c. 10–12 m thick and up to 180 m in length that may date to c. 200 CE, from radiocarbon ages on marine shell found in the wall fill (Sand 1996; Sand pers. comm. 22 September 2020), but additional dating is required to confirm the structure's early age. Hnakudotit is only 500 m from another large fort called Waninetit (Dubois 1970), suggesting fort placement was to control a roadway or to protect clan boundaries. It is only within the past 1000 years that fortifications appear to have been regularly constructed in Fiji and adjacent island groups such as Tonga, Samoa, Futuna and 'Uvea (Burrows 1936; Clark et al. 2017; Sand 1993, 2008).

Injuries consistent with interpersonal violence and warfare have been identified in human remains, predominantly those of males, dating to the second millennium CE in Papua New Guinea (Nebira) and the Polynesian outlier of Taumako in the Solomon Islands (Scott and Buckley 2010). Piercing wounds from bone-tipped projectiles were present in the Taumako burial group (Buckley 2000), while blunt force cranial trauma was found in both Taumako and Nebira, but was particularly high among Nebira males (38.5 per cent), consistent with inter-group conflict and warfare (Scott and Buckley 2010). In Tonga, high rates of fractured radii in the people interred in the 'Atele burial mounds point to ritualised violence, possibly from combat sports such as boxing, club fights and controlled displays of public violence known to have been held at chiefly and community gatherings (Scott and Buckley 2014). The funeral ceremonies of Tongan high chiefs involved combat sports as well as public displays of self-harm that could involve the mourner cutting, burning, clubbing, spearing or stabbing themselves to demonstrate grief and affection for the deceased, and amputation of finger joints to influence the gods was common (Clark and Langley 2020; Martin 1991; Statham 2013). Interestingly, Pardoe (2014:127) notes self-harm in the funerary behaviour of Aboriginal groups on the Central

Murray and Darling Rivers. Elite sacrifice is suggested from human remains interred at the burial site of the paramount chief Roy Mata in Vanuatu (c. 1600 CE), whose regime traditionally involved political reorganisation and warfare (Luders 2001).

In 'Uvea in West Polynesia, the remains of more than 150 people were buried together at the Petania burial mound around a beach rock burial vault, which is a mortuary structure used in Tonga for the interment of elites (Clark 2016; Sand and Valentin 1991). Oral traditions suggest the individuals belonged to a Tongan colony who were massacred, with the number of dead representing around 5 per cent of 'Uvea's pre-European population. However, Sand et al. (2006) note there was little evidence for violent death at the Petania site, although the presence of poorly healed forearm fractures among 'Uvean males was probably the result of aggressive behaviour. The massacre of Tongan colonists and fighters is widespread in traditional history from many parts of the Pacific, including Vanuatu, Fiji, Anuta, Futuna, 'Uvea, Samoa and Niue (e.g. Burrows 1936:126, 1937:29; Churchill 1911:46; Feinberg 1998; Loeb 1926; Smith 1903:11).

East Polynesia

Colonisation of East Polynesia 1000–700 years ago, most likely from 'homeland' West Polynesia, involved long-distance voyaging and some level of limited post-colonisation contact among widely dispersed island groups. This is shown by the distribution of Samoan stone adzes over 5000 km from Pohnpei to the Cook Islands (Clark et al. 2014; Weisler et al. 2016) and the settlement of more than 20 Polynesian outlier communities in Melanesia and Micronesia (Kirch 1984). Traditional history is unambiguous in describing the existence of warfare in many parts of Polynesia (Hommon 2013; Tau and Anderson 2008), which could be accompanied in places by the remains of specialised built sites such as linear defences, observation posts, palisaded compounds, war temples and large community fortifications made in earth, stone and wood (Best 1993; Irwin 1985; Kolb and Dixon 2002). Just as in Melanesia and Micronesia, defensive structures made of earth and stone were not universal among Polynesian societies (Green 1967, see below). Fortifications capable of community protection are most abundant in Aotearoa/New Zealand (Anderson this volume), reasonably frequent in Rapa Iti (Kennett and McClure 2012) and the Marquesas (Molle and Marolleau this volume), but rare or absent almost everywhere else. The islands/groups where fortifications are reasonably common share complicated topographies where the natural defensive properties of the land can be enhanced by group investment in construction (Field 2004). Islands or archipelagos consisting of atolls with a small land area and flat topography, such as the Tuamotus and Northern Cooks, do not have numerous built fortifications, yet neither do many rugged volcanic islands in Polynesia including most of Hawai'i, Southern Cooks, Society Islands, Australs (excluding Rapa Iti) and Mangareva—illustrating that a decision to make fortifications was not influenced solely by physical geography.

On Rapa Nui/Easter Island, warfare was once seen as a prime mover for social change and cultural disintegration as a result of significant inter-group conflict, reported in oral traditions and seen in some archaeological data. This view has been questioned largely in response to Diamond's (2005) well-known view that a human-induced environmental catastrophe on Rapa Nui led to societal collapse. Injuries to human remains, *mata'a* obsidian flakes suggested to have been hafted to projectile and thrusting weapons, and cave refuges are no longer seen to offer support for the existence of endemic warfare and social breakdown (Stevenson and Williams 2018). There are only a few potentially defensive sites on Rapa Nui (Green 1967; Martinsson-Wallin this volume) and a recent paper by DiNapoli et al. (2019) suggests that:

> Several emerging and independent lines of evidence show that there is little empirical support for violent warfare, including little evidence for the production of lethal weapons, limited instances of lethal skeletal trauma, and a lack of fortifications.

While the archaeological data does not support large-scale warfare on Rapa Nui, as in most of Australia and the Pacific, there is good evidence for significant inter-group conflict probably involving raiding and aggression between prehistoric communities (Martinsson-Wallin this volume). The largest and most contentious defensive site on Rapa Nui is the 'Poike Ditch', which spans the eastern part of the island. In local oral traditions the area was a battle and massacre location associated with two groups known as the *Hanau e'epe* and *Hanau momoko*. The north–south ditch consists of a series of linear ditch segments nearly 2 km in total length (Reanier and Ryan 2003). Investigations by Smith (1990) suggest the ditch was a natural geological fault where the fill had been dug out and deposited on the upslope side in a number of mounds or as a rampart. The site was originally interpreted as a fortification due to oral traditions of inter-group conflict (Routledge 1919:280–282), but researchers now suggest the feature could have been used for horticulture or was a cooking place for workers at the nearby Rano Raraku statue quarry. In a recent scholarly review of Rapa Nui warfare and conflict, DiNapoli et al. (2020) note that the Poike Ditch is of geological origin, but make no mention of the fact that sediment from the natural depression was excavated and placed in a mound/rampart on the upslope side of the ditch. The ditch was dug out to at least 2 m depth and is possibly over 3 m in depth, implying an upslope mound/rampart 2–3 m in height prior to erosion and ditch infilling (see Smith 1990:33). The earthwork at Poike, based on Smith's (1990) cross-section, therefore created a vertical obstacle 4–6 m in height with a gradient of 0.25–0.35 that could have slowed attackers.

While the Poike feature may have been used for agriculture, water control or cooking, it is highly suggestive of a defensive earthwork, consisting of sections separated by gates/entrances that utilised the natural ditch to physically define and limit access to the eastern part of the island. New excavations and study of this enigmatic site are needed to resolve its age and function, along with other possible defensive sites (see Martinsson-Wallin this volume).

An extensive study of Rapa Nui human remains (minimum number of individuals, MNI = 469) mostly dating to 1647 CE or later did not find evidence to support organised lethal warfare, yet found a high rate of male cranial vault fractures (30.4 per cent) especially among young adult males (37.7 per cent), likely caused by thrown stones and in some cases from clubs (*paoa*). Lithic fragments, probably of obsidian, were found in two crania, suggesting that *mata'a* were employed as weapons (Owsley et al. 2016:236, Figure 13.10). Geiseler (in Ayres 1995:72) noted that even in the late nineteenth century, after substantial population decline, obsidian *mata'a* points were hafted to spears and caused wounds that were hard to heal, while Flas (2015) suggests that *mata'a* were hafted as spears only after substantial post-contact population collapse. However, Johann Forster (1982:470) in 1774 CE recorded that: 'The Natives have a kind of Spear consisting of a Stick, to which a black sharp Flint is fixed, which they constantly wrap', suggesting that *mata'a* were hafted multipurpose tools that could be used as weapons.

Clearly, violence was not unknown to Rapa Nui (Bahn 2015), but whether these skeletal injuries resulted from post-contact intensification in violence (see below) or from traditional forms of Rapa Nui combat between individuals and groups (raiding, feuding, ambushes, ritual combat) needs further study. According to the careful ethnographer Métraux (1940:74):

> References to intertribal wars are frequent in Easter Island folklore. They reflect real conflicts between tribes (*mata*) whose quarrels and feuds ended only after the advent of the missionaries.

Resource shortfalls, warfare and exceptionalism

Many archaeological studies posit resource shortages as a reason for conflict and warfare in the past, as outlined by the philosopher Thomas Hobbes (1588–1679 CE). Such conflicts have been termed 'wars of necessity':

> The most frequent cause why men want to hurt each other arises when many want the same thing at the same time, without being able to enjoy it in common or to divide it. The consequence is that it must go to the stronger. But who is the stronger? Fighting must decide. (in Thivet 2008:707)

Spectacular evidence for early violence among hunter-gather groups is dated to c. 10 000 years ago at the Nataruk site in Kenya: the site includes 12 individuals found over 260 m of palaeoshoreline, 10 of whom had likely experienced violent injury, including blunt force trauma to the head and injuries from lithic bladelets and microliths, which were found embedded in bone or found within skeletons. The Nataruk remains have been interpreted as a 'massacre' from a raid for 'resources' such as territory and stored food, and for women; the injuries seen to testify to a 'standard' antagonistic inter-group response (Mirazón Lahr et al. 2016). In the development of complex societies, the link between resource restrictions and conflict was highlighted in Carneiro's (1970, 1988) elegant model of circumscription theory. Competition for limited agricultural land and population growth in the model were the catalysts for inter-group wars that led to the formation of centralised political systems (chiefdoms) run by the victors. Over time, both the size of the political units and the geographic scale they controlled increased, eventually leading to the formation of early/archaic states.

Archaeological explanations of conflict from resource shortfalls/unpredictability are complicated because ideally, we would like to know which basic/essential resources were diminished, and by what amount, and we would like to be able to identify the cause(s) of resource declines. Population growth/pressure (see Shankman 1991) and climate events acting together or independently are commonly invoked mechanisms that can cause shortfalls. Numerous studies suggest that societies throughout the world experienced significant subsistence declines (Zhang et al. 2007, but see Oka et al. 2017), especially from drought, and increased conflict was the result (e.g. Buckley et al. 2010; Haug et al. 2003; Huang and Su 2009; Kaniewski et al. 2013), although the hypothesis is not without criticism (e.g. Caldararo 2015; Dittmar et al. 2019:75). The role of population pressure/density on land as a direct cause of conflict has also been queried in several archaeological and cross-cultural studies (Groube 1970:162; Keeley 1996:118–121; Nolan 2003:28; Robarchek and Robarchek 1992).

A simple feedback system in which climate-driven changes to subsistence lead to societal 'collapse' has been suggested for north-west Australia from 3200–1300 years ago (McGowan et al. 2012), and has been proposed across the Pacific when cooling associated with the 'Little Ice Age' led to a drop in sea level. Nunn (2007a, 2007b) has argued that between the Medieval Warm Period and the Little Ice Age there was a century or two of rapid cooling in the Pacific, termed the 'AD 1300 event'. This marked a rapid transition from a warmer to a cooler, stormier period, when sea levels dropped 60–80 cm from cyclical variation in solar irradiance. The combination of rapid sea level fall and increased storminess is argued to have caused a dramatic reduction of up to 80 per cent in available food resources (Nunn 2003:224, 2007c:121). This disturbance to the resource base resulted in increased competition and conflict across the Pacific, represented in some areas by the construction of fortifications and in others by a shift from open settlement locations to occupation of naturally defensible areas. Other signs of aggression were a rise in violent social practices such as cannibalism and headhunting (Nunn 2007a, 2007b).

In Australia, ethnographic sources examined by Allen (2014:106) indicate that basic resources were highly defended and entire groups were sometimes eliminated in conflicts over them, with the caveat that sacred places (frequently waterholes) were often the 'resource' involved. The indivisible nature of many cultural and subsistence resources suggests that explanations of conflict that highlight access to basic resources may be too narrow. In Central Australia, Kimber (1990:163) notes that conflicts were probably more frequent in well-watered areas where population density was highest and during journeys that crossed clan boundaries to procure red ochre and the *pituri* stimulant. Other ethnographies, such as the accounts of William Buckley (Morgan 1980), mention that many conflicts were over women, in addition to those involved in long-distance expeditions to obtain stone axes, and payback for death attributed to 'magic'. The latter is not mentioned by Allen (2014) as a reason for inter-group violence yet the application of 'magic' could involve revenge killings, surprise raids and the deaths of men, women and children (Curr 1883:311–320). The main point is that resource shortages are seldom mentioned as a reason for Aboriginal conflict by ethnographic observers and in some cases inter-group aggression took place when food sources 'seemed inexhaustible' (Morgan 1980).

Similarly, among Pacific societies the ethnographic motivations for conflict and warfare only rarely mention basic resources, particularly land, among a range of reasons (Anderson this volume; Younger 2008, 2009). For the Maori, cultivable land, fishing grounds and eel weirs were causes of friction, but so too were murder, magic, infringement of *tapu* (traditional prohibitions) and slights to an individual/group (Ballara 1976). Land is a basic resource necessary for subsistence and group survival, but when developed through cultivation and land management practices such as arboriculture and intensified dryland and irrigated agricultural systems, the land and the people who work it are frequently viewed as a political resource that is sought or destroyed to strengthen the position of leaders, communities and states relative to others (see Earle 1997; Parry 1981). For many groups and societies, control and/or management of 'basic resources' is not strictly about group survival and is often prompted by a desire to maintain and expand existing economic and social systems.

The traditional motivation for raids, headhunting and wars in the Marquesas was to obtain human sacrifices for local deities as well as reciprocal conflict to avenge those who had been sacrificed by rival groups (Dening 1978; Molle and Marolleau this volume). Insults to tribes and chiefs could also result in wars where individuals and groups could enhance their prestige. Wars appear only rarely to have led to control over land, with agreed battle sites located in upland valleys. Inter-group conflict might be stopped when a sacrifice was taken, plunder was obtained, the enemies' religious images were stolen or a truce was called to hold agricultural or funerary ceremonies (Handy 1923:123–141). Raiding and warfare in Palau (1000–1800 CE) was strongly linked to the political position of chiefs and villages, with headhunting raids used to obtain traditional money (*udoud*) used in chiefly politics. Pitched battles were undertaken to become the paramount village in a district, to acquire prestige items and valuables, and to create a tribute relationship with weaker settlements. Punitive wars were also made to stop lower ranked villages from challenging the district hierarchy (Liston and Tuggle 2006; Parmentier 1987).

Conflict to maintain, and if possible, extend influence through subjugation of tribute-paying villages is also reported from Fiji, with wars between rival chiefs challenging for political supremacy. Wars also occurred within chiefly families for leadership, and conflict could be precipitated by insults, portable valuables, the breaking of traditional laws and, as in the Marquesas, the common use of human sacrifices to appease war gods. As Wilkes observed during a visit to Fiji in 1840 CE:

> The wars of the Feejeeans [Fijians] usually arises from some accidental affront or misunderstanding, of which the most powerful party takes advantage to extend his dominions or extend his wealth. (Wilkes 1985:78)

According to Clunie (2003:7), the most serious and destructive conflicts in Fiji were between tribal confederations headed by paramount chiefs who were personal enemies, which could result in sacking and the depopulation of large tracts of land and entire islands. Traditional history in Tonga, where a centralised polity developed (1200–1800 CE), is unequivocal in linking warfare with political upheaval, particularly attempts at regime change when members of the paramount Tuʻi Tonga line were assassinated c. 1450–1500 CE (Clark 2016; Parton et al. this volume). A similar situation is noted for late pre-contact Hawaiʻi, where warfare was common after the death of a king when the heir was challenged by collateral kinsmen (Kirch 2010:71). Insults and disputes over high titles, especially following the assassination of a paramount chief, are recorded as the main cause of war in Samoa (Krämer 1995:392).

The above examples suggest two serious limitations to the idea that 'resource shortfalls' were a primary driver of conflict and warfare in the past (see also Ember and Ember 1992; Younger 2008, 2014). First, archaeological explanations that link conflict/warfare with resource shortages frequently diverge from instances of inter-group aggression in emic accounts as well as explanations for aggression put forward by external observers. For instance, Dye (2014:64) has noted that in several Hawaiian traditions a consequence of severe drought and famine was a food-sharing ethic rather than social disruption and war. A review of pre-contact warfare in Melanesia identified conflict over land rights, women, and individual and group prestige that was necessary to assert identity. Not only was Melanesian warfare largely characterised by an 'absence of territorial ambition', conflict also appeared to be driven by a desire for political stability and balance with reciprocity a fundamental aspect of inter-group violence in many societies (Younger 2014). In islands near Malekula in Vanuatu, wrote Layard (1942:588), wars were made 'almost entirely on questions involving the prestige of one group against another, in order to maintain the existing order of society by wreaking vengeance on any who seek to disturb it', with violence mainly over women, insults, trade and kinship relations, or resources such as pigs.

One reason for diverging views about the cause of conflict in archaeology, compared with other disciplines and sources, might be that the ecological and population circumstances leading to conflict are of such complexity and duration that they cannot be recognised by the participants/observers themselves (Vayda 1970:570, 1976). Resource declines in the past might therefore be deduced from archaeological and environmental records. However, this seems unlikely given: (1) A general absence of high-precision environmental archives for many conflict locations; (2) An incomplete and often mute archaeological record regarding the motivation for conflict; and (3) An untested assumption that indigenous groups are unable to perceive the reason(s) why they engage in conflict.

The second limitation to the idea of resource scarcity as a driver of warfare is that a connection between conflict and resource scarcity is largely absent from records of societal aggression from classical antiquity through to the modern era. If writers of history concerned with large and small conflicts from Herodotus and Thucydides through to Clausewitz (1984) and Hintze (1975) fail to mention basic resources as a reason for inter-group aggression, then we might consider whether archaeology and some strands of evolutionary archaeology have adequately established a causal connection. Is the appeal to resource shortfalls to explain conflict in archaeology justified by our data? Are conflicts involving ancient communities, states and empires really so different from those of recent times? The historian of contemporary warfare Betz (2019:32) has observed that major NATO installations in Afghanistan were 'located about one day's march apart, essentially where Alexander the Great placed variants of them 2,500 years before'. He might have added that conflict in this region, then as now, was not over the acquisition of basic resources (see Arrian and de Sélincourt 1976). Appeals to 'historical uniqueness' (Weiner 1971:666) and 'chronocentrism' (Fowles 1974) need to be scrutinised carefully, both when archaeological reasons for conflict in the past diverge from the causes of conflict and warfare outlined in detailed historical accounts spanning thousands of years and when they are not strongly supported by analyses of recent conflict. Wimmer and Min (2006:894) caution against explanations of warfare based on modern 'unprecedented' circumstances, which 'represents yet another example of the widespread tendency among social scientists to perceive their own times as unique and exceptionally dynamic'.

A final point about resource shortages as an explicator of aggression in the archaeological record is the question of event order. Declining food yields/basic resources are often seen as the prime mover for societal disruption that leads directly and quickly to systemic intergroup conflict (e.g. Nunn 2003, 2007a, 2007b). Historical observations, however, suggest that in several instances the impacts of famine and resource shortfalls were created or made significantly worse by conflict and warfare (see also Zhang et al. 2007). During the late eighteenth and nineteenth centuries in Tonga, political upheaval and assassination led to polity fragmentation and civil war c. 1792–1852 CE. During this lengthy interval it was observed that famines and subsistence shortfalls were a direct and predictable outcome of conflict (see also Layard 1942:599):

> they usually made war by attacking the taro and yam-grounds; these they plunder and destroy, which ultimately produces a famine, not only to their enemies but to themselves. (Wilkes 1985:28)

In modern times some of the worst famines and declines in food production, such as those that affected Syria, Sudan, Somalia, Ethiopia and Cambodia, have been caused or intensified by prolonged wars and repressive or poor governance (e.g. Clarke 2000). The relationship between resources and conflict is complicated, as in Syria where drought caused the relocation of around 250 000 farmers to urban areas, which directly contributed to the outbreak of serious and ongoing civil war. Even in this instance, political instability, mismanagement and drastic water reductions caused by river damming contributed to the severity of drought, forced migration and conflict (Al-Muqdadi 2019). In short, conflict to secure basic resources is often used to explain violence in the archaeological record whether there is sufficient evidence for it or not (see Dittmar et al. 2019:75). An outcome of this is that we know little about why some societies appear to deal with significant climate and drought events while others experience warfare, fragmentation and collapse.

Culture contact and conflict

If initial meetings are a guide to future relations, then European arrival in much of Australia and the Pacific was highly discouraging, with many encounters characterised by violence and death. One of the earliest but least known events occurred during the first European crossing of the Pacific Ocean by a small fleet under Ferdinand Magellan, which reached Guam in 1521 CE after a voyage of more than three months. After the local Chamorro people had taken items from the ships, they took the skiff from Magellan's flagship, whereupon the captain became 'very irritated' and took ashore an armed party of 40 men that burned 40–50 houses and killed seven or eight people. The account of Antonio Pigafetta (Pigafetta and Robinson 1906:92) records that before the punitive party left the ship, the killing of Chamorro people was anticipated: 'some of our sick men begged us that if we killed men or women, we should bring their entrails so that the sick men would be cured immediately'. The crew were suffering from severe scurvy and while there is no evidence that the dead were mutilated it is perhaps unlikely that such an atrocity would be recorded in an account meant for an elite and Catholic readership in Europe. Nonetheless, in an inversion of popular expectations, first contact in the Pacific almost certainly involved a plan by Europeans to cannibalise slain Pacific Islanders.

Other expeditions and brutalities followed. Soon after Mendaña's arrival in the Marquesas (1595 CE), the bodies of three murdered Marquesan men were displayed on shore to demonstrate the effectiveness of Spanish weapons and 200 Marquesan people were estimated to have been killed in under three weeks (Markham 2016:24, 26). On Santo in Vanuatu, first contact by Quirós (1606 CE) involved a plan to teach indigenous people Spanish and 'to catch some natives so as to establish peace and friendship'. Inevitably, this approach failed to foster cordial relations and soon after the Spanish landed, a local man was killed and his beheaded body hung in a tree, presumably as a warning not to attack the new arrivals, which predictably resulted in escalating cross-cultural violence (Markham 2016:242).

Serious conflict was not universal during the phase of European exploration from the sixteenth to the late eighteenth century, but was more common than not. To cite two instances that occurred long before James Cook's well-known voyages to the Southern Hemisphere (1768–1779 CE), Janzoon's 1606 CE voyage in the *Duyfken* to northern Australia and New Guinea involved resistance by the Wik-Mungkan people and killings on both sides (Mutch 1942; Sutton 2008), while in southern New Guinea also in 1606 CE, food, converts and 'plunder' were taken from Mailu Island after major fighting and storming of the local fort, where, Prado relates: 'I was sorry to see so many dead children' (Stevens and Barwick 2010:153).

Early contact was accompanied by violence in other Pacific Islands, including Chuuk (1565 CE), Tonga (1616 CE), New Zealand (1642 CE), Society Islands (1767 CE), Rapa Nui (1722 CE), Hawai'i (1778–1779 CE) and Samoa (1787 CE). It is necessary to understand a strong association between violence and conflict during early contact and subsequent colonial activity in Australia and the Pacific, as archaeological studies can add nuance and new interpretations to historical records, and cross-cultural conflict may be important aspect of inter-group contact in the past.

There are at least two modes of conflict in early contact records. The first has been characterised as a result of the shock of the new, and the idea that when 'different worlds collide', violence is a likely outcome. Reasons for friction include the European need to reprovision after long ocean passages, views of indigenous people as 'savages' (noble or ignoble), difficulty in communicating and understanding social norms, and local demand for exotic materials. Other aspects were also important as both pre-Enlightenment and Enlightenment voyages were crewed almost entirely by males, many of whom had military or naval backgrounds and who were trained in the use of weapons. The small size of crews relative to island populations and their extreme isolation from aid meant that violence was often used as a form of boundary maintenance.

The fact that visiting ships were armed and usually crewed entirely by males equipped with weapons suggests that Europeans were seen as potential raiders or aggressors because many indigenous societies associated the arrival of armed all-male groups with raiding and inter-group conflict (Clark 2017). Such a perception would have been reinforced by the performance of military drills and the demonstration of weapons that, while designed to avert conflict, may have had the opposite effect, in addition to behaviours and ceremonies that were viewed as assertions of sovereignty. This was the case after Spanish arrival at Big Bay on Santo in Vanuatu (Markham 2016:243) and at Tahiti, where a well-armed shore party from the *Dolphin* took formal possession of the archipelago by erecting a naval pennant on a pole (Robertson 1973). It can also be seen in Aboriginal (Gweagal) resistance to Cook's landing at Botany Bay, summarised in his observation that 'all they seem'd to want was for us to be gone' (Cook in Beaglehole 1968:306), and in Vanuatu where Cook pondered how exploration might be viewed by the 'discovered':

its impossible for them to know our real design, we enter their Ports without their daring to make opposition, we attempt to land in a peaceable manner, if this succeeds its well, if not we land nevertheless and maintain the footing we thus got by the Superiority of our fire arms, in what other light can they than at first look upon us but as invaders of their Country. (Cook in Beaglehole 1969:493)

Early contacts that involved conflict should, in many instances, be viewed as an entirely predictable response to territorial intrusion (e.g. Dillon 1829:145) rather than mutual 'misunderstanding' from the collision of different cultures.

The second and more complicated dimension of conflict during the subsequent phase of colonial emplacement and expansion has been well canvassed (e.g. Morrison et al. 2019) and we confine ourselves to comments about changes to 'traditional' conflict and warfare, especially the issue of whether indigenous violence intensified in the colonial era. Conflicts within and between indigenous groups are argued to have been relatively common in Australia and the Pacific, and there is a considerable literature, and debate, about the expression, frequency and scale of 'traditional' conflicts in post-contact settings. The severity of inter-group violence witnessed may be related to demand for new goods in post-contact tribal societies (Blick 1988). Guns, glass, metal and many other new items were rapidly incorporated into Aboriginal societies (Harrison 2002a, 2002b; May et al. 2017). The seemingly innocuous addition of new items of material culture was studied by Sharp (1952), who found that the introduction of steel axes to the Yir Yoront undermined gender, kinship and totemic relations and contributed to high levels of social and psychological stress, which was linked with the possibility of symbolic, if not actual, aggression.

Rates of lethal aggression among hunter-gathers outlined by Gat (2015) may therefore be influenced by social destabilisation due to contact and colonialism. Fry (2006), in contrast, has argued that within-group murder/feud was more common in Aboriginal societies, while inter-group conflict, raiding and warfare were rare. The topic of conflict is largely absent from recent scholarship (see Allen 2014) including Bruce Pascoe's (2014) influential *Dark Emu*, except in relation to European invasion and settlement. If agriculture and other resources underpinned Aboriginal sedentism and higher population densities, as Pascoe suggests, then these factors in particular areas might also have led to significant conflict and inter-group warfare. We currently lack robust data and archaeological frameworks to distinguish between the range of plausible alternatives due, in part, to the entirely appropriate cultural and political sensitivities concerning the study of Indigenous remains (see Pardoe this volume). Nonetheless, we think it probable that some ethnohistoric records of Aboriginal inter-group violence were influenced by social instability, shrinking territory and a colonial environment where institutional discrimination and marginalisation was accompanied by violence and massacre on the frontier.

Turning to the Pacific, an increase in internal conflict is seen in several island groups after European contact (DiNapoli et al. 2020; Martin 1990). Some of the significant contributors to violence include demographic decline and social upheaval from introduced diseases, the introduction of metal weapons (hand and projectile), and the erosion of political and religious belief systems as colonial and foreign influence grew. In Aotearoa/New Zealand, Anderson (this volume) found that warfare was intensified by differential access to European muskets and cannons (see Vayda 1970), as is also reported in Vanuatu (Layard 1942:602–603), Hawai'i (D'Arcy 2000), Tonga (Martin 1990) and Fiji (Clunie 2003), although the impact of new weapons was not universal even within an archipelago (Shineberg 1966).

Traditional conflict in many parts of Oceania was frequently reciprocal, with impasses common and shifts in power and territory difficult to maintain. The introduction of new weapons to a segment of the population could be a decisive element, as in Palau where the paramount chief of Koror (*Ibedul*) successfully defeated his enemies in four engagements with the help a shipwrecked English crew equipped with cutlasses, pistols and muskets and, at times, a swivel gun (Clark and de Biran 2010). In Tonga, a fort at Nuku'alofa that had resisted traditional warfare for 11 years was taken in 1806 CE with the help of guns, cannons and crew forcibly taken from the *Port au Prince* (Martin 1991:82), and European mercenaries and their muskets in Fiji had a 'profound influence' on the rise of the Bau polity (Parry 1977:22). The demand for guns in Oceania was met by land, pigs, sandalwood and bêche-de-mer, and also women, creating new economic systems and port settlements that depended on foreign vessels (Quimby 2011).

Introduced diseases were disrupting populations in Australia and the Pacific at or soon after European contact (e.g. Crosby 1986; Richards 2004; Shell 1999). The first recorded epidemic in Tonga was in the 1790s (Martin 1991:66) after the arrival of missionaries who recorded that: 'Till the Europeans visited them, they had few disorders among them … The case at present is wofully [sic] altered' (Wilson 1799:381). Traditional history in Fiji links two major pandemics with early contact by the *Argo* (1800 CE), which brought a wasting sickness (*lila balavu*), and the *El Plumier* (1802 CE), associated with dysentery (*thokandra*) (Im Thurn and Wharton 2010). The historical demographer McArthur (1967:96) suggested that epidemic transmission may have been slower in Tonga due to sporadic contact between islands, yet there were high rates of intra- and inter-archipelago voyaging during the peak of the sandalwood trade in Fiji (1802–1812 CE), when European and American ships competed for the valuable timber. The point here is that Tongans had long travelled to Fiji to procure sandalwood and had European trade goods to exchange for Fijian products such as the large double canoes that not only increased chiefly trade but, like European vessels, were the means of spreading disease. This is shown by the arrival of an epidemic (*ngangau*) that killed many people in Tonga in 1811 CE and which likely originated in the Fijian sandalwood trade and was brought to Tonga in two canoes procured in Fiji (Statham 2013:85–86).

New weapons, economies and diseases contributed to social instability, as did the arrival of foreign ideologies and belief systems that competed with, and undermined, traditional power structures (Dening 1978). This is exhibited in the Pacific by the number of monarchies, both nominal and substantive, that emerged in the contact era in Hawai'i, Tonga, Fiji, Samoa, New Zealand and the Society Islands. These employed European weapons and influence to try and create new nation-states, including several that had imperial aspirations (Gunson 1969). The adoption of European political systems to exert control over an entire archipelago is noteworthy, as war group size and conflict causalities appear to scale with population size (Oka et al. 2017). In Fiji, the rise of the Bau chiefdom in the 1840s instituted conflicts with other polities that involved 'warfare on a scale and of a barbarity hitherto unknown' (Derrick 1974:75; also Sahlins 1991), while in Hawai'i battles for regional consolidation by Kamehamea I involved conflict at 'unprecedented levels' (Kennedy and Brady 1997:651).

New trade and exchange networks brought diseases and were accompanied by social reordering due to the arrival of different forms of Christianity, most of which were highly critical of the indigenous gods and religious customs that were interwoven through traditional socio-economic structures. Chiefly power and authority in Oceania derived from practical and religious roles, particularly those that maintained the health and wellbeing of the people. Introduced epidemics eroded traditional leadership directly by killing leaders and indirectly by showing that when faced with serious diseases the gods, chiefs and traditional medicines were ineffectual or worse: in Polynesian societies it was common for disease and death to be viewed as divine punishment for religious transgression (Burrows 1937:92; Martin 1991:331). In contrast, Christian missionaries were offering a non-elite religion and showing its power through the efficacy of foreign medicines. The connection between exotic medical treatment and support for Christianity was apparent to at least some missionaries:

> its [medicine] skilful and successful application is one of the best means of gaining influence among the people and predisposing them to regard with favour his endeavours to direct their minds to the heavenly Physician. (Ellis 1844:159)

Thus, in parts of the Australia–Pacific region, indigenous conflicts appear to have occurred at either a higher frequency, a greater intensity or a larger scale after culture contact and colonialism, although we are yet to fully understand all of the factors and reasons involved in a rise in internal conflict. For example, traditional kinship and ranking systems may have had a significant role in promoting conflict when several individuals had a valid claim to leadership positions in sociopolitical systems that were weakened by colonialism. Societal decline accompanied by conflict was often a reason for extending European control, including through punitive expeditions, which eventually reduced violence from the imposition of colonial rule (Bedford this volume; Best 1993; Irwin et al. 2019).

The impact of colonialism in Oceania suggests that previous significant episodes of non-European culture contact—which may have included elements of colonialism, such as the arrival of migrant communities—could be represented in an archaeological record of heightened violence. There are many potential examples of indigenous 'colonial' conflict that would benefit from archaeological investigation. These include aggression between Polynesian migrants from Tikopia and the Melanesian inhabitants of Vanikoro (Stanbury and Green 2004:138); the use of force and coercion by the Saudelur dynasty on Pohnpei, which traditionally overcame local opposition and instituted centralised control from the monumental Nan Madol site (Hanlon 1988); the overthrow of Tongan rule in Samoa by the founders of the Mālietoa title (Gifford 1929:52); the role of warfare in the powerful Roy Mata chiefdom of Vanuatu, which recent aDNA results suggest was influenced by Polynesian migration (Lipson et al. 2020); and Macassan conflicts with North Australian Indigenous communities (Macnight 1972:288).

Warfare and conflict as punctuated events

Historians have long commented that many conflicts appear as episodic and punctuated events (e.g. regional conflicts, the life cycle of empires and world wars), particularly in complex societies where cycles of violence and warfare are viewed as intrinsic drivers of system change. The Chinese dynastic cycle and Ibn Khaldun's (1332–1406 CE) model of state development associate political and moral corruption with economic and leadership collapse. Strong political systems begin with experienced military–civil leaders who overthrow corrupt and/or disorganised regimes and govern fairly, allowing a cohesive society to emerge and prosper. Over time, corruption and poor management, especially from self-interested and hereditary elites, increasingly burden the productive populace, which weakens and fragments society. Conflict and warfare, whether internal, external or a combination of both, resets the unbalanced political system to begin the next cycle. In Turchin's (2006) war–peace–war cycle, highly unified groups form at metaethnic frontiers, which separate groups and peoples with very different belief systems from one another. Competition and warfare at ethnic frontiers foster high social cohesion (Ibn Khaldun's *asabiya*), which drives military success and imperiogenesis. Eventually the number, and demands, of elites grows too large, social cohesion is lost and internal war breaks out, causing the 'death' of expansive states and empires. Scheidel (2017) also identified a progression from secular 'integrative' societies marked by relative equality (high cohesion) to later states where there was drastic inequality. Severe inequality can only be reversed, in Scheidel's persuasive analysis, by extreme violence from one of four sources (catastrophic epidemic/pandemic, complete economic collapse, mass-mobilisation warfare, transformative revolutions). Historical studies support the idea that poor governance, growing inequality, the enrichment of elites and increasing inflation/taxation precede conflict and collapse of complex societies primarily through destruction of the peasant–agrarian foundation (Tainter 2009:150–151; Yu-Ch'uan 1936).

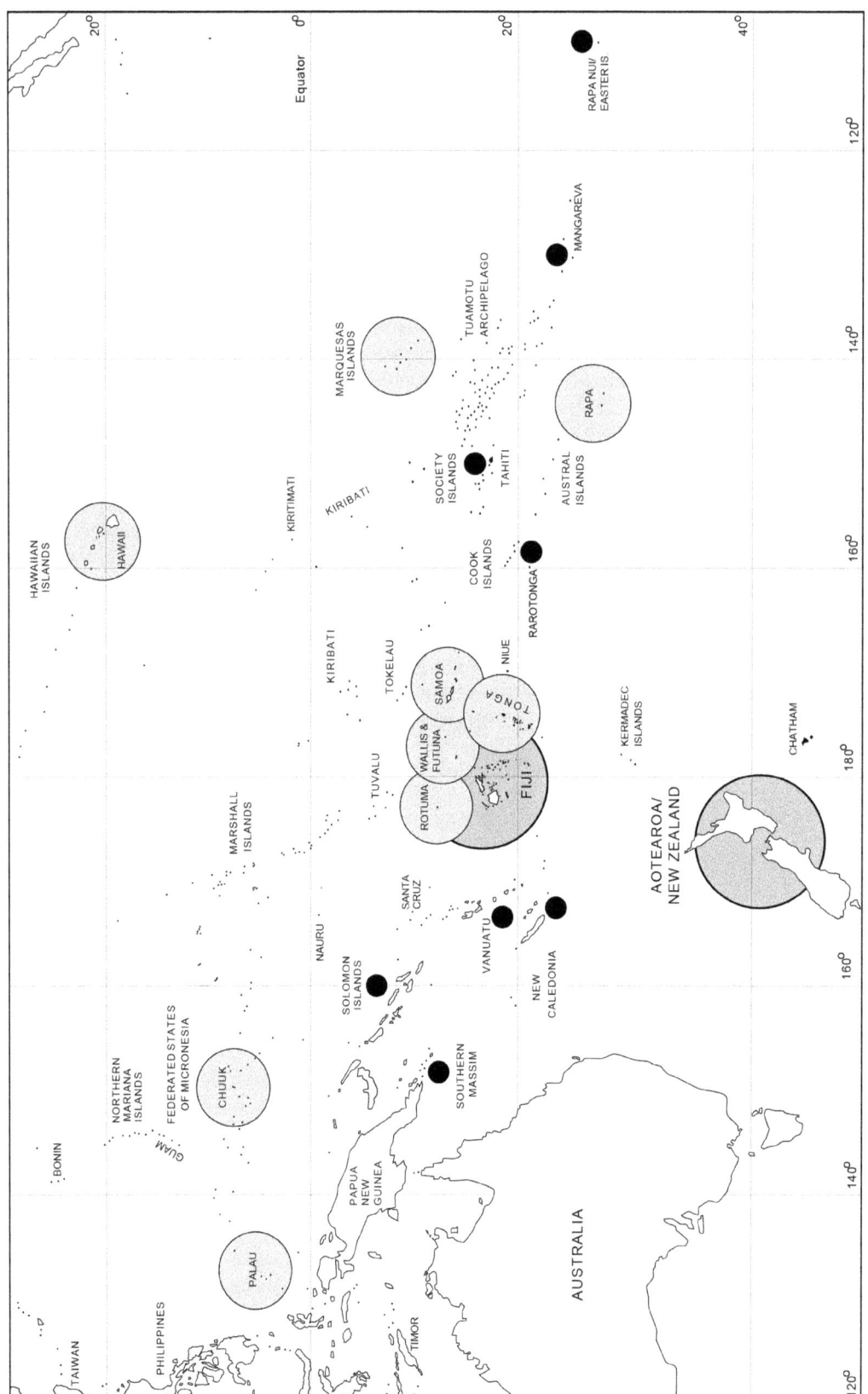

Figure 1.1. Relative abundance of fortified/defensive sites in the Pacific.

Based on Field and Lape (2010:Table 1) with additions as noted in the text (does not include west New Guinea forts mentioned by Wright et al. 2013). Note the presence of forts throughout Fiji–West Polynesia.

Source: Geoffrey Clark.

In contrast, some archaeologists and historians associate peaks of inter-group conflict in the past with reduced agricultural productivity caused by climate forcing, particularly colder and drier periods (Zhang et al. 2007), such as in the Little Ice Age (LIA, c. 1450–1850 CE). It is difficult to examine whether conflict in Australia and the Pacific has peaks and troughs that correlate with climate events although the potential exists for detailed chronological analyses of violence in rock art images, human remains and weapons to compare with palaeoclimate records. Fortifications have been used to examine a connection between climate events and conflict in the Indo-Pacific, with important work by Field and Lape (2010:121) indicating that in the tropical Pacific 'fortification construction is linked to drought, or more specifically, to subsistence systems that are significantly impacted by drought'. Elsewhere, Di Cosmo et al. (2018) present evidence that a seven-decade-long drought did not cause the Uyghur empire to collapse, wage war or decompose into simpler sociopolitical units, while the role of drought in the demise of the Khmer empire is also questioned (Caldararo 2015).

The link between fortification building and the LIA was based on the age and location of 8761 fortifications in the Pacific Islands (Field and Lape 2010:Table 1, excluding forts in Okinawa, Indonesia and Timor). The majority of fortifications in the study were in Aotearoa/New Zealand (6796) and Fiji (1523), comprising 95 per cent of the total. Smaller but significant numbers of fortifications/defensive sites are found in Palau (Babeldoab 253), Samoa (46), Tonga (39), Rapa Iti (35), Chuuk (26), 'Uvea (22), Hawaiian Islands (16) and Rotuma (14). In other areas there were only a few fortifications (Maupiti 1, Rarotonga 1, Marquesas 4, Maré Island 1, New Georgia 1). Since the data was compiled, additional fortifications (Figure 1.1) have been identified in ethnohistorical records, and archaeological and remote sensing surveys (e.g. Wright et al. 2013) including in the southern Massim (Irwin et al. 2019), Solomon Islands (Codrington 1901:301; Sheppard et al. 2000), Vanuatu (Layard 1942:596), New Caledonia (Sand 1996; pers. comm.), Fiji (Burley et al. 2016), Tongatapu (Parton et al. 2018), Mangareva (Green 1967) and the Marquesas (Molle and Marolleau this volume).

Fortified sites generally contain defensive structures that impede or control movement, such as walls, ditches, banks, causeways and pits in sites that vary in scale from large hillfort–ridgeline complexes to linear fortifications, enclosure defences (*enceinte*), observation posts and refuges (e.g. defended caves, landscape high points). Ritual and/or high-status structures in defended areas can also be used for controlling movement with built architecture. Best (1993) and Keeley et al. (2007) discuss features of defensive constructions, particularly ditches made for agriculture, water management and transport. On Rotuma the 'fortifications' listed by Field and Lape (2010) were described by Ladefoged (1993:253) as 'possible' defensive lookouts located on hilltops, as the sites did not have typical earth or stone defensive constructions. It is probable that many archaeological settlements, and perhaps the hill sites on Rotuma, were once defended by wooden palisades that have perished (e.g. Suggs 1961:163). It is also useful to note that inter-group raiding and warfare in several island groups did not necessarily involve earth and stone defences, but relied instead on placing warriors/young men in strategic locations, as in Palau (Babeldoab) and Yap, where men's houses guarded road and wharf access to villages (Liston this volume, see Younger 2009). Similarly, in Guam in 1526 CE, where built defensive sites were rare/absent:

> They make war among themselves. The weapons they have are slings, and fire-hardened sticks. They also place at the tip of some sticks the shinbones of men they have killed in battle, and which they also use to fight with. (Urdaneta in Lévesque 1992:465)

The location of sites on high points and in association with significant communication corridors (marine and terrestrial) is suggestive of strategic control and/or observation, whereas substantial fortifications indicate a community-scale military/defensive role (e.g. Clausewitz 1984; Parton et al. this volume; Reepmeyer et al. this volume).

Some of the fortifications listed by Field and Lape (2010), such as the earthworks in Palau and stone forts in New Caledonia, clearly predate the LIA, while others were made in the eighteenth–nineteenth centuries after European contact (see also western New Guinea forts in Wright et al. 2013). Detailed study of early fortifications would help to show whether climate events and potential resource shortfalls coincide with the development of elaborate defensive structures in New Caledonia and Palau prior to the LIA. Recent fortifications dating to the nineteenth century include the majority of Tongan earthwork fortifications built after the collapse of centralised rule, which caused a lengthy civil conflict among regional chiefs and their followers (Gifford 1929; Statham 2013; Parton et al. 2018), an unknown number of Fijian forts associated with significant conflict among nineteenth-century political confederacies (e.g. Burley et al. 2016), and forts used in post-contact warfare in Samoa (Davidson 1974:241; see also Best 1993). More than 500 fortifications were made during the New Zealand Wars (1843–1881 CE), with 322 made by Europeans and 183 by Maori (Prickett 2016). It is feasible therefore that a proportion of defensive sites listed by Field and Lape (2010) were constructed in response to social destabilisation following European contact rather than in reaction to LIA conditions. In addition to the structures already mentioned, post-contact fortifications were also probably made and used on Chuuk (Rainbird 1996:470), New Georgia (Sheppard et al. 2000:25–26), Marquesas (Suggs 1961:163), Hawai'i (Kennedy and Brady 1997), Society Islands (Green 1967:103–104), 'Uvea (Burrows 1937:83–84), Rotuma (Howard and Kjellgren 1994) and the northern Marianas (Burney 1813:308).

Nonetheless, many defensive sites and fortifications in Oceania were constructed during the LIA and warfare appears to have been endemic in several areas well before European contact (Knauft 1990). Fortifications in Oceania have a patchy distribution (Groube 1970:133) that is largely inconsistent with direct cultural transmission, with one important exception. For instance, the ridgeline forts of Rapa Iti do not occur on other Austral Islands, and in Palau early and late defences (e.g. those in the Rock Islands) are not found on Yap or the Marianas. There is no obvious source for the *pā* earthworks of New Zealand in Central Polynesia (Green 1967), and *pā* were not introduced to the Chatham Islands that were settled by Maori (Anderson this volume). An alternative to direct transmission is that the practice of surrounding settlements and compounds with wooden palisades/fences (PPN **kolo*) was an early and widespread development. Palisades were eventually combined with ditch and bank earthworks, or the settlement boundary in rocky areas could be rendered in stone. Excavations in Fiji–West Polynesia show that earth and stone residential and burial structures date to at least 1000 CE (Best 1984; Field 2004; Frimigacci and Sand 2016). In Tonga, earth mounds were commonly formed by excavating a ditch around a residence, with the soil used to create a raised house foundation, suggesting that the architectural elements of palisade/ditch and bank fortifications were in place by the time East Polynesia was colonised (Wilmshurst et al. 2011), but were only brought together to make fortifications in some island groups.

The exception to the patchy distribution of forts noted above is a well-defined cluster in the Fiji–West Polynesia area consisting of Fiji, Rotuma, Tonga, 'Uvea, Futuna and Samoa (Figure 1.1). Within this area, interaction in the past 1000 years appears to have been relatively common. Warfare involving Tongan arrivals is noted in the traditional histories of these islands and is supported by significant linguistic, traditional and archaeological data (e.g. Burrows 1937; Krämer 1995; Sand 1993; Schmidt 2000). From a Tongan perspective, warfare in traditional and historical records has a punctuated expression, with internal and external conflict strongly correlated (i.e. Ross 1985). The most recent conflict phase in the late eighteenth–nineteenth centuries involved polity fragmentation, significant warfare and the construction of fortifications throughout the Tongan archipelago. External conflicts included Tongan involvement in 'wars' in Fiji (Martin 1991), culminating in the Tongan chief Ma'afu's control of east and northern Fiji before the archipelago became a British crown colony in 1874 CE (Spurway 2015). An earlier phase of warfare occurred in Tonga c. 1450–1500 CE, when the Tuʻi Tonga Takalaua was murdered by two chiefs from a neighbouring chiefdom (Parton et al. this volume). Oral traditions record that Takalaua's son, Kauʻulufonuafekai, then undertook a vigorous military campaign involving fortifications, which subdued dissent within Tonga (Tongatapu, ʻEua, Haʻapai, Vavaʻu, Niuatoputapu, Niuafoʻou) and abroad to Samoa, ʻUvea and Futuna (Gifford 1929:54–56; Statham 2013:29–30).

We do not suggest that all conflict in Fiji–West Polynesia can be condensed into two time periods, but note that in two instances instability in the centralised system of Tonga led to major civil conflicts that had significant external impacts including warfare and the construction and use of fortifications. The role of the LIA in these conflicts requires island-specific high-resolution climate records and an emphasis on the archaeological investigation of defensive sites, yet neither traditional history nor ethnohistory currently suggest that climate change was a decisive factor in outbreaks of conflict. In Aotearoa/New Zealand and Fiji, where most Pacific fortifications were made, there are interesting parallels in their defensive sites and features such as proximity to intensively gardened arable land, indications of significant population growth, high rates of internal migration and, in the protohistoric era at least, an increase in the density and size variation of fortifications indicating larger political units and confederations (Anderson this volume; Parry 1997).

The impetus for these defensive configurations is likely a response to external threats (Best 1984:658; Irwin 1985; Parry 1977), especially from inter-regional conflict and migration. It is worth noting that during the LIA—a proposed period of climatic and societal stress—populations appear to have increased in both subtropical and tropical islands, and complex societies, which arguably reached the level of archaic states, emerged in Tonga, Hawaiʻi, Tahiti and perhaps Pohnpei. Population agglomeration, whether from making war, defending against it or migrating from it, can stimulate the formation of new sociopolitical systems with high levels of social cohesion.

Conclusion

Carneiro (1970) theorised that the development of complex societies, leading to early states, involved inter-group warfare for limited agricultural land, and archaeological findings support the view that coercion and warfare were involved in state formation (e.g. Clark et al. 2017; Marcus 1998; Spencer 2003; Stanish and Levine 2011). However, the archaeological identification of violence does not tell us whether these seminal conflicts were over arable land. Cyclical theories of conflict in human history suggest that warfare was involved in the expansion and collapse of several societies, implying that conflict is an entrenched and almost inescapable aspect of human history, as in Allison's (2015) 'Thucydides trap', where rising and ruling powers battle for primacy. As rates of violent death in the second millennium CE are now held to be lower than they were in the past, it has been argued that warfare is essentially responsible for the development of large populations ruled by stable governments: that stamping out internal violence creates the conditions for mass economic prosperity (Morris 2014). To return to the quote by Samuel Johnson, violence and conflict may, under certain lights, be conceived as a 'good thing', but this counterintuitive reframing of violence only emphasises how little we know about its deployment and societal influence in the past, particularly in relation to the formation of complex societies. In addition, because many conflicts have a punctuated expression, it may be the case that while larger political entities tend to have an overall lower frequency of warfare, when outbreaks of violence occur, they can result in greater social disruption and a larger number of overall deaths.

In Australia and the Pacific, the construction of detailed chronological records of aggression is an important research issue, but to develop a better understanding of conflict requires, among other things, detailed climate–environment sequences and the investigation of group sociopolitical structure and interactions. Environmental shortfalls and resource scarcity play a part in conflict, yet so too do the social and political structures of human groups, which while difficult to identify archaeologically are central to understanding variation in the frequency and scale of aggression. Thomas Hobbes and Jean-Jacques Rousseau had contrasting and influential views about human nature and violence in the past, but their ideas were simply thought experiments about human behaviour that can now be tested against increasingly detailed sets of archaeological and environmental data. In 1932, Freud exchanged pessimistic views with Einstein on how conflict seemed innate to human nature:

> In some happy corners of the earth, they say, where nature brings forth abundantly whatever man desires, there flourish races whose lives go gently by: unknowing of aggression or constraint. This I can hardly credit; I would like further details about these happy folk. (Freud in Isaacson 2008:597)

It is a truism that is not always appreciated in archaeology that the resources available to every society are 'limited' and therefore that resource shortfalls in the past must be a primary driver of conflict. Yet the frequency and scale of violence varies significantly among contemporary groups located in comparable subsistence environments and which share a similar technology, population number, density and social hierarchy (Knauft and Shankman 1992; Nolan 2003:28; Robarchek and Robarchek 1992). The manner in which different leadership, belief and social systems incentivise competition and inter-group violence are also aspects that need archaeological consideration, particularly in areas where conflict appears to have been endemic (Knauft 1990).

In parts of Fiji, warfare was used to subjugate villages that were then incorporated into unstable regional polities to provide the subsistence and material goods for higher ranked settlements (Clunie 2003; Parry 1977). Ranked villages also existed in Palau and may be manifested in the dense *pā* landscapes of New Zealand (e.g. Irwin 1985; Liston this volume). It was not land *per se* that was sought in these conflicts, but the ability to control human labour and productivity that materialised chiefly and community power—this may well be the principal driver of endemic internal/territorial conflict. A great advantage of our region is the presence of rich ethnographic and historic records that can be integrated with archaeological data to examine culture contact and colonialism in different landscapes (e.g. Barker et al. 2020; Bedford this volume; May et al. 2017). As we have noted, European culture contact has likely had a significant impact on the scale and intensity of some conflicts. This needs to be taken into account by researchers, but does not necessarily lessen the value of textual records for understanding indigenous conflict, and of course, such material is critical for tracking the complicated and long-term impacts of contact, colonialism and globalisation. We have also identified that societal instability and outbreaks of conflict, both internal and external, were often an outcome of ongoing culture contact and migration (Anderson this volume; Bamforth 1994), which are aspects of human life with a deep past. Globalisation in the relatively recent era was accompanied by the spread of pathogens that contributed to social instability and high rates of violence and conflict that led to millions of deaths (e.g. Tavares et al. 2019).

Historical records and comparative analyses of conflict and warfare including traditional perspectives are an important but often underutilised resource to understand violence in the archaeological record, whether at a single site or in records that extend across landscapes and encompass long periods. Finally, studies of traditional weapons, art, vocabulary and performances, along with an examination of the defensive properties of sites (Reepmeyer et al. this volume) are needed to establish the social dimensions and traditional practices of conflict in our region.

References

Allen, M.W. 2014. Hunter-gatherer violence and warfare in Australia. In M.W. Allen and T.L. Jones (eds), *Violence and warfare among hunter-gatherers*, pp. 97–111. Left Coast Press, California. doi.org/10.4324/9781315415970-5.

Allison, G. 2015. The Thucydides trap. Are the U.S. and China headed for war? *The Atlantic*, 24 September.

Al-Muqdadi, S.W.H. 2019. Developing strategy for water conflict management and transformation at Euphrates–Tigris Basin. *Water* 11:2037. doi.org/10.3390/w11102037.

Ambrose, W. 1988. An early bronze artifact from Papua New Guinea. *Antiquity* 62:483–491. doi.org/10.1017/s0003598x00074585.

Amhurst, Lord and B. Thomson 1901. *The discovery of the Solomon Islands by Alvaro de Mendana in 1568*. Translated from the original Spanish manuscripts. 2 volumes. The Hakluyt Society, London.

Anderson, A.J. 2000. Slow boats from China: Issues in the prehistory of Indo-Pacific seafaring. In S. O'Connor and P. Veth (eds), *East of Wallace's Line: Studies of past and present maritime cultures of the Indo-Pacific region*, pp. 13–50. Balkema, Rotterdam.

Arrian and A. de Sélincourt 1976. *The campaigns of Alexander*. Penguin Classics, Hammondsworth and Baltimore.

Ayres, W. (ed.) 1995. *Geiseler's Easter Island report: An 1880s anthropological account*. Asian and Pacific Archaeology Series No. 12. University of Hawai'i Press, Honolulu.

Bahn, P. 2015. The end of the moai–did they fall or were they pushed? In N. Cauwe and M. De Dapper (eds), *Easter Island: Collapse or transformation? A state of the art*, pp. 135–152. Royal Academy for Overseas Sciences and Royal Museums of Art and History, Brussels.

Ballara, A. 1976. The role of warfare in Maori society in the early contact period. *Journal of the Polynesian Society* 85(4):487–506.

Bamforth, D.B. 1994. Indigenous people, Indigenous violence: Precontact warfare on the north American Great Plains. *Man* 29(1):95–115. doi.org/10.2307/2803512.

Barber, I. 2012. Gardens of Rongo: Applying cross-field anthropology to explain contact violence in New Zealand. *Current Anthropology* 53: 799–808. doi.org/10.1086/667834.

Barker, B., L.A. Wallis, H. Burke, N. Cole, K. Lowe et al. 2020. The archaeology of the 'Secret War': The material evidence of conflict on the Queensland frontier, 1849–1901. *Queensland Archaeological Research* 23:25–41. doi.org/10.25120/qar.23.2020.3720.

Beaglehole, J.C. (ed.) 1968. *The journals of Captain James Cook on his voyages of discovery. Volume I: The voyage of the* Endeavour, *1768–1771*. The Hakluyt Society, Cambridge.

Beaglehole, J.C. (ed.) 1969. *The journals of Captain James Cook on his voyages of discovery. Volume II: The voyage of the* Resolution *and* Adventure, *1772–1775*. The Hakluyt Society, Cambridge. doi.org/10.4324/9781315086156.

Bedford, S., D. Haskell-Crook, M. Spriggs and R. Shing. 2020. Encounters with stone: Missionary battles with idols in the southern New Hebrides. *Journal of Pacific Archaeology* 11(2):21–33.

Best, S. 1984. Lakeba: The prehistory of a Fijian Island. Unpublished PhD thesis. University of Auckland, Auckland.

Best, S. 1993. At the halls of the mountain kings. Fijian and Samoan fortifications: Comparison and analysis. *Journal of the Polynesian Society* 102(4):385–447.

Betz, D. 2019. Citadels and marching forts: How non-technological drivers are pointing future warfare towards techniques from the past. *Scandinavian Journal of Military Studies* 2(1):30–41. doi.org/10.31374/sjms.25.

Blick, J.P. 1988. Genocidal warfare in tribal societies as a result of European-induced culture conflict. *Royal Anthropological Institute of Great Britain and Ireland* 23(4):654–670. doi.org/10.2307/2802598.

Bocquentin, F. and O. Bar-Yosef 2004. Early Natufian remains: Evidence for physical conflict from Mt. Carmel, Israel. *Journal of Human Evolution* 47:19–23. doi.org/10.1016/j.jhevol.2004.05.003.

Brooks, C.C. 1981. A contribution to the geoarchaeology of Truk, Micronesia. *Asian Perspectives* 24(1):27–42.

Brown, P. 1989. *Coobool Creek: A morphological and metrical analysis of the crania, mandibles and dentitions of a prehistoric Australian human population.* Terra Australis 13. Research School of Pacific Studies, The Australian National University, Canberra.

Buckley, B.B., K.J. Anchukaitis, D. Penny, R. Fletcher, E.R. Cook et al. 2010. Climate as a contributing factor in the demise of Angkor, Cambodia. *Proceedings of the National Academy of Sciences USA* 107(15):6748–6752. doi.org/10.1073/pnas.0910827107.

Buckley, H.R. 2000. A possible fatal wounding in the prehistoric Pacific Islands. *International Journal of Osteoarchaeology* 10(2):135–141. doi.org/10.1002/(SICI)1099-1212(200003/04)10:2<135::AID-OA518>3.0.CO;2-O.

Burke, H. and L.A. Wallis 2019. *Frontier conflict and the Native Mounted Police in Queensland Database.* doi.org/10.25957/5d9fb541294d5.

Burley, D.V., T. Freeland and J. Balenaivalu 2016. Nineteenth-century conflict and the Koivuanabuli fortification complex on Mali Island, Northern Fiji. *Journal of Island and Coastal Archaeology* 11(1):107–121. doi.org/10.1080/15564894.2015.1050132.

Burney, J. 1813 [1967]. *A chronological history of voyages and discoveries in the South Seas. Part 3: From the Year 1620, to the Year 1688.* Da Capo Press and N. Israel, Amsterdam and New York.

Burrows, E.G. 1936. *Ethnology of Futuna.* Bernice P. Bishop Museum Bulletin 138. Bishop Museum, Honolulu.

Burrows, E.G. 1937. *Ethnology of Uvea (Wallis Island).* Bernice P. Bishop Museum Bulletin 145. Bishop Museum, Honolulu.

Caldararo, N. 2015. Beyond zero population: Ethnohistory, archaeology and the Khmer, climate change and the collapse of civilizations. *Anthropology* 3(2):1000154. doi.org/10.4172/2332-0915.1000154.

Campbell, I.C. 2009. Chiefs, agitators and the navy: The Mau in American Samoa. *Journal of Pacific History* 44(1):41–60. doi.org/10.1080/00223340902900779.

Carneiro, R.L. 1970. A theory of the origin of the state. *Science* 169:733–738.

Carneiro, R.L. 1988. The Circumscription Theory. Challenge and response. *American Behavioral Scientist* 31(4):497–511. doi.org/10.1177/000276488031004010.

Carson, M.T. 2017. Cultural spaces inside and outside caves: A study in Guam, western Micronesia. *Antiquity* 91(356):421–441. doi.org/10.15184/aqy.2016.233.

Chappell, D.A. 1993. Frontier ethnogenesis: The case of New Caledonia. *Journal of World History* 4(2):307–324.

Chippindale, C., B. Smith and P.S.C. Taçon 2000. Visions of Dynamic power: Archaic rock-paintings, altered states of consciousness and 'Clever Men' in Western Arnhem Land (NT), Australia. *Cambridge Archaeological Journal* 10(1):63–101. doi.org/10.1017/s0959774300000032.

Churchill, W. 1911. *The Polynesian wanderings; tracks of the migration deduced from an examination of the proto-Samoan content of Efaté and other languages of Melanesia*. The Carnegie Institution of Washington, Washington.

Clark, G. 2005. A 3000-year culture sequence from Palau, western Micronesia. *Asian Perspectives* 44:349–380. doi.org/10.1353/asi.2005.0020.

Clark, G. 2016. Chiefly tombs, lineage history, and the ancient Tongan state. *Journal of Island and Coastal Archaeology* 11(3):326–343. doi.org/10.1080/15564894.2015.1098754.

Clark, G. 2017. Violence and early maritime encounters in the Pacific. In C. Beaule (ed.), *Frontiers of colonialism*, pp. 208–235. University of Florida Press, Florida. doi.org/10.2307/j.ctvx06wxq.15.

Clark, G. and A. de Biran 2010. Geophysical and archaeological investigation of the survivor-camp of the *Antelope* (1783) in the Palau Islands, Western Pacific. *International Journal of Nautical Archaeology* 39(2):345–356. doi.org/10.2307/j.ctvx06wxq.15.

Clark, G. and M. Langley 2020. Ancient tattooing in Polynesia. *Journal of Island and Coastal Archaeology* 15(3):407–420. doi.org/10.1080/15564894.2018.1561558.

Clark, G., C. Reepmeyer, N. Melekiola, J. Woodhead, W.R. Dickinson and H. Martinsson-Wallin 2014. Stone tools from the ancient Tongan state reveal prehistoric interaction centres in the Central Pacific. *Proceedings of the National Academy of Sciences USA* 111(29):10491–10496. doi.org/10.1073/pnas.1406165111.

Clark, G., P. Parton, C. Reepmeyer, N. Melekiola and D. Burley 2017. Conflict and state development in ancient Tonga: The Lapaha earth fort. *Journal of Island and Coastal Archaeology* 13(3):405–419. doi.org/10.1080/15564894.2017.1337658.

Clarke, P. 2000. Food security and war in Afghanistan. *Development* 43(3):113–119.

Clarkson, C., Z. Jacobs, B. Marwick, R. Fullagar, L. Wallis et al. 2017. Human occupation of northern Australia by 65,000 years ago. *Nature* 547:306–310. doi.org/10.1038/nature22968.

Clausewitz, C.V. 1984. *On war*. Princeton University Press, Princeton.

Clunie, F. 2003. *Fijian weapons and warfare*. Bulletin of the Fiji Museum No. 2. The Fiji Museum, Suva.

Codrington, R.H. 1901. *The Melanesians: Studies in their anthropology and folklore*. Clarendon Press, Oxford.

Connor, J. 2002. *The Australian frontier wars, 1788–1838*. University of New South Wales Press, Sydney.

Cork, E. 2005. Peaceful Harappans? Reviewing the evidence for the absence of warfare in the Indus Civilization of north-west India and Pakistan (c. 2500–1900 BC). *Antiquity* 79:411–423. doi.org/10.1017/s0003598x0011419x.

Crosby, A.W. 1986. *Ecological imperialism: The biological expansion of Europe, 900–1900*. Cambridge University Press, Cambridge, New York and Melbourne.

Cummins, H.G. 1977. Holy war: Peter Dillon and the 1837 massacres in Tonga. *Journal of Pacific History* 12(1):25–39. doi.org/10.1080/00223347708572311.

Curr, E.M. 1883. *Recollections of squatting in Victoria, then called the Port Phillip District (from 1841 to 1851)*. George Robertson, Melbourne, Sydney and Adelaide.

Daly, M. 2012. The Bible and the sword: John Thomas and the Tongan civil war of 1837. *Wesley and Methodist Studies* 4:71–90.

D'Arcy, P. 2000. Maori and muskets from a pan-Polynesian perspective. *New Zealand Journal of History* 34(1):117–132.

Davidson, J.M. 1974. Samoan structural remains and settlement patterns. In R.C. Green and J.M. Davidson (eds), *Archaeology in Western Samoa*, Volume II, pp. 225–243. Bulletin of the Auckland Institute and Museum Number 7, Auckland.

DeGusta, D. 1999. Fijian cannibalism: Osteological evidence from Navatu. *American Journal of Physical Anthropology* 110:215–241. doi.org/10.1002/(sici)1096-8644(199910)110:2<215::aid-ajpa7>3.0.co;2-d.

Dening, G. 1978. Institutions of violence in the Marquesas. In N. Gunson (ed.), *The changing Pacific. Essays in honour of H.E. Maude*, pp. 134–141. Oxford University Press, Melbourne.

Derrick, R.A. 1974. *A History of Fiji*. Volume One. Government Press, Suva.

Diamond, J. 2005. *Collapse: How societies choose to fail or survive*. Penguin Group, Victoria.

Di Cosmo, N., A. Hessl, C. Leland, O. Byambasuren, H. Tian et al. 2018. Environmental stress and steppe nomads: Re-thinking the history of the Uyghur empire (744–840) with paleoclimate data. *Journal of Interdisciplinary History* 48(4):439–463. doi.org/10.1162/jinh_a_01194.

Dillon, P. 1829. *Narrative and successful result of a voyage in the South Seas, performed by order of the Government of British India to ascertain the actual fate of La Pérouse's expedition*. Volume II. Hurst, Chance, and Co., London.

DiNapoli, R.J., C.P. Lipo, T. Brosnan, T.L. Hunt, S. Hixon et al. 2019. Rapa Nui (Easter Island) monument (*ahu*) locations explained by freshwater sources. *PLoS ONE* 14(1):e0210409. doi.org/10.1371/journal.pone.0210409.

DiNapoli, R., C. Lipo and T. Hunt 2020. Revisiting warfare, monument destruction, and the 'Huri Moaiá' phase in Rapa Nui (Easter Island) culture history. *Journal of Pacific Archaeology* 12(1):1–24. Available at: pacificarchaeology.org/index.php/journal/article/view/313.

Dittmar, J.M., E. Berger, X. Zhan, R. Mao, H. Wang and H.-Y. Yeh 2019. Skeletal evidence for violent trauma from the bronze age Qijia culture (2,300–1,500 BCE), Gansu Province, China. *International Journal of Paleopathology* 27:66–79. doi.org/10.1016/j.ijpp.2019.08.002.

Douglas, B. 1980. Conflicts and alliance in a colonial context: Case studies in New Caledonia 1853–1870. *Journal of Pacific History* 15(1):21–51. doi.org/10.1080/00223348008572386.

Dubois, M.-J. 1970. Les grands refuges de guerre de Hnaened à Maré, Nouvelle-Calédonie. *Journal de la Société des Océanistes* 26:55–60. doi.org/10.3406/jso.1970.2284.

Dye, T. 2014. Wealth in old Hawai'i: Good-year economics and the rise of pristine states. *Archaeology in Oceania* 49(2):59–72. doi.org/10.1002/arco.5034.

Earle, T. 1997. *How chiefs come to power: The political economy in prehistory*. Stanford University Press, Stanford.

Ella, S. 1899. The war of Tonga and Samoa and the origin of the name Malietoa. *Journal of the Polynesian Society* 8(4):231–234.

Ellis, W. 1844. *The history of the London Missionary Society*. Volume I. John Snow, London.

Ember, C.R. and M. Ember 1992. Resource unpredictability, mistrust, and war: A cross cultural study. *Journal of Conflict Resolution* 36:242–262. doi.org/10.1177/0022002792036002002.

Evans, R. and W. Thorpe 1992. Power, punishment and penal labour: Convict workers and Moreton Bay. *Australian Historical Studies* 98(25):90–111. doi.org/10.1080/10314619208595895.

Eyre, E.J. 1984. *Autobiographical narrative of residence and exploration in Australia 1832–1839.* Calaban Books, London.

Feinberg, R. 1998. *Oral traditions of Anuta: A Polynesian outlier in the Solomon Islands.* Oxford University Press, New York and Oxford.

Fibiger, L., T. Ahlström, P. Bennike and R.J. Schulting 2013. Patterns of violence-related skull trauma in Neolithic southern Scandinavia. *American Journal of Physical Anthropology* 150:190–202. doi.org/10.1002/ajpa.22192.

Field, J.S. 2004. Environmental and climatic considerations: A hypothesis for conflict and the emergence of social complexity in Fijian prehistory. *Journal of Anthropological Archaeology* 23:79–99. doi.org/10.1016/j.jaa.2003.12.004.

Field, J.S. and P.V. Lape 2010. Paleoclimates and the emergence of fortifications in the tropical Pacific Islands. *Journal of Anthropological Archaeology* 29:113–124. doi.org/10.1016/j.jaa.2009.11.001.

Filihia, M. 1999. Rituals of sacrifice in early post-European contact Tonga and Tahiti. *Journal of the Polynesian Society* 34(1):5–22. doi.org/10.1080/00223349908572888.

Flas, D. 2015. The mata'a and the 'Collapse Hypothesis'. In N. Cauwe and M. De Dapper (eds), *Easter Island: Collapse or transformation? A state of the art*, pp. 59–75. Royal Academy for Overseas Sciences and Royal Museums of Art and History, Brussels.

Forster, J.R. 1982. *The* Resolution *journal of Reinhold Forster 1772–1775.* Volume III. Edited by M.E. Hoare. The Hakluyt Society, London.

Fowles, J. 1974. On chronocentrism. *Futures* 6(1):65–68.

Frederickson, C., M. Spriggs and W. Ambrose 1993. Pamwak rockshelter: A Pleistocene site on Manus Island, Papua New Guinea. In M.A. Smith, M. Spriggs and B. Fankhauser (eds), *Sahul in review*, pp. 144–154. Occasional Papers in Prehistory 24. Department of Prehistory, The Australian National University, Canberra.

Frimigacci, D. and C. Sand 2016. *Archéologie de 'Uvea Mama'o.* Institut d'archéologie de la Nouvelle-Calédonie et du Pacifique, Nouméa, Nouvelle Calédonie.

Fry, D. 2006. *The human potential for peace: An anthropological challenge to assumptions about war and violence.* Oxford University Press, Oxford.

Fujita, M., S. Yamasaki, C. Katagiri, I. Oshiro, K. Sano et al. 2016. Advanced maritime adaptation in the western Pacific coastal region extends back to 35,000–30,000 years before present. *Proceedings of the National Academy of Sciences USA* 113(40):11184–11189. doi.org/10.1073/pnas.1607857113.

Fullagar, R., J. McDonald, J. Field and D. Donlon 2009. Deadly weapons: Backed microliths from Narrabeen, New South Wales. In M. Haslam, G. Robertson, A. Crowther, S. Nugent and L. Kirkwood (eds), *Archaeological science under a microscope: Studies in residue and ancient DNA analysis in Honour of Thomas H. Loy*, pp. 258–270. ANU E Press, Canberra. doi.org/10.22459/ta30.07.2009.19.

Gapps, S. 2018. Contested waterways: Aboriginal resistance in early colonial Sydney. *Signals* 123:22–27.

Gat, A. 2015. Proving communal warfare among hunter-gatherers: The quasi-Rousseauan error. *Evolutionary Anthropology* 24:111–126. doi.org/10.1002/evan.21446.

Gifford, E.W. 1929. *Tongan society.* Bernice P. Bishop Museum Bulletin 61. Bernice P. Bishop Museum, Honolulu.

Gilchrist, R. 2003. Towards a social archaeology of warfare. *World Archaeology* 35(1):1–6.

Green, R. 1967. Fortifications in other parts of tropical Polynesia. *New Zealand Archaeological Association Newsletter* 10:96–113.

Green, R.C. 1979. Lapita. In J. Jennings (ed.), *The prehistory of Polynesia*, pp. 27–60. Australian National University Press, Canberra.

Grguric, N.K. 2008. Fortified homesteads: The architecture of fear in frontier South Australia and the Northern Territory, ca. 1847–1885. *Journal of Conflict Archaeology* 4(1–2):59–85. doi.org/10.1163/157407808X382764.

Groube, L.M. 1970. The origin and development of earthwork fortifications in the Pacific. In R.C. Green and M. Kelly (eds), *Studies in Oceanic culture history*, Volume I, pp. 133–164. Pacific Anthropological Records Number 11. Bernice P. Bishop Museum, Honolulu.

Gunson, N. 1969. Pomare II of Tahiti and Polynesian imperialism. *Journal of Pacific History* 4:65–82. doi.org/10.1080/00223346908572146.

Haddon, A.C. 1928. The cult of Waiet in the Murray Islands, Torres Strait. *Memoirs of the Queensland Museum* 9(2):127–135.

Handy, E.S.C. 1923. *The native culture in the Marquesas. Volume 9: Bayard Dominick expedition.* Bernice P. Bishop Museum, Honolulu.

Hanlon, D. 1988. *Upon a stone altar: A history of the island of Pohnpei to 1890.* University of Hawai'i Press, Honolulu. doi.org/10.2307/j.ctvp2n4g9.

Harrison, R. 2002a. Archaeology and the colonial encounter: Kimberley spear points, cultural identity and masculinity in the north of Australia. *Journal of Social Archaeology* 2(3):352–377. doi.org/10.1177/146960530200200304.

Harrison, R. 2002b. Australia's iron age: Aboriginal post-contact metal artefacts from old Lamboo Station, Southeast Kimberley, Western Australia. *Australasian Historical Archaeology* 20:67–76.

Haug, G.H., D. Günther, L.C. Peterson, D.M. Sigman, K.A. Hughen et al. 2003. Climate and the collapse of Maya civilization. *Science* 299(5613):1731–1735. doi.org/10.1126/science.1080444.

Hill, G.B. and L.F. Powell (eds). 1934. *Boswell's life of Johnson. Volume 1. The life (1709–1763).* Clarendon Press, Oxford.

Hintze, O. 1975. Military organization and the organization of the state. In F. Gilbert (ed.), *The historical essays of Otto Hintze*, pp. 179–215. Oxford University Press, New York.

Hitchcock, G. 2017. The final fate of the La Pérouse expedition? The 1818 account of Shaik Jumaul, a Lascar castaway in Torres Strait. *The Journal of Pacific History* 52(2):217–235. doi.org/10.1080/00223344.2017.1335370.

Hommon, R.J. 2013. *The ancient Hawaiian state: Origins of a political society.* Oxford University Press, New York.

Howard, A. and E. Kjellgren 1994. Martyrs, progress and political ambition: Re-examining Rotuma's 'religious wars'. *Journal of Pacific History* 29(2):131–152. doi.org/10.1080/00223349408572768.

Huang, C.C. and H. Su 2009. Climate change and Zhou relocations in early Chinese history. *Journal of Historical Geography* 35(2):297–310. doi.org/10.1016/j.jhg.2008.08.006.

Hudjashov, G., P. Endicott, H. Post, N. Nagle, S.Y.D. Ho et al. 2018. Investigating the origins of eastern Polynesians using genome-wide data from the Leeward Society Isles. *Scientific Reports* 8:1823. doi.org/10.1038/s41598-018-20026-8.

Hutchinson, D.L. 1996. Brief encounters: Tatham mound and evidence for Spanish and native American confrontation. *International Journal of Osteoarchaeology* 6:51–65. doi.org/10.1002/(sici)1099-1212 (199601)6:1<51::aid-oa257>3.0.co;2-e.

Igler, D. 2015. Hardly Pacific: Violence and death in the Great Ocean. *Pacific Historical Review* 84(1):1–18.

Im Thurn, E. and L.C. Wharton (eds) 2010. *Journal of William Lockerby, sandalwood trader in the Fijian Islands during the years 1808–1809: With an introduction and other papers connected with the earliest European visitors to the islands*. Hakluyt Society, London. doi.org/10.4324/9781315556451.

Irwin, G. 1985. *Land, pā and polity. A study based on the Maori fortifications of Pouto*. New Zealand Archaeological Association Monograph 15. New Zealand Archaeological Association, Auckland.

Irwin, G., B. Shaw and A. McAlister 2019. The origins of the Kula Ring: Archaeological and maritime perspectives from the southern Massim and Mailu areas of Papua New Guinea. *Archaeology in Oceania* 54:1–16. doi 10.1002/arco.5167.

Isaac, B. and G. Isaac 2011. Unexpected trajectories: A history of Niuean throwing stones. *Journal of the Polynesian Society* 120(4):369–401.

Isaacson, W. 2008. *Einstein: His life and universe*. Pocket Books, London, Sydney, New York, Toronto.

Jones, T., V.A. Levchenko, P.L. King, E. Troitzsch, D. Wesley et al. 2017. Radiocarbon age constraints for a Pleistocene–Holocene transition rock art style: The Northern Running Figures of the East Alligator River region, western Arnhem Land, Australia. *Journal of Archaeological Science: Reports* 11:80–89. doi.org/10.1016/j.jasrep.2016.11.016.

Kaniewski, D., E. Van Campo, J. Guiot, S. Le Bruel, T. Otto et al. 2013. Environmental roots of the Late Bronze Age crisis. *PLoS ONE* 8(8):e71004. doi.org/10.1371/journal.pone.0071004.

Keate, G. 1788, *An account of the Pelew Islands, situated in the western part of the Pacific Ocean. Composed from the journals and communications of Captain Henry Wilson and some of his officers, who, in August 1783, were there shipwrecked, in the* Antelope, *a packet belonging to the Honourable East India company*. 3rd edition. G. Nichol, London. doi.org/10.5962/bhl.title.160285.

Keeley, L.H. 1996. *War before civilization: The myth of the peaceful savage*. Oxford University Press, New York.

Keeley, L.H., M. Fontana and R. Quick 2007. Baffles and bastions: The universal features of fortifications. *Journal of Archaeological Research* 15(1):55–95. doi.org/10.1007/s10814-006-9009-0.

Kennedy, J. and J.E. Brady 1997. Into the netherworld of island earth: A reevaluation of refuge caves in ancient Hawaiian society. *Geoarchaeology* 12(6):641–655. doi.org/10.1002/(sici)1520-6548 (199709)12:6<641::aid-gea6>3.0.co;2-z.

Kennett, D.J. and S.B. McClure 2012. The archaeology of Rapan fortifications. In A. Anderson and D.J. Kennett (eds), *Taking the high ground. The archaeology of Rapa, a fortified island in remote East Polynesia*. ANU E Press, Canberra. doi.org/10.22459/ta37.11.2012.12.

Kimber, R.G. 1990. Hunter-gatherer demography: The recent past in Central Australia. In B. Meehan and N. White (eds), *Hunter-gatherer demography*, pp. 160–175. University of Sydney, Sydney.

Kirch, P.V. 1984. *The evolution of the Polynesian chiefdoms*. New Studies in Archaeology. Cambridge University Press, Cambridge.

Kirch, P.V. 2010. *How chiefs became kings. Divine kingship and the rise of archaic states in ancient Hawai'i*. University of California Press, Berkeley. doi.org/10.1525/9780520947849.

Kirch, P.V. and R.C. Green 2001. *Hawaiki, ancestral Polynesia: An essay in historical anthropology*. Cambridge University Press, Cambridge. doi.org/10.1017/cbo9780511613678.

Kissel, M. and N.C. Kim 2018. The emergence of human warfare: Current perspectives. *American Journal of Physical Anthropology* 168(S67):141–163. doi.org/10.1002/ajpa.23751.

Kituai, A. 1988. Innovation and intrusion: Villagers and policemen in Papua New Guinea. *Journal of Pacific History* 23(2):156–166. doi.org/10.1080/00223348808572586.

Knauft, B.M. 1990. Melanesian warfare: A theoretical history. *Oceania* 60(4):250–311. doi.org/10.1002/j.1834-4461.1990.tb01557.x.

Knauft, B.M. and P. Shankman 1992. Warfare, Western intrusion and ecology in Melanesia. Comments by Knauft and Shankman. *Man* 27(2):399–403.

Knuckey, G. 1992. Patterns of fracture upon Aboriginal crania from the recent past. In N.W. Bruce (ed.), *Living with civilisation*, pp. 47–58. Proceedings of the Australasian Society for Human Biology 5. Centre for Human Biology, University of Western Australia, Perth.

Kolb, M.J. 2006. The origins of monumental architecture in ancient Hawai'i. *Current Anthropology* 47(4):657–665. doi.org/10.1086/506285.

Kolb, M.J. and B. Dixon 2002. Landscapes of war: Rules and conventions of conflict in ancient Hawai'i (and elsewhere). *American Antiquity* 67(3):514–534. doi.org/10.2307/1593824.

Krämer, A. 1995. *The Samoa Islands. Volume II: Material Culture*. Translated by Dr Theodore Verhaaren. University of Hawai'i Press, Honolulu.

Kwai, A.A. 2017. *Solomon Islanders in World War II: An Indigenous perspective*. State, Society and Governance in Melanesia Series. ANU Press, Canberra. doi.org/10.22459/siwwii.12.2017.

Kyle, B., J.S. Field and M. Kenyhercz 2009. Post-Lapita health, lifestyle, and mortuary behaviour in Fiji: A brief report. *Rapa Nui Journal* 23(1):28–39.

Ladefoged, T.N. 1993. Evolutionary process in an oceanic chiefdom. Intergroup aggression and political integration in traditional Roruman society. Unpublished PhD thesis. University of Hawai'i, Honolulu.

Layard, J. 1942. *Stone men of Malekula*. Chatto and Windus, London.

Lévesque, R. 1992. *History of Micronesia. A collection of source documents. Volume 1: European discovery*. Lévesque Publications, Quebec.

Lilley, I. 2010. Near Oceania. In I. Lilley (ed.), *Early human expansion and innovation in the Pacific*, pp. 13–45. International Council on Monuments and Sites, Paris.

Lipo, C.P., T.L. Hunt, R. Horneman and V. Bonhomme 2016. Weapons of war? Rapa Nui *mata'a* morphometric analyses. *Antiquity* 90(349):172–187. doi.org/10.15184/aqy.2015.189.

Lipson, M., M. Spriggs, F. Valentin, S. Bedford, R. Shing et al. 2020. Three phases of ancient migration shaped the ancestry of human populations in Vanuatu. *Current Biology* 30(24):P4846–4856.e6. doi.org/10.1016/j.cub.2020.09.035.

Liston, J. and M. Miko 2011. Oral tradition and archaeology: Palau's earth architecture. In J. Liston, G. Clark and D. Alexander (eds), *Pacific island heritage: Archaeology, identity & community*, pp. 181–204. Terra Australis 35. ANU E Press, Canberra. doi.org/10.22459/ta35.11.2011.13.

Liston, J. and H.D. Tuggle 2006. The archaeology of warfare: Prehistories of raiding and conquest. In E.N. Arkush and M.W. Allen (eds), *The archaeology of warfare: Prehistories of raiding and conquest*, pp. 148–183. University of Florida Press, Florida.

Litster, M. and L. Wallis 2011. Looking for the proverbial needle? The archaeology of Australian colonial frontier massacres. *Archaeology in Oceania* 46(3):105–117.

Loeb, E.M. 1926. *History and traditions of Niue*. Bernice P. Bishop Museum Bulletin 32. Bishop Museum, Honolulu.

Luders, D. 1996. Legend and history: Did the Vanuatu-Tonga kava trade cease in A.D. 1447. *Journal of the Polynesian Society* 105(3):287–310.

Luders, D. 2001. Retoka revisited and Roimata revised. *Journal of the Polynesian Society* 110(3):110: 247–288.

Macknight, C.C. 1972. Macassans and Aborigines. *Oceania* (42):283–321. doi.org/10.1002/j.1834-4461.1972.tb01183.x.

Marcus, J. 1998. The peaks and valleys of ancient states: An extension of the Dynamic Model. In G.M. Feinman and J. Marcus (eds), *Archaic states*, pp. 59–94. School of American Research Press, Santa Fe.

Markham, C. 2016. *The Voyages of Pedro Fernandez de Quirós, 1595 to 1606*. Volumes I–II. Translated and edited by Sir Clements Markham. Routledge, London and New York. doi.org/10.4324/9781315551548.

Martin, J. 1991. *Tonga islands: William Mariner's account*. 5th edition. Vava'u Press, Nuku'alofa.

May, S.K., D. Wesley, J. Goldham, M. Litster and B. Manera 2017. Symbols of power: The firearm paintings of Madjedbebe (Malakunanja II). *International Journal of Historical Archaeology* 21:690–707. doi.org/10.1007/s10761-017-0393-6.

McArthur, N. 1967. *Island populations of the Pacific*. Australian National University Press, Canberra.

McBryde, I. 1978. Wil-im-ee Moor-ring: Or, where do axes come from? Stone axe distribution and exchange patterns in Victoria. *Mankind* 11(3):354–382. doi.org/10.1111/j.1835-9310.1978.tb00666.x.

McDonald, J.J., D. Donlon, J.H. Field, R.L.K. Fullagar, J.B. Coltrain et al. 2007. The first archaeological evidence for death by spearing in Australia. *Antiquity* 81:877–885. doi.org/10.1017/s0003598 x00095971.

McGowan, H., S.K. Marx, P. Moss and A.M. Hammond 2012. Evidence of ENSO mega-drought triggered collapse of prehistoric Aboriginal society in northwest Australia. *Geophysical Research Letters* 39(22):L22702. doi.org/10.1029/2012gl053916.

McNiven, I. 1998. Enmity and amity: Reconsidering stone-headed club (Gabagaba) procurement and trade in Torres Strait. *Oceania* 69(2):94–115. doi.org/10.1002/j.1834-4461.1998.tb02697.x.

McNiven, I. 2018. Ritual mutilation of Europeans on the Torres Strait frontier. *Journal of Pacific History* 53(3):229–251. doi.org/10.1080/00223344.2018.1499007.

Métraux, A. 1940. *Ethnology of Easter Island*. Bernice P. Bishop Museum Bulletin 160. Bernice P. Bishop Museum, Honolulu.

Meyer, C., C. Lohr, D. Gronenborn and K.W. Alt 2015. The massacre mass grave of Schöneck-Kilianstädten reveals new insights into collective violence in Early Neolithic Central Europe. *Proceedings of the National Academy of Sciences USA* 112(36):11217–11222. doi.org/10.1073/pnas.1504365112.

Mirazón Lahr, M., F. Rivera, R.K. Power, A. Munier, B. Copsey et al. 2016. Inter-group violence among early Holocene hunter-gatherers of West Turkana, Kenya. *Nature* 529:394–398. doi.org/10.1038/nature16477.

Mitchell, S. 2000. Guns or barter? Indigenous exchange networks and the mediation of conflict in post-contact western Arnhem Land. In A. Clarke and R. Torrence (eds), *The archaeology of differences: Negotiating cross-cultural engagements in Oceania*, pp. 187–220. Routledge, London.

Montenegro, A., R.T. Callaghan and S. Fitzpatrick 2016. Using seafaring simulations and shortest-hop trajectories to model the prehistoric colonization of Oceania. *Proceedings of the National Academy of Sciences USA* 113(45):12685–12690. doi.org/10.1073/pnas.1612426113.

Morgan, J. 1980. *The life and adventures of William Buckley: Thirty-two years a wanderer among the Aborigines of the unexplored country round Port Philip*. Australian National University Press, Canberra.

Morris, I. 2014. *War! What is it good for? Conflict and the progress of civilization from primates to robots*. Farrar, Straus and Giroux, New York.

Morrison, M., A. Della-Sale and D. McNaughton 2019. War capitalism and the expropriation of country: Spatial analysis of Indigenous and settler-colonial entanglements in North Eastern Australia, 1864–1939. *International Journal of Historical Archaeology* 23:204–234. doi.org/10.1007/s10761-018-0463-4.

Moyle, R.M. 1984. *The Samoan journals of John Williams 1830 and 1832*. Pacific History Series 11. Australian National University Press, Canberra, London, New York.

Mutch, T.D. 1942. *The first discovery of Australia with an account of the voyage of the 'Duyfken' and the career of Captain Willem Jansz*. Reprinted from the *Journal of the Royal Australian Historical Society*, Vol. 28, Part 5. Sydney.

Neich, R. 2007. Tongan figures: From goddesses to missionary trophies to masterpieces. *Journal of the Polynesian Society* 116:213–278.

Nicole, R. 2010. *Disturbing history: Resistance in early colonial Fiji*. University of Hawai'i Press, Honolulu.

Nolan, P.D. 2003. Toward an ecological–evolutionary theory of the incidence of warfare in preindustrial societies. *Sociological Theory* 21(1):18–30. doi.org/10.1111/1467-9558.00172.

Nunn, P.D. 2003. Nature–society interactions in the Pacific Islands. *Geografiska Annaler, Series B: Human Geography* 85 (4):219–229. doi.org/10.1111/j.0435-3684.2003.00144.x.

Nunn, P.D. 2007a. *Climate, environment and society in the Pacific during the last millennium*. Elsevier, Amsterdam.

Nunn, P.D. 2007b. The AD1300 event in the Pacific Basin. *The Geographical Review* 97(1):1–23.

Nunn, P.D. 2007c. Holocene sea-level change and human response in Pacific Islands. *Earth and Environmental Science Transactions of the Royal Society of Edinburgh* 98:117–125. doi.org/10.1017/s1755691007000084.

O'Connor, S., A. McWilliam and S. Brockwell (eds) 2020. *Forts and fortification in Wallacea*. Terra Australis 53. ANU Press, Canberra. doi.org/10.22459/TA53.2020.

O'Driscoll, J. 2017. Hillforts in prehistoric Ireland: A costly display of power? *World Archaeology* 49(4):506–525. doi.org/10.1080/00438243.2017.1282379.

Oka, R.C., M. Kissel, M. Golitko, S.G. Sheridan, N.C. Kim et al. 2017. Population is the main driver of war group size and conflict casualties. *Proceedings of the National Academy of Sciences USA* 114:E11101–E11110. doi.org/10.1073/pnas.1713972114.

Orchiston, D.W. and L.C. Horrocks 1975. Contact and conflict: The Rowe massacre in early Protohistoric New Zealand. *Historical Studies* 16(65):519–538. doi.org/10.1080/10314617508595522.

Owsley, D.W., K.G. Barca, V.E. Simon and G.W. Gill 2016. Evidence for injuries and violent death. In V.H. Stefan and G.W. Gill (eds), *Skeletal biology of the ancient Rapanui (Easter Islanders)*, pp. 222–252. Cambridge University Press, Cambridge. doi.org/10.1017/cbo9781139151856.013.

Pagliaro, J.B., J.F. Garber and T.W. Stanton 2003. Re-evaluating the archaeological signatures of Maya ritual and conflict. In K.M. Brown and T.W. Stanton (eds), *Ancient Mesoamerican warfare*, pp. 75–89. Walnut Creek, AltaMira.

Pang, B.K. 2003. In the wake of the ruling chiefs: Forest use on the island of Hawai'i during the time of Kamehamea I. Unpublished PhD thesis. University of Hawai'i, Honolulu.

Pardoe, C. 2014. Conflict and territoriality in Aboriginal Australia: Evidence from biology and ethnography. In M.W. Allen and T.L. Jones (eds), *Violence and warfare among hunter-gatherers*, pp. 112–132. Left Coast Press, California. doi.org/10.4324/9781315415970-6.

Parke, E. 2020. The Christian converts who are setting fire to sacred Aboriginal objects. *ABC News*, 20 September. www.abc.net.au/news/2019-09-20/the-christian-converts-who-are-setting-fire-to-sacred-aboriginal/11527402.

Parmentier, R.J. 1987. *The sacred remains: Myth, history, and polity in Belau*. The University of Chicago Press, Chicago.

Parry, J.T. 1977. *Ring-ditch fortifications in the Rewa Delta, Fiji: Air photo interpretation and analysis*. Bulletin of the Fiji Museum, No. 3. The Fiji Museum, Suva.

Parry, J.T. 1981. *Ring-ditch fortifications II: Ring-ditch fortifications in the Navua Delta, Fiji: Air photo interpretation and analysis*. Bulletin of the Fiji Museum, No. 7. The Fiji Museum, Suva.

Parry, J.T. 1997. *The north coast of Viti Levu Ba to Ra air photo archaeology and ethnohistory*. Bulletin of the Fiji Museum, No. 10. The Fiji Museum, Suva.

Parton, P., G. Clark, C. Reepmeyer and D. Burley 2018. The field of war: LiDAR identification of earthwork defences on Tongatapu Island, Kingdom of Tonga. *Journal of Pacific Archaeology* 9(1):11–24.

Pascoe, B. 2014. *Dark emu: Aboriginal Australia and the birth of agriculture*. Scribe publications, Brunswick and London.

Pearson, W.H. 1970. The reception of European voyagers on Polynesian islands, 1568–1797. *Journal de la Société des Océanistes* 27:121–154. doi.org/10.3406/jso.1970.2151.

Petchey, F., G. Clark, I. Linderman, P. O'Day, J. Southon et al. 2018. Forgotten news: Shellfish isotopic insight into changing sea-level and associated impact on the first settlers of the Mariana Archipelago. *Quaternary Geochronology* 48:180–194. doi.org/10.1016/j.quageo.2018.10.002.

Pietrusewsky, M., M.T. Douglas, E.E. Cochrane and S. Reinke 2007. Cultural modifications in an adolescent earth-oven interment from Fiji: Sorting out mortuary practice. *Journal of Island and Coastal Archaeology* 2:44–71. doi.org/10.1080/15564890701228579.

Pigafetta, A. and J.A. Robinson 1906. *Magellan's voyage around the world by Antonio Pigafetta: The original text of the Ambrosian MS., with English translation, notes, bibliography, and index, by James Alexander Robertson with portrait, and facsimiles of the original maps and plates*. Volumes I and II. Arthur H. Clark, Cleveland.

Price, N. and R. Knecht 2012. Peleliu 1944: The archaeology of a South Pacific D-Day. *Journal of Conflict Archaeology* 7(1):5–48. doi.org/10.1179/157407812X13245464933786.

Prickett, N. 2016. *Fortifications of the New Zealand Wars*. New Zealand Department of Conservation Te Papa Atawahi, Wellington.

Quimby, F. 2011. The *Hierro* commerce: Culture contact, appropriation and colonial entanglement in the Marianas, 1521–1668. *Journal of Pacific History* 46(1):1–26. doi.org/10.1080/00223344.2011.573630.

Rainbird, P. 1996. A place to look up to: A review of Chuukese hilltop enclosures. *Journal of the Polynesian Society* 105:461–478.

Reanier, R.E. and D.P. Ryan 2003. Mapping the Poike Ditch. In J. Loret and J.T. Tanacredi (eds), *Easter Island: Scientific exploration into the world's environmental problems in microcosm*, pp. 207–221. Springer, Boston. doi.org/10.1007/978-1-4615-0183-1_14.

Reynolds, H. 1981. *The other side of the frontier: Aboriginal resistance to the European invasion of Australia*. UNSW Press, Sydney.

Richards, R. 2004. The earliest foreign visitors and their massive depopulation of Rapa-iti from 1824 to 1830. *Journal de la Société des Océanistes* 118:3–10. doi.org/10.4000/jso.67.

Robarchek, C.A. and C.J. Robarchek 1992. Cultures of war and peace: A comparative study of Waorani and Semai. In J. Silverberg and J.P. Gray (eds), *Aggression and peacefulness in humans and other primates*, pp. 189–213. Oxford University Press, New York and Oxford.

Robertson, G. 1973. *An account of the discovery of Tahiti from the journal of George Robertson Master H.M.S. Dolphin*. Folio Press, London.

Ross, M.H. 1985. Internal and external conflict and violence: Cross-cultural evidence and a new analysis. *Journal of Conflict Resolution* 29:547–579. doi.org/10.1177/0022002785029004001.

Routledge, K. 1919. *The mystery of Easter Island*. Hazell, Watson and Viney, London.

Rowley, C.D. 1970. *The destruction of Aboriginal society*. Aboriginal policy and practice—Volume 1. Australian National University Press, Canberra.

Ryan, L. 2010. Settler massacres on the Port Phillip Frontier, 1836–1851. *Journal of Australian Studies* 34(3): 257–273. doi.org/10.1080/14443058.2010.498091.

Sahlins, M. 1991. The return of the event, again: With reflections on the beginnings of the Great Fijian War of 1843 to 1845 between the Kingdoms of Bau and Rewa. In A. Biersack (ed.), *Clio in Oceania*, pp. 37–100. Smithsonian Institution Press, Washington.

Salcedo, H.C. 2015. Environmental violence and its consequences. *Latin American Perspectives* 204(42):19–26.

Sand, C. 1993. A preliminary study of the impact of the Tongan maritime chiefdom on the late prehistoric society of 'Uvea, western Polynesia. In M.W. Graves and R.C. Green (eds), *The evolution and organization of prehistoric society in Polynesia*, pp. 43–51. New Zealand Archaeological Association Monograph No. 19. New Zealand Archaeological Association, Auckland.

Sand, C. 1996. Structural remains as markers of complex societies in southern Melanesia during prehistory: The case of the monumental forts of Maré Island (New Caledonia). In I.C. Glover and P. Bellwood (eds), *Indo-Pacific prehistory: The Chiang Mai papers. Bulletin of the Indo-Pacific Prehistory Association* 15:37–44.

Sand, C. 2001. Changes in non-ceramic artefacts during the prehistory of New Caledonia. In G.R. Clark, A.J. Anderson and T. Vunidilo (eds), *The archaeology of Lapita dispersal in Oceania*, pp. 75–92. Terra Australis 17. Pandanus Press, Canberra.

Sand, C. 2008. Prehistoric maritime empires in the Pacific: Ga'asialilil ('Elili) and the establishment of a Tongan colony on 'Uvea (Wallis, Western Polynesia). In A. Di Piazza, E. Pearthree, and C. Sand (eds), *At the heart of ancient societies: French contributions to Pacific archaeology*, pp. 73–105. Les Cahiers de l'Archeólogiá en Nouvelle-Calédonie Volume 18. Noumea, New Caledonia.

Sand, C. and F. Valentin 1991. First results of the excavation of the burial mound of Petania, Uvea, Western Polynesia. *Indo-Pacific Prehistory Association Bulletin* 11:236–246.

Sand, C., F. Valentin and D. Frimigacci 2006. Sépultures à caveau en Polynésie occidentale: Des traditions orales à l'archéologie. *Journal de la Société des Océanistes* 122–123:13–25. doi.org/10.4000/jso.511.

Schamberger, K. 2017. Difficult history in a local museum: The Lambing Flat riots at Young, New South Wales. *Australian Historical Studies* 48(3):436–441. doi.org/10.1080/1031461X.2017.1331693.

Scheidel, W. 2017. *The great leveler: Violence and the history of inequality from the Stone Age to the twenty-first century.* Princeton University Press, Princeton.

Schmidt, H. 2003. Loanword strata in Rotuman. In H. Andersen (ed.), *Language contacts in prehistory: Studies in stratigraphy*, pp. 201–240. John Benjamins, Amsterdam and Philadelphia. doi.org/10.1075/cilt.239.16sch.

Scott, R.M. and H.R. Buckley 2010. Biocultural interpretations of trauma in two prehistoric Pacific Island populations from Papua New Guinea and the Solomon Islands. *American Journal of Physical Anthropology* 142:509–518. doi.org/10.1002/ajpa.21250.

Scott, R.M. and H.R. Buckley 2014. Exploring prehistoric violence in Tonga: Understanding skeletal trauma from a biocultural perspective. *Current Anthropology* 55(3):335–347. doi.org/10.1086/676477.

Shankman, P. 1991. Culture contact, cultural ecology, and Dani warfare. *Man* 26(2):299–321. doi.org/10.2307/2803834.

Sharp, L. 1952. Steel-axes for Stone Age Australians. *Human Organization* 11(2):17–22. doi.org/10.17730/humo.11.2.a105413403436788.

Shaw, B., J. Field, G.R. Summerhayes, S. Coxe, A.C.F. Coster et al. 2020. Emergence of a Neolithic in highland New Guinea by 5000 to 4000 years ago. *Science Advances* 6(13):eaay4573/. doi.org/10.1126/sciadv.aay4573.

Shell, R.J. 1999. The Marianas population decline: 17th century estimates. *Journal of Pacific History* 34(3):291–305. doi.org/10.1080/00223349908572914.

Sheppard, P.J., R. Walter and T. Nagaoka 2000. The archaeology of head-hunting in Roviana Lagoon, New Georgia. *Journal of the Polynesian Society* 109:9–38.

Shineberg, D. 1966. The sandalwood trade in Melanesian economics, 1841–65. *The Journal of Pacific History* 1:129–146. doi.org/10.1080/00223346608572084.

Sissons, J. 2011. History as sacrifice: The Polynesian iconoclasm. *Oceania* 81: 302–315. doi.org/10.1002/j.1834-4461.2011.tb00110.x.

Skoglund, P., C. Posth, K. Sirak, M. Spriggs, F. Valentin et al. 2016. Ancient genomics and the peopling of the Southwest Pacific. *Nature* 538(7626):510–513. doi.org/10.1038/nature19844.

Smith. C. 1990. The Poike ditch in retrospect. *Rapa Nui Journal* 4(3):33, 36–37.

Smith, P. 2000. Into the Kimberley: The invasion of the Sturt Creek Basin (Kimberley region), Western Australia) and evidence of Aboriginal resistance. *Aboriginal History* 24:62–74. doi.org/10.22459/ah.24.2011.04.

Smith, S.P. 1903. Niue Island, and its people. *Journal of the Polynesian Society* 12(1):1–21.

Spencer. C.S. 2003. War and early state formation in Oaxaca, Mexico. *Proceedings of the National Academy of Sciences USA* 100(20):1185–1187.

Spurway, J. 2015. *Ma'afu, prince of Tonga, chief of Fiji. The life and times of Fiji's first Tui Lau*. ANU Press, Canberra. doi.org/10.22459/MPTCF.02.2015.

Stanbury, M. and J. Green (eds) 2004. *Laperouse and the loss of the* Astrolabe *and the* Boussole *(1788): Reports of the 1986 and 1990 investigations of the shipwrecks at Vanikoro, Solomon Islands.* The Australian National Centre of Excellence for Maritime Archaeology Special Publication No. 8, Australasian Institute for Maritime Archaeology Special Publication No. 11, Fremantle.

Stanish, C. and A. Levine 2011. War and early state formation in the northern Titicaca basin, Peru. *Proceedings of the National Academy of Sciences USA* 108(34):1901–13906. doi.org/10.1073/pnas.1110176108.

Statham, N. (ed.) 2013. *A history of Tonga. As recorded by Rev. John Thomas*. Bible Society in Korea, Seoul.

Stevens, H.N. and G.F. Barwick (eds) 2010. *New light on the discovery of Australia as revealed by the journal of Captain Don Diego de Prado y Tovar*. Ashgate Publishing Company, Surray and Burlington. doi.org/10.4324/9781315597997.

Stevenson, C.M. and C. Williams 2018. The temporal occurrence and possible uses of obsidian *mata'a* on Rapa Nui (Easter Island, Chile). *Archaeology in Oceania* 53:92–102. doi.org/10.1002/arco.5145.

Suggs, R.C. 1961. *The archaeology of Nuku Hiva, Marquesas Islands, French Polynesia*. Anthropological Papers of the American Museum of Natural History 49, Part 1. American Museum of Natural History, New York.

Summerhayes, G.R., M. Leavesley, A. Fairburn, H. Mandui, A. Field et al. 2010. Human adaptation and plant use in Highland New Guinea 49,000 to 44,000 years ago. *Science* 330(6000):78–81. doi.org/10.1126/science.1193130.

Sutton, P. 2008. Stories about feeling: Dutch–Australian contact in Cape York Peninsula, 1606–1675. In P. Veth, P. Sutton and M. Neale (eds), *Strangers on the shore: Early coastal contacts in Australia*, pp. 35–59. National Museum of Australia Press, Canberra.

Taçon, P. and C. Chippindale 1994. Australia's ancient warriors: Changing depictions in the rock art of Arnhem Land, N.T. *Cambridge Archaeological Journal* 4:211–248. doi.org/10.1017/s0959977300001086.

Tainter, J.A. 2009. *The collapse of complex societies*. New Studies in Archaeology. Cambridge University Press, Cambridge.

Tau, T.M. and A. Anderson (eds) 2008. *Ngāi Tahu: A migration history. The Carrington text*. Bridget Williams Books, Wellington.

Tavares, G.M., G. Reales, M.C. Bortolini and N.J.R. Fagundes 2019. Measuring the impact of European colonization on Native American populations in Southern Brazil and Uruguay: Evidence from mtDNA. *American Journal of Human Biology* 31:e23243. doi.org/10.1002/ajhb.23243.

Tcherkézoff, S. 2003. A long and unfortunate voyage towards the 'invention' of the Melanesia/Polynesia distinction 1595–1832. *Journal of Pacific History* 38(2):175–196. doi.org/10.1080/0022334032000120521.

Thivet, D. 2008. Thomas Hobbes: A philosopher of war or peace? *British Journal for the History of Philosophy* 16(4):701–721. doi.org/10.1080/09608780802407407.

Torrence, R., S. Kelloway and P. White 2013. Stemmed tools, social interaction, and voyaging in early-mid Holocene Papua New Guinea. *Journal of Island and Coastal Archaeology* 8(2):278–310. doi.org/10.1080/15564894.2012.761300.

Turchin, P. 2006. *War and peace and war: The rise and fall of empires*. PI Press, New York.

Turner, G. 1861. *Nineteen years in Polynesia: Missionary life, travels, and researches in the islands of the Pacific*. John Snow, London.

Valentin, F., G. Clark, P. Parton and C. Reepmeyer 2020. Mortuary practices of the first Polynesians: Formative ethnogenesis in the Kingdom of Tonga. *Antiquity* 94(376):999–1014. doi.org/10.15184/aqy.2020.89.

Vayda, A.P. 1970. Maori and muskets in New Zealand: Disruption of a war system. *Political Science Quarterly* 85(4):560–584. doi.org/10.2307/2147596.

Vayda, A.P. 1976. *War in ecological perspective: Persistence, change, and adaptive processes in three Oceanian societies.* Plenum Press, New York and London. doi.org/10.1007/978-1-4684-2193-4.

Vilar, M.G., C.W. Chan, D.R. Santos, D. Lynch, R. Spathis et al. 2012. The origins and genetic distinctiveness of the Chamorros of the Mariana Islands: An mtDNA perspective. *American Journal of Human Biology* 25(1):116–122. doi.org/10.1002/ajhb.22349.

Wallis, L.A., N. Cole, H. Burke, B. Barker, K. Lowe et al. 2017. *Rewriting the history of the Native Mounted Police in Queensland.* Nulungu Insights No. 1. Nulungu Research Institute, The University of Notre Dame, Sydney.

Walter, R., T. Thomas and P. Sheppard 2004. Cult assemblages and ritual practice in Roviana Lagoon, Solomon Islands. *World Archaeology* 36(1):142–157. doi.org/10.1080/0043824042000192614.

Walth, C.K. (ed.) 2016. *Archaeological investigations at the Naton Beach site, Tumon, Guam. Volume II: The osteological analysis of the human remains.* SWCA Environmental Consultants, New Mexico.

Webb, S. 1991. *The palaeopathology of Aboriginal Australia.* Cambridge University Press, Cambridge.

Webster, D. 1998. Warfare and status rivalry: Lowland Maya and Polynesian comparisons. In G.M. Feinman and J. Marcus (eds), *Archaic states*, pp. 311–351. School of American Research Press, Santa Fe.

Weiner, M. 1971. The Macedonian syndrome: An historical model of international relations and political development. *World Politics* 23(4):655–683. doi.org/10.2307/2009855.

Weisler, M., R. Bolhar, J. Ma, E. St. Pierre, P. Sheppard et al. 2016. Cook Island artifact geochemistry demonstrates spatial and temporal extent of pre-European interarchipelago voyaging in East Polynesia. *Proceedings of the National Academy of Sciences USA* 113(29):8150–8155. doi.org/10.1073/pnas.1608130113.

Wesley, D., T. Jones, S. O'Connor, J. Fenner and W. Dickinson 2014. Earthenware of Malara, Anuru Bay: A reassessment of potsherds from a Macassan trepang processing site, Arnhem Land, Australia, and implications for Macassan trade and the trepang industry. *Australian Archaeology* 79(1):14–25. doi.org/10.1080/03122417.2014.11682015.

Westaway, M., D. Williams, R. Wright, R. Wood, J. Olley et al. 2016. The death of Kaakutja: A case of peri-mortem weapon trauma in an Aboriginal man from north-western New South Wales, Australia. *Antiquity* 90(353):1318–1333. doi.org/10.15184/aqy.2016.173.

Wilkes, C. 1985. *United States Exploring Expedition. Volume III: Tongataboo, Feejee group, Honolulu.* Fiji Museum, Suva.

Williams, A.N., S. Ulm, A.R. Cook, M.C. Langley and M. Collard 2013. Human refugia in Australia during the Last Glacial Maximum and Terminal Pleistocene: A geospatial analysis of the 25–12 ka Australian archaeological record. *Journal of Archaeological Science* 40:4612–4625. doi.org/10.1016/j.jas.2013.06.015.

Wilmshurst, J.M., T.L. Hunt, C.P. Lipo and A. Anderson 2011. High-precision radiocarbon dating shows recent and rapid initial human colonization of East Polynesia. *Proceedings of the National Academy of Sciences USA* 108(5): 1815–1820. doi.org/10.1073/pnas.1015876108.

Wilson, J. 1799. *A missionary voyage to the Southern Pacific Ocean, performed in the years 1796, 1797, 1798 in the ship* Duff, *commanded by Captain James Wilson.* Chapman, London.

Wimmer, A. and B. Min. 2006. From empire to nation-state. Explaining wars in the modern world, 1816–2001. *American Sociological Review* 71(6):867–897.

Winter, O., G. Clark, A. Anderson and A. Lindahl 2012. Austronesian sailing to the northern Marianas, a comment on Hung et al. (2011). *Antiquity* 86(333):898–910. doi.org/10.1017/s0003598x00047992.

Worthy, T.H. and G. Clark 2009. Bird, mammal and reptile remains. In G.R. Clark and A.J. Anderson (eds), *The early prehistory of Fiji*, pp. 231–258. Terra Australis 31. ANU E Press, Canberra. doi.org/10.22459/ta31.12.2009.10.

Wright, D., T. Denham, D. Shine and M. Donohue 2013. An archaeological review of western New Guinea. *Journal of World Prehistory* 26:25–73. doi.org/10.1007/s10963-013-9063-8.

Yokoyama, Y., T.M. Esat, W.G. Thompson, A.L. Thomas, J.M. Webster et al. 2018. Rapid glaciation and a two-step sea level plunge into the Last Glacial Maximum. *Nature* 559:603–607. doi.org/10.1038/s41586-018-0335-4.

York, R. and G. York 2014. *Slings and slingstones: The forgotten weapons of Oceania and the Americas.* Kent State University, Ohio.

Younger, S.M. 2008. Conditions and mechanisms for peace in precontact Polynesia. *Current Anthropology* 49:927–934. doi.org/10.1086/591276.

Younger, S.M. 2009. Violence and warfare in the pre-contact Caroline Islands. *Journal of the Polynesian Society* 118(2):135–164.

Younger, S.M. 2014. Violence and warfare in precontact Melanesia. *Journal of Anthropology* 2014:658597. doi.org/10.1155/2014/658597.

Yu-Ch'uan, W. 1936. The rise of land tax and the fall of dynasties in Chinese history. *Pacific Affairs* 9(2):201–220. doi.org/10.2307/2751407.

Zhang, D.D., P. Brecke, H.F. Lee, Y.-Q. He and J. Zhang 2007. Global climate change, war, and population decline in recent human history. *Proceedings of the National Academy of Sciences USA* 104:19214–19219. doi.org/10.1073/pnas.0703073104.

2

War is their principal profession: On the frequency and causes of Maori warfare and migration, 1250–1850 CE

Atholl Anderson

Introduction

In 1835 CE, Charles Darwin (1909:422) went walking in the Bay of Islands, northern New Zealand, and was 'surprised to find that almost every hill which I ascended, had been at some former time more or less fortified'. He then heard about the forts (*pa* in Maori) and fighting from the missionary William Williams, including a droll anecdote about a chief who started a war so as not to waste a barrel of deteriorating gunpowder. Darwin's (1909:423) comment that 'a more warlike race of inhabitants could not be found in any part of the world' was of a piece with most others that had preceded it. Abel Tasman in 1642 CE 'found the natives to be of a malignant and murderous nature' (McNab 1914:35), Joseph Banks wrote in 1770 CE that Maori lived in a 'state of war' (Beaglehole 1962:31), William Anderson in 1777 CE that 'war is their principal profession' (Beaglehole 1967:814), John Nicholas, in 1814 CE (1817 I:29), that Maori were 'barbarians of the most ferocious and implacable disposition', and the missionary Thomas Kendall in 1820 CE that 'war is all their glory' (Wright 1959:119).

These impressions involved a widely accepted assumption that the Maori state of war reflected an unattained level of 'civilisation', a term that entered the English language only in 1767 CE (O'Brien 1993). Banks described Maori as 'uncivilized', and in an 'uncultivated state of nature' (Beaglehole 1962:12), and Johann Forster (1778 CE in Thomas et al. 1996:159; also Darwin 1909:424) admired Tahitians, but saw Maori as barbarians of a 'ferocious and uncultured disposition', if with some redeeming qualities of warrior courage and independence. It followed that their warfare was correspondingly fierce, merciless and unremitting. Anderson (Beaglehole 1967:814) asserted that Maori 'public contentions are frequent and rather perpetual', fought with no quarter given or prisoners taken, and conclude with cannibalism. If not quite a Hobbesian vision of savage pandemonium it did fit contemporary British expectations that clan societies emerging from barbarism into civilisation, not least those in Scotland and Ireland, were torn by constant rivalry and frequent war, such as in John Millar's 1771 CE conjectural history (Smith 2009).

Direct observations of Maori fighting, however, were exceedingly few (e.g. Banks 1769 in Beaglehole 1962:427), compared to inferences drawn from seeing war canoes (*waka taua*), companies of armed men, captives and sometimes dead bodies or baskets of human flesh.

The impressions conveyed by those were inflamed at times by calculated Maori scaremongering (Thompson 1997:115), particularly on the matter of cannibalism (Anderson et al. 2014:148–150). The fullest historical evidence of warfare is from the Bay of Islands, where European observations of large war parties departing and returning were combined with eyewitness accounts by their Maori chieftains of what transpired on those expeditions (e.g. Marsden 1820–1824 in Elder 1932:265–267, 355–359, 389–390). The records describe at least one major foray a year from 1807 to 1818 CE, rising to two or three per year up to 1828 CE (Crosby 1999:29–31). This is a high frequency of warfare; in fact, level 4 on the five-point scale used by Ember et al. (2013:53).

These conflicts, however, were part of the so-called 'musket wars', implying the proposition that early access to firearms, axes, potatoes and other goods of European origin by the Bay of Islands people led to more frequent expeditionary wars against tribes that had few or no such commodities. Attacked tribes then hastened to acquire firearms and turn on less fortunate groups again, so that a front of asymmetric military and economic advantage rolled across New Zealand. Irrespective of debate about this hypothesis (Anderson et al. 2014:175–177; Ballara 1998:234–239; Crosby 1999:13; Fitzpatrick 2007; Wright 2011), it is undeniable that involvement of a European presence muddies the waters for using historical data from the contact period to represent the frequency and scale of Maori war during the 600 preceding years of exclusive Maori habitation (c.f. Ferguson and Whitehead 1992; Gat 2015), the period of particular interest here.

The prehistory of Maori warfare, insofar as it can be discerned, might shed some light upon how the historical conflicts developed, but it is at least as important for thinking about the role of warfare in the larger-scale development of Maori society. Was the apparently endemic and destructive warfare perceived by early Europeans a longstanding condition in Maori society? Had warfare been a continuously prominent feature of Maori society from the beginning? What does the long-term shape of Maori war suggest about the relevance of potential causes or influences, some operating at centennial scales or larger? These issues are discussed here, initially by considering some existing models of Maori war, then by reference to archaeological evidence and lastly through a new approach to the long-term frequency of Maori war using traditional histories. Warfare is taken as armed combat between territorially defined groups that were formed to defend against violence or project it (paraphrasing Ember et al. 2013:39 and Roscoe 2016:15) and who could act as non-kin toward enemies even if those were closely related. For example, warfare occurred repeatedly in the Kai Huanga (i.e. the 'eat relatives') feud among Ngai Tahu, 1824–1830 CE (Tau and Anderson 2008:162–171), despite close kinship relations among the combatants.

Current hypotheses about the causes and frequency of Maori war

Explanatory hypotheses of Maori warfare refer variously to intrinsic biological predispositions, societally embedded motivations or extrinsic demographic and ecological imperatives; the three general themes, in fact, of most explanations of warfare among small-scale societies (e.g. Ferguson 2008; Wilson and VanDerwarker 2016).

Biological predisposition

The most venerable and universal of all models of war is encapsulated in the truism that men are violent by nature. This has been discussed widely in terms of 'coalitional aggression', manifested by ingroup–outgroup construction of the social landscape and expressed as 'male warrior' psychology (Fry and Söderberg 2013; McDonald et al. 2012), with its benefits for individual evolutionary fitness (Glowacki and Wrangham 2015; Lehmann and Feldman 2008). Related hypotheses have referred to physiological mechanisms involved in aggressive responses to perceived threat (Berns and Atran 2012), and one of these proposed a 'warrior gene' as particularly influential in Maori violence.

Gene MAOA (the monoamine oxidase enzyme) controls the breakdown of human mood-regulating neurotransmitters such as adrenaline, dopamine, norepinephrine and serotonin. Through different histories of genetic selection, alleles of MAOA have evolved with varying levels of activity, and therefore of breakdown rates. MAOA-L, the allele often identified as the warrior gene, has low activity and in populations where it is relatively common it leaves high levels of neurotransmitters that are associated with elevated expressions of bold, impulsive or aggressive male behaviour.

A study of 46 Maori men found that the warrior gene occurred in 70 per cent of cases compared to 40 per cent of a non-Maori sample (Hall et al. 2006; Lea and Chambers 2007). This finding was interpreted as reflecting 'ancient episodes of positive selection and genetic bottlenecks … due to both environmental pressures during the migrations and behavioural characteristics of Polynesian voyagers', the latter epitomised by a 'warrior tradition' (Lea and Chambers 2007:3). Application of the warrior gene hypothesis to relatively high levels of violence in the contemporary Maori male population provoked criticism on methodological grounds (Crampton and Parkin 2007; Merriman and Cameron 2007) and for fear of social and political repercussions (Hook 2009; Perbal 2013).

Nevertheless, the basic idea is plausible as a contributory factor to conflict. Research in controlled experimental conditions outside Polynesia has shown 'a clear demonstration of the relationship between MAOA-L and actual behavioral aggression' (McDermott et al. 2009:2121). In similar research (Eisenberger et al. 2007 in McDermott et al. 2009:2121), the finding that 'MAOA-L individuals showed greater activity in the dorsal anterior cingulate cortex (dACC), an area that has been associated with distress related to rejection or status challenges' suggests a potentially relevant connection to historical Maori behaviour concerning protection of *mana* (ritual and social standing derived mainly from ancestry) that frequently led to war.

Societally embedded compulsion

Early European observers understood the sociopolitical context of Maori warfare. James Cook (1774 CE, in Beaglehole 1961:578) wrote that the population in Queen Charlotte Sound was 'under no regular form of government, or so united as to form one body politick', and that its chiefs had 'no right or power to command obedience'. Anderson (1777 CE, in Beaglehole 1967:813) added that 'no people can be more susceptible of an injury done them, and none more ready to resent it'. Later, Nicholas (1817:306) put the two points together in writing of the Bay of Islands being:

> divided as a nation by the form of their government, they [Maori] are split into rival associations, who are taught from their infancy to cherish a spirit of ferocious hostility against each other; and implacable vengeance becomes a necessary duty, to which they are reconciled by habit, while they indulge it without remorse.

That the 'necessary duty' of war arose from fastidious regard for *mana* among politically fragmented communities remains the dominant explanatory narrative today in historical and anthropological scholarship.

Among Maori, acts of crime or violence, including spoken or observed slights to *mana* and breaches of *tapu* (ritual proscription) were regarded as compromising the spiritual relationship between an offended descent group and its ancestors and gods. Rebalancing or repair of that relationship required some form of reciprocal action; against the original perpetrators preferably, against their kin or, in the event that neither were possible, against available non-kin. Such reciprocity (*utu*) 'was a fundamental principle of all Maori interaction … a necessity, not an option, for Maori political and social groups which had been attacked' (Ballara 2003:26). There were means of obtaining it short of war, such as recompense in stored foods or valuables, chiefly marriages, or stripping raids (*taua muru*, hostile plundering expedition) in which offenders allowed themselves to be dispossessed of goods and slaves. These occurred more often among closely related descent groups or within political alliances underwritten by the *mana* of powerful chiefs.

However, while Maori recognised kinship links between clans at a notionally tribal (*iwi*) level, and the largely sentimental appeal of common origins in one or another of the ancient colonising canoes (*waka*), effective responsibility in *utu*, as in other matters, rested principally at the level of the clan or *hapu*. Lacking any higher authority capable of mediation, clans had usually to reach, independently or with allies, for 'the ultimate sanction in the Maori system [which] was force applied in warfare' (Ballara 2003:73). It was delivered by the war party (*taua toto*, hostile expedition for blood) and such actions were thought on all sides to be no less than *tika*—correct, proper and just. The argument advanced by Maori, then, was that 'wars were fought to restore the *mana* of groups and their allies damaged by an injury of some kind' (Ballara 2003:26). This sociopolitical model provides a robust explanation of historical Maori warfare at the familial or clan level, suggesting that it was at least a continual activity, but it offers little insight into patterns of war at larger scales of analysis.

Demographic and ecological imperatives

While 'even economic sources of dispute or competition were subordinated to the political and spiritual consequences of clashes over tapu, mana and utu' (Ballara 2003:163), some warfare was motivated nonetheless by disputes about territory. These were difficult to resolve because Maori property inheritance was tied to ambilineal reckoning of descent—that is, through both male and female lines, potentially legitimating claims from both within and outside the local group and creating a continually fertile source of dispute (Anderson et al. 2014:100–107). Arguments turned upon demonstration of genealogical precedence, but their resolution, including by warfare, often meant that some people had to move away. Andrew Vayda has argued that such warfare-induced dispersal was fulfilling underlying demographic and ecological imperatives. Fundamentally, those derived from resource scarcity and revolved around the proposition 'that war is almost always incited by food shortages' (Keeley 2016:295).

Vayda (1970:568) deplored 'the general failure of ethnographers to note the systemic relations between the fighting undertaken for revenge and the fighting undertaken for territory'. As he saw it (Vayda 1974:188), 'fighting for revenge … became fighting for territory whenever some attacked groups failed to defend themselves stoutly or to retaliate adequately'. In such actions, Maori were:

> without their necessarily knowing it [performing] essential operations of a system whereby the overall population of New Zealand could grow and be dispersed and whereby access to the resources sustaining this process could be regulated. (Vayda 1970:570)

Clearance of primary rainforest using stone axes was so arduous that it was more economical for a group experiencing population pressure on its established gardens to capture cut-over or cleared land elsewhere than to fell more forest within its own territory (Vayda 1960:113). This strategy created 'a chain-reaction process of aggressive territorial expansion' in which stronger groups expanded at the expense of weaker neighbours and it operated more or less continuously and adaptively to maintain the dispersal of the growing Maori population (Vayda 1970:563).

The difficulty of clearing primary forest is overstated in Vayda's model. Clearance was achieved principally by fire rather than felling and, instead of replanting the clearings of former owners, Maori preferred to clear virgin forest to expose the most fertile soils (Ballara 2003:18). Most importantly, the notion of incremental territorial expansion through warfare is not supported by Maori traditional history or historical observation. Conflicts occurred between neighbouring families and clans, but organised warfare was conducted primarily against groups at some distance away, usually non-kin.

These ethnographic perspectives on Maori warfare draw attention to mechanisms that imply it was a habitual, random or unpatterned activity, because its propensity was inherent (warrior gene), socially contingent (protection of mana) or ecologically constituted by land clearance (resource competition). Whether they are relevant to understanding the long-term history of pre-European Maori warfare, and of influences or causes operating beyond the local level that might have been involved in shaping its trajectory, is a matter that can be approached first through archaeological evidence.

Archaeological considerations

Archaeological remains support the elucidation of long-term trends in prehistoric warfare in Europe and elsewhere (e.g. Armit 2011; Carman and Harding 1999), but material evidence of pre-European Maori fighting is scarce. Most of the numerous *patu* (hand clubs with sharp edges that were used as thrusting and slashing weapons) in museum collections are from ethnographic collecting, especially those (*mere*) made of jade, which were also marks of rank. Other weapons, including various types of long blades, lances and darts were made of hardwood. Maori did not use bow and arrow or stone-tipped projectiles of any kind. In Maori rock art there are no unequivocal depictions of fighting and very few in which the numerous human figures are shown with weapons. On the rare occasions in which weapons of stone or bone have been documented archaeologically, they have come from sites dated after about 1500 CE (e.g. Skinner 1974:155). Archaeological remains of burnt houses and other structures are quite common, but settlements burned accidentally or were torched upon the death of high-ranking people.

Evidence of mortal wounds occurs infrequently on Maori skeletal remains, and no mass graves of victims of violence are recorded (Houghton 1980). Taking of trophy heads, and heads for sale to Europeans, is well-known historically but specific skeletal marks of decapitation are not recorded archaeologically, and nor is unequivocal skeletal evidence of cannibalism. This might reflect only a scarcity of detailed forensic examination using large samples of Maori skeletal remains; a consequence largely of customary Maori disapproval of human bones being subjected to analysis.

Archaeological evidence of the long-term frequency of Maori warfare, therefore, is almost entirely confined to analysis of *pa*. Of 7022 recorded *pa*, 98 per cent are in the North Island, all but a few within the boundary of *kumara* (sweet potato) cultivation (Figure 2.1), but the ensuing assumption that population growth associated with agricultural development accounts for *pa* construction is problematic at first sight. A Maori population of about 100 000 at 1800 CE (Anderson 2017 contra Chapple 2017) would have a population density of only 0.3–1.1 people per km^2 within the horticultural boundary, compared to about 15 per 1 km^2 for the rest of East Polynesia as a whole, where relatively few forts were built (Anderson 2013). Seasonality of production might have been a crucial difference. Most tropical root crops would produce twice a year or more often and there was, in addition, a wide range of additional food plants, many cropping all year round. Periodic warfare could result in some crop or store losses, but far from all. In temperate New Zealand, however, only one crop of *kumara* (and a few other tubers) was produced each year at a predictable time. Protection of that single harvest for food and seed tubers, and also rich patches of wild plant foods, was consequently more critical, perhaps inducing *pa* construction at lower population densities than elsewhere (Anderson 2013).

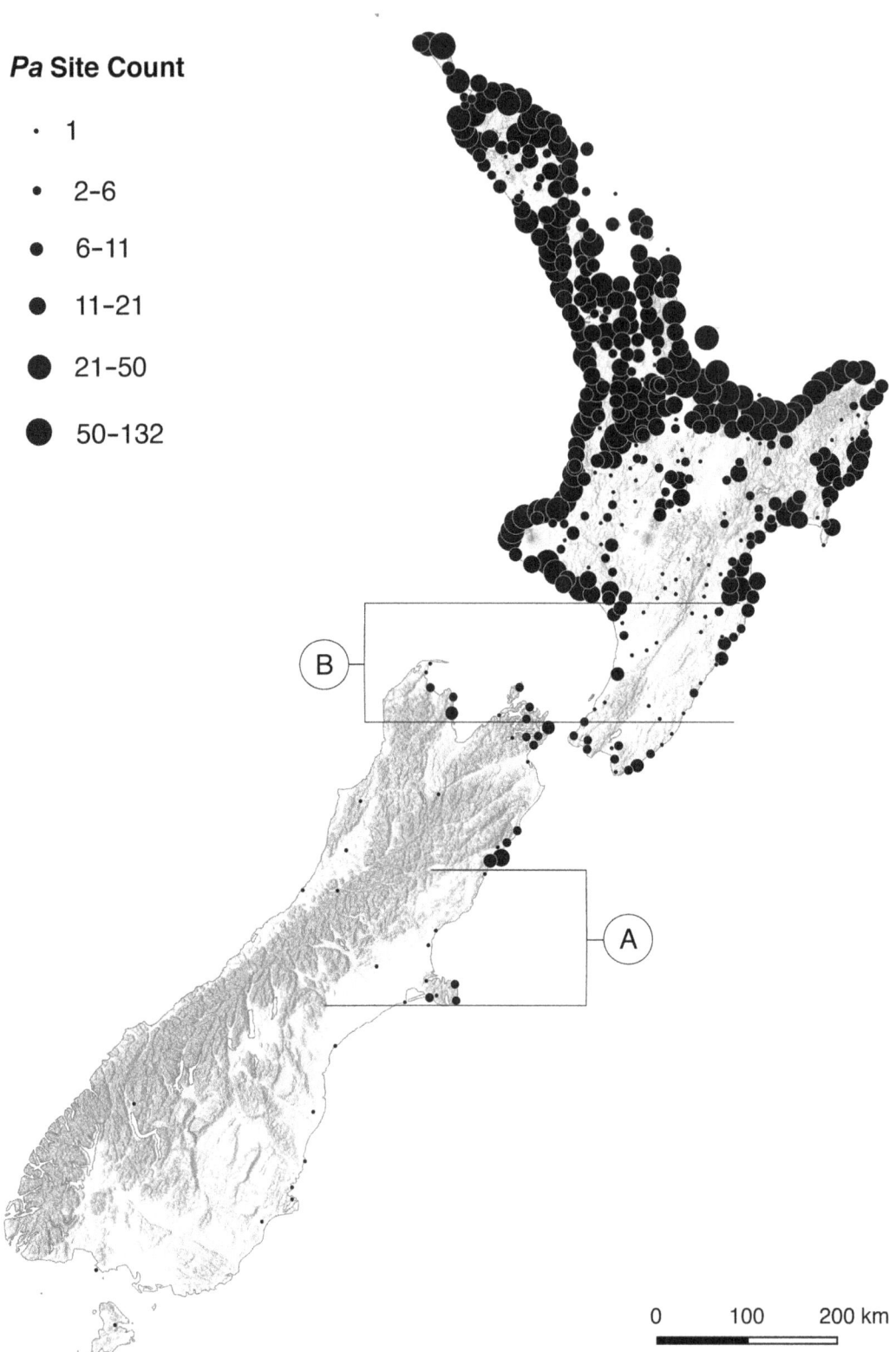

Figure 2.1. Distribution of pa sites and approximate latitudinal spans of marginal cultivation at the fourteenth century (A) and sixteenth century (B).

Source: Atholl Anderson.

This hypothesis gains theoretical support from research on 'the trade-off between the defensive value of military strength and the commuting costs of the food quest' (Roscoe 2016:35). At very low and very high population densities, dispersed settlement patterns are favoured for small-scale societies, but at medium densities (c. 10–40 people per 1 km^2 in contact-era New Guinea), nucleated defensive settlement is preferred (Roscoe 2016:32–35). As the population density per km^2 of arable land in the northern North Island was 11 people, compared to 99–120 people per 1 km^2 in tropical East Polynesia, the difference might have been that the Maori population density suited nucleated defence, while elsewhere in East Polynesia the threshold for nucleation was generally exceeded. This density-dependent model could be valid for most *pa* construction, but not all. Some *pa* were built well beyond the agricultural boundary, in areas of low population density, as far south as Foveaux Strait.

Other potential explanations for *pa* building include materialisation of group power by construction size and complexity, and defence of key localities for mobility and exchange. Both can be manifestations of 'costly signalling' (e.g. O'Driscoll 2017) that refer implicitly to military power. In addition, construction for symbolic, ideological or religious purposes cannot be ruled out. Monumental construction was associated with the late prehistoric cult of Oro (a war deity) in Tahiti, and with Lono (an agricultural deity) in Hawai'i, and it is not impossible that *pa* construction reflects, if only partly, a late prehistoric change of Maori religious orientation, perhaps associated with Rongo (the agricultural deity).

Pa building began about 1500 CE and as nearly all radiocarbon dates from them have medians after 1600 CE, and most of those after 1700 CE, an increasing rate of *pa* construction is implied (Irwin 2013; Schmidt 1996). However, as less than 2 per cent of *pa* have been radiocarbon dated these trends might not prove representative. All types of *pa* were built contemporaneously. There is accumulating evidence that groups of *pa* were set out in landscapes to provide extensive interlinking defence arrangements. On north Kaipara head, 20 *pa* sites were built at the same time in the eighteenth century and are set in a strategic pattern, indicating either a large group migration, or a concerted response to external threat by a large resident group (Irwin 1985). On Ponui Island the distribution of *pa* built in the early sixteenth century indicates a similarly short span of *pa* building and a strategic defensive system for the island as a whole (Irwin 2013). *Pa* landscapes in Taranaki produced comparable evidence (Prickett 1982, 1983).

Tightening of territoriality after about 1500 CE, implicit in *pa* construction, is also documented by attenuation of early long-distance exchange networks involving obsidian and stone adzes (e.g. Turner 2004). A similar conclusion can be inferred for ritual behaviour. The small, paved-stone ritual features that existed in East Polynesia at the time of migration to New Zealand are recorded from a number of early Maori sites. It can be argued that while they, and also cemeteries, were safe from hostile destruction in early open settlements, the tensions arising from growing population density on and around horticultural lands created a need for later groups to protect their ritual assets. Burials were hidden away in caves and forest, and ancestor carvings, godsticks, bundled bones and other sacred things were taken into *pa*, which became sanctuaries for clan spirits as much as safe storage and protection for people (Anderson 2014).

These data and interpretations suggest that most *pa* were intended primarily for defence of agricultural groups and their tangible and intangible assets. It is worth noting that the only other population of Polynesians in the New Zealand region that survived into historical times, the Moriori of the Chatham Islands, had no agriculture, had proscribed warfare and built no *pa*. It was only with Maori invasion of the Chathams in the 1820s CE that some *pa* were built (Anderson 2014). Maori construction of *pa* in mainland New Zealand after 1500 CE, then, can be seen as a response to warfare, or its threat, resulting from competitive pressure on cultivable land and other resources. Whether long-term change in the relative frequency of warfare actually followed this pattern is a matter than can be addressed independently through oral traditions.

Long-term frequency of Maori migratory war in oral traditions

Maori oral traditions were organised iteratively, by generations, and the narratives associated with ancestors often followed a convention of receding causation in which each event was seen as the consequence of a previous event of the same kind, and that of an earlier event, and so on in multigenerational chains. There was no reflexive commentary or recognition of trans-tribal patterns of war. If larger processes were at work on the shape of war, they were not recognised or understood, or they were simply extraneous to the purpose and practicality of keeping an oral account of clan ancestry and fortunes. As warfare and other conflicts had to be committed to memory in these oral traditions, many episodes of localised conflict have probably been discarded over the years, and it might be expected that proportionately fewer of the older events were retained. With no way of knowing such patterns of discard, or of variation in the extent of discard between group traditions, any comparative analysis based only on references to conflict would be rendered nugatory.

It is better to choose another kind of activity that was more certain to be remembered and that was associated closely with elevated levels of warfare. Group migrations in which clans, or sections of clans, moved into new localities were almost inevitably hostile incursions involving warfare that induced migration and subsequent warfare, among other actions, that produced residential rights for newly arrived migrants. Furthermore, as oral traditions were the foundation of property ownership, sustaining rights in new territories required remembering the genealogies and narratives that supported each case. Migrations, then, can be taken as an index of the frequency of notable warfare; of events which had high status and lasting significance for the groups concerned (c.f. Thorpe 2003:146).

The Maori evidence is particularly useful in elucidating the frequency of migration warfare, and spatio-temporal patterns in it, because the evidence came from hundreds of independent groups. As clans were highly dispersed at low population densities in the comparatively huge landmass of New Zealand, and effective Maori political authority peaked at the clan level, the numerous individual traditions were never reduced to the relatively few aristocratic or monarchical lines that came to dominate traditional histories in state-level Tonga, Hawai'i and Tahiti.

The singular abundance and detail of Maori traditions invited some early scepticism about their historical validity, but Edward Shortland, among others in the early nineteenth century who were fluent in Maori and worked with Maori on the practical problems of land tenure to which the traditions were recognised on all sides as crucial evidence, showed that there was remarkable consistency among numerous and widely separated clan records. He concluded that the traditions were historical in the common sense of that term and observed that they distinguished carefully between mythological, fabulous and historical narratives recognising, for example, a distinction between supernatural and historical locations of Hawaiki, the Maori homeland (Anderson et al. 2014:40–49). A recent test of the historicity of genealogies examined 156 migration canoe genealogies for their estimates of the age of initial colonisation and found that initial migrants arrived 1280–1370 CE (Anderson et al. 2014:60–64). The overlap of ancestral names between Tahitian, Cook Islands and Maori genealogies immediately before the period of migration supports this interpretation, and it is also congruent with radiocarbon dated events in archaeology and palaeoecology that are markers of initial human colonisation in New Zealand (Anderson et al. 2014:32–34). With that assurance of the general historicity of Maori traditions, a method of estimating the ages of migrations recorded in them was devised.

Working method

The relative incidence of migratory warfare was estimated in the following way (further detail in Anderson et al. 2014:60–64, 104–105, 111–117). For each group, generally a clan but sometimes known only under a later tribal name, genealogies were collated that showed continuously successive generations between named ancestors who arrived in initial colonising canoes and historical figures who lived in the early nineteenth century. For some groups, marriages and other interactions across groups were needed to reconstruct full genealogies. A generation interval of 30 years was adopted, after Fenner (2005) who used large historical datasets to calculate generation length (combining the mean age at parturition for females and the mean age at paternity for males) for small-scale societies, obtaining figures of 28–30 years. For combined agricultural–foraging societies his data suggest about 29.5 years, here rounded to 30, which is significantly longer than the 20 or 25 years commonly used hitherto in analysis of Polynesian genealogies. Historical evidence that described the period of flourishing of an early-nineteenth-century ancestor was used to set the dates for the latest generation, and then successive 30-year intervals were allocated to each preceding ancestor. The approximate accuracy of this procedure was checked by comparing the positions occupied in different genealogies by ancestors who interacted with each other in traditions from different sources. The chronological intervals for ancestors who were involved in specific migrations and associated warfare recorded in the traditions were noted, and these periods were plotted for the different clan or group lineages to determine whether there were cross-lineage correlations of the same phases of migration and war.

This method was applied to genealogies and traditions of groups originally in the eastern North Island who ended up in the South Island. I looked also at the migration and warfare of the *Tainui* canoe people who colonised the Waikato region, to see whether there was similar temporal patterning in the incidence of migratory warfare (Anderson 2013). The genealogies and traditions were taken primarily from Tau and Anderson (2008) for the eastern migrations; Jones and Biggs (1995) for those in the Waikato District; and Crosby (1999) for historical migrations into the southern North Island and northern South Island.

Migration and warfare

Relatively high migration frequency can be observed as three phases (Figure 2.2).

Phase I: Colonising migration

In the first phase, New Zealand became inhabited, for the first time, by migrants arriving in 12–20 canoes from 'Hawaiki', meaning in this case the Cook, Society or Austral Islands. Maori traditions say that 'in the time of Houmai-tawhiti there had been a great war, and thence there were many battles fought in Hawaiki'. In one of these, 'Uenuku and Toi-te-huatahi went to make war on Tama-te-kapua and his people, and some fell on both sides' after which Uenuku's people were defeated by Houmai-tawhiti (Grey 1954 (1855):99–104). Uenuku's son, Kahuiterangi (later known as Paikea, 'the whale rider') migrated to New Zealand and was the progenitor of Ngati Porou, Ngai Tahu and other tribes originating in the eastern North Island. Tamatekapua brought the *Arawa* canoe to New Zealand and its crew populated much of the Bay of Plenty. The *Tainui* canoe under Hoturoa arrived at the same time and its people occupied the Waikato region. More canoes arrived in the same period, about 1280–1340 CE and took possession of other districts, mostly in the North Island. Some conflicts are recorded, but almost no warfare.

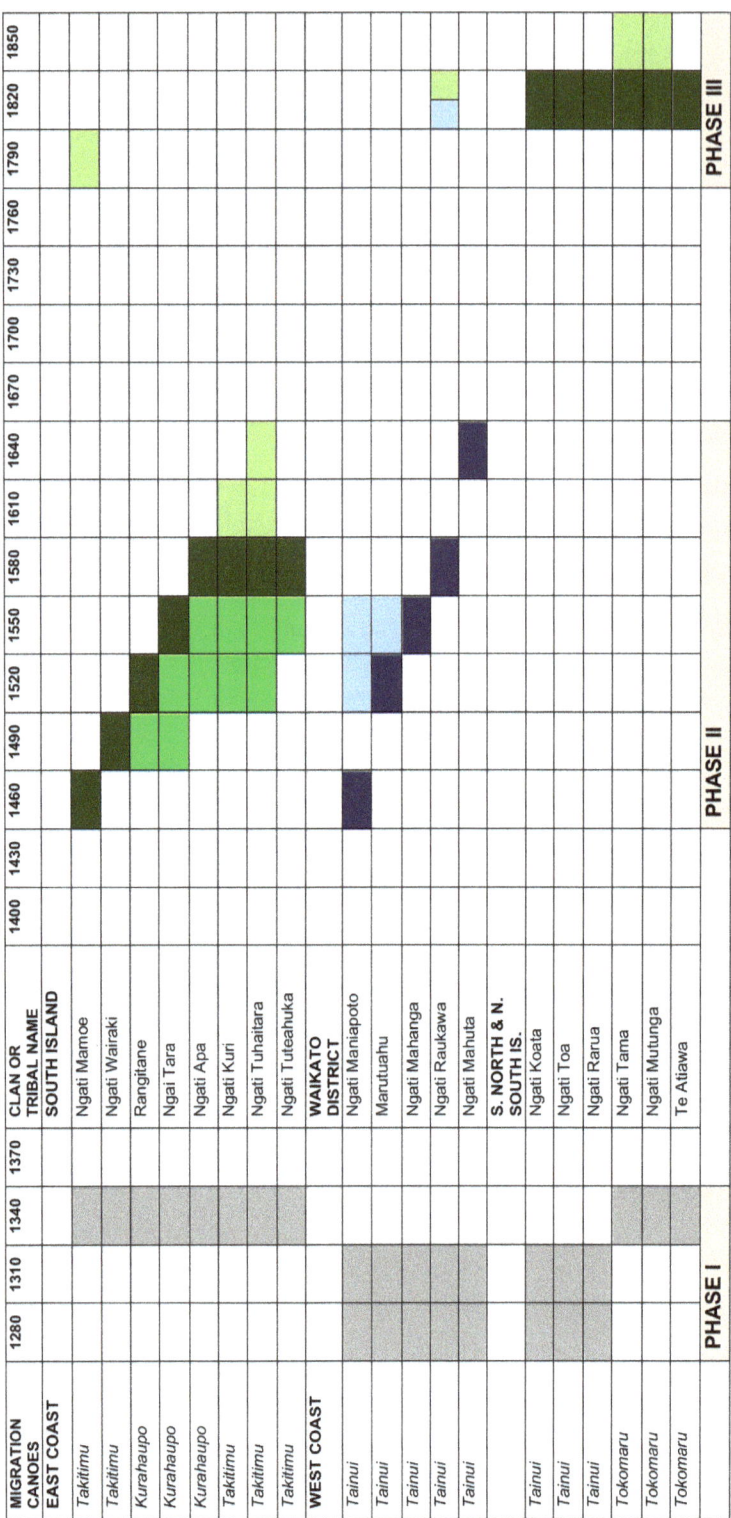

Figure 2.2. Temporal distribution of traditional Maori migrations by groups originating on the east and west coasts of the North Island, and their canoe ancestors from East Polynesia.

Key: grey = colonisation canoe landings; dark green = migration into the South Island; mid-green = preceding migrations in North Island; light green = subsequent migrations in South Island or to Chatham and Auckland islands; dark blue = migrations into interior of Waikato and Auckland districts; light blue = subsequent migrations in North Island. Migration phases shown in pink.

Source: Atholl Anderson.

Phase II: Early tribal migration

The second phase refers to migration within New Zealand. The group names that follow combine the terms 'Ngati', 'Ati' or 'Ngai' (clan or tribe), with an identifying ancestral name, such as 'Tahu' or 'Wairaki'. The migrations were primarily from the East Coast of the North Island into the lower North Island and then into the South Island. Ngati Mamoe migration to the South Island began after the death of Tukapua in the fifteenth century (Figure 2.3). Ngati Wairaki migrated from the East Coast, probably with Ngati Tumatakokiri, as both spent some time in the Taupo region and ended up in Whanganui, from where Ngati Wairaki migrated to the western South Island under Tuaroaroterangi about 1500 CE.

Ngati Kahungunu and Ngai Tahu migration began with the killing near Gisborne of the great-grandsons of Kahungunu, which split the community. Rakaihikuroa and his son, Taraia, took their people, and Ngati Ira under Te Aomatarahi (Rakaihikuroa's uncle) to Hawkes Bay about 1500 CE, while Rakaipaka, half-brother of Rakaihikuroa, and the descendants of Tahumutu known as Ngai Tahu moved to Wairoa. Ngati Kahungunu migration to Hawkes Bay compelled remaining Ngati Mamoe to move south into the Wairarapa, while conflict there between incoming Ngati Kahungunu and resident Ngai Tara led many of the latter to move to Wellington about 1500–1530 CE. With Rangitane migrating south-west to Manawatu, some by way of southern Wairarapa, and Ngati Ira coming from Poverty Bay, the influx of migrants threatened to overwhelm Ngai Tara and Rangitane in the Wairarapa. They began migrating to the South Island during the mid-sixteenth century under Te Rerewa and others.

Following another conflict, many Ngai Tahu and Ngati Ira migrated to Wairarapa and Wellington in the mid-sixteenth century. Some of Rakaipaka's children, notably Rakaitekura, Tuhiku and Waitai, moved to Wellington, and soon after to the South Island. Within the same generation, conflict among newly arrived groups of Ngati Kahungunu, Ngati Ira, Ngai Tahu and Ngati Porou in the Wellington district led to a series of migrations into the South Island at the end of the sixteenth century led by Tutekawa, Te Ao Hikuraki, Puraho and Tuteahuka, among others. These were mostly groups of Ngai Tahu allegiance. They fought Ngati Mamoe, and each other, in the South Island as migration continued there until the early seventeenth century (Tau and Anderson 2008:153–161).

Although many different groups were involved in this phase of migration, the shape of their movement followed the same general pattern. That observation prompts the question of whether there were broader imperatives of migration than the particular conflicts involved, and a test of that is to consider Maori migration history elsewhere. I looked at the situation of the Tainui groups for comparison. The Tainui traditions show that until six to eight generations (180–240 years) after the arrival of the *Tainui* canoe, there was relatively little conflict and almost no migration into the inland Waikato (Jones and Biggs 1995). Archaeological data confirm the relative absence of inland settlement at this time (Anderson 2016). Then, from the late fifteenth century to the mid-sixteenth century, there was territorial expansion east, north-east and south-east from Kawhia (Figure 2.2), with emerging political divisions among the main lineages, derived from Tawhao, Tuhianga and Puhanga. Tawhao divided the Kawhia lands between Whatihua and Turongo, with the latter required to live inland. He settled in the upper Waipa valley and soon after, more coastal groups under Rereahu and Hotunui moved into the Waikato valley, then later to the Firth of Thames, where Marutuahu began a vigorous campaign to establish authority over eastern Hauraki. Maniapoto lived mainly in the Waitomo district; his younger brother Matakore, and also Mahanga, in the Waipa valley (Jones and Biggs 1995).

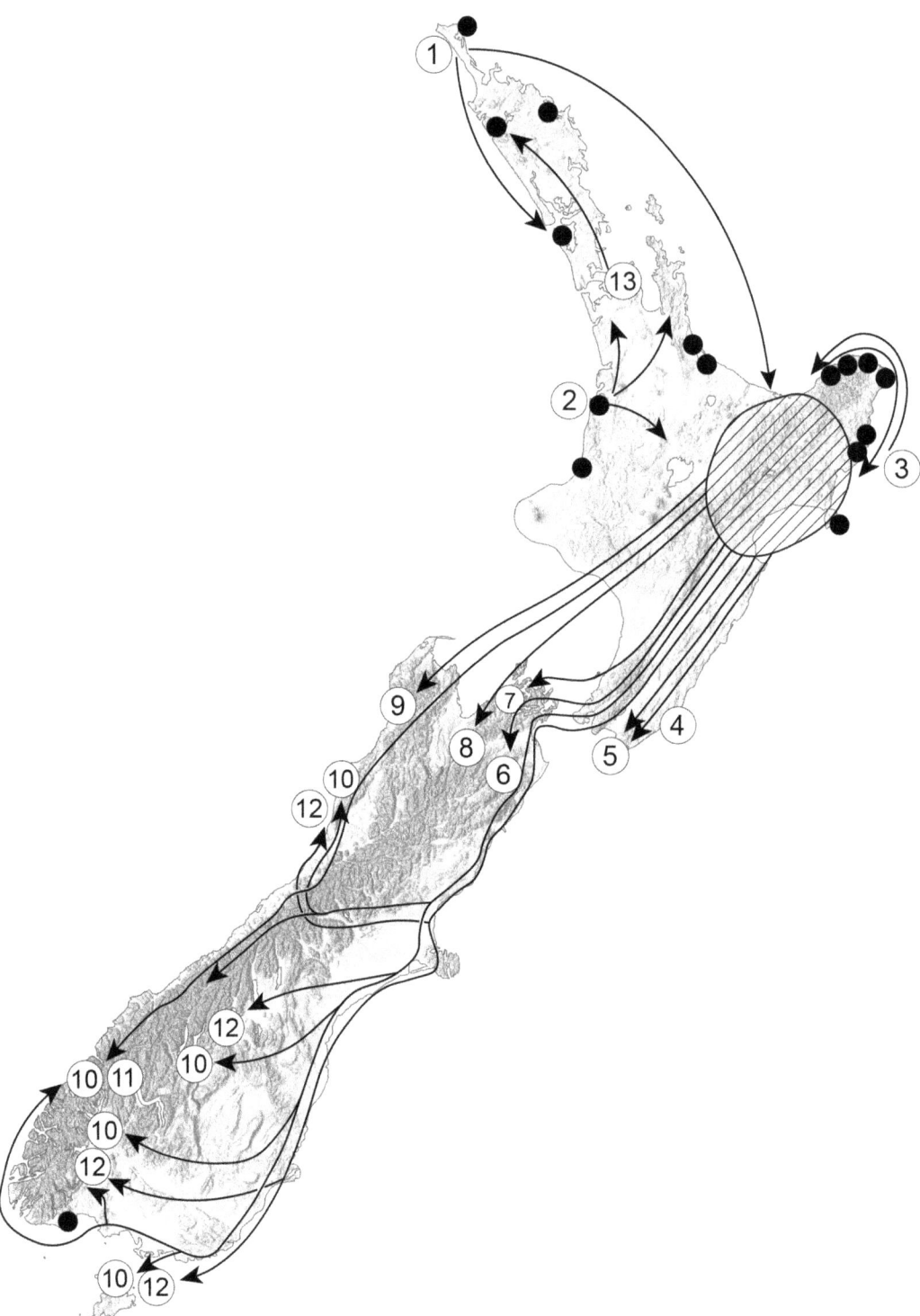

Figure 2.3. Phase I and II migrations.

Black dots = main landing places of colonising canoes (Phase I). Oval area with diagonal lines = approximate area of origin of most Phase II migrations. Arrows show direction of migrations. Groups involved: 1 Ngati Awa; 2 Tainui; 3 Ngai Te Rangi; 4 Ngati Kahungunu; 5 Ngati Ira; 6 Rangitane; 7 Ngai Tara; 8 Ngati Apa; 9 Ngati Tumatakokiri; 10 Ngati Mamoe; 11 Ngati Wairangi; 12 Ngai Tahu; 13 Te Uri o Pou.

Source: Atholl Anderson.

A brief survey of some other northern traditions suggests that migrations occurred in the sixteenth century in other regions as well. Marutuahu and his sons forced Te Uri o Pou out of Hauraki and they migrated north to Hokianga. In Nga Puhi tradition, the first big migration occurred in the mid-sixteenth century when early Nga Puhi expansion caused the migration of Northland Ngati Awa to the Bay of Plenty and Taranaki. The Ngati Apa migration from the Bay of Plenty occurred at the same time, reaching the south-west coast of the North Island about 1550 CE. Long migrations in this phase had ceased by the early seventeenth century.

Phase III: Late tribal migration

The latest migrations derived also from warfare in the North Island, especially in the northern half. Warfare seems to have increased in the Waikato region in the eighteenth century, with conflict beginning between Ngati Raukawa and other Waikato groups, and then further north between Waikato and Nga Puhi about 1750 CE. In the Waikato, warfare came to a head with the battle of Hingakaka ('the fall of parrots', referring to the great loss of chiefs), probably in 1807 CE. This was the largest battle ever fought in New Zealand, with about 13 000 warriors involved. It is important to note that neither this battle, nor many others until about 1815 CE, involved muskets, and also that both the locality (inland Waikato) and the reasons for the battle (Jones and Biggs 1995: 348) preclude any suggestion that it was fought over access to European goods and services. It was a traditional affair. On one side were most of the resident *Tainui* canoe descendants belonging to the Waikato and Ngati Maniapoto people, with allies from Northland Ngati Whatua. The attacking force, 7000–10 000 strong, centred around Ngati Raukawa, a people of *Tainui* and East Coast descent, and it included the west coast *Tainui* people of Ngati Toa; Te Ati Awa, Ngati Ruanui, and Whanganui from Taranaki; and groups of Te Arawa, Ngai Tuhoe, Ngati Kahungunu and Ngati Porou from Bay of Plenty–East Coast (Jones and Biggs 1995:348–357). All had accumulated grievances of *utu* and *mana* against Waikato, but Waikato won and that had major repercussions for those *Tainui* groups who had opposed them.

In 1816–1821 CE, long-distance campaigns in which muskets were used by Nga Puhi, Ngati Whatua (Auckland) and Waikato virtually encircled the North Island. Ngati Toa joined the 1819 CE Ngapuhi campaign, called Amiowhenua ('encircle the land'), but alliance with Ngapuhi, who were generally in opposition to Waikato, on top of opposition at Hingakaka, brought overwhelming retaliation by Waikato and Ngati Maniapoto. Ngati Toa, and their neighbouring tribes Ngati Koata and Ngati Rarua, were forced to migrate south. They were joined successively by the Taranaki tribes Ngati Tama, Ngati Mutunga and Te Atiawa, which became exposed by the evacuation of northern allies. A large section of Ngati Raukawa, defeated again by Waikato and under pressure from Hauraki migrants fleeing Ngapuhi, also migrated south, eventually ending up alongside their Ngati Toa allies on the south-west coast of the North Island (Crosby 1999:90–93, 136–149, 160–161, 182–185, 200–206). In 1827 CE, Te Rauparaha (Ngati Toa) led a campaign against the tribes in the northern South Island, and in 1829–1832 CE against Ngai Tahu to the south. The result of these events was that the southern North Island and northernmost South Island became occupied largely by people from the groups defeated at Hingakaka (Figure 2.4). There were some other, smaller migrations around this time. In the South Island, Ngai Tahu and Ngati Mamoe reached an accommodation, sealed by marriage, about 1790 CE, but some Ngati Mamoe, unable to accept this, migrated into the western lakes and fiords (Tau and Anderson 2008:152–158).

Figure 2.4. Phase III migrations. Oval area with diagonal lines shows approximate area of origin of most Phase III migrations.

Arrows show direction of migration. Groups involved: 1 Ngati Raukawa; 2 Ngati Koata; 3 Ngati Toa; 4 Ngati Rarua; 5 Ngati Tama; 6 Ngati Mutunga; 7 Te Atiawa.

Source: Atholl Anderson.

Long-term patterns of warfare and migration

1. In the three cases here, rising warfare eventually triggered migration. From the perspective of the traditions, disputes about resources, the deaths of significant individuals on the East Coast, and rebellion against senior clans in the Waikato—each initiated phases of relatively intensive warfare. As that proceeded, some groups shifted out of the areas of contention. The traditions say, or imply, that they were compelled to move by the fortunes of war.

2. Migration occurred incrementally. In Phase I, the canoes left individually or in small fleets, probably over a period of decades, because some genealogies begin later than others—for example, those for the *Takitimu* canoe (Anderson et al. 2014:63). Similar serial or staggered migration occurs in Phase II (Figure 2.2), where early Ngai Tahu were effectively forced to move across Cook Strait and then their success in capturing territory from Ngati Mamoe encouraged other related clans to follow suit. In the Waikato, it is not so clear that migration inland was compelled by war so much as a means, initially, of separating competing lineages (Jones and Biggs 1995), but movement by other clans proceeded serially. In Phase III, obligate Ngati Toa migration from Kawhia prompted its allied clans to follow suit in a domino process.

3. Nearly all migrations were from north to south; from the tropical to the temperate zone, from warmer to cooler districts in New Zealand; from higher to lower population densities and from reliable to marginal agriculture, or beyond into foraging. There were attractions to the south, notably jade and comparatively abundant wild food resources in the South Island, and Ngati Toa were interested in the trading opportunities with Europeans that were emerging in Cook Strait, but the overall pattern is nevertheless one expected of involuntary or obligatory migration—that is, exile (Anderson 2006).

The phases of migration are spaced fairly evenly across the pre-European era (Figure 2.2): Phase I about 1280–1340 CE, Phase II about 1460–1640 CE and Phase III beginning around 1820 CE. The phases are separated by intervals of less frequent warfare, lasting a century or more, and the peaks of activity occur about 1300, 1500–1600 and 1820 CE, approximately 200 years apart. This suggests that while warfare might have been endemic at the ethnographic level, at a larger scale it may not have been an inescapable part of social existence (Ferguson 2008:34).

These observations beg numerous questions, including whether the patterns noted here would be sustained in a more comprehensive study of Maori traditions. That remains to be seen, but if the current data are assumed as representative, then the principal issue raised is this: why were there pulses in the incidence of migration and associated warfare?

Discussion

One of the more striking aspects of the migration war data is that they do not show a general directional trend, such as migration increasing in frequency from early to late across the pre-European era, the inverse, no change in time or simply random activity. Instead, they are patterned as three separate peaks more or less equidistant in time. This raises a question as to whether the activity was in some way cyclical. The notion of regularities, oscillations or cycles in cultural activity, and of the interlinking or coupling of different cycles derived from diverse variables of cultural and natural origin—the historiographical interests of cliodynamics (Turchin 2011)—is so intuitively plausible that it is worth noticing such phenomena even when they are unable to be satisfactorily explained. Human behaviour operates on multiple scales, from the quotidian to the *longue durée* in historical terms, and even longer on archaeological time scales. The oscillation of multiple trajectories means that, at certain junctures, imperatives from one level influence behaviour at another. In that context, the periodicity of migration and warfare needs to be considered in terms of potential endogenous governors and exogenous drivers such as population growth, climate change and political development.

Endogenous periodicity of migration and war

It has been conjectured that Oceanic migration in general involved repeated cycles, each a binary phase of settlement stability and mobility, in which the overall trajectory of repetition was accelerating and being driven endogenously in some way (Anderson 2001). One way could be that migration propensity, whether genetic or cultural in origin, was heritable. If so, it could become proportionately more frequent with successive migrations of daughter populations through demographic bottlenecks, increasing the frequency of migration over the long term (Anderson 2013). Generally decreasing intervals of migration between Lapita (c. 3100 years ago), marginal West Polynesia (c. 2000 years ago), Central East Polynesia (c. 1100 years ago) and South Polynesia (c. 700 years ago) offers some evidence potentially relevant to this proposition (Anderson 2001), and that migration peaks at approximately 200-year intervals in New Zealand adds more. Speculating further, a propensity to migrate might be linked to genetic traits for boldness that were also expressed as a willingness to make war.

A similar kind of explanation for modulated warfare frequency might be an approximate periodicity in the accumulation of grievances. Some grievances between the crews of migration canoes were brought to New Zealand, for instance an offence that resulted in the burning of the *Arawa* canoe, but marriages between early canoe communities helped to prevent any serious trouble for some generations. In time, however, the closeness of individual and group descent, and a proportionate ability to meet or know other people in a district population, declined with population growth (Roscoe 1993) so that kin become increasingly non-kin and liable to be regarded as potentially hostile. It can be conjectured that ramifying political divisions thus increased the accumulation of grievances for all groups increasing, in turn, the frequency of war and migration required to resolve them. As the colonising canoes all arrived within a relatively short period, it would not be surprising to find in a comprehensive analysis of Maori traditions that warfare increased at about the same rate everywhere, peaked in about the sixteenth century, declined as grievances were resolved by war and migration, and then increased again to a peak during the late eighteenth and early nineteenth century.

Population growth

Changes in Maori population growth rates, and in population density, affected resource competition and might have impelled variation in the frequency of migration and war. Opinions vary about the shape of Maori population growth up to the turn of the nineteenth century, but the process was probably logistic—that is, dependent upon availability of resources (Anderson 2016). Computer simulation of Maori population growth, assuming a logistic curve and beginning with 200–400 men and women in the late thirteenth century, indicates that the growth rate declines about the sixteenth century (Whyte et al. 2005). Summed probability distribution of radiocarbon dates, although prone to some methodological problems (Dye 2016), shows that Maori population overall increased up to the sixteenth century and then plateaued until 1800 CE (Brown and Crema 2019). In central New Zealand a small secondary spurt of population growth occurred up to 1650 CE, possibly reflecting the southward migrations discussed here, while in southern New Zealand the population peaked around 1400 CE and remained low thereafter (Brown and Crema 2019). Density-dependent decline in the population growth rate, beginning in the sixteenth century, is consistent with an origin of *pa* construction in the northern North Island, given that this reflected warfare arising from population pressure on agricultural land.

The interlinkage of population dynamics with war among small-scale societies ('internal' warfare) is well known. Turchin and Korotayev (2006:123) argue that population size and warfare intensity 'should oscillate with long periods (ranging from one to three centuries depending on parameter values) and that these two variables should be phase-shifted with respect to each other', with peaks of warfare following peaks of population growth. In the Maori case, if migration was driven by warfare that increased with population growth, then a model could be sketched as follows. In central East Polynesia, population pressure resulted in warfare that induced migration, beginning in the thirteenth century and at least some migrants went to New Zealand. There, low population at colonisation and for a century or more later, precluded warfare, but growing population density and warfare frequency eventually induced migration southward into regions of lower population density. This suppressed territorial competition in areas of migration origin, and thereby warfare frequency, until a continuing rise in population density led to increasing warfare and migration again in the early nineteenth century.

Climate change

Climate change is another potential influence upon variation in migratory war. Increased warfare in non-state societies has been shown as a common response to climatically induced change in the distribution or productivity of food resources (Burtsev and Korotayev 2004:32; Ember et al. 2013:35). A conjunction between population decline, climate cooling and subsistence reorganisation has been shown as a periodic phenomenon in Holocene Britain and Ireland (Bevan et al. 2017), and increased warfare at such times was recognised by Zhang et al. (2007) in European and temperate zone Chinese historical records 1000–1900 CE. A similarly reciprocal relationship of enhanced conflict and episodes of environmental shock is described for drought-prone tropical regions by von Uexkull et al. (2016). It is apparent that a crucial factor was not just change in the geographical extent and productivity of resources, but rather the confidence that people could have in their availability—that is, in levels of food uncertainty.

Could something similar have occurred in New Zealand? Initial colonisation occurred during the 'Polynesian Warm Period', which persisted, with fluctuations, up to about 1400 CE. There was then a fairly sudden, substantial, decline into the Little Ice Age (LIA), coldest and wettest at 1500–1670 CE, which gradually ameliorated up to about 1850 CE. Across the LIA as a whole, mean summer temperature dropped by 0.6 °C, and in winter by about 1 °C, in New Zealand, but the drop was especially sharp and deep during the beginning of the LIA, where some data show a 1.5 °C fall (Anderson 2016). Such changes are comparable in scale to those that had profound effects on European rural economy and society.

Kumara will not grow in soil temperatures of less than 15 °C, which put the southern limit of cultivation during the colonisation era at about 43° south (North Canterbury). A fall in mean annual temperature of 1.0–1.5 °C at sea level by the sixteenth century is equivalent to moving the cultivation limit 145 km further north, and a fall of 1.5 °C in mean summer temperature is the equivalent of shifting it 220 km north, to 41° south, the southern North Island. In that case, agriculture had probably become marginal almost as far north as Hawkes Bay (Anderson 2016), which might account in some degree for the origin of sixteenth-century warfare and migration on the East Coast. Heavy rainfall was also problematic for *kumara*, especially in the autumn and early winter before the crop was lifted, and also through dampness when the crop was stored in covered pits. Rainfall increased substantially over most of New Zealand in the coldest years of the LIA, 1400–1560 CE, and it is quite possible that it led to frequent rotting of *kumara* in the ground, creating a crisis of the same kind, if not on the same scale, as the Irish potato famine.

Political reorganisation

Whether political reorganisation was also involved in the patterning of war is open to question. By the eighteenth century, at least, exclusive clan control of territoriality seems to have weakened in the northern North Island as some groups achieved a level of political consolidation that foreshadowed the rise of modern tribes. This process has been seen, variously, as the beginnings of a change toward a class society, the developing primacy of political over kinship relationships and a move toward settlement or community-ordered societies (Anderson et al. 2014:125–126 and references therein). How far back it goes is hard to tell but if, for example, the sixteenth-century ousting of Ngati Awa from Northland is seen as an early move in the rise of Nga Puhi, then it might have begun to emerge at the time of the Phase II migrations.

Any greater political complexity can be ruled out by an absence of demographic prerequisites. State-like reorganisation occurred in Hawai'i but the historical population there was four times larger than in New Zealand and its gross population density was 65 times greater (Anderson 2016). Nevertheless, in Northland, the district of highest population density, early nineteenth-century accumulation of fine goods and services extracted by Nga Puhi from client groups in Thames and Bay of Plenty, the construction of large formal houses (*whare whakairo*) and *hakari* (feasting) display stages, and the carrying of high chiefs in chairs of state suggest that political innovation was heading in a similar direction. The Waikato groups were favouring lines of descent that continued into the later nineteenth-century Maori King movement, and among highly dispersed Ngai Tahu, issues of political integration as a tribe under a paramount chief were apparent by the late eighteenth century. It is possible that these political changes influenced the rise of warfare frequency before and during the Phase III migrations.

Slavery could also have played a part. The introduction of potatoes and other European crops facilitated Maori agrarian commerce which, in turn, underwrote the logistics of the large, musket-armed raids of the early nineteenth century, and was reinforced by the capture of slaves (Fitzpatrick 2007). There is no traditional evidence about the pre-European development of slavery and it is known only by its historical occurrence (Petrie 2015). However, a combination of extensive, unused, allophanic soils suited to agricultural expansion in the northern North Island, and a medium-density population level in that region by the sixteenth century or so, were conditions in which slavery is predicted to emerge (Lagerlöf 2009). It may be no coincidence, then, that most of the Phase II and Phase III migrations began around the margins of the main horticultural territories; that is, from districts of relative disadvantage, including in military strength, where slaves would probably have been sought by the more powerful and populous groups who were developing extensive agricultural estates (Anderson 2016).

Conclusions

Existing models of Maori conflict are essentially ethnographic in conception and offer little insight into the patterning of warfare and what might have shaped it, at centennial or greater scales of consideration. In addition, the significance to warfare of *pa*, practically the only source of archaeological data, is to some extent enigmatic. Fortunately, there is an alternative archive of pertinent data contained in numerous, independent, genealogically dated, oral traditions of clan and tribal history extending across the pre-European era. In order to extract a sense of the frequency and intensity of warfare from these data, it has been assumed that there is a covariance between elevated warfare and phases of migration, as suggested by traditional evidence that migration was generally involuntary and accompanied throughout by warfare. The main result of a pilot study of East Coast and Waikato traditions is that migration and associated war appear to have fluctuated at a centennial scale and were possibly cyclic, with phase peaks at about 200-year intervals. More comprehensive research is needed to determine whether this result is valid for Maori as a whole.

Turning to the original questions, warfare was frequent when Europeans arrived and it continued during the early nineteenth century, for entirely valid traditional reasons. It became more frequent and intensified by differential access to European commodities, including muskets and potatoes and, to that extent, early European impressions of Maori warfare cannot be taken as representative of its long-term state. The frequency and assumed intensity of warfare, as measured by the frequency of associated long-distance migration, was not constant through Maori history, nor did it follow a simple trajectory of incidence. Warfare was infrequent, at least, for up to two centuries after colonisation, and it may have declined also between migration phases II and III. Warfare was more frequent immediately prior to the thirteenth-century colonising migrations, again in the sixteenth century and then in the early nineteenth century.

Several potential explanations of periodic oscillations in Maori migration and warfare have been discussed. The current state of evidence and understanding of these does not encourage a preference for any one, or combination, of them as explaining the long-term patterning in Maori war. Nevertheless, setting them out emphasises the necessity of examining not only inherent propensities, if these exist, and the sociopolitical particularities of warfare in Maori society, but also contextual influences in demography and environment that vary on centennial or larger scales. Lastly, the archaeology of Maori warfare, including but not exclusively of the *pa* sites, is in great need of sustained attention for, in the final analysis, it must be the arbiter of our hypotheses.

References

Anderson, A.J. 2001. Mobility models of Lapita migration. In G.R. Clark, A.J. Anderson and T. Vunidilo (eds), *The archaeology of Lapita dispersal in Oceania*, pp. 15–23. Terra Australis 17. The Australian National University, Canberra.

Anderson, A.J. 2006. Islands of exile: Ideological motivation in maritime migration. *Journal of Island and Coastal Archaeology* 1:33–48. doi.org/10.1080/15564890600579858.

Anderson, A.J. 2013. Patterns and processes of migration in Maori tradition. Biennial Te Rangikaheke Memorial Lecture to the New Zealand History Association Conference, Otakou Marae.

Anderson, A.J. 2014. Monumentality and ritual behaviour in South Polynesia. In H. Martinsson-Wallin and T. Thomas (eds), *Studies in global archaeology* 24, pp. 273–296, University of Uppsala, Uppsala.

Anderson, A.J. 2016. The making of the Maori middle ages. *Journal of New Zealand Studies* NS23:2–18.

Anderson, A.J. 2017. Using numbers from somewhere else: Comment on New Zealand numbers from nearly nowhere: 80,000 to 100,000 Maori circa 1769. *New Zealand Journal of History* 51:122–125.

Anderson, A.J., J. Binney and A. Harris 2014. *Tangata Whenua: An illustrated history*. Bridget Williams Books, Wellington.

Armit, I. 2011. Violence and society in the deep human past. *British Journal of Criminology* 51:499–517. doi.org/10.1093/bjc/azq076.

Ballara, A. 1998. *Iwi: The dynamics of Maori tribal organization from c. 1769 to c. 1945*. Victoria University Press, Wellington.

Ballara, A. 2003. *Taua: 'Musket wars', 'land wars' or tikanga? Warfare in Maori society in the early nineteenth century.* Penguin, Auckland.

Beaglehole, J.C. (ed.) 1961. *The journals of Captain James Cook on his voyages of discovery. Volume II: The voyage of the* Resolution *and* Adventure, *1772–1775*. The Hakluyt Society, Cambridge.

Beaglehole, J.C. (ed.) 1962. *The* Endeavour *journal of Joseph Banks*, Volume II. Angus and Robertson, Sydney.

Beaglehole, J.C. (ed.) 1967. *The journals of Captain James Cook on his voyages of discovery. Volume III: The voyage of the* Resolution *and* Discovery, *1776–1780*. The Hakluyt Society, Cambridge. doi.org/10.4324/9781315086149.

Berns, G.S. and S. Atran 2012. The biology of culture conflict. *Philosophical Transactions of the Royal Society B* 367:633–639.

Bevan, A., S. Colledge, D. Fuller, R. Fyfe, S. Shennan and C. Stevens 2017. Holocene fluctuations in human population demonstrate repeated links to food production and climate. *Proceedings of the National Academy of Sciences USA* 114:E10524–E10531. doi.org/10.1073/pnas.1709190114.

Brown, A.A. and E.R. Crema 2019. Maori population growth in pre-contact New Zealand: Regional population dynamics inferred from summed probability distributions of radiocarbon dates. *Journal of Island and Coastal Archaeology*. doi.org/10.1080/15564894.2019.1605429.

Burtsev, M.S. and A. Korotayev 2004. An evolutionary agent-based model of pre-state warfare patterns: Cross-cultural tests. *World Cultures* 15:28–36.

Carman, J. and A. Harding (eds) 1999. *Ancient warfare: Archaeological perspectives*. The History Press, Stroud.

Chapple, S. 2017. New Zealand numbers from nearly nowhere: 80,000 to 100,000 Maori circa 1769. *New Zealand Journal of History* 51:104–121.

Crampton, P. and C. Parkin 2007. Warrior genes and risk-taking science. *New Zealand Medical Journal* 120(1250):U2439.

Crosby, R.D. 1999. *The musket wars: A history of inter-iwi conflict 1806–45*. Reed, Auckland.

Darwin, C. 1909. *Voyage of the Beagle*. Collier, New York.

Dye, T.S. 2016. Long-term rhythms in the development of Hawaiian social stratification. *Journal of Archaeological Science* 71:1–9. doi.org/10.1016/j.jas.2016.05.006.

Elder, R.J. 1932. *The letters and journals of Samuel Marsden 1765–1838*. Coulls Somerville Wilkie and Reed, Dunedin.

Ember, C.R., T.A. Adem and I. Skoggard 2013. Risk, uncertainty and violence in eastern Africa, a regional comparison. *Human Nature* 24:33–58. doi.org/10.1007/s12110-012-9157-5.

Fenner, J.N. 2005. Cross-cultural estimation of the human generation interval for use in genetics-based population divergence studies. *American Journal of Physical Anthropology* 128:415–423. doi.org/10.1002/ajpa.20188.

Ferguson, R.B. 2008. Ten points on war. *Social Analysis* 52:32–49.

Ferguson, R.B. and N.L. Whitehead 1992. The violent edge of empire. In R.B. Ferguson and N.L. Whitehead (eds), *War in the tribal zone: Expanding states and indigenous warfare*, pp. 1–30. School of American Research Press, Santa Fe.

Fitzpatrick, J. 2007. The Columbian exchange and the two colonizations of Aotearoa New Zealand. *Food, Culture and Society* 10:211–238. doi.org/10.2752/155280107x211421.

Fry, D.P. and P. Söderberg 2013. Lethal aggression in mobile forager bands and implications for the origins of war. *Science* 34:270–273. doi.org/10.1126/science.1235675.

Gat, A. 2015. Proving communal warfare among hunter-gatherers: The quasi-Rousseauan error. *Evolutionary Anthropology* 24:111–126. doi.org/10.1002/evan.21446.

Glowacki, L. and R. Wrangham 2015. Warfare and reproductive success in a tribal population. *Proceedings of the National Academy of Sciences USA* 112:348–353. doi.org/10.1073/pnas.1412287112.

Grey, Sir G. 1954 (1855). *Polynesian mythology*. First published 1855. Whitcombe and Tombs, Christchurch.

Hall, D., M. Green, G. Chambers and R. Lea 2006. Tracking the evolutionary history of the warrior gene in the South Pacific. Unpublished paper presented at the 11th International Human Genetics Meeting, Brisbane, 6–10 August.

Hook, G.R. 2009. 'Warrior genes' and the disease of being Maori. *MAI Review* 2009(2).

Houghton, P. 1980. *The first New Zealanders*. Hodder and Stoughton, Auckland.

Irwin, G.J. 1985. *Land, pā and polity: A study based on the Maori fortifications of Pouto*. New Zealand Archaeological Association Monograph 15. New Zealand Archaeological Association, Auckland.

Irwin, G.J. 2013. Wetland archaeology and the study of late Maori settlement patterns and social organization in northern New Zealand. *Journal of the Polynesian Society* 122:311–332. doi.org/10.15286/jps.122.4.311-332.

Jones, P., H. Te and B. Biggs 1995. *Nga Iwi o Tainui: The traditional history of the Tainui people*. Auckland University Press, Auckland.

Keeley, L.H. 2016. Food for war, war for food and war on food. In A.M. VanDerwarker and G.D. Wilson (eds), *The archaeology of food and warfare*, pp. 291–302. Springer, New York. doi.org/10.1007/978-3-319-18506-4_13.

Lagerlöf, N.-P. 2009. Slavery and other property rights. *The Review of Economic Studies* 76:319–342.

Lea, R. and G. Chambers 2007. Monoamine oxidase, addiction, and the 'warrior' gene hypothesis. *New Zealand Medical Journal* 20(1250):U2439.

Lehmann, L. and M. Feldman 2008. War and the evolution of belligerence and bravery. *Proceedings of the Royal Society B* 275:2877–2885. doi.org/10.1098/rspb.2008.0842.

McDermott, R., D. Tingley, J. Cowden, G. Frazzetto and D. Johnson 2009. Monoamine oxidase A gene (MAOA) predicts behavioral aggression following provocation. *Proceedings of the National Academy of Sciences USA* 106:2118–2123. doi.org/10.1073/pnas.0808376106.

McDonald, M.M., C.D. Navarrete and M. van Vugt 2012. Evolution and the psychology of intergroup conflict: The male warrior hypothesis. *Philosophical Transactions of the Royal Society B* 367:670–679. doi.org/10.1098/rstb.2011.0301.

McNab, R. 1914. *Historical records of New Zealand*. Volume II. Government Printer, Wellington.

Merriman, T. and V. Cameron 2007. Risk-taking: Behind the warrior gene story. *New Zealand Medical Journal* 120(1250):U2440.

Nicholas, J.L. 1817. *Narrative of a voyage to New Zealand: Performed in the Years 1814 and 1815 in company with the Rev. Samuel Marsden*. Black, London. doi.org/10.1017/CBO9780511707001.

O'Brien, K. 1993. Between enlightenment and stadial history: William Robertson on the history of Europe. *Journal of Eighteenth-Century Studies* 16:53–64. doi.org/10.1111/j.1754-0208.1993.tb00155.x.

O'Driscoll, J. 2017. Hillforts in prehistoric Ireland: A costly display of power? *World Archaeology* 49(4):506–525. doi.org/10.1080/00438243.2017.1282379.

Perbal, L. 2013. The 'warrior gene' and the Maori people: The responsibility of the geneticists. *Bioethics* 27:382–387. doi.org/10.1111/j.1467-8519.2012.01970.x.

Petrie, H. 2015. *Outcasts of the gods: The struggle over slavery in Maori New Zealand*. Auckland University Press, Auckland.

Prickett, N.J. 1982. Maori fortifications of the Tataraimaka District, Taranaki. *Records of the Auckland Institute and Museum* 19:1–52.

Prickett, N.J. 1983. Maori fortifications of the Okato District, Taranaki, *Records of the Auckland Institute and Museum* 20:1–39.

Roscoe, P.B. 1993. Practice and political centralization: A new approach to political evolution. *Current Anthropology* 34:111–140.

Roscoe, P. 2016. War and the food quest in small-scale societies: Settlement-pattern formation in contact era New Guinea. In A.M. VanDerwarker and G.D. Wilson (eds), *The archaeology of food and warfare*, pp. 13–39. Springer, New York. doi.org/10.1007/978-3-319-18506-4_2.

Schmidt, M. 1996. The commencement of pa construction in New Zealand prehistory. *Journal of the Polynesian Society* 105:441–451.

Skinner, H.D. 1974. *Comparatively speaking: Studies in Pacific material culture 1921–1972*. Otago University Press, Dunedin.

Smith, C. 2009. The Scottish Enlightenment, unintended consequences and the science of man. *Journal of Scottish Philosophy* 7:9–28.

Tau, T. M. and A.J. Anderson (eds) 2008. *Ngai Tahu: A migration history. The Carrington text*. Bridget Williams Books, Wellington.

Thomas, N., H. Guest and M. Dettelbach (eds) 1996. *Observations made during a voyage around the world: Johann Reinhold Forster*. University of Hawai'i Press, Honolulu.

Thompson, C.A. 1997. A dangerous people whose only occupation is war: Maori and Pakeha in 19th century New Zealand. *The Journal of Pacific History* 32:109–119. doi.org/10.1080/00223349708572831.

Thorpe, I.J.N. 2003. Anthropology, archaeology, and the origin of warfare. *World Archaeology* 35:145–165. doi.org/10.1080/0043824032000079198.

Turchin, P. 2011. Toward cliodynamics—an analytical, predictive science of history. *Cliodynamics* 2:167–186. doi.org/10.21237/c7clio21210.

Turchin, P. and A.V. Korotayev 2006. Population dynamics and internal warfare: A reconsideration. *Social Evolution and History* 5:112–147.

Turner, M. 2004. Functional and technological explanations for the variation amongst early New Zealand adzes. *New Zealand Journal of Archaeology* 26:57–101.

Vayda, A.P. 1960. *Maori warfare*. Polynesian Society Maori Monograph 2. Polynesian Society, Wellington.

Vayda, A.P. 1970. Maoris and muskets in New Zealand: Disruption of a war system. *Political Science Quarterly* 85(4):560–584. doi.org/10.2307/2147596.

Vayda, A.P. 1974. Warfare in ecological perspective. *Annual Review of Ecological Systems* 5:183–193.

Von Uexkull, N., M. Croicu, H. Fjelde and H. Buhaug 2016. Civil conflict sensitivity to growing-season drought. *Proceedings of the National Academy of Sciences USA* 113:12391–12396. doi.org/10.1073/pnas.1607542113.

Whyte, A., S. Marshall and G. Chambers 2005. Human evolution in Polynesia. *Human Biology* 77:157–177. doi.org/10.1353/hub.2005.0045.

Wilson, G.D. and A.M. VanDerwarker 2016. Toward an archaeology of food and warfare. In A.M. VanDerwarker and G.D. Wilson (eds), *The archaeology of food and warfare*, pp. 1–12. Springer, New York. doi.org/10.1007/978-3-319-18506-4_1.

Wright, H. 1959. *New Zealand, 1769–1840: Early years of western contact*. Harvard University Press, Cambridge Massachusetts.

Wright, M. 2011. *Guns and Utu: A short history of the musket wars*. Penguin, Auckland.

Zhang, D.D., P. Brecke, H.F. Lee, Y.-Q. He and J. Zhang 2007. Global climate change, war, and population decline in recent human history. *Proceedings of the National Academy of Sciences USA* 104:19214–19219. doi.org/10.1073/pnas.0703073104.

3

Violence and warfare in Aboriginal Australia

Colin Pardoe

Archaeological interest in the nature, distribution and change in societies over the course of our evolution must include attention to violence as well as cooperation; barriers as well as links. Our understanding of the forms of evidence in the archaeological record has improved over the years, as has our conceptualisation of violence and warfare situated within and between societies. The disentangling of violence and warfare is particularly important and considerable research has been carried out on this matter (for an introduction to the literature, see Allen and Jones 2014; Keeley 1996; Leblanc 2014; Leblanc and Register 2003; Shackelford and Hansen 2013). Mark Allen, in his introduction to the book *Violence and warfare among hunter-gatherers* (Allen and Jones 2014:15), noted that archaeology and social anthropology generally had been in the midst of a moratorium on research into violence during the 1970s and 1980s, and instead had emphasised 'ecological balance and intergroup harmony'. Since that time, considerable research efforts have seen an integrated approach of many strands of evidence—something not seen in studies of territoriality, for instance. The phenomenon we call warfare requires archaeological and skeletal data that become increasingly difficult to find and interpret with increasing antiquity.

For the reader with less background in the history of archaeology and biological anthropology in Australia, it is necessary to point out that the availability of skeletal remains as a source of evidence and knowledge of the past has more or less disappeared. This has not been complete by any means, as we shall see in the next section of this chapter, but the skeletal evidence must be understood in its historical context. The study of human skeletal remains in an archaeological framework more or less disappeared during the late 1980s and early 1990s. While archaeologists were attempting to figure out an archaeology that would work and be of benefit in Australia, and in particular to Indigenous communities, archaeologists had to come to terms with issues of ownership and control. This took a lot of effort from all parties and it was a major transformation in ways of thinking about science, practice and legislation.

My point in this is to explain that such evidence as we have from skeletal remains (pathology, demography, morphology, evolutionary and more) has remained at the same state as when there were more of us studying large samples and making regional and even continental comparisons. Those studies from several decades past are as valid as ever in their data and many interpretations, but many have slipped from archaeological memory. Where once the evidence from skeletal remains was a very important component of archaeological thought and model-building (see for instance, the amount of information used in White and O'Connell's 1982 *Prehistory of Australia* that came only from burials, skeletal remains and their study), it has now almost completely disappeared.

Evidence of violence from skeletal remains

Evidence from skeletal remains is often considered to be pivotal to the investigation of violence. A split skull or spear point in the ribs is not generally questioned. Such examples of trauma are, however, fairly rare. It is difficult to extrapolate to population frequencies without large amounts of data, and in parts of the world where such evidence has been found (California and parts of Europe) the nature of violence in those societies has contributed to a better understanding of territoriality, resource pressure and demography.

The research by Webb (1984, 1989, 1995) on palaeopathology across Aboriginal Australia has made a major contribution and is the main source of our information. His analyses have considered similar kinds of violence. In a later publication (Pardoe 2014), I recast his data into different regional and tribal groupings, adding data from my studies over the years. Two of the more common osteological markers of violence were quantified and examined in more detail—cranial depression fractures and parrying fractures of the forearm—both of which are features that occur across Australia (Webb 1995), and the latter across the globe.

The difficulty in interpreting these traumas is in determining whether we might differentiate our categorisations of 'warfare', 'domestic violence', 'stylised single combat', et cetera. Given the archaeological, biological and ethnohistorical record in the central Murray River region, this seemed to be the place to examine these data sets (see Pardoe 2014).

Cranial depression fractures

Cranial depression fractures are somewhat enigmatic. They occur elsewhere in the world, but nothing like what is seen in Aboriginal Australia. These are thumb-sized depressions in the outer table of the skull, always on the upper and more central part of the vault, where the skull has no overlying muscle. They are typically smooth and appear more like an indent than a cracking fracture of bone. It is probable that they result from being hit by a piece of wood—the waddy being a particularly popular implement across the country (the waddy being a stick with a naturally occurring knob on the end—usually a Mulga or Black Box sapling). As with so many examples of trauma to the skeleton, people are often amazed at such damage. The damage rarely intrudes to the inner table and is usually not visible internally. It is inconceivable that concussion and perhaps hematoma would not follow, but to all intents and purposes, these traumatic incidents are not seen as life-threatening or disabling in the long term.

Given the distribution of these fractures across the country and by sex, we are drawn to think of single reasons for their occurrence. Mourning, or 'sorry business', has been suggested given historical documentation of self-harm by relatives at the grave. There is some justification for this idea when one examines the distribution of dents across the skull, allowing for handedness of the person wielding the stick.

Stylised single combat has been suggested as a possibility (Brown 1989), although this would not necessarily account for both sexes. Interpersonal violence is a likely cause for many of these dents. Their shape varies, but many are in the form of a groove rather than circular dent, suggesting being hit with a stick—either a woman's digging stick or a man's spear being obvious sources. The antiquity of this pattern of violence, from whatever causes, extends from the terminal Pleistocene, where depression fractures are present among both men and women in the Coobool Creek sample and Nacurrie Man (Brown 1989, 2009). There is a notable increase in incidence by the Late Holocene, particularly among men (Table 3.1).

Table 3.1. Change in occurrence of violence from the Early to Late Holocene in what is now traditional Barapa territory, as measured by cranial trauma of the vault.

Locality	Men (%)	Women (%)
Coobool Creek (~10 000 years)	10.7	18.8
Central Murray River (~2000 years)	18.1	21.9
% increase	7.4	3.1

Source: Data from Webb (1984) and Brown (1989).

We should not necessarily expect to find a single cause for cranial depression fractures. It seems likely that these several causes—trial by ordeal, stylised single combat and interpersonal violence—all contributed to a widespread pattern persisting for thousands of years. What has become clear, however, is that these depressed fractures would not result from night raids, payback or revenge killings, or open warfare.

Parrying fractures

Parrying fractures are seen throughout the world, where the arm is raised in self-defence against a blow from a weapon. When a right-handed assailant strikes, the victim might raise the left arm in defence more often than not. The incidence of parrying fractures is greater for the left side in all groups examined.

Parrying fractures are probably the result of face-to-face combat or to ward off an unexpected or sudden blow. The incidence by side confirms a supposition that most would result from a direct blow from a right-handed assailant who would generally be in the victim's line of sight. This could be the result of a direct blow on an unprotected arm or glancing off a shield. From the data (Pardoe 2014; Webb 1989) it is difficult to distinguish between domestic violence (within or between the sexes), trial by ordeal, or warfare. It would seem least likely that parrying fractures would result from revenge killings of individuals or night raids on a sleeping group. These are invariably planned assassinations with an element of surprise that few people survive.

Investigations of the individual

A more considered investigation of skeletal biology and ethnohistory did not hold out much hope for relying on the former to inform us about violence in the past (Pardoe 2014). Combined with concerns about the validity of ethnohistory being pushed back into antiquity, is there any hope for investigating violence as part of ancient society? The difficulty of investigating violence using skeletal pathology does not diminish the validity of skeletal studies in general but does require caution when looking for trends. And yet, each life and the meagre facts and inferences we are able to make prove fascinating. Here is where a more personal approach does allow us to form a view of what violence in the ancient world might have looked like. A lot like ours, as it turns out.

Detailed examination of an individual from excavation through to study in the laboratory has been rarely possible in Australia, but the effects have always been instructive. What we properly hesitate to call a burial proved to be the opportunistic spearing, killing and dismemberment of the body in what is now suburban Sydney (MacDonald et al. 2007). An individual from Burkes Bridge in what is now Barapa territory, on the north side of the Murray River from Kow Swamp, was also probably killed by a spear or pointed weapon entering the skull (Webb 1984, 1995). Instances of stabbing, apparently while the victim was asleep (Pardoe 2014), accord with historical accounts (Warner 1969 (1937)) of night raids and revenge killings.

A particular form of trauma has been observed just a few times, over the course of more than 10 000 years, but these are a good example of ongoing detailed studies that as well as documenting shocking injuries that could be sustained only in a fight, give us some indication of the use of such implements as fighting boomerangs, wielded in a similar fashion and with similar results to a sword. One could imagine that such trauma would only be sustained in a deadly fight or open warfare. The individual from Burkes Bridge, again in Barapa territory, suffered a blow to the side of the head, either from a spear or possibly a fighting stick. Although undated, the preservation of the skeleton indicates early Holocene – terminal Pleistocene data. Another individual, also undated, but probably mid to later Holocene from Barapa territory, was hit across the left side of the head.

A man buried on the banks of the Darling River in Barkandji territory had been savagely attacked, again probably with a fighting boomerang (Westaway et al. 2016). There have been several examples of severe cranial trauma caused almost certainly by a fighting boomerang. Several instances among the Barapa of the Murray River give a time depth of more than 10 000 years.

Conclusion

This short review has focused on only a couple of features indicative of violence. An ecologically based perspective fits well with current thinking and research on violence in prehistory, where we are concerned with matters that affect societies and the individuals that make them. Research in Australia has not shown systematic patterns related to environment at a very general or continental level.

When we turn to chronology, we see glimpses of what looks like considerable trauma from fighting with weaponry—enough to suggest that it was common in the early Holocene. At the same time, the incidence of cranial depression fractures marginally increases among women, and considerably more among men, suggesting that open combat increased by the Late Holocene.

While we might wish for population-based evidence for violence (percentages of fractures and the like) that accords with other population studies of skeletal remains, we must use the relatively rare occurrences to infer violence and warfare in the Australian archaeological record. Based on the present evidence, violence would appear to be common across several categories including domestic, trial by ordeal, warfare and revenge (Pardoe 2014). Nowadays, when my colleagues encounter skeletal remains, they often feel the best of what I always have felt—privilege, curiosity and always learning.

References

Allen, W. and T.L. Jones (eds) 2014. *Violence and warfare among hunter-gatherers.* Left Coast Press, California.

Brown, P. 1989. *Coobool Creek: A morphological and metrical analysis of the crania, mandibles and dentitions of a prehistoric Australian human population.* Terra Australis 13. Research School of Pacific Studies, The Australian National University, Canberra.

Brown, P. 2009. Nacurrie 1: Mark of ancient Java or a mother's caring hands in terminal Pleistocene Australia? *Journal of Human Evolution* 59:168–187. doi.org/10.1016/j.jhevol.2010.05.007.

Keeley, L.H. 1996. *War before civilization: The myth of the peaceful savage.* Oxford University Press, New York.

Leblanc, S. 2014. Forager warfare and our evolutionary past. In M.W. Allen and T.L. Jones (eds), *Violence and warfare among hunter-gatherers*, pp. 26–46. Left Coast Press, California. doi.org/10.4324/9781315415970-2.

Leblanc, S. and K. Register 2003. *Constant battles: The myth of the peaceful noble savage.* St Martin's Press: New York.

McDonald, J., D. Donlon, J. Field, R. Fullagar, J. Coltrain et al. 2007. The first archaeological evidence for death by spearing in Australia. *Antiquity* 81:877–885. doi.org/10.1017/s0003598x00095971.

Pardoe, C. 2014. Conflict and territoriality in Aboriginal Australia: Evidence from biology and ethnography. In M.W. Allen and T.L. Jones (eds), *Violence and warfare among hunter-gatherers*, pp. 112–132. Left Coast Press, California. doi.org/10.4324/9781315415970-6.

Shackelford, T. and R. Hansen (eds) 2013. *The evolution of violence.* Springer, New York.

Warner, W.L. 1969 (1937). *A black civilization: A study of an Australian tribe*. First published 1937. Peter Smith, Massachusetts.

Webb, S.G. 1984. Prehistoric stress in Australian Aborigines. PhD thesis. The Australian National University, Canberra.

Webb, S.G. 1989. *Prehistoric stress in Australian Aborigines: A paleopathological study of hunter-gathering population.* British Archaeological Reports International Series 490. Oxford, England.

Webb, S.G. 1995. *Palaeopathology of Aboriginal Australians: Health and disease across a hunter-gatherer continent.* Cambridge University Press, Cambridge. doi.org/10.1017/cbo9780511552182.

Westaway, M., D. Williams, R. Wright, R. Wood, J. Olley et al. 2016. The death of Kaakutja: A case of peri-mortem weapon trauma in an Aboriginal man from north-western New South Wales, Australia. *Antiquity* 90(353):1318–1333. doi.org/10.15184/aqy.2016.173.

White, P., and J.F. O'Connell 1982. *A prehistory of Australia, New Guinea and Sahul.* Academic Press, Sydney.

4

Warfare in Rapa Nui (Easter Island)

Helene Martinsson-Wallin

Introduction

Evidence of massacre, trauma on human skeletal remains, finds of used weapons, depictions of fighting on rock carvings and pottery, destruction of monuments, built defensive structures such as earth forts, and descriptions of warfare and violence in oral traditions point to the existence of organised warfare in pre-text societies (Kolb and Dixon 2002). The aim of this chapter is to review and discuss the evidence of warfare and violence in pre- and protohistoric Rapa Nui (Easter Island) using data from oral traditions, the analysis of material culture and information from human skeletal remains.

Rapa Nui is a small and remote island situated in the East Pacific (Figure 4.1). Archaeological research shows that a Polynesian population settled the island around 700–1000 years ago (DiNapoli et al. 2020; Hunt and Lipo 2006; Martinsson-Wallin and Crockford 2002). The Western world's first knowledge of Rapa Nui came when the Dutch Captain Roggeveen sighted it on Easter Day 1722 CE. Diamond (2005) has since portrayed Rapa Nui as a place of precolonial societal and ecological collapse. This image has recently been challenged by research that suggests that Rapa Nui was a nonviolent society (Hunt and Lipo 2011) and was highly resilient (Haoa Cardinali et al. 2017). Instead of social collapse from ecological degradation, it has been argued that European colonial activity caused unrest and the decline of traditional Rapa Nui society (Delsing 2004; Griffero 1998:365–367; Martinsson-Wallin 2007).

Based on archaeology, oral traditions and early historical accounts, Rapa Nui was probably a largely isolated society in prehistory. Archaeological and geological investigations (Martinsson-Wallin 2004; Mieth and Bork 2010; Wosniak 1998) have shown that the land was covered by an extensive endemic palm forest which was gradually cut down, in part so that agriculture and ceremonial sites could be built. This, in tandem with agriculture, caused soil erosion and environmental degradation. Traditional history collected in the nineteenth and early twentieth centuries point to competition and conflict over resources that set off warfare, violence and societal collapse (Métraux 1940; Routledge 1919; Thomson 1889).

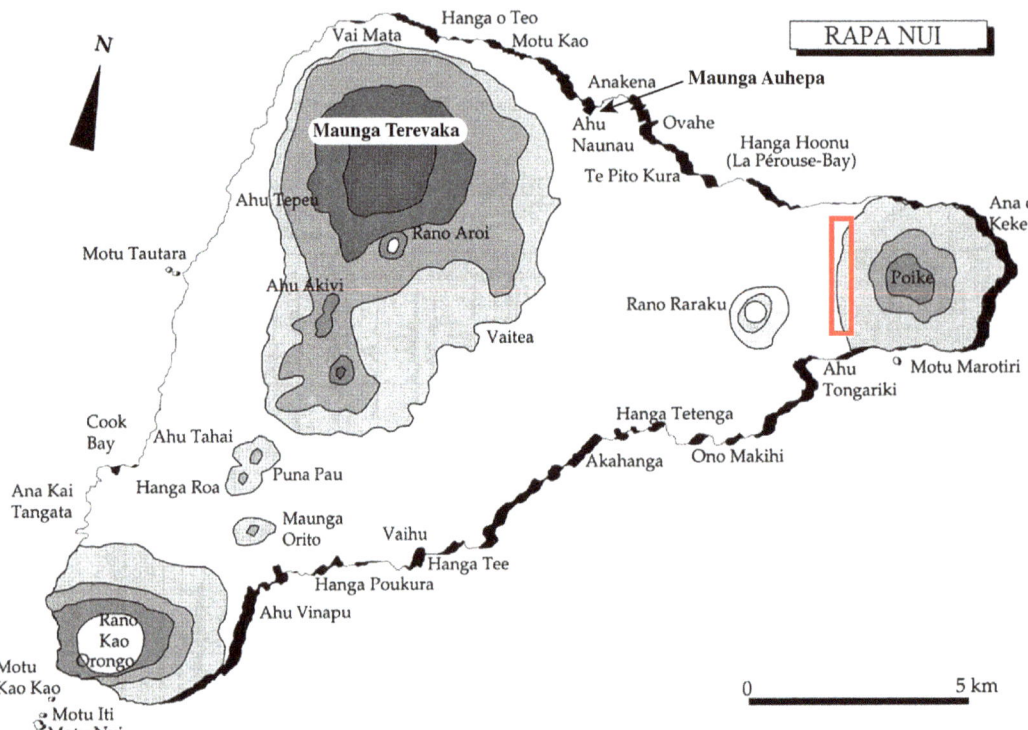

Figure 4.1. Map of Rapa Nui with main locations mentioned in text.
Rectangle marks the location of the Poike Ditch.
Source: Helene Martinsson-Wallin.

Archaeological excavations and surveys from the 1950s CE onward indicate extensive destruction of ceremonial sites, the rebuilding of monuments, and a special type of obsidian 'spearhead', called *mata'a* (Figure 4.2) that is distributed on or close to the surface. Heyerdahl and Ferdon (1961) interpret this artefact as evidence for violence that involved destruction of the monuments (a phase known as *huri moai*) and community raiding. However, recent use-wear analysis of *mata'a* suggest that these tanged obsidian blades were probably multipurpose tools used for cutting, scraping and peeling plant material, and therefore their use as a spearhead in interpersonal conflict is unlikely (Church and Ellis 1996; DiNapoli et al. 2020; Hunt and Lipo 2011:96–99; Lipo et al. 2016).

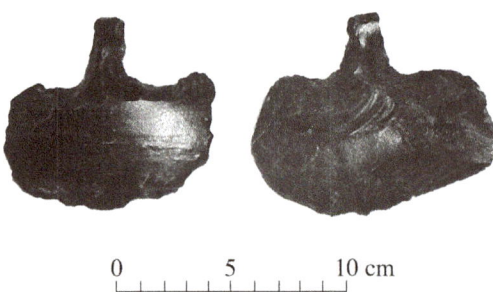

Figure 4.2. Two *mata'a* showing tanged attachment and crescent-shaped cutting edge.
Source: Helene Martinsson-Wallin.

The collapse theory of Diamond (2005), focused on environmental degradation, precolonial endemic warfare and societal collapse, is the subject of current debate. There are several lines of evidence to support the view that precolonial Rapa Nui experienced environmental degradation and internal fighting, but also that the traditional society showed high levels of resilience until it was severely impacted by European colonial encounters (Martinsson-Wallin 2007; Wallin and Martinsson-Wallin 2010). The prehistoric Rapa Nui society might not, therefore, have been such a violent place as previous research suggests. Hostility and fights have undoubtedly occurred, but the question is whether precolonial Rapa Nui organised and engaged in regular conflict and warfare or not.

The massacre of the 'Long Ears'—Oral tradition and archaeology

Oral tradition

A well-known legend narrates the massacre of the group called *Hanau eepe* ('Long Ears') by the *Hanau momoko* ('Short Ears'). The former group is said to have chased the latter into the so-called Poike Ditch, which was then set on fire and the people killed (Métraux 1940:69–71). The massacre of the 'Long Ears' and the battle of the Poike Ditch, written in the nineteenth century, could indicate that a massacre and internal warfare or violent actions occurred in ancient Rapa Nui. Legends and vernacular history can accurately record past events that are, however, often rephrased in a metaphorical way, which differs from the concept of history based on a linear chronology of events. Fader Sebastian Englert (1974) thought that the Poike battle was a real event, which he dated with genealogies to the end of the seventeenth century CE. However, the story has been interpreted in different ways. Thor Heyerdahl thought that the 'Long Ears' were the original settlers from South America, named for their extended ear lobes. The expansion of ear lobes also prevailed in the precolonial Marquesas Islands and Heyerdahl stressed a connection between pre-Columbian South America and East Polynesia during his one-year visit to Marquesas in 1937–1938 (Heyerdahl 1974). Heyerdahl further thought that the 'Long Ears' in Rapa Nui were subsequently conquered and slaughtered by the 'Short Ears' who came to Rapa Nui from Polynesia in a second migration (Heyerdahl 1961). Heyerdahl writes (1961:33) that local traditions recorded by Palmer in 1868 CE indicate two different groups of people on the island. Palmer was a surgeon aboard the British battleship *Topaze*, which took a statue (*Hoa hakananai'a*) from a house in Orongo. Since then, the British Museum has displayed this statue, but there are currently indigenous attempts to return it. The *Topaze* visited the island around the time when the first missionaries came to Rapa Nui and there are textual records about life and culture by several (Eyraud 1864; Roussel 1926 (1869); Zumbohm 1879–1880). Métraux (1940:74) thought that the Poike massacre was a 'fairly recent theme' and discussed the 'short and long ear' groups as different societal classes. Thus, he interprets the massacre as an internal 'revolution' by the 'commoners' to overthrow the ruling chiefs (Martinsson-Wallin 1994; Métraux 1940:70; Van Tilburg 1994:38). Métraux (1940:73) also suggested the story was 'partially an etiological myth'.

Initial visits by European navigators in the eighteenth century and their writings made the enigmatic Rapa Nui known across the globe. Knowledge about the island increased with the number of ship visits in the eighteenth and nineteenth centuries. Foerster and Lorenzo (2015) have collected extensive data on travel logs from protohistoric visits by whalers, slave traders, and from military, scientific and commercial ship visits from the eighteenth century onwards. This data shows that there were a large number of ship visits, which affected the Rapa Nui in profound and mostly negative ways. The population size diminished drastically due to slave raids, diseases and hostility, and the demographic decline probably affected the cultural reservoir of traditional history, which might have led to unwillingness to part with indigenous knowledge. The impact of external contacts since the eighteenth century certainly caused trauma in the society and could be one of the reasons that contributed to the onset of Rapa Nui warfare and the destruction of ceremonial sites, including the toppling of *moai* statues. There are several historical reports that the Rapa Nui were throwing stones at European arrivals in the nineteenth century when they tried to come ashore. The missionary Eyraud also noted in 1864 CE that he had to flee for his life due to hostilities when the time of Mataveri (the birdman cult) started at Orongo. The impact of colonial contact might also have created room for the invention of new cult activities or the hybridisation/creolisation of old traditions (Wallin and Martinsson-Wallin 2010).

In the period between 1877 and 1886 CE, Alexander Salmon, who was a half-Tahitian resident engaged by the Tahitian Maison Brander farm, recorded traditional history. He and a local Rapa Nui, Juan Tepano Huki (born c. 1876 CE), became the two most important informants about Rapa Nui oral history, including providing information about the massacre at the Poike Ditch. Their information has been used repeatedly by researchers, but has been interpreted in different ways (e.g. Heyerdahl 1961:33; Van Tilburg 1994:33). The English Commander Clark made the first-known interview with Salmond in 1882 CE (Heyerdahl 1961). Thomson (1889:528–529), a paymaster in the US Navy who visited the island in 1886 CE, was the first to record the story of the 'Long Ears'. The information was obtained from Salmon: in one narrative the 'Long Ears' arrived during the rule of the third *ariki* (high chief), and in another version the two groups arrived together during the initial colonisation by *Hotu-matua*, who was the ancestor of the 'Short Ears', and *Hinelilu*, who was the ancestor of the 'Long Ears'.

According to Métraux (1940:71), the 'Short Ears' tilled the soil and planted food, and it was the 'Long Ears' who built the *moai* and *ahu* monuments. Thomson (1889:528–29) states that the two groups were from different races and the 'Long Ears' settled the eastern part of the island and lived on Poike and in Hanga-nui in boat-shaped houses with stone foundations (*hare paenga*). The 'Short Ears' lived on the western part of the island at Hangaroa, Mataveri, Vinapu and Vaihu, and had houses made with a light frame and straw, but also lived in caves. Martinsson-Wallin (1994:132–133) suggests that the *Hoto-matua* legend could be a late influence from Mangareva from the time when the missionaries returned a large group of Rapa Nui, which resulted in hostilities involving commercial use of the island as a sheep and cattle farm.

Archaeological evidence

Excavations of the Poike Ditch by Smith (1961) did not find human remains consistent with a massacre, but he did report several charcoal horizons. Smith excavated six test pits in two segments of the ditch and mound/rampart running in a north–south direction at c. 60 m above sea level on the western slope of the Poike peninsula (Smith 1961:386; Reainer and Ryan 2003:217, Figure 7). All test pits yielded charcoal and one of the pits that contained the most was extended to a c. 30 x 1.5 m trench traversing the ditch and mound/rampart in an east–west direction. Two charcoal samples provided dates of 1570 ± 100 BP and 280 ± 100 BP. Heyerdahl and his team interpreted the older determination as representing the earliest human occupation of the island (Heyerdahl 1961). This date was refuted on stratigraphic grounds by Martinsson-Wallin (1994) and Martinsson and Crockford (2002:245, 249, Table 1), but the early age persisted in scholarly work until Wilmshurst et al. (2011) concluded that Rapa Nui was probably colonised as late as the fourteenth century CE. Radiocarbon dates generally support an initial colonisation around the twelfth–thirteenth century CE, although the radiocarbon sequence is yet to be finalised (Martinsson-Wallin and Crockford 2002; Martinsson-Wallin et al. 2013). The more recent date of 280 ± 100 BP from the Poike Ditch could indicate human activities around the sixteenth or seventeenth centuries CE, as suggested by oral traditions, but when calibrated (at 2 sigma) the radiocarbon result has a broad range of 1450–1890 cal. BP. Smith adds that there were no finds of *mata'a* in the excavations, but three sling stones were found in the Poike Ditch excavations:

> the absence of the *mataa*, or obsidian spear head used in warfare, suggest that the war between the Hanau Eepe and the Hanau Momoko marked the end of the Middle period when the *mataa* seems to have been unknown or rare, and the beginning of the Late Period [c. 1680 CE] when it is common. (Smith 1961:391)

Excavations by Vargas in 1991 CE suggests the ditch may date to around the twelfth century CE (Bahn and Flenley 1992:168; Van Tilburg 1994:78), but the estimate is not supported by published radiocarbon dates. Additional excavation and dates on new charcoal samples would shed more light on the age and extent of burning at Poike. Smith later revised his interpretation of the Poike Ditch and argued that the charcoal derived from a massive earth oven that was made to feed the workers in the nearby *moai* quarries at Rano Raraku (Smith 1990). Digital mapping of the trench by Reainer and Ryan (2003:207–221) showed that the ditch and mounds/banks stretch over 300 m in a north–south direction along the western slope of the Poike peninsula.

Due to the oral tradition of a massacre, the Poike Ditch was mentioned by Routledge (1919:281) in a footnote that interprets the ditch as a natural geological formation, while the upslope mounds of soil along the ditch might have been the remains of a fortification. DiNapoli et al. (2020:8) dismiss the Poike Ditch as an earthwork fortification and state that: 'there is not a single recorded instance of such a feature on Rapa Nui'. Furthermore, they indicate that: 'its form is likely geologic in origin' without discussing the mound/rampart stratigraphy resulting from excavation of the ditch (Smith 1961:Figures 97 and 98).

The geologist Chubb (1933) notes that the Poike peninsula is geologically different from the rest of Rapa Nui and is the oldest volcanic formation. The ditch is probably a remnant of a rugged coastline when Poike was an ancient islet (Chubb 1933), which only later fused with the Terevaka lava flow and was incorporated into Rapa Nui. Subsequently the trench filled with erosion soil from the steep slopes of Poike, and survey indicates the ditch is 20 m above the base of the lower slope (Reainer and Ryan 2003).

The traditional history stating that the stone foundation houses (*hare paenga*) should only occur in the east side of the island and thus only belong to the 'Long Ears' is clearly not true. These types of house foundations occur all over the island, but only in close relationship with ceremonial sites such as *ahu* (see for example Håkansson 2017). The inland areas display other types of house foundations, especially around Vaitea and towards the hills of Terevaka (Stevenson 1997). It is true that there are fewer *hare paenga* houses in Hangaroa, but since all the people were forced to move there during the European colonial times, the area has been subjected to urban development. There are, for example, records that a large *ahu* with cut stones in Hangaroa harbour was demolished (Englert 1974) and stone foundation houses have likely been destroyed by development.

Recent surveys at Poike (site visit and oral information by Sonia Haoa Cardinali in November 2017) showed the area appears to have been intentionally cleared of stones, since it looks different from other parts of the island where stones frequently occur on the surface. Some 'fields of stones' in other parts of Rapa Nui are agricultural inventions, so-called 'rock gardens' that cover the ground to keep it moist and fertile for agricultural purposes (Stevenson and Haoa 2008). Archaeological remains are few on Poike and in a ruined state. Large-scale soil erosion is evident on the south side across from Moto Marotiri and there are traces that monuments close to the cliff edges have fallen into the sea or are actively eroding (Cauwe et al. 2006). The monuments in the area on the north-west side of Poike, like Ahu Mahatua (one of the larger monuments on the island), have also been largely destroyed.

Archaeological evidence does not support the massacre of 'Long Ears' from fire at the Poike Ditch. However, stone 'crematorium' structures, which are attached to the majority of ceremonial sites, do contain burnt human remains. Dates for crematoria show that this burial custom may have a lengthy history on Rapa Nui (Martinsson-Wallin In prep; Martinsson-Wallin and Crockford 2002; Martinsson-Wallin et al. 2013). Evidence of human cremation is found all over the island at or near ceremonial sites. Cremations could be a traditional burial custom, but Palmer (1870) thought that the cremated human bones found at the two-headed statue at Vinapu were offerings, while oral traditions suggest that cannibal activities and cremation were connected (Heyerdahl 1961:73). From a settlement pattern perspective, the crematoria might be seen as representing 'waste' since they were placed on the sea side of the ceremonial site. On the other hand, the area on the sea side of the ceremonial sites that is between the land and sea was a liminal zone controlled by the *ariki*, which was *tapu* at certain times of the year (Ayres 1975). The crematoria were carefully built structures that were lined with small rounded *poro* stones, red scoria and coral, which is not consistent with 'waste' deposition of cannibalised human remains. Sometimes cremated bones are found in small stone cists in the wing of the *ahu*, as for example at Ahu Ra'ai (Martinsson-Wallin et al. 1998). Ayres (1973) reports that there were cremation pits and small cists in the ramp at Ahu Ko-te Riki in Tahai. Crematoria and the cremated bones they hold have not been studied in any detail and have often been interpreted as the result of cannibalism.

A second site that may have been fortified/defended is a small hill called Maunga Auhepa at Anakena. The hill has a levelled summit with a lower terrace around it, 1 m below the top and 2 m wide, that connects with an entrance ramp to the east. The artificial nature of the hill was recognised by Routledge (1919:295 and Figure 97) and Brown (1924:59, 213), but Métraux (1937:137) thought it natural. Test trenching of Maunga Auhepa showed that the lower terrace was made by the cut-and-fill technique, with some fill derived from levelling the summit. Smith (1961:278) suggested that the terrace may have been defensive and the hill possibly used as a refuge.

Oral traditions and evidence of other forms of hostility and violence

Yet another frequently cited legend points to constant hostilities and raids among clan groups that belonged to the Ko-Tu'u (western side) and Hoto-iti (eastern side) of the island, respectively (Métraux 1940:74–86).

> The western tribes attacked the eastern or vice versa. When one party felt that it was overwhelmed and that victory (*ao*) was with their adversaries, the warriors fled and tried to take refuge in caves (*he opo ki roto ki te ana, he pipiko*) or on the rocks or islets off the coast. The old men, the woman, and the children scattered and hid in caves or in deserted places. (Métraux 1940:150)

Routledge's (1919:289) informant, Kariera, suggests these events occurred in the eighteenth century CE, but the conflict chronology is unclear. According to oral traditions, the onset of these 'wars' seems to centre on cannibal activities and fighting between the Tupahotu and Miru clans (Métraux 1940:74–84). There are two versions of the story of hostilities and they both focus on a man called Kainga (a synonym for an extended family group glossed as 'people who eat together'). The geographical areas where conflict occurred appear to be close to Poike, Tongariki and the islet of Morotiri, but the legends also narrate that areas of the Miru clan were raided and people had to flee to the Moto Kaviti and Moto Nui on the west side of the island (Figure 4.1).

Elsewhere, I have suggested that the clan areas Ngatimo and Ngaure may be relatively recent divisions with the territorial fractioning tied to raids and hostilities (Martinsson-Wallin 1994:103). Based on dating of ceremonial sites in the La Perouse area it has been suggested that primary and secondary ceremonial sites were associated with senior and junior chiefs who engaged in conflict over land (Martinsson-Wallin and Wallin 2014; Wallin and Martinsson-Wallin 2008). Disputes over access, power and utilisation of resources are likely to have contributed to hostility and violence among kinship groups (Martinsson-Wallin 1994:105).

Figure 4.3. The statue *Paro* at Ahu Te Pito Kura.
Source: Helene Martinsson-Wallin.

The destruction of the Rapa Nui monuments and the statues also indicates violent social activity and the possibility of warfare. However, erosion and cyclones have also caused damage to ceremonial sites. For example, a tsunami hit Ahu Tongariki in 1960s, but in that instance photos of the site prior to the tsunami show already toppled statues. Based on historical data from eighteenth-century accounts of early navigators, compared with nineteenth-century accounts like those of Kotzebue (1821) in 1817, Petit-Thouars (1841) in 1837 and the first missionary accounts (Eyraud 1864), the last standing statue must have been pulled down between 1838 and 1864 CE (Métraux 1940:86), well after European contact. An informant of Routledge (1919:173) told her that the large statue called *Paro* (Figure 4.3) at Ahu Te Pito Kura was the last left standing. The Rapa Nui refer to the protohistoric toppling of the *moai* and destruction of *ahu* as the *huri moai* time. Oral traditions that include hostility and fighting often mention raids and revenge for stealing food, and include stories of cannibalism and the use of fire. Métraux (1940:149) writes that:

> there was constant rivalry between the tribes, particularly between those of the eastern and western part of the island … The first act of war was to burn the hut of one's opponent.

Thomson (1889:475) stated that 'every able-bodied man was supposed to be a warrior', but accounts by Routledge (1919:224) and Métraux (1940:138) indicate that there were men called *matatoa* (*toa toa*) who were the leaders of ordinary fighters (*paoa*). The fighters threw stones and used obsidian spears (*mata'a*) and wooden clubs (*ua, paoa*).

Métraux (1940:149) reports that young children learned the art of war through mock fights using a blunt blade. Barthel (1958) visited the island in 1957 CE and give a detailed account of the legends and use of the *mata'a*. The *matatoa* at times took over the role of the *ariki* (chief) of the clan and this might have happened when statues were toppled as a result of intercommunity raiding and during the rise of the birdman cult (Wallin and Martinsson-Wallin 2010).

The missionary Roussel (1926 (1869)) gives an account of a war party who painted themselves black and spent a sleepless night before combat, hiding their belongings before leaving. Women and children accompanied the war party with chants and stayed on the side of the nearest hill to witness the battle. The warriors ambushed their enemies, damaged huts and sugar cane plots, and carried away the defeated. The defeated were struck with cudgels, buried alive, cooked in earth ovens, cut up with axes and some were trodden on and beaten until they died. Thomson (1889) mentions that while there were frequent hostilities there were relatively few victims in battle, but the robbing of women and killing of children and the disabled occurred. Thomson (1889), Routledge (1919) and Métraux (1940) also note that survivors hid in caves and remote places.

Examination of ceremonial sites demonstrates that monuments are complex as they have often been destroyed and rebuilt, with features added over time (Martinsson-Wallin 1994). Elsewhere I have argued that the protohistoric *huri moai* time is not the initial phase of statue and monument destruction in Rapa Nui (Martinsson-Wallin 2000). This is because the restructuring of ceremonial sites included the incorporation of already mutilated smaller statues concealed inside the *ahu* or incorporated in the *ahu* wall. The excavations of Ahu Nau Nau at Anakena (Skjølsvold 1994) yielded such statues from the inside of the *ahu* platform and another example is seen at Ahu Tongariki (Martinsson-Wallin 2000). Ayres et al. (2014), who excavated *ahu* Ura Urenga te Mahina, close to Akahanga, argued that the fallen *moai* were still venerated after toppling and were intentionally 'buried' by covering them with stones.

It is common for symbols from a belief system to be incorporated and amalgamated with new symbols when belief systems change. External factors and culture contact often trigger a change in symbols that indicate significant societal change. It is not unlikely that there was more than one external pre-European contact on Rapa Nui. Martinsson-Wallin et al. (2013) have argued that the monument-building of the *ahu* is earlier in Rapa Nui than that of *marae* in the Society Islands, even if the early colonisers who settled Rapa Nui came from Polynesian islands such as Mangareva, the Austral Islands or the Tuamotus (Martinsson-Wallin and Crockford 2002; Martinsson-Wallin and Wallin 1999). We argue that the typical *marae/ahu* complex could have developed first in Rapa Nui and the concept spread to the Society Islands sometime in the fifteenth century CE (Martinsson-Wallin et al. 2013). The current radiocarbon dates for ceremonial sites in Rapa Nui and Central Polynesia support this idea and challenge the current opinion that there was a single colonisation event and that ancient Rapa Nui was a remote isolated island with no external contacts after initial colonisation.

The intentional destruction in the late prehistoric and protohistoric phase of the ceremonial sites and toppling of statues (considered as gods and *ariki*) was very likely tied to the inter-group hostility and endemic warfare mentioned in oral traditions. However, both internal and external factors likely contributed to these conflicts. The abundance of obsidian tanged *mata'a* found on the surface or close to the surface in Rapa Nui have been taken as evidence for hostility and fighting (see discussion below). Another sign of warfare is the possible occurrence of fortifications. In Rapa Nui, there are no ring forts and only one possible hill fort at Anakena. Instead, it seems that many caves have served as forts/refuges and the small islets (*motu*) were also places of refuge. It is not clear whether inland parts of the island also served as refuges as in Tahiti. The Poike Ditch and mounds/embankments discussed above may have been a linear fortification.

Weapons in oral traditions, historical accounts and archaeology

Beechey (1831:49) writes that when he tried to go ashore, the Rapa Nui threw stones with great accuracy and several of the new arrivals received severe blows from stones thrown from the shore. The blow was less severe if the stones were thrown underhand (*patu raro*) compared with an overhand throw (Métraux 1940:165). Métraux (1940:165) thought that the sling (*maea-taea*) was a new invention brought from Tahiti in protohistoric times. Some human bone remains from various burial sites in Rapa Nui show trauma that results from precolonial violence. Owsley et al. (2016) conducted osteological analysis on human remains that indicated blows from stones or clubs were present on several skulls.

Longer clubs called *ua* (c. 1.5–2 m long) had a face with inlaid eyes of bone and obsidian with carved long ears at the club end (Métraux 1940:168). The *ua*, according to Thomson's (1859:475) informant, was a sign of authority and parade staff for a chief, but could also be used as a weapon according to Roussel (1926 (1869):426). Shorter clubs (*paoa*), usually with a carved head of a human or a lizard at one end, are said to have been used in raids and warfare while the wooden swords called *puhi* are suggested to be recent (Métraux 1940:169–170). Métraux (1940:171) examined similar items in other parts of Polynesia and concluded that staffs were signs of authority. The *paoa* had similarities with the *patu* of the Maori in New Zealand according to Cook (1777:291) and Forster (1777:536), but Métraux (1940:172) thought the resemblance coincidental. The short club has also been discussed by Ramirez (1990/1991:53–54) as similar to the South American war club (*clava*) of the Mapuche.

The obsidian spearhead—*mata'a*

The main type of weapon indicative of warfare in late prehistoric and protohistoric times is the obsidian spearhead with tang for hafting called *mata'a* (Figure 4.2). These artefacts are found on or close to the current ground surface. The only morphological studies by Lipo et al. (2010, 2016) concluded that:

> Blade shape, it appears, freely varied and was probably conditioned by the happenstance of the flake selected for the artefact in the first place. This pattern suggests that mata'a were not used extensively as weapons given the lack of a specific pattern in shape driven by the function of stabbing or inflicting other serious injuries. (Lipo et al. 2010:2560)

Lipo et al. (2010) also suggest that their seriation analysis shows differences in craft tradition at different locations and this suggests there was not a large-scale social network on the island. The *mata'a* analysed by Lipo et al. (2010, 2016) were mainly from museum collections and were not found in stratigraphic sequences and thus no radiocarbon dates can be used to assess artefact age. Smith made the only chronological analysis of *mata'a* based on archaeological excavations in the mid-1950s. In the excavation of two habitation caves, Smith found:

> The most important discovery is the correlation of the *mataa* and European trade goods with the final occupation in both sites Puapua II and O-hae II. In earlier occupations, Puapua I and O-hae I European trade items are absent, the *mataa* is rare or absent, and other artefacts appear in slightly different proportions. (Smith 1961:270)

Routledge (1919:223) writes about the *mata'a*:

> Legends tell of continual wars between Hot-iti and Kotuu. In recent times, general fighting seems to have been constant and took place even between members of one clan. A wooden sword, or paoa, was used, but the chief weapon was made from obsidian, and took from it the name 'mataa'.

When I surveyed *ahu* structures around the island in 1991 CE (Martinsson-Wallin 1994), I could see *mata'a* distributed on the ground everywhere. Thus, archaeological excavations and survey have shown that this type of artefact is tied to the last prehistoric and the protohistoric phase and occurs across the island.

According to Thomson (1889:474) and Métraux (1940:165–168), there were two types of spears used in conflict; a throwing spear or javelin (*kakau*) that was used as a missile and a thrusting spear or pike for close fighting (*vero*). According to Routlege's informant, there were 14 different shapes of spearhead; one of which was named 'tail of a fish', another 'backbone of a rat' and a third 'leaf of banana'. Based on Skinner (unpublished manuscript), Métraux (1940:168) provided six morphological types of *mata'a* and also noted that the *mata'a* is depicted on rongorongo plates. Barthel's (1958) account mentions the *mata'a* have important social and magical aspects and gives detailed accounts of how the obsidian spearhead was attached, along with techniques used in handling and throwing hafted weapons.

According to the Rapa Nui, these weapons were increasingly effective when treated with magic (*tohu*), and if a weapon killed someone the obsidian point received the title of *mataa ika* (Barthel 1958:17). Martinsson-Wallin and Wallin (2001) noted that human sacrifices to the gods were called *ika* (fish) with the body hung by the mouth with a large fishhook. The number of windings with the *hau* fibre, which attached a spearhead to the haft, could be used to mark clan identity. This made it easier to identify particular weapons and obtain revenge (Barthel 1958:17). To make it ready for war, the owner of a *mata'a* weapon attached two feathers to the hafting on each side of the spearhead and with the assistance of the *aku aku* (family spirit), told the weapon the reason for the approaching fight/war.

Recent study of use-wear on *mata'a* in museum collections indicates the artefacts were probably used as multipurpose tools and their use as interpersonal weapons is questionable (Church and Ellis 1996; Hunt and Lipo 2011:96–99). Barthel (1958:18) note that it is likely that the initial use of the *mata'a* was as a multipurpose tool, which subsequently transformed into a weapon.

Osteological analysis by Owsley et al. (2016) found few traces of trauma on human skeletal remains that might have been inflicted by *mata'a* and therefore question the use of the *mata'a* as a weapon in large-scale warfare and massacre, but add that lethal cuts and wounds inflicted by a *mata'a* would be unlikely to leave a mark in skeletal remains. The Spanish who visited and annexed the island in 1770 CE reported that:

> We observed sundry wounds on the body, which we thought to have been inflicted by cutting instruments of iron or steel, we found that they proceeded from stones which are their only defence and offense, and as most of these are sharp edged they produce the injury referred to. (Ruiz-Tagle 2005:63)

Hunt and Lipo (2011:96–107) have a lengthy discussion about the lack of evidence for warfare in Rapa Nui and instead picture the island as having a mostly peaceful past. They state that the *mata'a* is not suited for combat since they have an asymmetric shape that makes them unfit to be used as projectiles or stabbing tools (Hunt and Lipo 2011:97). Based on a quantitative analysis of measurements of a sample of 118 *mata'a* and an additional 249 measurements from photos of *mata'a*, Lipo et al. (2016:182) conclude that obsidian artefacts were not used as lethal weapons in warfare. Lipo et al. (2016:180) also suggest that 'there is in essence no evidence that *mata'a* blade shape was constrained by functional performance, location or obsidian source'.

In contrast to Hunt and Lipo (2011:96–99) and Lipo et al. (2016), Barthel (1958:17–19) mentions that the Rapa Nui were very skilled in the art of using various types of hafted *mata'a* in raids between clan groups and the use of such weapons involved ritual and magic. An oral account obtained by Sonia Haoa Cardinali (pers. comm. 24 January 2019) says the *mata'a* were used as projectiles in a dangerous game where an individual had to catch the *mata'a* between the palms of the hand or between the cheek and the palm of one hand. Even if the sample of *mata'a* reported by Church and Ellis (1996) served as multipurpose tools it cannot be ruled out that they were also used as weapons in interpersonal conflict and raids. In her study of pre-state European warfare and warriorhood, Vandkilde (2013:43) stresses that function is both variable and independent of material form.

Evidence of cutting and scraping on *mata'a* may be connected with the defleshing of human bones as a mortuary practice or may be the result of cannibalism, as many traditional societies engaged in ritual cannibalism (Obeyesekere 1992). The use-wear analysis of Church and Ellis (1996) that indicated cutting and scraping of plant material could be from the reuse of *mata'a*, just as a coral eye once used in a *moai* statue was reused as an oil lamp (Martinsson-Wallin 1996). Other types of material culture said to be connected to war and warriors on Rapa Nui were the *Hau kurakura*, which was a small crown of red (*kura*) feathers made from the feathers from a rooster's neck (Métraux 1940:223).

Evidence of warfare and weapons in rock carvings and rongorongo plates

Extensive survey of rock carvings by Lavachery (1935) and Lee (1992) shows they depict anthropomorphic figures, birdmen, birds, marine creatures, terrestrial creatures, ceremonial objects and ornaments, watercraft, items of material culture, plants and celestial phenomena. Lee (1992:28–43) made an analysis of rock art patterns and their spatial distribution by placing carvings in 12 different groups. There are no carvings that depict war scenes, but some designs resemble *mata'a* and perhaps show a hafted axe. On the rongorongo boards there are designs that might show a person holding a spear, club or axe (Métraux 1940:401).

Evidence of warfare and trauma on human skeletal remains

Injuries in human skeletal remains can be indicative of regular warfare and violence such as intra-family fights, feuding and homicide. It can be difficult to identify what kind of hostile acts have caused a particular trauma, since periods of intensified war often coincide with increased interpersonal violence (Vandkilde 2013:52).

Owsley et al. (1994) studied human skeletal remains from Rapa Nui in the late 1980s, with an extended study by Owsley et al. (2016) containing detailed data on bone trauma and injury. The more recent study shows that in comparison to a reference group of individuals from other Polynesian islands, the people from Rapa Nui had a higher percentage of bone injuries and these injuries could result from interpersonal violence (Owsley et al. 2016: 244). The analysis was based on a large sample of human skeletal remains from museum collections collected in the nineteenth and twentieth centuries CE, but some derive from archaeological excavations in the 1950s–1980s. Dates on the bones, and obsidian hydration dates, indicate the majority of the skeletal remains derive from the late prehistoric and protohistoric phases (after 1647 CE) with only a few dating older. Cranial bones make up a large part of the sample, reflecting colonial collecting strategies (Owsley et al. 2016:228). Of the 4169 analysed craniofacial bones, around 3.1 per cent display traumatic injuries, with the majority of injuries involving the frontal bone (Owsley et al. 2016:231). Blunt force trauma was the main injury identified and was probably caused by thrown stones, while a few crushing injuries were probably from clubs (Owsley et al. 2016:235).

Most of the bone injuries do not seem to have been the primary cause of death as only a few were classed as potentially lethal. Only two remains had obsidian embedded in the bone, with a few other injuries probably caused by *mata'a* (Owsley et al. 2016:236). Some of the postcranial bones also show pre-mortem damage with most injuries to the lower arm bone (ulna). The analysis also shows that in relation to gender and age, the evidence for violence was mostly found in the remains of young males. According to Owsley et al. (2016) the injuries are not compatible with oral traditions of massacres and extensive fighting, but show that lethal violence could be inflicted by stones, clubs and obsidian blades especially in late prehistoric and protohistoric Rapa Nui society.

Archaeological investigations show that human remains were deposited in crematoria placed on the sea side of the majority of the *ahu* structures. Radiocarbon dates from 10 crematoria at various sites on the island indicate that this burial custom could have been part of *ahu* design by the twelfth–thirteenth centuries CE (Martinsson-Wallin In prep; Martinsson-Wallin and Crockford 2002:Table 1; Martinsson-Wallin et al. 2013; Navarro 2017). Only a few studies have examined cremated bone deposits and it is not known whether there are intentional injuries on the remains. Unfortunately, many of the crematoria are deteriorating and the human bones are weathering and eroding without any cultural management plan or archaeological investigation. A radiocarbon dating program on cremation inhumations and study of cremated bones for evidence of trauma could provide additional information about conflict and violence in Rapa Nui's past.

Warfare and violence in traditional societies

Researchers in sociology and anthropology have long discussed the role of warfare in human history and whether humans commonly resorted to lethal violence in the past. Vandkilde (2013:41) defines warfare as 'collective, violent social interaction, which is built upon cultural logic and waged against other groups'. She further notes that 'actions of war vary from raiding to large-scale military actions; its precise form and content depending on the specific societal setting'. Thorpe (2003:146) defines warfare 'as organized aggression between autonomous political units'. Current discussions on warfare are often tied to neo-Darwinian views and the idea that human culture and behaviour largely result from biological imperatives combined with adaptation to environmental constraints. A neo-Darwinian analysis by DiNapoli et al. (2018) uses economic dependability and costly signalling to compare the chance of conflict and warfare in Rapa Iti and Rapa Nui. They suggest that on Rapa Iti resources were highly defendable and led to the occurrence of fortifications on Rapa Iti, but not on Rapa Nui. This view assumes that the 'fortifications' on Rapa Iti were restricted to defence; a ritual function is not considered, as suggested by a shrine at Morongo Uta (Ferdon 1965:74–75).

According to Thorpe (2003:147), there are three basic ideas for why humans use violence and conflict: territorial disputes, reproductive competition and status competition. In a diachronic study of violence and warfare in the hunter-gatherer Jomon culture, Nakato et al. (2016) conclude that violence and warfare was never common, but a small increase in the frequency of violent death occurred when society moved towards greater complexity and people become more sedentary. Kolb and Dixon (2002), in their study of warfare landscapes in Hawai'i, identified four categories of architectural site that result from organised conflict: ritual structures (war temples), fortifications, defensive settlement patterns and places of refuge. Helbling (2006) suggests that to wage war is in certain instances a less risky strategy than peace as you cannot trust your allies. In the case of Rapa Nui and in other Polynesian societies, there is an in-built power struggle between senior and junior chiefs, and shifting allegiances between different groups were common (Martinsson-Wallin and Wallin 2014).

Several Polynesian societies, such as Tonga, Hawai'i, Society Islands and Samoa, have archaeological remains indicating organised warfare. Tonga has ring forts, while Samoa has defensive sites including modified hilltops and ridges that were strategic points of defence and/or served as places of refuge (Clark et al. 2016; Green and Davidson 1969). Kolb and Dixon (2002:512) argue that war temples and the creation of refuge places indicates warfare in precolonial Hawai'i. In Hawai'i, there are relatively few prehistoric human skeletal remains that have been examined and only a few artefacts are associated with war and hostility, but oral tradition and ethnohistorical accounts suggest warlike activity was relatively common. In Rapa Nui, and to some extent in Samoa, caves and lava tubes were places of refuge. It is possible that some of the large mounds (*maota*) in Samoa might also have served as ritual sites in times of war (Martinsson-Wallin 2014).

Kolb and Dixon (2002) suggest that some of the war temples in Hawai'i date to the fourteenth century CE and that large-scale warfare became more frequent in Hawai'i during the European contact era. The high chiefs (*ali'i*) managed and organised conflict, and groups of trained warriors mostly from the commoner class were led by junior chiefs (Kolb and Dixon 2002). The endemic wars of Hawai'i were, according to Kolb and Dixon (2002), highly ritualised events and included the conquest of land, raiding to obtain valuables and the capture of elite human sacrifices who were offered to the war god. The leeward islands of Hawai'i experienced a rise in the influence of the war gods (*Kuka'ilimoku* and *Kanevila*) consistent with expansionary warfare.

In Tonga, indications of ancient and European contact-era warfare are found in oral traditions as well as in a large number of earthwork ring forts, some of which date to the thirteenth–fourteenth century CE (Clark et al. 2018). In the Society Islands, the rise of the war god *Oro* and the associated cult involving human sacrifice at the *marae* temples, along with the rise of places of inland refuge, indicates escalating warfare around the sixteenth century CE (Wallin 1993). In Samoa, the rise of the chiefly title of Mālietoa, estimated by genealogies to date to the fourteenth–fifteenth century CE, indicates increasing warfare, which is mentioned in oral traditions that refer to constant fights over land and chiefly titles (Meleisea and Meleisea 1987).

Conclusion

Oral traditions of the Poike Ditch massacre and fights between the Ko-Tu'u and Hoto-iti clans, as well as cannibalism, point to the presence of violence on Rapa Nui in late prehistoric and protohistoric times. These activities seems to have escalated in the seventeenth century CE. Based on osteological analysis of human remains and use-wear on *mata'a* artefacts, Hunt and Lipo (2011:98–107) suggest prehistoric Rapa Nui was a peaceful island. This view contrasts with oral traditions, extensive finds of *mata'a* and the widespread destruction of monuments. In bringing various types of data together we must ask whether a society like Rapa Nui, which was highly competitive, was at the same time peaceable? Early contact with Europeans almost certainly increased inter-group hostility and placed stress on the social system, with the rise of the birdman cult possibly an attempt to stabilise fragmenting social relationships (Wallin and Martinsson-Wallin 2010).

Revenge, food, women and competition between different clans/extended family groups (*kainga*) and frictions between chiefs and the *matatoa* (young warriors) seem to be important traditional factors that sparked hostility. Ethnohistorical accounts note that hostile actions could involve stone throwing, but also that the Rapa Nui had weapons including wooden clubs and spears with obsidian points. Archaeological data that indicate hostility and violence include the destruction of ritual sites and the toppling and mutilation of the large *moai* statues, as well as the mutilation and incorporation of smaller statues in ceremonial sites. The chronology of these events is unclear, but radiocarbon and obsidian hydration dates from archaeological excavation and references to genealogies point to a late seventeenth century CE age, associated by the Rapa Nui with the *huri moai* (statue-toppling) phase, which continued during the protohistoric and colonial periods. This is supported by examples of small statues found mutilated and incorporated in *ahu* structures prior to the last *huri moai* events (Martinsson-Wallin 2000). When placed in a neo-evolutionary framework, the archaeological data for conflict suggest that it was less costly for the Rapa Nui to compete though conspicuous consumption than to invest in larger and more elaborate *moai* and *ahu* structures (DiNapoli et al. 2017). The initial construction of *ahu* sites on Rapa Nui dates to around the eleventh–twelfth century CE, with some structures showing at least three phases of construction/rebuilding. Destruction of smaller and stylistically more diversified statues that were incorporated in the *ahu* could point to early '*huri moai*' in the fourteenth–sixteenth centuries CE. The obsidian tool/spearhead called *mataʻa* is likely to belong to the late prehistoric and protohistoric era.

Human skeletal remains from different sites (mainly those connected with *ahu* sites) display injuries from fights and the effect of weapons. The frequency of such injuries is around 3 per cent of the skeletal sample. The majority of these injuries occur in the remains of young males, but many wounds were unlikely to have been lethal. The frequency of violence is however higher than in the other Polynesian reference groups. In general, the evidence to date does not point to massacres or instances of intensive warfare.

Turning to the *mataʻa*, it was likely a multipurpose tool, including use as a spearhead/knife in raids and interpersonal combat. The recent use-wear analysis of the *mataʻa* contrasts with vernacular history and traditions of *mataʻa* being used by warriors. Further use-wear studies using a larger sample of this type of artefact is required.

Large-scale warfare is often connected with complex societies while violence in small-scale traditional societies is often associated with raids, threats and ritual warfare. In Hawaiʻi, the rise of war gods and war temples suggests ritualised endemic warfare in prehistoric and protohistoric society. In Rapa Nui, there do not appear to be ceremonial sites exclusively dedicated to war or to particular war gods. The birdman cult and associated god *Make Make* is primarily a fertility cult that appears to be unrelated to war. However, the link between fertility and warfare is seen in the veneration of the god *Oro*, who became important in the Society Islands in the sixteenth century CE (Wallin 1993). Cannibal activities narrated in Rapa Nui oral traditions have probably occurred, but it is likely these activities were of a ritual kind associated with revenge and the usurping of a group's *mana*. It is not clear whether cannibalism is associated with human remains found in crematoria at *ahu* sites. Current research suggests that crematoria could date to the initial building of *ahu* (Martinsson-Wallin In prep).

There are no formal fortifications on Rapa Nui, with the possible exception of the Poike earthwork and Maunga Auhepa, but there are many places of refuge. Several known caves have walls made to hide the entrance. The use of caves very likely indicates that they were hiding places for smaller segments of society as a result of raids and revenge between extended families (*kainga*). The use of caves and islets as hiding places and refuge is not necessarily an outcome of warfare, but does suggest that hostile activity and raids occurred.

There is no evidence for conflict from petroglyphs or on the rongorongo plates. This might be because the petroglyphs have a symbolic meaning and were used for ritual purposes in the communication between gods and people.

To conclude, endemic hostilities, raids and cannibal activities occurred in Rapa Nui especially in late prehistoric and protohistoric times. The archaeological material does not support large-scale massacres or highly organised warfare as narrated in oral traditions. Oral history narrates power struggles over land and resources where the junior chiefs acted as warriors (*matatoa*). It is likely that fights involved power struggles between senior and junior branches of extended families in a clan as well as between different clans, which may have led to statue mutilation and toppling.

In comparison to other Polynesian societies such as Hawai'i and Tonga, the endemic hostilities and conflict on Rapa Nui seem to have involved a relatively small number of combatants and were less organised. The toppling of the *moai* statues is probably a sign of community defeat while stronger clans may have been able to protect their statues. Warlike activities are likely to be tied to societal stress when the Rapa Nui experienced competition and resource shortages from drought and social upheaval from external culture contact.

References

Ayres, W. 1973. The cultural context of Easter Island religious structures. Unpublished PhD thesis. Tulane University, New Orleans.

Ayres, W. 1975. *Easter Island: Investigations in prehistoric cultural dynamics*. NSF Grant Report. University of South Carolina.

Ayres, W., J. Wozniak and J. Ramirez 2014. The stone statues at Urauranga te Mahina, Rapa Nui. In H. Martinsson-Wallin and T. Thomas (eds), *Monuments and people in the Pacific*, pp. 343–372. Studies in Global Archaeology 20. Department of Archaeology and Ancient History, Uppsala University, Uppsala.

Bahn, P. and J. Flenley 1992. *Easter Island: Earth Island*. Thames and Hudson, London.

Barthel, T. 1958. Obsidian waffen von der Osterinsel. *Jahrbuch des museums für völkerkunde zu Leipzig* XVII/1958:14–21.

Beechey, F.W. 1831. *Narrative of a voyage to the Pacific and Beerings Strait*. 2 volumes. Carey and Lea, Philadelphia.

Brown, J.M. 1924. *The riddle of the Pacific*. T. Fisher Unwin, London.

Cauwe, N., D. Huyge, J. De Meulemeester, M. De Dapper, W. Claes et al. 2006. Ahu Motu Toremo Hiva Vie et mort de monuments cultuels sur l'île de Pâques. *Anthropologica et Prehistorica* 117:89–114.

Chubb, L. 1933. *Geology of the Galapagos, Cocos and Easter Island*. Bernice P. Bishop Museum Bulletin 110. Bernice P. Bishop Museum, Honolulu.

Church, F. and G. Ellis 1996. A use-wear analysis of obsidian tools from an *Ana Kionga*. *Rapa Nui Journal* 10(4):81–88.

Clark, G., C. Reepmeyer and N. Melekiola 2016. The rapid emergence of the archaic Tongan state: The royal tomb of Paepaeotelea. *Antiquity* 90(349):1038–1053. doi.org/10.15184/aqy.2016.114.

Clark, G., P. Parton, C. Reepmeyer, N. Melekiola and D. Burley 2018. Conflict and state development in ancient Tonga: The Lapaha earth fort. *Journal of Island and Coastal Archaeology* 13(3):405–419. doi.org/10.1080/15564894.2017.1337658.

Cook, J. 1777. *A voyage towards the South Pole, and round the world: Performed in His Majesty's ships the* Resolution *and* Adventure, *in the years 1772, 1773, 1774, and 1775*. W. Strahan and T. Cadell, London.

Delsing, R. 2004. Colonialism and resistance in Rapa Nui. *Rapa Nui Journal* 18(1):24–30.

Diamond, J. 2005. *Collapse: How societies choose to fail or survive*. Penguin Books, London.

DiNapoli, R.J., A. Morrison, C. Lipo, T. Hunt and B. Lane 2018. East Polynesian islands as models of cultural divergence: The case of Rapa Nui and Rapa Iti. *Journal of Island and Coastal Archaeology* 13(2):157–160. doi.org/10.1080/15564894.2016.1276490.

DiNapoli, R.J., C.P. Lipo and T.L. Hunt 2020. Revisiting warfare, monument destruction, and the 'Huri Moai' phase in Rapa Nui (Easter Island) culture history. *Journal of Pacific Archaeology*. EPUB 2020. pacificarchaeology.org/index.php/journal/article/view/313.

Englert, S. 1974. *La Tierra de Hoto Matua: Historia y etnologia de la Isla de Pascua*. 3rd edition. Edatorial Universitaria, Santiago de Chile.

Eyraud, E. 1864. Letter from missionary Eugenio Eyraud after nine months stay at Rapa Nui. Translated by Dina Tricca and Angélica Alister C. *Easter Island Travel*. www.easterisland.travel/easter-island-facts-and-info/history/ship-logs-and-journals/eugenio-eyraud-1864/.

Ferdon, E.N. 1965. Report 4: A summary of Rapa Iti fortified villages. In T. Heyerdahl and E.W. Ferdon (eds), *Reports of the Norwegian Archaeological expedition to Easter Island and the East Pacific. Volume 2: Miscellaneous papers*, pp. 69–87. Monographs of the School of American Research and the Kon-Tiki Museum 24. Forum Publishing, Stockholm.

Foerster, R. and S. Lorenzo 2015. *Expediciones a Rapa Nui 1791–1892*. Rapa Nui Press, Chile.

Forster, G. 1777. *A voyage round the world in His Britannic Majesty's sloop,* Resolution *commanded by Captain James Cook during the years 1772–1775*. B. White, J. Robson and P. Elmsly, London.

Green, R.C. and J.M. Davidson (eds) 1969. *Archaeology in Western Samoa*. Volume 1. Auckland Institute and Museum Bulletin 6. Auckland.

Griffero, A. 1998. Colonialism and Rapanui identity. In C. Stevenson, G. Lee and F. Morin (eds), *Proceedings of the Fourth International Conference on Easter Island and East Polynesia*, pp. 365–367. Easter Island Foundation, Los Osos.

Håkansson, O. 2017. Stratified Polynesia: A GIS-based study of prehistoric settlements in Samoa and Rapa Nui. Unpublished MA thesis. Uppsala University, Uppsala.

Haoa Cardinali, S., K. Ingersoll, D. Ingersoll and C. Stevenson (eds) 2017. *Cultural and environmental change on Rapa Nui*. Routledge Studies in Archaeology. Cambridge University Press, Cambridge. doi.org/10.4324/9781315294452.

Helbling, J. 2006. War and peace in societies without central power: Theories and perspectives. In T. Otto, H. Thrane and H. Vandkilde (eds), *Warfare and society: Archaeological and social anthropological perspectives*, pp. 113–139. Aarhus University Press, Aarhus.

Heyerdahl, T. 1961. An introduction to Easter Island. In T. Heyerdahl and E.N. Ferdon (eds), *Reports of the Norwegian archaeological expedition to Easter Island and the East Pacific. Volume 1: Archaeology of Easter Island*, pp. 21–90. Monographs of the School of American Research and the Kon-Tiki Museum 24. Forum Publishing, Stockholm.

Heyerdahl, T. 1974. *Fatuhiva–Back to nature*. Allen and Unwin, London.

Heyerdahl, T. and E. Ferdon (eds) 1961. *Reports of the Norwegian archaeological expedition to Easter Island and the East Pacific. Volume 1: Archaeology of Easter Island*. Monographs of the School of American Research and the Kon-Tiki Museum 24. Forum Publishing, Stockholm.

Hunt, T. and C. Lipo 2006. Late colonization of Easter Island. *Science* 311:1603–1606.

Hunt, T. and C. Lipo 2011. *The statues that walked: Unraveling the mystery of Easter Island*. Free Press, New York.

Kolb, M.J. and B. Dixon 2002. Landscapes of war: Rules and conventions of conflict in ancient Hawai'i (and elsewhere). *American Antiquity* 67(3):514–534. doi.org/10.2307/1593824.

Kotzebue, O. 1821. *A voyage of discovery into the South Sea and Beering's Strait*. London.

Lavachery, H. 1935. *Île de Pâques*. Bernard Grasset, Paris.

Lee, G. 1992. *Rock art of Easter Island: Symbols of power, prayers to the God*. UCLA Institute of Archaeology, Los Angeles.

Lipo, C, T. Hunt and B. Hundtoft 2010. Stylistic variability of stemmed obsidian tools (*mata'a*), frequency seriation, and the scale of social interaction on Rapa Nui (Easter Island). *Journal of Archaeological Science* 37(10):2551–2561. doi.org/10.1016/j.jas.2010.05.015.

Lipo, C., T. Hunt, R. Horneman and V. Bonhomme 2016. Weapons of war? Rapa Nui *mata'a* morphometric analyses. *Antiquity* 90:172–187. doi.org/10.15184/aqy.2015.189.

Martinsson-Wallin, H. 1994. *Ahu–The ceremonial stone structures of Easter Island: Analysis of variation and interpretation of meanings*. Aun 19. Societas Archaologica Upsaliensis, Uppsala.

Martinsson-Wallin, H. 1996. The eyes of the Moai–Lost and re-discovered. *Rapa Nui Journal* 10(2):41–44.

Martinsson-Wallin, H. 2000. 'No stone unturned' … a reflection on the recycling of worked stones on Rapa Nui. In P. Wallin and H. Martinsson-Wallin (eds), *Essays in honour of Arne Skjølsvold: 75 Years*, pp. 44–60. The Kon-Tiki Museum Occasional Papers 5. The Kon-Tiki Museum Institute for Pacific Archaeology and Cultural History, Oslo.

Martinsson-Wallin, H. 2004. Archaeological excavation at Vinapu (Rapa Nui). *Rapa Nui Journal* 18(1):7–9.

Martinsson-Wallin, H. 2007. Arkeologi, politik och identitet. Kulturell identitet i ett långtidsperspektiv på Påskön. In B. Pettersson and P. Skoglund (eds), *Arkeologi och Identitet. Nordic Tag 2005*. Lund University, Lund.

Martinsson-Wallin, H. In prep. Analysing and dating cremated bones from ceremonial sites in Rapa-Nui (Easter Island). Unpublished manuscript in possession of the author.

Martinsson-Wallin, H. and S. Crockford 2002. Early settlement of Rapa Nui. *Asian Perspectives* 40(2):244–278. doi.org/10.1353/asi.2001.0016.

Martinsson-Wallin, H., P. Wallin and R. Solsvik 1998. *Archaeological excavations at ahu Ra'ai, La Pérouse, Easter Island Oct–Nov 1997*. Kon-Tiki Field Report Series 2. The Kon-Tiki Museum, Oslo.

Martinsson-Wallin, H. and P. Wallin 1999. Excavation at Anakena: The Easter Island settlement sequence and change of subsistence? In P. Vargas (ed.), *Easter Island and East Polynesian prehistory*, pp. 179–186. Universidad de Chile. Insituto Estudio Isla de Pascua, Santiago.

Martinsson-Wallin, H. and P. Wallin 2001. The 'fish' for the gods. *Rapa Nui Journal* 15(1):7–10.

Martinsson-Wallin, H. 2014. Archaeological investigations in independent Samoa – 'tala eli' of Laupule mound and beyond. In H. Martinsson-Wallin and T. Thomas (eds), *Monuments and people in the Pacific*, pp. 245–272. Studies in Global Archaeology 20. Uppsala University, Sweden.

Martinsson-Wallin, H. and P. Wallin 2014. Spatial perspectives on ceremonial complexes: Testing traditional land divisions. In H. Martinsson-Wallin and T. Thomas (eds), *Monuments and people in the Pacific*, pp. 318–342. Studies in Global Archaeology 20. Uppsala University, Sweden.

Martinsson-Wallin, H., P. Wallin, A. Anderson and R. Solsvik 2013. Chronogeographic variation in initial East Polynesian construction of monumental ceremonial sites. *Journal of Island and Coastal Archaeology* 8(3):405–421. doi.org/10.1080/15564894.2013.834009.

Meleisea, M. and P. Schoeffel Meleisea 1987. *Lagaga–A short history of Western Samoa*. Oceania Printers, Suva.

Métraux, A. 1937. *Easter Island sanctuaries: Analytic and comparative study*. Etnologiska Studier 5. Elanders Boktryckeri Aktiebolag, Gothenburg.

Métraux, A. 1940. *Ethnology of Easter Island*. Bernice P. Bishop Museum Bulletin 160. Bernice P. Bishop Museum, Honolulu.

Mieth, A. and H.R. Bork 2010. Humans, climate or introduced rats–Which is to blame for the woodland destruction on prehistoric Rapa Nui (Easter Island)? *Journal of Archaeological Science* 37:417–426. doi.org/10.1016/j.jas.2009.10.006.

Nakato, H., K. Tamura, Y. Arimatsu, T. Nakagawa, N. Matsumoto and T. Matsugi 2016. Violence in the prehistoric period of Japan: The spatio-temporal pattern of skeletal evidence for violence in the Jomon period. *Biology Letters* 12:20160847. doi.org/10.1098/rsbl.2016.0847.

Navarro, S. 2017. The crematorium of Hanga Hahave on Rapa Nui (Easter Island): What stories can the skeletal remains reveal. Unpublished MA thesis. Department of Archaeology and Ancient History, Uppsala University.

Obeyesekere, G. 1992. *The apotheosis of Captain Cook*. Princeton University Press and Bishop Museum Press, Honolulu.

Owsley, D.W., G.W. Gill and S.D. Ousley 1994. Biological effects of European contact on Easter Island. In C.S. Larsen and G.R. Milner (eds), *The wake of contact: Biological responses to conquest*, pp. 161–177. Wiley-Liss, New York.

Owsley, D., K. Barca, V. Simon and G. Gill 2016. Evidence for injuries and violent death. In V. Stefan and G. Gill (eds), *Skeletal biology of the ancient Rapanui (Easter Islanders)*, pp. 222–252. Cambridge University Press, Cambridge. doi.org/10.1017/cbo9781139151856.013.

Palmer, J.L. 1870. A visit to Easter Island, or Rapa Nui. *Royal Geographical Society Proceedings* 14:108–119. doi.org/10.2307/1798641.

Petit-Thouars, A. du. 1841. *Voyage autour de Monde sur la frégate La Venus, pendant les Années 1836–1839*. Gide, Paris. doi.org/10.5962/bhl.title.39468.

Ramirez, J.-M. 1990/1991. Transpacific contacts: The Mapuche connection. *Rapa Nui Journal* 4(4):53–55.

Reainer, R. and D. Ryan 2003. Mapping the Poike Ditch. In J. Loret and J. Tanacredi (eds), *Easter Island: Scientific exploration into the world's environmental problems in microcosm*, pp. 207–221. Springer, Boston. doi.org/10.1007/978-1-4615-0183-1_14.

Roussel, R.P. 1926 (1869). Île de Pâques ou Rapanui. *Extrait des Annales des Sacré-Coeurs* 305:355–360, 307:423–430, 308:462–466, 309:495–499. First published in 1869.

Routledge, K. 1919. *The mystery of Easter Island*. Hazell, Watson and Viney, London.

Ruiz-Tagle, E. 2005. *The first three expeditions*. Rapanui Press, Santiago.

Skjølsvold, A. 1994. Archaeological investigations at Anakena, Easter Island. *The Kon-Tiki Museum Occasional Papers* 3:1–121.

Smith, C. 1961. The Poike Ditch. In T. Heyerdahl and E. Ferdon (eds), *Reports of the Norwegian Archaeological expedition to Easter Island and the East Pacific. Volume 1: Archaeology of Easter Island*, pp. 385–391. Monographs of the School of American Research and the Kon-Tiki Museum 24. Forum Publishing, Stockholm.

Smith, C. 1990. The Poike Ditch in retrospect. *Rapa Nui Journal* 4(3):33–37.

Stevenson, C. 1997. *Archaeological investigations on Easter Island Mauga Tari: An upland agricultural complex*. Easter Island Foundation, Los Osos.

Stevenson, C. and S. Haoa 2008. *Prehistoric Rapa Nui: Landscape and settlement. Archaeology at Hanga Ho'onu*. Bearsville Press, Los Osos.

Thomson, W. 1889. The Pito te Henua, or Easter Island. *Report of the U.S. National Museum*, pp. 447–552. Smithsonian Institute, Washington.

Thorpe, I.J. 2003. Anthropology, archaeology, and the origin of warfare. *World Archaeology* 35:145–165. doi.org/10.1080/0043824032000079198.

Vandkilde, H. 2013. Warfare in northern European Bronze Age society. In S. Ralph (ed.), *The archaeology of violence: Interdisciplinary approaches*, pp. 32–62. IEMA Proceedings Volume 2. State University of New York Press, New York.

Van Tilburg, J. 1994. *Easter Island: Archaeology, ecology and culture*. British Museum Press, London.

Wallin, P. 1993. *Ceremonial stone structures. The archaeology and ethnohistory of the marae complex in the Society Islands, French Polynesia*. Societas Archaeologica Upsaliensis 18. Uppsala.

Wallin, P. and H. Martinsson-Wallin 2008. Religious structures in the Hanga Ho'onu region. In C.M. Stevenson and S. Haoa-Cardinali (eds), *Prehistoric Rapa Nui: Landscape and settlement archaeology at Hanga Ho'onu*, pp. 127–161. Easter Island Foundation, Los Osos.

Wallin, P. and H. Martinsson-Wallin 2010. Monumental structures and the spirit of chiefly actions. *Time and mind* 4(1):43–58. doi.org/10.2752/175169711x12893985693630.

Wilmshurst, J.M., T.L. Hunt, C.P. Lipo and A.J. Anderson 2011. High-precision radiocarbon dating shows recent and rapid initial human colonization of East Polynesia. *Proceedings of the National Academy of Sciences USA* 108(5):1815–1820. doi.org/10.1073/pnas.1015876108.

Wosniak, J. 1998. Settlement patterns and subsistence on the northwest coast of Rapa Nui. In C. Stevenson, G. Lee and F.J. Morin (eds), *Easter Island in Pacific context. South Seas symposium: Proceedings of the Fourth International Conference on Easter Island and East Polynesia*, pp. 185–192. Easter Island Foundation, Los Osos.

Zumbohm, G. 1879–1880. Lettres du R.P. Gaspard Zumbohm au directeur des Annales sur la mission de l'île de Pâques. *Annales de la Congrégation des Sacrés-Coeurs de Jésus det de Marie* 5, Paris.

5

Traditional places in conflict and their historic context: Ritidian, Guam

Boyd Dixon, Andrea Jalandoni and Maria Kottermair

Introduction

The term 'traditional places in conflict' in the title does not imply that pre-Contact Period village sites such as Ritidian on the island of Guam in the Mariana Islands of Micronesia (Figure 5.1) were deliberately constructed to be settings of defence or animosity. Rather, non-indigenous participant observers recorded traditional conflict before the late seventeenth century in contested spaces between indigenous Chamorro village sites, and often quite literally 'on the beach' (Flexner 2014:49). Some traditional villages on Guam may then have assumed a role in conflict when Spanish, American and Japanese forces imposed their will upon the resident population.

When the first Austronesian voyagers reached the shores of Ritidian c. 1500 BCE, the mean sea level was approximately 1.8 m higher than present (Dickinson 2000, 2001), towards the end of the Holocene Epoch. The high sea level then began to drop from c. 1100 BCE until around 100 CE when it reached near present-day levels. The first inhabitants at Ritidian were therefore restricted to a narrow beach area, but the gradually retreating sea exposed more beach to inhabit by the Latte Period (1000–1521 CE), allowing for more native vegetation and farming areas, and encouraging reef and sand dune development that supported marine food abundance and protection from tidal surges (Carson 2010, 2012, 2014). Today, *latte* structures at Ritidian and across the Mariana Islands are one of the most distinguishable aspects of Chamorro culture, a symbol with which the local people identify themselves even today. The *latte* are composed of two parts, stone columns (*haligi*) and caps or tops (*tasa*). The stone pillars and their caps held up an A-framed structure probably made of wood and thatch. Archaeological evidence at Ritidian and early historic archival documents suggest the *latte* buildings served various related functions such as family housing, canoe and domestic implement storage, household food production, and ancestor veneration (Bayman et al. 2010; Dixon et al. 2006; Reinman 1977; Thompson 1940).

Bayman et al. (2012) investigated two adjacent *latte* sets, located on the west side of Ritidian, and demonstrated different but interrelated domestic activities during the early Contact Period (1521–1668 CE). Each *latte* building had its own economic specialty and both were probably gender-specific. Nearby, there are four known caves at the cliff line with multicoloured pictograms. Not all the figures are identifiable, although there are some anatomically correct anthropomorphic images in black, red and white pigment. While none of the pictograms have yet been precisely dated, the black and red images are suspected to be Pre-Latte in date, while the white images are suspected to date to the Latte Period (Carson 2017).

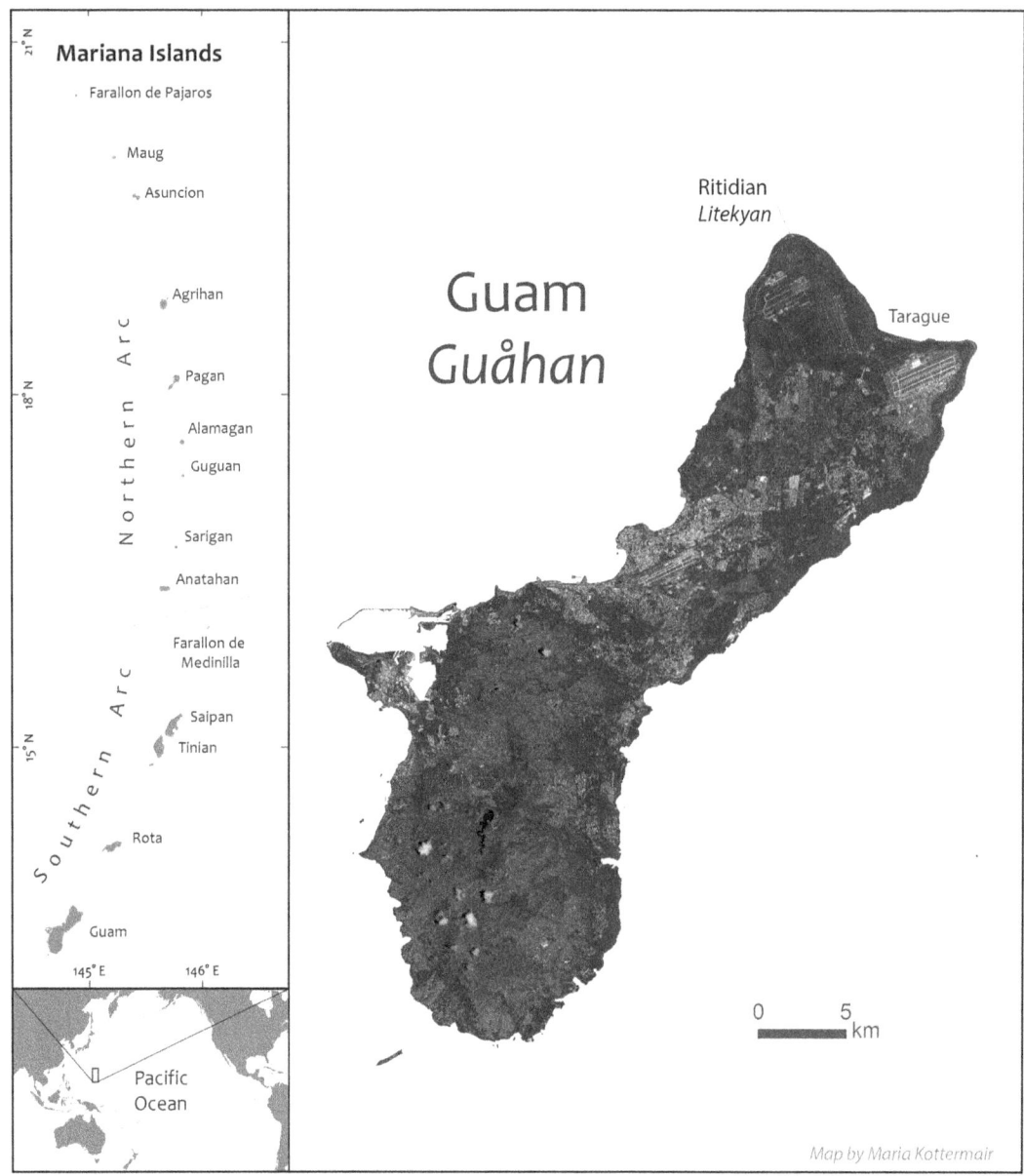

Figure 5.1. Guam and Ritidian with the Northern Mariana Islands.
Source: Maria Kottermair.

The site of Ritidian is also historically significant for the wealth of archival documentation of the early interaction between the Spanish clergy and the Chamorro residents. Archaeological evidence of a stone church or priest residence in Ritidian has recently uncovered valuable information about the tenuous early Spanish Colonial Period (Jalandoni 2011). In 1674 CE, construction of a church dedicated to St Francis Xavier began at Ritidian, and was completed the following year in 1675 CE by the Jesuits, presumably using native labour and materials. In December 1675 CE, Brother Diaz was murdered in an altercation with the *urritaos* (young native men) over a cultural difference in premarital behaviour, after Brother Diaz and an assistant tried to burn the *guma urritao* or single men's house (Farrell 2011). The murder of Brother Diaz then led the Chamorro to burn the church, residences and schools, as well as abandoning the village to take refuge in Rota.

While the village was abandoned, members of the rival village of Tarague burned the remains of Ritidian, cut down food-bearing trees and destroyed crops. The Chamorro eventually returned to Ritidian by 1681 CE and a stone church dedicated to San Miguel was built in nearby Jinapsan to service several of the surrounding villages. That church and priest residence were subsequently burned down and rebuilt twice. In 1684 CE, the resident priest, Fr Angelis, was killed at Ritidian during a Chamorro revolt. The area of Ritidian was again abandoned for almost a century when the Spaniards forced the Chamorro to relocate to southern Guam (Jalandoni 2011).

Pre-Contact conflict: 1500 BCE–1521 CE

The traditional causes of pre-Contact conflict on Guam and at Ritidian are many, likely rooted in the growth of relatively small early Pre-Latte Period Chamorro populations on islands of finite resources, in a fluctuating global climate. Archaeological evidence of initial settlement of the Mariana archipelago c. 1500 BCE is relatively sparse and not clustered within individual islands, suggesting that maritime settlers of the archipelago targeted a wide range of natural habitats to maximise survival upon landing (Dixon and Dega, In press). These settings included inland estuaries and marshes, cliff lines with caves, native forests and soils, and beach dunes with shallow lagoons and offshore reefs. Recent DNA research and similarities in material culture with Southeast Asia suggest multiple origins to the Marianas, which probably originated along a cultural corridor from the Philippines to Sulawesi and island Melanesia beginning between 1500–1100 BCE (Vilar et al. 2016). This settlement strategy of 'social distancing', targeting various habitats upon arrival, may therefore have been a long-practised mechanism to avoid initial conflict between various seafaring families and clans of uncertain lineage.

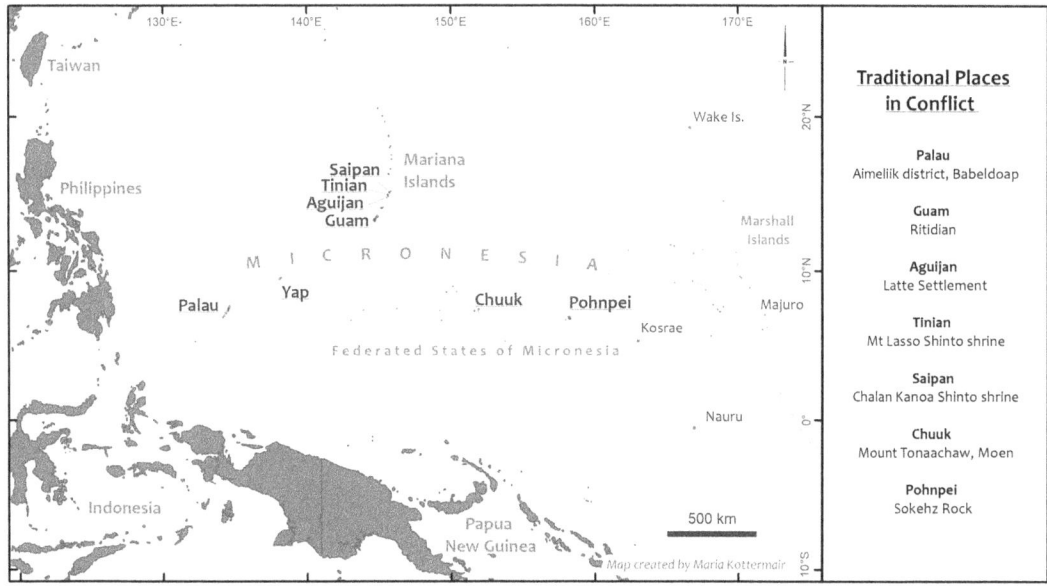

Figure 5.2. Selected traditional places in conflict across Micronesia.
Source: Maria Kottermair.

By the Latte Period, it can be assumed that some altercations accompanied the gradual infilling of early island environments, but there is no evidence of pre-Contact fortifications or defensive site locations on Guam such as existed elsewhere across Micronesia (Figure 5.2) until well after European contact. The symbolic projection of coercion, force and violence has been surmised at Palauan crowns and ring-ditches from 600 BCE to 1000 CE (Liston and Tuggle 2006), and at Chuukese hill forts c. 1300 CE (Nunn 2007; Rainbird 2004). Historic-era conflict is associated with the Chamorro island stronghold of Aguijan in 1695 CE during the Spanish Contact Period

(Butler 1992), at Sokehz Rock on Pohnpei during the German administration and rebellion in 1911 CE (Hezel 2016), and during the World War II American invasion of 1944 CE at the traditional Japanese Shinto shrines of Mt Lasso on Tinian (Farrell 2012) and Chalan Kanoa in Saipan (Russell 1984). Ritidian and all these sites, whether pre-Contact, historic or early twentieth century, were also at times a place of elite ritual, reverence, habitation, burial and/or cultivation claimed by native or non-indigenous peoples (cf. Liston 2014).

Traditional warfare and conflict was relatively common on Guam in the contact era, but left little direct evidence apart from bone spear points and shaped sling stones (Dixon 2011).

The Latte Period (between 1000 and 1668 CE) is distinguished from the preceding Pre-Latte Period (between 1500 BCE and 1000 CE) (Carson 2014) by a greater number of sling stones in archaeological sites, consistent with pre-contact conflict (Hornbostel 1924–25; Morgan 1988; York and York 2014). Unlike the massive terraces and hilltop crowns the early Palauans built for several reasons including their defence (Liston 2009), Latte Period settlements were built with little apparent concern for defence (Russell 1998). Many *latte* sets or house foundations are found on ridge tops in the interior of southern Guam (Dixon and Gilda 2011), but these sites likely occupied settings connected to ancient footpaths from which the occupants could farm arable soils and wetlands and gather native forest resources.

Artefacts of Latte Period warfare are relatively easy to identify in the archaeological record since there were no large animals to hunt in the Mariana Islands, and these weapons were mentioned respectfully by early Spanish visitors and settlers to Guam. Sling stones of baked clay, limestone, mudstone and basalt, such as those found at Pagat Village (Craib 1986), were deadly at close range, and were an effective way to keep the enemy at a distance. While sling stones are commonly found around most coastal Latte Period villages, including at Ritidian Point (Thompson 1932:49), clusters of them denoting possible manufacture for broader distribution are mostly restricted to southern Guam where raw materials occur naturally in the cliffs and uplands above coastal villages. Sling stones were also modified for use as net sinker weights, gaming pieces, amulets or ornaments, and as burial goods (York and York 2014).

When combat or the element of surprise was called for, fire-hardened or barbed human-shinbone tipped spears such as those found at Ritidian (Dixon and Jalandoni 2019) could dispatch many a warrior who returned home to find his wounds infected from poison on the spear tips. Magellan's chronicler Antonio Pigafetta noted that:

> When our people wounded any of the islanders with their arrows, (of which weapon they had no conception), and chanced to pierce them through, the unfortunate sufferers endeavoured to draw out these arrows from their bodies, now by one end, now by another; after which they looked at them with astonishment, and sometimes died of their wounds. (Pigafetta in Lévesque 1992:214)

Indeed, what is believed to be the first of the 'Ladrones' or Chamorro warriors ever depicted c. 1590 CE was naked and without body armour or tattoos (Figure 5.3) in the Boxer Codex (Dasmarinas 1595).

It is probably safe to assume that by the time late Latte Period populations had increased, so had the demand for firewood, construction materials, forest fruits, native herbs and agriculturally produced foods (Dixon and Schaefer 2014). Changes in late pre-Contact settlement, from a primarily coastal orientation to a more inland focus, are noted across much of the Pacific between roughly 1300 and 1800 CE (Nunn et al. 2007), in many cases interpreted as a response to the Little Ice Age and its effects on sea level, temperature and rainfall. In the Marianas archipelago, however, it would be difficult to portray these climatic changes as related to societal upheaval and conflict, since existing coastal settlements appeared to grow in size at much the same time as substantial new settlements appeared in the interior of the larger islands (Dixon et al. 2011a).

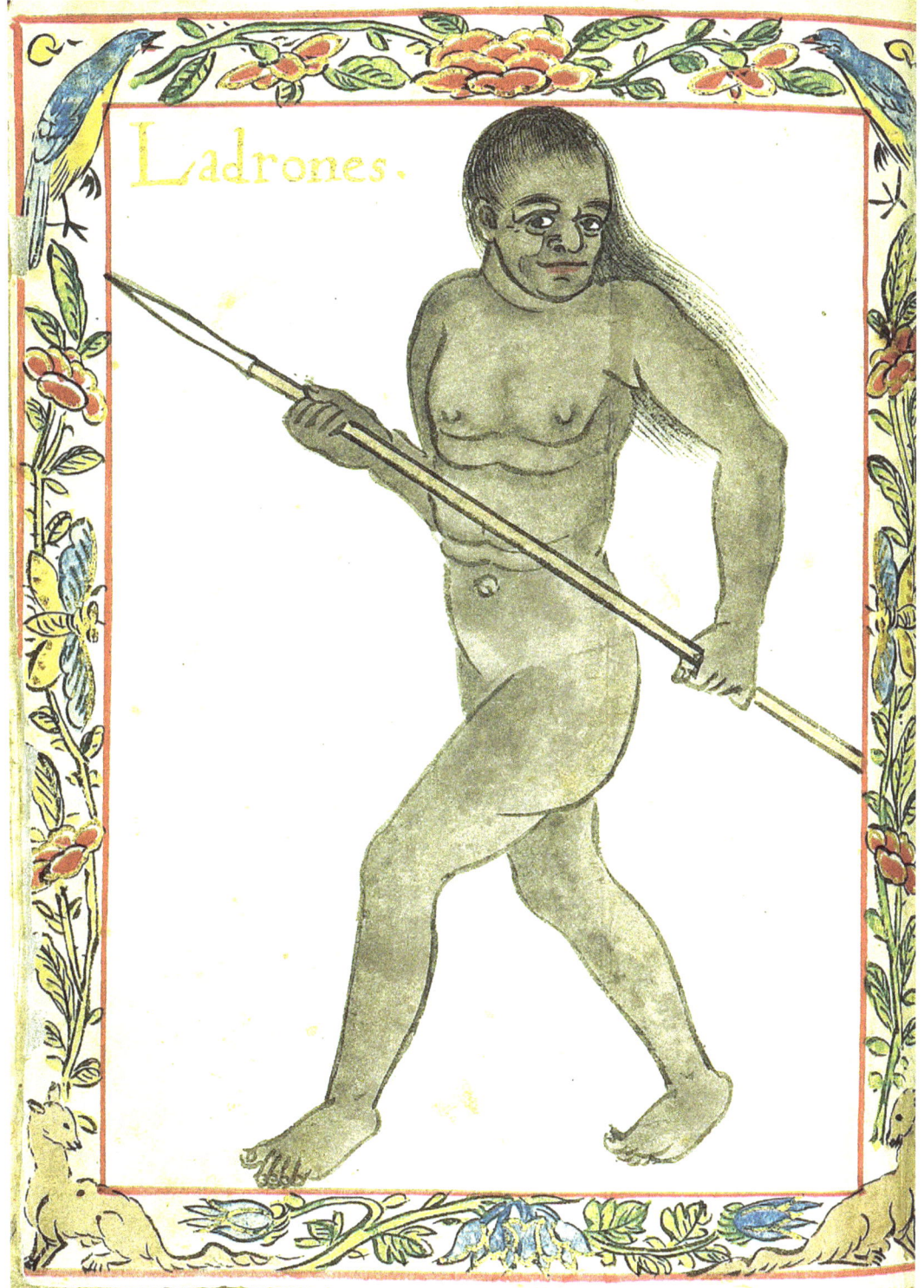

Figure 5.3. First depiction of a Chamorro warrior, c. 1590–1591 CE.
Source: Boxer Codex, attributed to Gomez Perez Dasmarinas (Dasmarinas 1595).

When assessing these possible changes after the arrival of Magellan in 1521 CE, the scenario is differently recorded between early historic accounts and later archival documents. One interpretation suggests that 'interactions between aliens and natives remained superficial and transient on the whole until the arrival of the Jesuit mission' (Underwood 1973:12) and 'no evidence exists that any extensive decline took place among the Chamorro either as a result of the introduction of diseases or in armed conflict, until a later period of history' (Underwood 1973:13). An opposing perspective maintains that 'it is difficult to believe that the Marianas population suddenly began to decline when the missionaries arrived in 1668' (Shell 1999:293), since 'there can be no serious doubt that the known epidemics, and lesser ones that may not have been recognised as such, took a disproportionate toll of infants, children and the frail and elderly' (Shell 1999:303).

The demographic effect of combat-related casualties on the pre-Contact population in the Mariana Islands is likewise not easy to assess. In one late Latte to Contact Period (1400–1668 CE) village on Saipan, with a skeletal MNI (minimum number of individuals) population of 93 individuals, a single barbed human bone spear point was encountered in a disturbed burial context containing one child and two adults at the village site of Afetna (Dixon et al. 2019), but the artefact's precise association was impossible to determine. In the late Latte Period village site at Anaguan in Garapan (Dega et al. 2017) on Saipan, with a skeletal population of over 416 MNI, one male was encountered with a single sling stone imbedded in his ribs, one male was found with a cache of 15 sling stones, and one male had over 150 sling stones at his side. Nine human bone spear points were also found in non-burial contexts.

At the Naton Beach Pre-Latte and Latte Period village site on Guam (DeFant 2009), with a skeletal population of 370 MNI, 'there was no evidence of death from warfare' (Walth 2016:i). One sling stone was found as a grave good in a Pre-Latte burial. Six were found with Latte Period adult males and females, and five were found with Latte Period subadults of indeterminable gender. Only two human bone spear points were encountered in Latte Period non-burial contexts. While these burial samples vary considerably in size and combat-related grave good volumes, they leave the impression that only a small percentage of the male population was ever directly involved in conflict.

Contact Period conflict: 1521–1668 CE

Historical accounts from the period of European contact with Guam, spanning the early sixteenth to late seventeenth centuries, document sporadic bellicose interactions with Chamorro, beginning with the first visit to the island by Ferdinand Magellan in 1521 CE. After settlement of the island in 1668 CE by Spanish clergy and militia or soldiers from the Philippines and Mexico, initial curiosity and goodwill were transformed into a largely confrontational relationship within a decade of native resistance to Spanish demands to abandon traditional culture and adopt imposed beliefs and behaviour. Small churches built in existing Chamorro villages at desirable beach settings often with protective cliffs (Figure 5.4) often became flashpoints of conflict by the 1680s CE, such as at Ritidian. Intervillage conflict before Spanish contact during the Latte Period was not unknown but is not believed to have risen above the level of clan or family feuds (Hezel 2015), rarely resulting in more than a few casualties.

A manuscript by Fray Peter Coomans written around 1672–1673 noted:

> Then, if envy would make them want to burn a house from a distance, they would stuff the perforated side of it [the sling] with tow burning with a very ferocious fire, which, with a swift movement became a flame, and sail away to seek shelter in enemy houses. (Coomans, in Lévesque 1995:99)

Figure 5.4. Ritidian Point to the south-east from the Guam National Wildlife Refuge.
Source: Mike Carson.

As protection from sling stones, he observed:

> Their defensive weapons are hardly more than palm mats, which they place like a hat on their heads by way of a helmet. They also used another [mat] which they tie around their chest by way of a breast-plate, leaving the rest of their body naked; this way they can more easily shoot their sling, or throw spears. (Coomans, in Lévesque 1995:99)

The simple but effective weapons used by Chamorro during conflict with the Spaniards and their militia were best suited to a style of warfare that involved small groups of warriors engaging briefly and often at some distance (Dixon 2011), with the goal being to inflict some damage to the enemy perhaps in an ambush, but then withdraw to fight another day. The goal seemed to be to take an aggressive stance if some insult could not be ignored, but then agree to terms that everyone could live with. In 1602 CE, Fray Juan Pobre was told by his informant Sancho on Rota that:

> When one kills another, if they are from the same town he absents himself from that town to go to another island so that the relatives will not kill him. He remains absent until from the killer's house or from that of his father or mother they take one or two palms of tortoise [shells] which is the thing that is most valued among them and with some big fish and rice they pay the father or mother or wife of the deceased for the death. Once this has been done, they send word to the exile and he can come freely and walk about fearlessly through his town and that is their form of justice. (Pobre, in Lévesque 1992:182)

Combat training did appear to be a necessary part of every Chamorro warrior's life when charged with defending his village and its elders. Fray Juan Pobre's informant Sancho noted that:

> The young men usually show off their strength in front of these chiefs and they wrestle arms open and make each other tumble. … and thus they test their strength or sometimes they move apart from each other and, although in jest they usually act as earnestly as in fencing.

> They take some spears at 10 or 12 paces, one throws at the other and although they are skilful at hitting correctly, they are more so in avoiding being hit, and many times they grab the spear in the air. (Pobre, in Lévesque 1992:181)

No mention is made, however, that any Chamorro village maintained a standing army or militia, nor were there obvious officers or insignias of rank during combat (Dixon 2011), as the Spanish would easily have recognised from their own military training.

Possible evidence of combat-related wounds has been suggested in Contact Period (1521–1668 CE) skeletal populations in the Mariana Islands, but such individuals were rarely buried with securely dated non-native Chamorro (Dixon et al. 2017). Acts of violence and Chamorro deaths were recorded during the early visits of Magellan and Legaspi (Farrell 2011), although actual contact was rather limited between Europeans and Chamorro since most close encounters occurred on shore during very short visits to replenish fresh food and water and conduct limited trade.

On the active volcanic island of Pagan, north of Saipan, bird-leg bone spearheads of *Phasionidae* sp., a Carnelian bead, Ming Dynasty blue and white porcelain sherds, and metal artefact fragments with wooden attachments were found in sealed Latte Period contexts with charcoal radiocarbon dates of 1325 ± 90 BP, 1495 ± 115 BP and 1665 ± 95 BP (Egami and Saito 1973:208), 'suggesting to the authors pre-Magallanes [Magellan] contact with Iron Age Southeast Asia, and perhaps an attempt to introduce chicken or pheasant' (Dixon et al. 2017:201). No burial evidence of conflict was noted.

Spanish colonial conflict: 1668–1898 CE

Events after the Spanish settled in the principal village of Hagåtña in 1668 CE eventually led to open conflict between soldiers and Chamorro warriors at more than one location. According to Hezel and Driver (1988:137), 'twelve priests, perhaps 20 of their lay helpers, and an uncounted number of soldiers and Chamorro warriors died in the periodic skirmishes that occurred over a 17-year period'. This violence eventually culminated in *la Reducción* between roughly 1684–1720 CE (Jalandoni 2011), when most Mariana and northern Guam populations were forcibly removed to six southern villages with a church and small Jesuit presence to enforce order and acculturation. As defined by Driver on Guam, *la Reducción* was:

> the method employed by the Spanish ecclesiastical and military authorities to convert or Christianize the indigenous inhabitants of an area and bring them from what they considered rustic living conditions into more highly organized communities that were centred around a church or mission. (Driver, in Jalandoni and Peterson 2013)

La Reducción was not well received by Chamorro residents of the villages being forced from their ancestral homes and the burial places of their kin, so their response was not the submission the Jesuits had hoped for, as later described by Velarde in 1759 CE:

> Another reason is that these natives love their independence so strongly that they tolerate nothing that restricts their freedom. The yoke of subjection is very hard on their pride and, though they all possess strange ways, the subjection causes some in desperation to take their own lives by hanging themselves. Some women practice sterilization or throw their new born babies into the sea. They believe that it is better to die than to live and experience true sadness or hardship. (Velarde 1987:16)

Ritidian, one of several well-populated villages situated on the north-western coast of Guam with a small church later known as the Casa Real (Reed 1952), became one traditional place in conflict at that time. Local warriors were trained in traditional martial arts and fighting techniques, including the use of sling stones and human bone pointed spears (Figure 5.5), but not the art of European warfare. Consequently, Chamorro warriors soon found themselves unable to repel newly arrived Spanish soldiers with Sergeant Major Joseph de Quiroga y Losada in 1679 CE, some in armour and perhaps mounted on a few horses, many armed with muskets or swords (Figure 5.6). The scale of combat involving civilians as targets and seizure of high-status warriors for public execution must have also been unnerving, accustomed as Chamorro were to a negotiated resolution after minimal casualties.

Figure 5.5. Limestone and volcanic sling stones and human bone spearpoints.
Source: Andrea Jalandoni.

Figure 5.6. Reconstruction of a Spanish raid on a Chamorro Village, c. 1680 CE.
Source: Don Farrell (2011:169).

In the same year, an enclave of resistors to Spanish mandates had gathered at the relatively inaccessible village and water cave of Hanum below the cliffs on the north-eastern side of Guam. After the Spanish attempt at a sunrise surprise was foiled by lookouts, the troops divided into four groups to cover native escape or resupply upon razing the village. García (2004:492) describes the results of this rout:

> The houses, with everything that could not be used by the victors, were consumed in flames. Fifty boats that were taken as the spoils of war were given to the friendly natives. Those they did not want were burned. The remaining booty was shared among the soldiers and the natives, except for the rice, which was kept for the general food supply and was taken by boat to Agadña.

During this same campaign, after Brother Diaz was killed and the first church was burned, the village of Ritidian was soon abandoned, presumably expecting swift Spanish retribution. The village was later resettled briefly, but the entire population was soon removed by Spanish soldiers to southern villages on Guam. The area was only repopulated as a rural ranch setting in the 1800s CE, when small ranches or *lanchos* and a limited population lived off subsistence farming and fishing or reef collecting. It is probable former Ritidian residents attended mass in Hagåtña or a nearby rural church on Sundays, but returned to their *lanchos* during the week, thus avoiding potential conflict with civilian and Spanish administration and clergy in Hagåtña. The implementation of the *lancho* system (Bayman et al. 2020) was undoubtedly encouraged by later colonial governments and clergy as a means to collect produce and wood from agricultural farms and nearby forests during the week, while indoctrinating the children in religious schools without the possible conflict of parental supervision.

Skeletal evidence of violence in the Mariana Islands during the early Spanish Colonial Period (1668–1720 CE) is difficult to date, in part because such apostate individuals would likely have been buried in a contested ceremony with failure to convert to Christian burial customs. One Chamorro male aged 50 excavated on the island of Tinian and given the name Taotao Tagga was found to have a healed wound to the face and cheek bone, likely inflicted by a metal weapon while the individual was in his 20s or 30s. 'The force of the blow was so strong that the cheek bone was displaced downward and outward where it meets the upper jaw' (Heathcote 2006:5). The date of his burial was postulated to have occurred well before 1695 CE when Chamorro were driven from the Aguijan stronghold (see Figure 5.2) to resettlement on Guam.

At the site of Achugao on the west coast of Saipan, fragments of a small metal flush loop bell were found just above the left side of the pelvis on a Latte Period burial, apparently having been attached to something around the waist (Butler 1995:345).

> The author argues that this particular specimen likely dates between the wreck of the *Nuestra Señora de la Concepción* on the south coast of Saipan in 1638 and the end of the Chamorro settlement of Saipan around CE 1730. (Dixon et al. 2017:201)

At Laulau House A on the east coast of Saipan, an iron spear point, a nail and an iron knife blade fragment were found beneath rocks packed around a *latte* stone (Spoehr 1957:167), 'suggesting a post-Contact ending date to the Latte Period occupation' (Dixon et al. 2017:201) at this site and perhaps at Achugao. No burial evidence of conflict was noted in either case.

First American administration conflict: 1898–1941 CE

At the end of the Spanish–American War in 1898 CE, Guam was ceded by Spain to the US Government with little conflict locally, but Guam did not become a US territory until 1950 CE. Between 1898 and 1941 CE, Guam served as a coaling and fuelling station for naval ships and other vessels, as the site of the trans-Pacific cable station, as the base for a strategic naval radio station, and as a landing place for the Pan-American trans-Pacific air clippers flying between San Francisco and Hong Kong. Despite being surrounded by Japanese-controlled islands, the United States did little in terms of military defence development (Peattie 1988), under the terms of their agreement with other colonial powers in the Pacific after World War I.

During the early twentieth century in northern Guam, many of the inland inhabitants were involved in the commercial production of dry coconut meat for the copra export market, as well as subsistence farming at small *lanchos* in the jungle (Dixon et al. 2016). This patchy quilt-like pattern of small farms and surrounding forests remained during the first half of American rule. Some grazing of cattle and growing cash crops also occurred in clearings along newly widened roads on the northern plateau prior to World War II.

By 1940 CE, an official census recorded a total of 80 farms in northern Guam, each averaging 7.1 hectares (Hunter-Anderson and Moore 2003), far more land than was needed to support one family on home gardening alone. Recent archaeological survey of these plateau areas within Andersen Air Force Base has recorded post–World War II refuse at several pockets of arable soil with coconut trees of considerable age near Pott's Junction, likely reflecting a better postwar economy for Chamorro farmers.

World War II and Cold War conflict: 1941 CE–present

Global conflict again manifested itself on the island in the mid-twentieth century with World War II and then the Cold War conflict, arguably still the prevailing paradigm today. There is no record of Japanese landings at Ritidian during their 1941 invasion of Guam, although Chamorro policemen from Saipan were landed at night to help the Japanese coordinate the takeover of civilian populations (Rogers 1995). One encampment of Japanese troops was placed at Pott's Junction to control access of the public, and one fortified anti-aircraft position was discovered in the jungle nearby (Dixon et al. 2016) to defend air space during the eventual invasion. Pre–World War II American fortification and then abandonment of Ritidian Point is also suggested by a 1944 CE Japanese map of the general area that shows a 'lookout' and 'remains of a battery' located at the end of the pre-existing vehicle road, probably replaced by a defensive overlook at the point by the Japanese.

At the end of combat with American troops to retake the island in August 1944 CE, small groups of Japanese stragglers sought refuge in the cliffs at the base of Ritidian Point, and limited evidence was found of abandoned weapons (Kurashina et al. 1990) and modified rock shelters for defence as stragglers rejoined ranks in Tarague until the war's end. The barrel and firing mechanism of a Japanese military rifle found in the Guam National Wildlife Reserve (Kurashina et al. 1990) indicate that armed stragglers likely passed along the coast at the end of the war, perhaps along the 'mule path circa 1 m wide' depicted on the 1944 CE Japanese map (Dixon et al. 2011b).

When Guam was recaptured in 1944 CE, the US military followed through with a massive military build-up, transforming Guam into an important communications, repair, resupply and air support centre for the remaining battles of the Pacific War. The construction of Northwest Field on the plateau (Figure 5.7) created one of several American air bases built to launch B-29 bombing raids on Japan and military targets across the western Pacific (Dixon et al. 2016). By the end of July 1945 CE, almost 80 per cent of the south taxiway and parking area was complete, but by 1948 CE, activity at Northwest Field had decelerated as a victim of shifting postwar missions. Northwest Field was vacated in the spring of 1949 CE, but its housing area remained in use until 1962 CE. In April 1975 CE, at the end of the Vietnam War, the base received almost 40 000 refugees and processed another 109 000 for onward transportation to the United States as part of Operation New Life.

Figure 5.7. B-29 over Northwest Field, Guam c. 1945.
Source: Judith Amesbury (2019:33).

Not long thereafter, Ritidian once again became a flashpoint of sociopolitical conflict throughout the 1960s and 1980s CE when the US Navy denied access to Chamorro owners and residents while clearing and developing infrastructure for a classified facility on the previous site of a *latte* set and the former Casa Real (Kurashina et al. 1990). The US Navy Sound Surveillance System or SOSUS was invented as a long-range, early warning listening system. This Cold War facility, when abandoned in the late 1980s, was deeded to the US Fish and Wildlife Service as part of the Ritidian Unit of the Guam National Wildlife Refuge (Jalandoni 2011). Former landowners were not allowed to return to their coastal property and access from the plateau above was curtailed at Pott's Junction until 1993 CE while construction of military support facilities proceeded. Conflict arose as fences were then erected and public hunting restricted, while access to the Guam National Wildlife Refuge is only allowed by appointment today.

Conclusions and continuations

Construction of various projects to support the US Department of Defense mission continues, including a live fire training range for the US Marines on the plateau above Ritidian. This has raised concern that the coastal setting will be closed from visitation within a live fire safety exclusion zone for much of the year, with growing resistance to such plans by many Chamorro and other island residents and members of the Government of Guam. Also surfacing are accounts of exposure to Agent Orange, stored and used by US veterans on Guam in the 1970s during the Vietnam War (Kime 2020) and the effects of atomic fallout on civilians from nuclear testing in Micronesia during the Cold War (National Research Council 2005:Appendix C). In 2020 CE, with new restrictions on Guam residents due to the COVID-19 pandemic, conflict over public access to Ritidian is stirring.

As can be seen from this Mariana Islands–focused reconstruction of native and resident conflict with Spanish, German, Japanese and American culture contact in Micronesia, resistance and accommodation to colonialisation has taken many forms, from armed uprising to political action and civil disobedience. So, while not constructed as such during the Latte Period, the village site of Ritidian on Guam has indeed been a 'traditional place of conflict' over several centuries. Perhaps too, community and international dialogue generated by such confrontation will reflect a positive and healing sense of the Chamorro place name of *Litekyan* or the 'stirring place' (Carson 2018), situated both literally and figuratively in this ever-changing sea of islands.

Acknowledgements

The authors would like to thank the following people for their support, including the generous invitation to contribute to *Archaeological perspectives on conflict and warfare in Australia and the Pacific,* and the opportunity to participate in the Australian Archaeological Association Annual Conference on the Gold Coast, 10–13 December 2019, 'Disrupting paradise: The archaeology of the driest inhabited continent on Earth'.

Dr Mirani Litster, The Australian National University; Prof. Geoffrey Clark, The Australian National University; Dr Sven Ouzman, The University of Western Australia; Dr Daryl Wesley, Flinders University; Dr Kelly Marsh, Guam Legislator; Dr Michael Carson, University of Guam; Dr William Jeffries, University of Guam; Dr David Atienza, University of Guam; Dr Patrick Nunn, University of the Sunshine Coast; Dr John Peterson, University of San Carlos; Dr Jim Bayman, University of Hawai'i at Mānoa; Don Farrell, Tinian; Scott Russell, CNMI Humanities Council; Judy Amesbury, Micronesian Archaeological Research Services; David DeFant, SEARCH Inc.; Richard Schaefer, IA LLC; Cherie Walth, SWCA Environmental Consultants; Dr Michael Dega, Scientific Consultant Services; Dr David Tuggle, retired; Aja Reyes, Cardno-GS; and the Chamorro archaeologists and University of Guam students who shared our research as friends and colleagues with staff at the Ritidian Unit of the Guam National Wildlife Refuge. Special thanks to Guampedia for their continued support.

The authors bear the responsibility for errors in fact or interpretation and for those supporters not mentioned here. Please note that this research does not represent the opinion or the policy of the US Fish and Wildlife Service or the US Navy and their subcontractors.

References

Amesbury, J. 2019. *Archaeology on the northern plateau of Guam*. Booklet prepared for the US Navy by Cardno-GS, Guam.

Bayman, J., M. Carson, J. Peterson, H. Kurashina and D. Doig 2010. University of Guam and University of Hawai'i Archaeological Field School at the Guam National Wildlife Refuge, Ritidian Unit, Territory of Guam: The 2009 & 2008 seasons. Unpublished report prepared for Guam National Wildlife Refuge.

Bayman, J., H. Kurashina, M.T. Carson, J.A. Peterson, D. Doig et al. 2012. Latte household economic organization at Ritidian, Guam National Wildlife Refuge, Mariana Islands. *Micronesica* 42(1/2):258–273.

Bayman, J., B. Dixon, S. Monton-Subias and N. Moragas Segura 2020. Colonial surveillance, *lancho*, and the perpetuation of intangible cultural heritage in Guam, Mariana Islands. In C. Beaule and J. Douglass (eds), *The global Spanish empire: Five hundred years of place making and pluralism*, pp. 222–241. University of Arizona Press, Tucson. doi.org/10.2307/j.ctv105bb41.14.

Butler, B. 1992. *An archaeological survey of Aguiguan (Aguijan) Northern Mariana Islands*. Micronesian Archaeological Survey Report Number 29. Division of Historic Preservation, Department of Community and Cultural Affairs, Saipan.

Butler, B. 1995. *Archaeological investigations in the Achugao and Matansa areas of Saipan, Mariana Islands*. Micronesian Archaeological Survey Report Number 30. Division of Historic Preservation, Department of Community and Cultural Affairs, Saipan.

Carson, M. 2010. Radiocarbon chronology with marine reservoir correction for the Ritidian archaeological site, Northern Guam. *Radiocarbon* 52(4):1627–1638. doi.org/10.1017/s0033822200056356.

Carson, M. 2012. Evolution of an Austronesian landscape: The Ritidian site in Guam. *Journal of Austronesian Studies* 3(1):55–86.

Carson, M. 2014. *First settlement of remote Oceania: Earliest sites in the Mariana Islands*. Springer, New York. doi.org/10.1007/978-3-319-01047-2.

Carson, M. 2017. Cultural spaces inside and outside caves: A study in Guam, Western Micronesia. *Antiquity* 91(356):421–441. doi.org/10.15184/aqy.2016.233.

Carson, M. 2018. *Lina'la' portraits of life at Litekyan*. Micronesian Area Research Center, University of Guam Press, Guam.

Coomans, P. 1995. History of the Mariana Island Mission for the 1667-1673 period. In R. Lévesque (ed.), *History of Micronesia: A collection of source documents. Volume 3: First real contact*. Document 1673L1. Lévesque Publications, Quebec.

Craib, J. 1986. Casas de los Antiguos: Social differentiation in protohistoric Chamorro society, Mariana Islands. Unpublished PhD thesis. University of Sydney, Australia.

Dasmarinas, G.P. 1595. *Boxer codex*. Record and manuscript at the Lilly Library, Indiana University, Bloomington.

DeFant, D. 2008. Early human burials from the Naton Beach site, Tumon Bay, Island of Guam, Mariana Islands. *Journal of Island and Coastal Archaeology* 3(1):149–153. doi.org/10.1080/15564890801990789.

Dega, M., D. Perzinski and J. Ferrugia 2017. *The Latte village of Garapan: Archaeological data recovery, Saipan Commonwealth of the Northern Mariana Islands*. Prepared for Imperial Pacific International (CNMI), LLC, Scientific Consulting Services, Inc., Honolulu.

Dickinson, W. 2000. Hydro-isostatic and tectonic influences on emergent Holocene paleoshorelines in the Mariana Islands, Western Pacific Ocean. *Journal of Coastal Research* 16:735–746.

Dickinson, W. 2001. Paleoshoreline record of relative Holocene sea levels on Pacific Islands. *Earth Science Review* 55:191–234. doi.org/10.1016/s0012-8252(01)00063-0.

Dixon, B. 2011. Ancient CHamoru warfare. Guampedia, last modified 24 April 2021. www.guampedia.com/ancient-guam-warfare.

Dixon, B. and M. Dega In press. Placing the early pre-Latte period site of San Roque on Saipan in its broader context: 1500–1100 B.C. In M. Napolitano and S. Fitzpatrick (eds), *When the wild winds blow: Micronesia colonization in Pacific context*. Society for American Archaeology, San Francisco.

Dixon, B. and L. Gilda 2011. A comparison of an inland Latte Period community to coastal settlement patterns observed on southern Guam. *People and Culture of Oceania* 27:65–86.

Dixon, B. and A. Jalandoni 2019. Traditional places in conflict: Ritidian, Guam. Paper presented at 'Disrupting paradise: The archaeology of the driest inhabited continent on Earth', the Australian Archaeological Association Annual Conference 2019, Gold Coast, 10–13 December.

Dixon, B. and R. Schaefer 2014. Reconstructing cultural landscapes for the Latte Period settlement of Ritidian: A hypothetical model in Northern Guam. In M. Carson (ed.), *Guam's hidden gem: Archaeological and historical studies at Ritidian,* pp. 64–73. British Archaeological Reports International Series, Oxford. doi.org/10.30861/9781407313054.

Dixon, B., T. Mangieri, E. McDowell, K. Paraso and T. Reith 2006. Latte Period domestic household activities and disposal patterns on the Micronesian island of Tinian, CNMI. *Micronesica* 39(1):55–71.

Dixon, B., H. Bartow, J. Coil, W. Dickinson, G. Murakami and J. Ward 2011a. Recognizing inland expansion of Latte Period agriculture from multi-disciplinary data on Tinian, Commonwealth of the Northern Mariana Islands. *Journal of Island and Coastal Archaeology* 6(3):375–397. doi.org/10.1080/15564894.2010.521539.

Dixon, B., R. Schaefer and T. McCurdy 2011b. *Level 1 archaeological reconnaissance of 800 acres within selected properties on Andersen Air Force Base, Guam. Volume 1: Narrative.* Cardno TEC Inc., Guam for SEARCH Inc., Honolulu.

Dixon, B., T. McCurdy, D. Welch, R. Jones and I. Nelson 2016. *Archaeological data recovery in support of construction for MILCON P-175, Andersen Air Force Base, Yigo, Guam.* Cardno TEC Inc., Guam.

Dixon, B., A. Jalandoni and C. Craft 2017. The archaeological remains of early modern Spanish colonialism on Guam and their implications. In M. Cruz Berrocal and C. Tsang (eds), *Historical archaeology of early modern colonialism in Asia–Pacific: The southwest Pacific and Oceanian regions*, Volume 1, pp. 195–218. University Press of Florida, Gainesville. doi.org/10.2307/j.ctvx07b3c.14.

Dixon, B., C. Walth, K. Mowrer and D. Welch 2019. *Afetna Point, Saipan: Archaeological investigations of a Latte Period village and historic context in the Commonwealth of the Northern Mariana Islands.* ArchaeoPress Access Archaeology, Oxford.

Egami, T. and F. Saito 1973. Archaeological excavation on Pagan in the Mariana Islands. *Journal of the Anthropological Society of Nippon* 81(3):203–226. doi.org/10.1537/ase1911.81.203.

Farrell, D. 2011. *History of the Mariana Islands to partition.* Public school system, Commonwealth of the Northern Mariana Islands, Saipan.

Farrell, D. 2012. *Tinian: A brief history.* Pacific Historic Parks, Honolulu.

Flexner, J. 2014. Historical archaeology, contact, and colonialism in Oceania. *Journal of Archaeological Research* 22:43–87. doi.org/10.1007/s10814-013-9067-z.

García, F. 2004 (1683). *The life and martyrdom of the venerable Father Diego Luis De San Vitores, S.J.* MARC Monograph Series No. 3. University of Guam Press, Guam.

Heathcote, G. 2006. *Taotao tagga': Glimpses of his life history, recorded in his skeleton.* Paper Number 3, Non-Technical Report Series. University of Guam, Mangilao.

Hezel, F. 2015. *When cultures clash: Revisiting the 'Spanish-Chamorro Wars'.* Northern Marianas Humanities Council, Saipan.

Hezel, F. 2016. *German rule in Micronesia.* FSM Historic Preservation Office, Pohnpei.

Hezel, F. and M. Driver 1988. From conquest to colonization: Spain in the Mariana Islands 1690–1740. *The Journal of Pacific History* 23(2):137–155. doi.org/10.1080/00223348808572585.

Hornbostel, H. 1924–25. Unpublished notes and catalogs. Library Department, Bernice P. Bishop Museum, Honolulu.

Hunter-Anderson, R. and D. Moore 2003. *Cultural resources Snake Barrier concept, Andersen Air Force Base, Guam.* Prepared for Innovative Technical Solutions, Inc. Walnut Creek, California by Micronesian Archaeological Research Services, Guam.

Jalandoni, A. 2011. The Casa Real site in Ritidian, Northern Guam: A historical context. *Philippine Quarterly of Culture and Society* 39:27–53.

Jalandoni, A. and J. Peterson 2013. Conflict at contact: Late 17th century Spanish missions and la Reducción in Northern Guam. Paper delivered at Society for American Archaeology Annual Meeting 3–7 April 2013, Honolulu, Hawaii.

Kime, P. 2020. Report claims Vietnam-era veterans were exposed to Agent Orange on Guam. *Military.com*, 11 May. www.military.com/daily-news/2020/05/11/report-claims-vietnam-era-veterans-were-exposed-agent-orange-guam.html.

Kurashina, H., J.A. Simons, J.A. Toenjes, J. Allen, S.S. Amesbury et al. (eds) 1990. *Archaeological investigations at the Naval Facility (NAVFAC) Ritidian Point, Guam, Mariana Islands.* Report prepared for United States Department of the Navy. Micronesian Area Research Center, University of Guam, Mangilao.

Liston, J. 2009. Cultural chronology of earthworks in Palau, Western Micronesia. *Archaeology of Oceania* 44:56–73. doi.org/10.1002/j.1834-4453.2009.tb00047.x.

Liston, J. 2014. Ritual use of Palau's monumental earthworks and leadership strategies. In H. Martinsson-Wallin and T. Thomas (eds), *Monuments and people in the Pacific*, pp. 101–128. Studies in Global Archaeology No. 20. Uppsala University, Sweden.

Liston, J. and H.D. Tuggle 2006. Prehistoric warfare in Palau. In E. Arkush and M.W. Allen (eds), *The archaeology of warfare: Prehistories of raiding and conquest*, pp. 148–183. University Press of Florida, Florida.

Morgan, W. 1988. *Prehistoric architecture in Micronesia.* University of Texas Press, Texas.

National Research Council 2005. *Assessment of the scientific information for the radiation exposure screening and education program.* The National Academies Press, Washington DC. www.nap.edu/catalog/11279/assessment-of-the-scientific-information-for-the-radiation-exposure-screening-and-education-program. doi.org/10.17226/11279.

Nunn, P. 2007. *Climate, environment and society in the Pacific during the last millennium.* Developments in Earth and Environmental Sciences 6. Elsevier, Amsterdam. doi.org/10.1016/s1571-9197(07)06001-6.

Nunn, P., R. Hunter-Anderson, M. Carson, F. Thomas, S. Ulm and M. Rowland 2007. Times of plenty, times of less: Last-millennium societal disruption in the Pacific Basin. *Human Ecology* 35(4):345–401. doi.org/10.1007/s10745-006-9090-5.

Peattie, M. 1988. *Nanyo the rise and fall of the Japanese in Micronesia 1885–1945.* University of Hawai'i Press, Honolulu.

Pigafetta, A. 1992. Magellan's voyage–primary account by Pigafetta–the Italian manuscript. In R. Lévesque (ed.), *History of Micronesia: A collection of source documents. Volume 1: European discovery.* Document 1521B1. Lévesque Publications, Quebec.

Pobre, J. 1992. The story of Fray Juan Pobre's stay at Rota in the Ladrone islands in 1602. In R. Lévesque (ed.), *History of Micronesia: A collection of source documents. Volume 3: First real contact.* Document 1602A. Lévesque Publications, Quebec.

Rainbird, P. 2004. *The archaeology of Micronesia.* Cambridge University Press, Cambridge.

Reed, E. 1952. *General report on archaeology and history of Guam.* Report prepared for Governor of Guam. US National Park Service, Washington, DC.

Reinman, F. 1977. *An archaeological survey and preliminary test excavations on the Island of Guam, Mariana Islands, 1965–1966*. Miscellaneous Publications No. 1. Micronesian Area Research Center, University of Guam, Mangilao.

Rogers, R. 1995. *Destiny's landfall: A history of Guam*. University of Hawai'i Press, Honolulu.

Russell, S. 1984. *From Arabawal to ashes: A brief history of Garapan Village, 1818 to 1945*. Micronesian Archaeological Survey Report Number 19. Division of Historic Preservation, Saipan.

Russell, S. 1998. *Tiempon I Manomofo'ona: Ancient Chamorro culture and history of the Northern Marianas Islands*. Micronesian Archaeological Survey Report 32. Division of Historic Preservation, Saipan.

Shell, R. 1999. The Marianas population decline: 17th century estimates. *The Journal of Pacific History* 34(3):291–305. doi.org/10.1080/00223349908572914.

Spoehr, A. 1957. *Marianas prehistory. Archaeological survey and excavations on Saipan, Tinian and Rota*. Fieldiana Anthropology 48. Chicago Natural History Museum, Chicago. doi.org/10.5962/bhl.title.3552.

Thompson, L. 1932. *Archaeology of the Marianas Islands*. Bernice P. Bishop Museum Bulletin 100. Bishop Museum Press, Honolulu.

Thompson, L. 1940. The function of Latte in the Marianas. *Journal of the Polynesian Society* 49:447–465.

Tomonari-Tuggle, M., T. Rieth, D. Tuggle, M. Bell and D. Knecht 2018. *A synthesis of archaeological inventory and evaluation efforts on the island of Guam. Volume II: AD 1521–1950*. Prepared by International Archaeology LLC, Honolulu.

Underwood, J. 1973. Population history of Guam: Context of microevolution. *Micronesica* 9(1):11–44.

Velarde, P.M. 1987. *The 'Reducción' of the Islands of the Ladrones, the discovery of the islands of the Palaos and other happenings*. Translated by E.F. Plaza and republished as Working Paper No. 51. Micronesian Area Research Center, University of Guam, Mangilao.

Vilar, M., F. Camacho, D. Santos, K. Lum and T. Schurr 2016. The origins and genetic distinctiveness of the Chamorros: A bi-parental analysis. University of Guam Presidential Lecture Series, 26 January 2016, Mangilao.

Walth, C. 2016. *Archaeological investigations at the Naton Beach site, Tumon, Guam. Volume II: The osteological analysis of human remains*. Prepared for Guam Hotel Okura, SWCA Environmental Consultants, Albuquerque.

York, R. and G. York 2014. *Slings and slingstones: The forgotten weapons of Oceania and the Americas*. Kent State University Press, Kent.

6

The *'enata* way of war: An ethnoarchaeological perspective on warfare dynamics in the Marquesas Islands

Guillaume Molle and Vincent Marolleau

Introduction

At the time of Western contact, warfare had become a critical feature of Polynesian chiefdoms, varying in both scale and intensity (Kirch 1984:197). East Polynesian societies have been described by early Western visitors as violent and often caught in a state of 'endemic warfare'. This has been archaeologically recognised through the emergence of fortified sites, some of which have developed in a unique way similar to the fortified villages or *pare* in Rapa Iti (Anderson and Kennett 2012). The famous Maori *pa* in Aotearoa/New Zealand have also captured the attention of scholars for more than a century (see Best 1975; Daugherty 1979).

The Marquesas group were among the Polynesian chiefdoms that cultivated a 'warrior spirit' (Dening 1978:134). Many observers related the blood thirst of the warriors, who proudly exhibited trophy skulls of their enemies, captured human victims for sacrifices at temples and led large, allied wars. But to what extent are these accounts trustworthy? And how do they really reflect the complex role of conflict and violence in the making of Marquesan culture? With the Tahitian chiefdoms, the traditional *'enata* society may be one of the best documented in central East Polynesia. *'Enata* is the indigenous word used to refer to the Marquesan people. Classic ethnographies (e.g. Handy 1923; Linton 1925) addressed the salience of conflicts; however, they attached little importance to understanding the societal dynamics both causing and deriving from warfare.

Kirch (1984:198) noted that Polynesian warfare has been extensively discussed through the lens of demographic and ecological pressures. These factors have long occupied a prominent position in historical narratives in New Zealand (Duff 1967; Vayda 1960, 1976) and Rapa Nui (McCoy 1979), and are found in a more nuanced fashion in studies of Hawai'i (Cordy 1974). Suggs (1961) drew on the correlation between population growth and land limitation to justify an intensification of warfare in the Marquesas Islands during this period of expansion. The ecological argument of environmental constraints was also employed by anthropologist Sahlins (1958). The harsh environmental conditions in the Marquesas guaranteed the emergence of such a perspective. The *fenua 'enata* (traditional territory) consists of 12 inhabited islands, which lack both coral reefs and lagoons (Figure 6.1). Valleys radiate from central volcanic cones and are circumscribed by steep slopes, while the cliffs plunge directly into the sea on the coastline. This particular environmental setting led Ottino (1996:60) to characterise the sociopolitical organisation as a 'valley system' in which the valley would form an exclusive and limited territory occupied, used and transformed by *'enata*. The rugged character of the Marquesan landscape is intensified by regular climatic crises and droughts, which severely impact vegetation development and crop culture (Allen 2010).

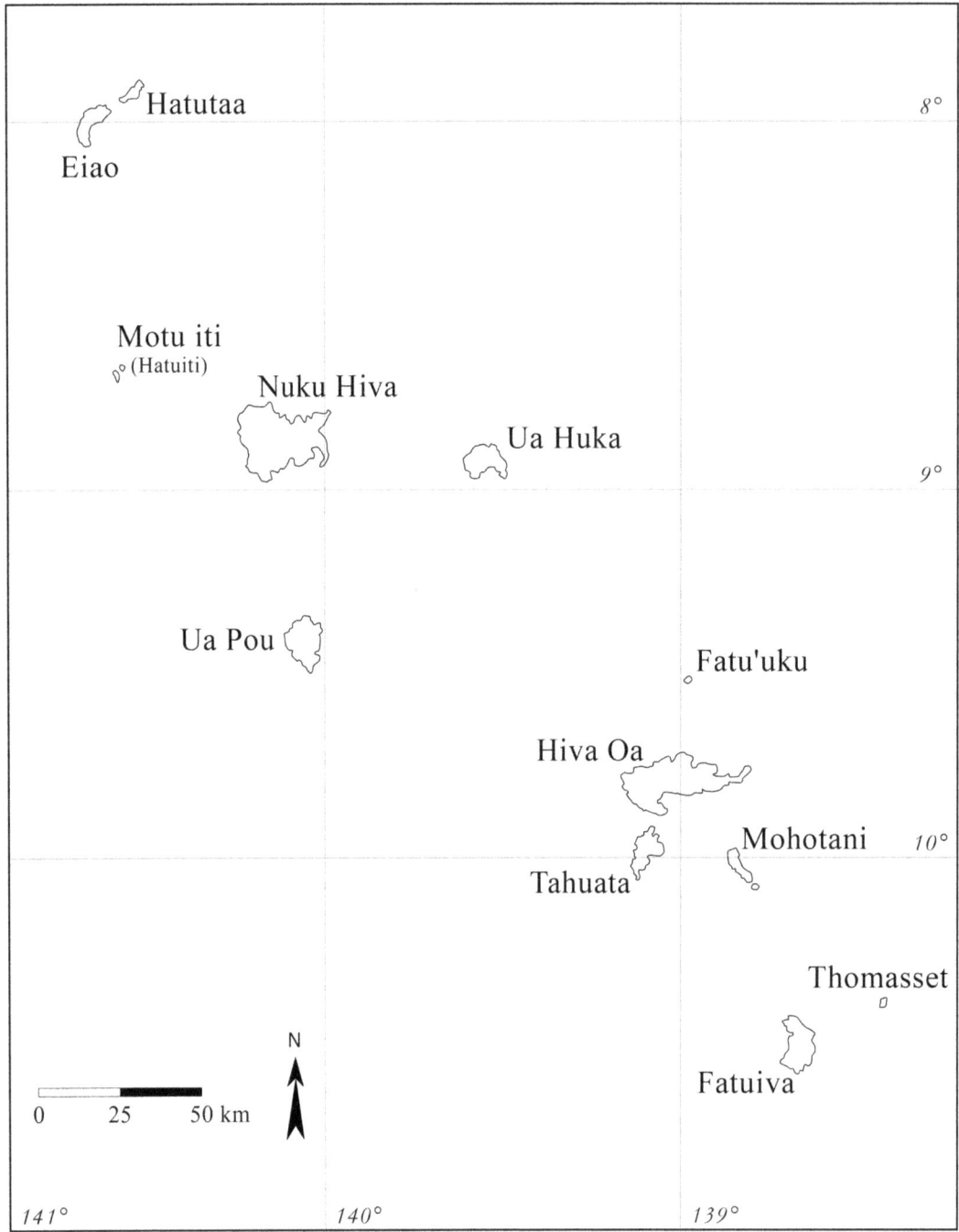

Figure 6.1. Map of the Marquesas Islands.
Source: Guillaume Molle and Vincent Marolleau, adapted from Molle (2011a).

It therefore makes sense to factor in ecological explanations to explain the emergence of warfare within the archipelago; however, as Kirch (1984:195) has argued, neither the cause nor function of warfare in Polynesia can be explained or understood from purely demographic or ecological perspectives. Kirch further insisted that internal sociopolitical dynamics facilitated the pursuit of *mana* and prestige, status achievement, usurpation of power and challenge to the chieftainship. Societal mechanisms as alternative instigators of conflict demand more detailed investigations of the local cultural context. The rich ethnohistorical material concerning the Marquesas also presents insights, which allowed Dening (1980) and Thomas (1990) to substantially enhance our understanding of *'enata* society prior to European contact—thus opening new avenues for exploring the nature and form of conflict in the archipelago from a refined systemic perspective (and building on an ambition of historical anthropology as described by Thomas (1996)), which we discuss in the first part of this chapter.

Despite substantial ethnohistorical information, the manner in which ancient warfare materialised in the archaeological record remains overlooked. This can be attributed to the limited evidence of material conflict in the archaeological record of the Marquesas. Reassuringly, researchers have recorded fortified sites and defensive features in the context of general surveys and settlement pattern analyses, which provided a basis for local classifications (Bellwood 1972; Green 1967; Sinoto 1970; Suggs 1961); however, no study has systematically focused on the archaeology of Marquesan warfare nor attempted to date the development of such sites. This clearly creates a gap in our general understanding of *'enata* chiefdoms that must be prioritised in future research. The second part of this chapter will synthesise available archaeological information about defensive sites while highlighting some theoretical and methodological considerations.

The ambition of our synthesis is nonetheless hampered by both the absence of clear chronological context for the development of fortified sites and the inherent limitations of ethnohistorical analysis in inferring early historical processes. This means that the proposed reconstruction of warfare dynamics concerns only the last pre-European period (roughly defined from the mid-seventeenth to late eighteenth century CE) when conflict became institutionalised. Forms of warfare and conflict may have existed in earlier *'enata* society as the Marquesas Islands may have been discovered as early as 900 CE based on results from the Hane site (Conte and Molle 2014), and the archipelago was surely occupied by 1000–1100 CE (Allen 2004; Rolett 1998). However, archaeological evidence for this is lacking and we can reasonably suppose that the causal mechanisms of early warfare, if they existed, differed from those operating at the time of Western contact.

Society, food and forms of conflict in the Marquesas Islands

The *'enata* chiefdoms

Anthropologists have examined the contribution of different societal dynamics to conflict in the Marquesas Islands. In his famous article on status rivalry and cultural evolution in Polynesia, Irving Goldman (1955) came to define the traditional Marquesan society as an archetype of the so-called 'open chiefdoms', placing the *'enata* culture in a transitioning phase towards a more stratified society. By setting status rivalry as the main cause for culture change, Goldman emphasised the role of outstanding warriors in counterbalancing the traditional chiefly authority and creating a fluid situation in which power could be achieved through 'military' performance. Marshall Sahlins (1958) also supported the notion of open chiefdom but further stressed the deterministic role of environmental settings in the emergence of Marquesan intertribal conflicts.

Nicholas Thomas (1990, 1996) later criticised Goldman's categorisation, notably for its overreliance on secondary ethnographic material collected by anthropologists E.S.C. Handy and R. Linton from the Bishop Museum (Handy 1923; Linton 1925). The detailed ethnohistorical analyses of Greg Dening (1980) and Thomas (1990) redressed previous inaccuracies and redefined the sociopolitical dynamics operating within the 'enata chiefdoms, while going beyond the simple notion of status rivalry. Among the critical points raised by Thomas especially is the competitive character of the 'enata society that manifested at both internal and external levels of the tribal organisation.

By European contact, 'enata chiefdoms (or mata'eina'a) displayed an organisation distinct from neighbouring groups. While Polynesian chiefs traditionally held both secular and sacred authority over the group, Marquesan haka'iki (chiefs) seem to have been progressively deprived of these functions, to the benefit of other leaders, who achieved higher rank through performance and strategy. Among these alternate leaders were the powerful tau'a who appropriated most of the religious authority. Tau'a were shamanistic priests chosen by the deities themselves during intense phases of inspiration. The spirit of the god was believed to reside in the tau'a's own stomach, thus creating a physical connection with the individual, now a very sacred figure. These inspired priests were in charge of many important rituals, including mortuary treatments of high-ranked individuals but also fertility renewal ceremonies through the placing or removing of tapu (Handy 1923:106). Allen (2010) has hypothesised that a series of environmental crises, including long periods of drought, may have diminished the confidence of people in the chief's ability to maintain equilibrium and ensure the survival of the group. 'Enata would have sought the intervention of tau'a, who held more prestige and authority thanks to their direct connection with the deities (Allen 2010:95). Tau'a were the most feared individuals in the tribe mostly because they decided on human sacrifices and would send a group of warriors to capture their victims. Interestingly, during the nineteenth century, powerful tau'a were also in charge of negotiating treaties with Europeans and peace treaties were often agreed upon in their name, another form of agency that they usurped from the chiefs (Molle 2011a).

Among the highest-ranked individuals in the group were the war leaders or toa. These were distinguished as professionals serving under a chief, compared to the common fighters, who were only summoned at times of war and otherwise had other daily activities. As the chief rarely participated in battle, the direction of combat fell into the hands of the toa in charge of gathering, leading and stimulating the men, as well as organising the defence of the community (Handy 1923:126). Due to their critical function within the group, the toa had many privileges, which placed them among the Marquesan elite. Such prestige was acquired by demonstrating prowess in combat for which they could be rewarded with land and servants. In addition to becoming landowners, accessing higher ranks allowed them to marry women of chiefly families, guaranteeing their social position through strategic alliances. Warriors also achieved higher rank by accumulating mana. Capturing enemies during war usually served sacrificial purposes, although it aided the toa in appropriating their mana by preserving their skulls—heads were said to be the seat of the soul essence (Delmas 1927; Gracia 1843). On many European engravings, warriors are depicted with their weapons such as the long and finely carved wooden head clubs (u'u), spears and slings, and war accessories (conch shells) and dresses (Figure 6.2). Weapons were not only tools for war but also symbolic artefacts charged with the mana of their owners and as such were often displayed in public events (see Mills 2009). The main insignias were the ta'avaha headdress, made of black cock's feathers atop a pearl-shell ornamented with tortoiseshell, and the white or red tapa cloak (Handy 1923:128). Weapons and accessories were kept in the warriors' house, a part of the chief's properties, where the toa shared their meals together and remained secluded in wartime.

Figure 6.2. Mouina, chief warrior of the Tayehs (Tei'i tribe, Nuku Hiva).
Source: Lithography by William Strickland after a drawing of David Porter, in Porter (1822).

As illustrated in this brief review, many tensions traversed the Marquesan organisation, firstly between hereditary chiefs and shamanistic priests, secondly between traditional leaders and achieved-status individuals. Among those, landowners (*akati'a*) seem to have formed a category of their own. By inheriting and/or acquiring parts of lands, *akati'a* capitalised means of production and played a pivotal role in the chiefdom. As a result, the dispersion of traditional chiefly powers that may have started as early as the fifteenth century ended into a 'broadening of the pool of potential secular leaders' (Allen 2010:96). *'Enata* society was consequently characterised by high performativity. Competitive performances, either at an individual or collective level, served the pursuit of prestige and manifested in both feasting cycles and warfare (Kirch 1991:131).

Feast, food and conflict

Feasts (*koina*) had become an essential feature of *'enata* lives by the eighteenth century. They celebrated various occasions such as harvests, betrothal, marriage or rites of passage for members of the chiefly family (Handy 1923:203). The most important was the memorialisation, and often deification, of great chiefs and *tau'a*. These lavish commemorative feasts (called *mau*) required much labour and resources, including human victims for sacrifices, which further demonstrated the power of the honoured individual.

These gatherings occurred at the tribal *tohua*, a large community place comprised of a central court surrounded by houses on stone platforms reserved for each social and gender category. The increasing importance of feasting cycles is reflected in the rapid development of *tohua* in all inhabited valleys of the archipelago (Linton 1925). Festivities could last for several days and involved dances, chants, sports competitions, and oratory and ritual performances. According to Western observers, the display of foodstuffs usually marked the peak of the event. Large quantities of food were brought to the *tohua* to be shared by members of the tribe with visitors from other communities (Crook 2007:83; Radiguet 1882:193; Thomas 1996:73). Generous providers, often landowners, used such occasions to exhibit their economic wealth and power. By offering crops, fruits, fish and sometimes prestigious goods such as pigs, they intended to rival and exceed those presented by the chiefs and, by doing so, to achieve status. Demonstration of this kind relates to a unique form of 'performative agency', which is not uncommon in Polynesian contexts (see Bell 1931). The display of food during feasts at the *tohua* allowed individuals and social groups to show generosity, thereby accumulating *mana* and prestige. Therefore, it relates to a form of nonviolent—and, in a way, invisible—conflict.

However, sometimes violent actions would result. Thomas (1990:78) argued that the two main forms of intertribal warfare, raids and conquests, derived from socio-economic endeavours stemming from the competitive nature of Marquesan feasts. Collective labour required to organise these events aimed to demonstrate the power of the community to visitors. The large-scale presentation of food tacitly obligated the invited groups to return the favour, a subtle but critical feature of the Polynesian exchange systems. They were then expected to host an event of at least equal or superior quality. This escalating intertribal competition, centred on food presentation, was a part of the higher stakes for chiefdoms engaging in a productive economy, of which a large part was eventually allocated to the *koina*. Intertribal competition appears to be a common incentive for raids, that first aimed to destroy resources (mostly breadfruit and coconut trees) of other communities, preventing them from fulfilling their obligation. Additionally, the uncertain nature of the Marquesan climate, with spatially and temporally variable rainfall, certainly influenced the production and social organisation (Allen 2010). From this constrained environmental context, *'enata* may have found another reason to conquer lands and resources.

Forms and consequences of conflict

It appears that conflict would arise from specific motives embedded into sociopolitical and religious strategies. Such a simple explanation could mask the complexity of *'enata* warfare. Western accounts convey a sense of 'disorganised' conflict, which almost certainly derives from intersections between personal and collective endeavours. Some individuals did not hesitate to engage in hostile activities for personal motivation, like retaliation or land dispute; on the other hand, large-scale conflict such as conquest, while primarily a community engagement, served personal endeavours of the involved individuals (chiefs, *toa*, priests).

However, the ethnohistorical records from the nineteenth century must be treated with caution as they also reflect new patterns of violence emerging within a society already destabilised by European contact and its dramatic consequences, especially demographic (Molle and Conte 2015). New forms of conflict arose following the installation of colonial administration and missionaries, and the breaking of the traditional *tapu* system and socio-religious order. Consequently, 'the violence Marquesans showed to outsiders (*te aoe*) was different from the violence they showed to themselves (*te enata*)' (Dening 1978:137).

Minor raids were conducted, mostly aimed at capturing unarmed and isolated individuals from an enemy tribe, wandering alone by the shore or in the valley (Crook 2007:84; Stewart 1833:273). These raids were often motivated by the capture of women and children, a quarrel between families or an act of revenge (Robarts 1974:60). However, most of these operations served to capture victims for human sacrifice (*heana*) held on the *me'ae*. In which case, they were called *e ika*, or 'fishing parties', which refers to the symbolic treatment of the victims—they were hanged by their jaw from banyan trees with large wooden or bone fish hooks (Dening 1980:55; Tautain 1896:448). These captures were usually commanded by the *tau'a* in charge of the sacrificial ceremonies and consisted of isolated ambushes conducted by a small group of warriors travelling quickly by land or sea. The practice of *e ika* was institutionalised within *'enata* chiefdoms and pertained to the overall *tapu* system that governed the communities (Dening 1978).

Other forms of conflict involved collective actions with larger groups of warriors entering deep into enemy territory, intending to either destroy or seize land and resources, often ending in bloodshed. Because these needed to be well coordinated, these operations were decided upon by the chief and his/her council, including executives *tuhuna*, warriors and *tau'a* (Clavel 1885:49; Handy 1923:56; Radiguet 1882:160; Winter 1882:298). Consequently, these forms of warfare had become institutionalised by the end of the eighteenth century.

As previously mentioned, the destruction of enemy crops and harvests were common motivators for raiding parties, although the number of warriors involved would have been limited as such actions required rapidity. These raids often took place at night, warriors moving through the valley and systematically 'destroying the breadfruit tree by stripping off the bark, and the cocoa nut tree by beating to pieces the heart which grows between the branches' (Crook cited in Thomas 1996:100; see also Robarts 1974:60). The *ma* pits, in which breadfruit paste was stored as a basic resource, were commonly targeted.

The open conflicts—skirmishes and wars of conquest—need be distinguished. The former occurred when no peaceful agreement could be reached. The decision to go to war was made and all were warned of the place and time of the upcoming battle. Various ceremonies accompanied the preparation of the warriors and included many offerings to the gods (Crook 2007:84; Delmas 1927:141; Jouan 1858:319; Handy 1923:131). Groups of warriors led by the *toa* reached the location, which was usually an open space in the uplands between valleys. The initial phase consisted of the mocking and provocation of adversaries through face pulling, shouting or the performance of belligerent dances (Handy 1923:132; Porter 1834: 188). Sometimes, only the *toa*, as the representative of the tribes, engaged in battle and the conflict abruptly ended, depending on the outcome of the fight. At other times, the remaining warriors rushed in to the fight, armed with their head clubs and spears. Such combat could last for some time, small groups chasing one another through the bushes, retreating then attacking again (Gracia 1843:84). Skirmishes of this kind were not particularly violent—if one or two warriors were killed then parties would retreat and regroup and the fight would continue the following day, until they called a truce.

Wars of conquest on the other hand, while not as frequent, were deadlier. Chiefdoms or alliances of chiefdoms would engage in conquest to seize enemy land and subjugate populations. These large-scale conflicts, in which all of the tribes of an island could be involved, epitomise organised and high-intensity warfare (Clavel 1885:49; Crook 2007:83; Stewart 1833:273). These massive assaults were carried out by both land and sea. Although there is no evidence of maritime warfare *per se*, attacks on the valleys by sea served both to push enemies inland and prevent escape. Descriptions of Marquesan war canoes differ between authors, some stating that they could be operated by 140 warriors (Handy 1923:160). This is likely an overstatement as Vancouver (1801:140) reported only 20 men on such canoes. Success in entering a valley consequently led to the slaughter of the whole population in addition to the systematic destruction of buildings and resources. Such massacres were considered a source of great prestige for the victors (Jouan 1858:126).

The degree of violence in Marquesan conflict is difficult to reconcile in light of contradictory Western accounts. Many depict an extremely violent *'enata* society (a character one could attribute to a colonialist attempt to denigrate islanders). Resident Lawson reported that the Naiki slaughtered 50 people from the Maku-oho tribe at a feast on Ua Huka in 1830 CE (Lawson 1867). Victims of *e ika* were also numerous and Dening (1980:248) proposed an estimate of 260 individuals known to have been sacrificed for the period between 1798 and 1842 CE. One must differentiate between the ferocious nature of such actions and their demographic impact. The modes of combat described above do not support the idea of conflicts as deadly as some authors have suggested. Instead, large-scale massacres took place only in the exceptional context of the 'extirpation' of some groups from their land (Crook 2007). Rather than a direct impact on mortality, warfare undeniably contributed to the geographic mobility of social groups within the archipelago, a proposition well supported in the literature (Fanning 1833; Jouan 1858; Porter 1822; Robarts 1974). Wars of conquest could lead to either the appropriation of the defeated group or their banishment. Regarding the relative fluidity of the *'enata* organisation and the permeability of social relationships, allegiances to chiefs seem to have been readily denied, which surely favoured group mobility. Robarts (1974) mentioned people frequently changing residencies, either abandoning their valleys for another, or adopting new leadership. Following war, people were often forced to flee and seek asylum with their relatives or allies (Gracia 1843:85; Kellum-Ottino 1971:32,147; Vincendon-Dumoulin 1843:238). The changing sociopolitical map of the Marquesas in the nineteenth century reveals such patterns of inter-valley and inter-island migrations (Pechberty 1995a, 1995b).

Related ethnohistorical accounts also seem to overstate the role of introduced guns in indigenous conflict during the nineteenth century. In 1813 CE, Captain David Porter of the US Navy arrived in Nuku Hiva, took possession of the whole group (an annexing gesture that was not recognised by his government) and constructed a fortified base in the bay of Taiohae. Having concluded an alliance with the local chief Keatonui, Porter found himself involved in a series of conflicts opposing the tribe of Taioahe with their Hapa'a and Taipi enemies. Following the American commodore's military success and the demonstration of the efficiency of his weapons, *'enata* started to no longer see rifles as simple commodities but rather as an exchanged artefact with high-ranked value, therefore giving rise to a new 'musket economy' (Thomas 1991:100). Over the next two decades, Marquesan chiefs acquired many guns that were redistributed among warriors and allied tribes and by 1840 CE, 'there were several thousand [muskets] on Nukuhiva alone and every warrior on Tahuata had two or three' (Dening 1980:244). The hand-to-hand fights progressively disappeared after the introduction of rifles, most efficient when used at a distance through gunports at the fortified sites. Yet, introduction of muskets did not necessarily contribute to an increase in mortality. For Radiguet (1882:135), traditional weapons like clubs, spears or slingshots caused more damage and lethal or incurable injuries than rifles, for which accuracy was often inconsistent among Marquesan warriors.

War-induced mortality is nuanced and should be examined from an integrated perspective. Early nineteenth-century accounts show a continuation, and sometimes intensification, of warfare throughout the archipelago while also focusing on the dramatic famines caused by droughts (see Allen 2010). The constant destruction of food resources during conflict accentuated precarious situations resulting from climatic uncertainties. Through a detailed examination of the Ua Huka case study, Molle and Conte (2015) have suggested that it was the systemic connection between these factors (warfare, drought and famines) rather than the violence of conflict itself that impacted local demographics. These dynamics were certainly well engaged at least from the seventeenth century, but were surely aggravated by the later introduction of European diseases, alcohol and opium (see Rallu 1990; Saura 2002: 61).

Tracking warfare in the archaeological landscape

Some considerations on the archaeological signals for warfare in the Marquesas

From an archaeological perspective, identifying 'enata forms of conflict is quite problematic as the common warfare proxies prove limited in the archipelago, particularly in relation to human remains. Analysis of skeletal trauma (see Scott and Buckley 2014), modes of inhumation and demographic representation in burials (Pietrusewsky 1986; see also Sand et al. 2006 for a case study on Wallis/'Uvea) could theoretically inform us on ancient warfare. However, the complexity of 'enata mortuary treatments, coupled with current issues of representation leave us very few clues to definitively identify the burials of warriors or war victims (Maureille and Sellier 1996; Molle 2011a; Vigneron 1985). Marquesan trophy skulls are the only 'artefacts' that attest to the special treatment of human remains connected to processes of war (Figure 6.3). Handy (1923:136) claimed that some raids focused on collecting skulls; however, dedicated headhunting is not clearly evidenced in the ethnohistorical literature and it may have occurred in the context of large-scale wars. That being said, trophy skulls provide us with little information about the form of conflict itself, but mostly represent an output embedded in socio-religious activities (see Boes and Sears 1996; Valentin and Rolland 2011).

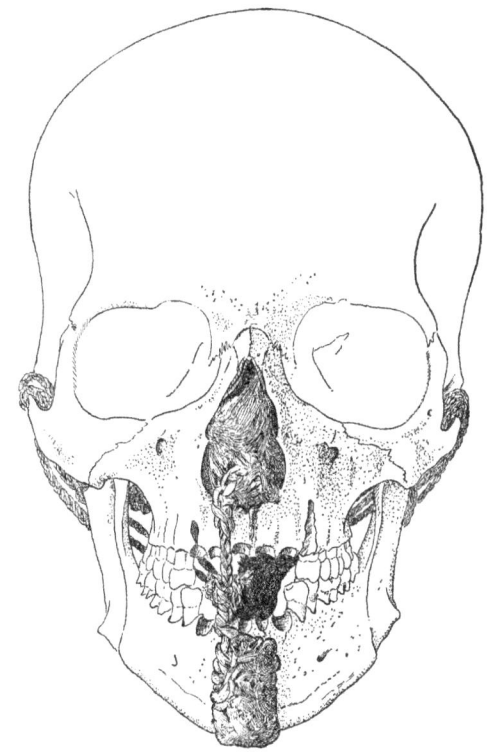

Figure 6.3. Marquesan trophy skull.
Source: Suggs (1961:169).

Archaeologists often rely on the monumental remains of warfare, even if these remains only relate to 'organised forms of conflict' to the exclusion of the other types of hostile interactions described above. Small-scale raiding parties and skirmishes left no particular material evidence. Conversely, the archaeological signature for warfare becomes more visible when it occurred at a larger scale and on a collective level. Both the multiplication and repetition of violent attacks may force a community to engage in the construction of war-oriented structures, for which collective labour is justified. This is connected to another bias in the archaeological record: those sites had defensive functions, either to stop or slow the enemies down and to provide refuge for the non-combatants of the group. Consequently, they exclusively inform the single perspective of the group that endured violence. On the other hand, identifying the agency of the aggressors is challenging as no traceable residues remain—the destruction of natural resources or even storage structures are impossible to detect in the Marquesan record. Yet, wars of conquest often resulted in the destruction of symbols of identity, such as temples. *Me'ae* sites, as critical places of interaction with gods and ancestors, were often targeted, the stone images placed down, platforms plundered and human remains stolen or destroyed (Stewart 1833:215). In 1897 CE, German ethnographer Karl von Den Steinen (1925–1928) recorded oral traditions connected to the *me'ae* Iipona in Puamau valley of Hiva Oa. Probably during the eighteenth century, a conflict erupted between three local chiefs from the Naiki tribe of Puamau and their neighbours from the west coast of the island. The Naiki were defeated and forced to flee the valley. It is said that the new occupants transformed the Iipona chiefly residence into a *me'ae* with platforms named after the victors. The site of Iipona is notably famous for its large red-tuff human figures or *tiki*, standing on the stone platforms. One example supposedly represents Takaii, a prestigious ancestor of the clan who took possession of the land after this war. Excavations suggest that the only broken figure found at the site, the one of Maiauto, one of the three Naiki chiefs who started the conflict, was intentionally left at the feet of Takaii as a reminder of his defeat (Ottino 1996:364). Such symbolic actions, especially when they occurred at sacred *me'ae* sites, would certainly reveal the behaviour of the victors, although difficult to recognise based on the archaeology alone. The supposed existence of pits serving as prisons for captives could also reflect the agency of attackers. Some pits have been identified as such, due to their large dimensions and greater width at the base, dissimilar to traditional *ma* storage pits (Butaud and Jacq 2010; Chavaillon and Olivier 2007:76, 165; Conte et al. 2001:89; Maric and Noury 2002:48) but we lack ethnohistorical information on this matter.

As a result, current limitations in the material record, partly deriving from the local forms of conflict, incite us to rather speak of an 'archaeology of defensive warfare' in the case of the Marquesas Islands.

Archaeology of defensive warfare

Probably from the sixteenth century CE onwards, increasing intertribal warfare and violence triggered the construction of 'defensive structures', a general term encompassing various types of sites. We hereafter define a defensive system as a combination of features scattered across the territory (usually the valley) that fulfilled three main functions: (1) observing and signalling the approach of enemies; (2) stopping or slowing down the progress of enemies; and (3) protecting resources and non-combatant members of the community. Although some defensive features may have been set up to protect individual properties, the implementation of such large-scale systems was a collective effort initiated by the ruling elite and involved community labour. As warfare became a highly dynamic process, defensive systems were likely subject to constant changes including rearrangements, reconstructions and relocations. Locations of these structures derive from their functions and thus tend to take advantage of environmental conditions and features.

They further demonstrate adaptive responses to the emergence of specific spatial patterns in the attacks, either by sea or by land. As such, they evidence the strategic use of territory and show critical developments in local settlement patterns, which archaeologists attempt to reconstruct.

Building on archaeological surveys throughout the archipelago, Table 6.1 summarises 'defensive structures' securely identified as such by various authors. In our current state of knowledge, 37 sites fall into this category. Larger numbers of sites on Ua Huka and Hiva Oa likely derive from more extensive surveys on these two islands. We then must acknowledge a potential bias towards Fatu Hiva and Tahuata, where systematic inventories are yet to be undertaken. As recordings are heterogeneous, we only retained the general types of site proposed by archaeologists. However, as discussed below, some sites may have had multiple functions, thus blurring the categories previously defined by Suggs (1961), Green (1967), Sinoto (1970) and Bellwood (1972).

Table 6.1. List of Marquesan defensive sites identified as such in the archaeological literature.

Island	Valley, ID of the site	Type	Archaeological features	References
Ua Huka	Hanaei, HNE-42 and -43	observation post	walled terraces	Molle 2011b
Ua Huka	Hanahouua, HNA-22	observation post	stone platform	Molle 2011b
Ua Huka	Vainaonao, VAN-34	observation post	stone platform	Molle 2011b
Ua Huka	Vainaonao, VAN-51	fortified site	stone walls and terraces	Molle 2011b
Ua Huka	Hane, HIT-2 and -3	observation post	walled terraces; *ua ma*	Molle 2011b; Maric and Noury 2002
Ua Huka	Hane, Penau ridge	transformed ridge	trenches; stone platforms	Sinoto 1970
Ua Huka	Hinitaihava, HTV-31 and -32	observation post	walled terraces	Molle 2011b
Ua Huka	Hiniaehi, Mouka Tapu	observation post	stone walls and platforms	Molle 2011b
Ua Huka	Vaikivi, VKV-8	breastwork	stone wall	Conte et al. 2001
Ua Huka	Teanaonamaui	fortified site	trenches; stone walls and platforms; *ua ma*	Butaud and Jacq 2010; Molle 2011a
Ua Huka	Mahaki	refuge/fortified site	trench; stone walls; *ua ma*	Molle 2011b; Molle and Marolleau, In press
Nuku Hiva	Taiohae, NTa1	observation post	trench; terrace	Suggs 1961
Nuku Hiva	Taiohae, NTa10	fortified site	trenches; stone platforms	Suggs 1961
Nuku Hiva	Taiohae, NTa11	fortified site	trenches; stone walls and platforms	Suggs 1961
Nuku Hiva	Hatiheu, Teaka'ua	fortified site	stone walls	Suggs 1961
Ua Pou	Hakahetau, site 73 (Vaiponiu)	'fort'	stone platform	Linton 1925
Ua Pou	Hakahetau, site 74 (Totamahiti)	'fort'	stone platform	Linton 1925
Ua Pou	Hakahetau, site 75 (Hapava)	'fort'/observation post/refuge site	stone walls and platforms	Linton 1925
Ua Pou	Hakahau, site 88 (Hautemumu)	'fort'	stone platform	Linton 1925
Ua Pou	Hakahau, site 89 (Kuatau)	'fort'	stone platform	Linton 1925
Ua Pou	Hakao'oka, Teniuaefiti	observation post/refuge site	stone platforms	Ottino and De Bergh 1990

Island	Valley, ID of the site	Type	Archaeological features	References
Hiva Oa	Atuona, B09-02-03	observation post	stone platform	Chavaillon and Olivier 2007
Hiva Oa	Atuona, B09-05	transformed ridge	trenches; stone platforms	Linton 1925; Chavaillon and Olivier 2007
Hiva Oa	Atuona, B09-30	transformed ridge	trenches; stone platforms; *ua ma*	Chavaillon and Olivier 2007
Hiva Oa	Tehutu, B08-05-03	observation post	stone platforms	Chavaillon and Olivier 2007
Hiva Oa	Taaoa, B05-02-19	observation post	walled terraces	Chavaillon and Olivier 2007
Hiva Oa	Taaoa, B05-03-01	fortified site	stone platforms	Chavaillon and Olivier 2007
Hiva Oa	Eiaone, B31-01	transformed ridge/refuge site	trenches; stone walls and platforms	Chavaillon and Olivier 2007; Millerstrom 1985
Hiva Oa	Hanaiapa	fortified site	stone walls, incl. loopholes	Sinoto 1970; Peltier 1973
Hiva Oa	Hanaiapa, Tauiti	fortified site	stone walls, incl. loopholes	Sinoto 1970; Peltier 1973
Hiva Oa	Hanaiapa, B39-06-01	fortified site	stone walls	Sinoto 1970; Peltier 1973; Chavaillon and Olivier 2007
Hiva Oa	Hanatekua, Pa 1	fortified site	stone walls, incl. loopholes	Bellwood 1972
Hiva Oa	Hanatekua, Pa 2	fortified site	stone walls and platforms	Bellwood 1972
Hiva Oa	Tahauku, B10-01-03	fortified site	stone walls	Chavaillon and Olivier 2007; Linton 1925
Hiva Oa	Hanamenu, B55-01	fortified site	stone platforms	Chavaillon and Olivier 2007
Hiva Oa	Hanamenu, site 162	'fort'	stone walls and platforms	Linton 1925
Hiva Oa	Hanapeteo, site 154	fortified site	stone walls, incl. loopholes; stone platforms	Linton 1925

Source: Authors' summary of data from citations throughout table.

Note: 'Fort' was the generic term used by Linton (1925) and he rarely distinguished between a fortified site, observation post and a refuge. As some of these sites have not been described since then, we chose to use his term until further studies can better detail structure function. *Ua ma* were storage pits for the fermented paste of the breadfruit. With the exception of sites reported by Linton (1925) and Suggs (1961), the site IDs used in this table come from the official recordings by the Direction de la Culture et du Patrimoine in Tahiti, in charge of the archaeological inventory of French Polynesia.

Observation posts

Observing the movement of enemies was crucial during wartime. As risk of violent raids or conquest increased, it became essential to spot any hostile movement by land or sea in order to alert the community and give them time to respond. Watchers usually beat drums or blew conch shell trumpets to warn people down in the valley. Identifying observations posts in the archaeological landscape is not easy and we often rely on the geographic location of sites to hypothesise a lookout function. Some simple low stone platforms or pavements have been recorded on high ridges between valleys or at elevated locations overlooking a valley. In Hanaei valley, Ua Huka, an isolated site on the northern crest comprised of a few stone borders and a flat area, can be found. The location offers a panorama not only of the valley itself from the coast to the inner caldera, but also of neighbouring valleys to the south. For these reasons it has been tentatively identified as an observation post (Molle 2011b:219). Local informants on Ua Huka also reported a series of small square platforms standing at regular intervals along the highest ridge surrounding Vaipaee, from where warriors would have maintained access to the valley under surveillance (Molle 2011b:104). A group of terraces and platforms standing on the narrow ridge overlooking the southern valleys of Ua Huka probably served the same function (Figure 6.4). We lack detailed descriptions of such structures in early historical accounts but it is likely that some lookouts were simply built with perishable materials, thus leaving no discernible remains. Furthermore, many strategic environmental features also served as natural observation posts and did not require any additional construction. An oral tradition on Ua Huka recalls that the promontory of Hatuana, at the south-east end of the island, served for controlling and preventing attacks from the Taipi coming on their canoes from Nuku Hiva (Kellum-Ottino 1971; Molle and Conte 2011).

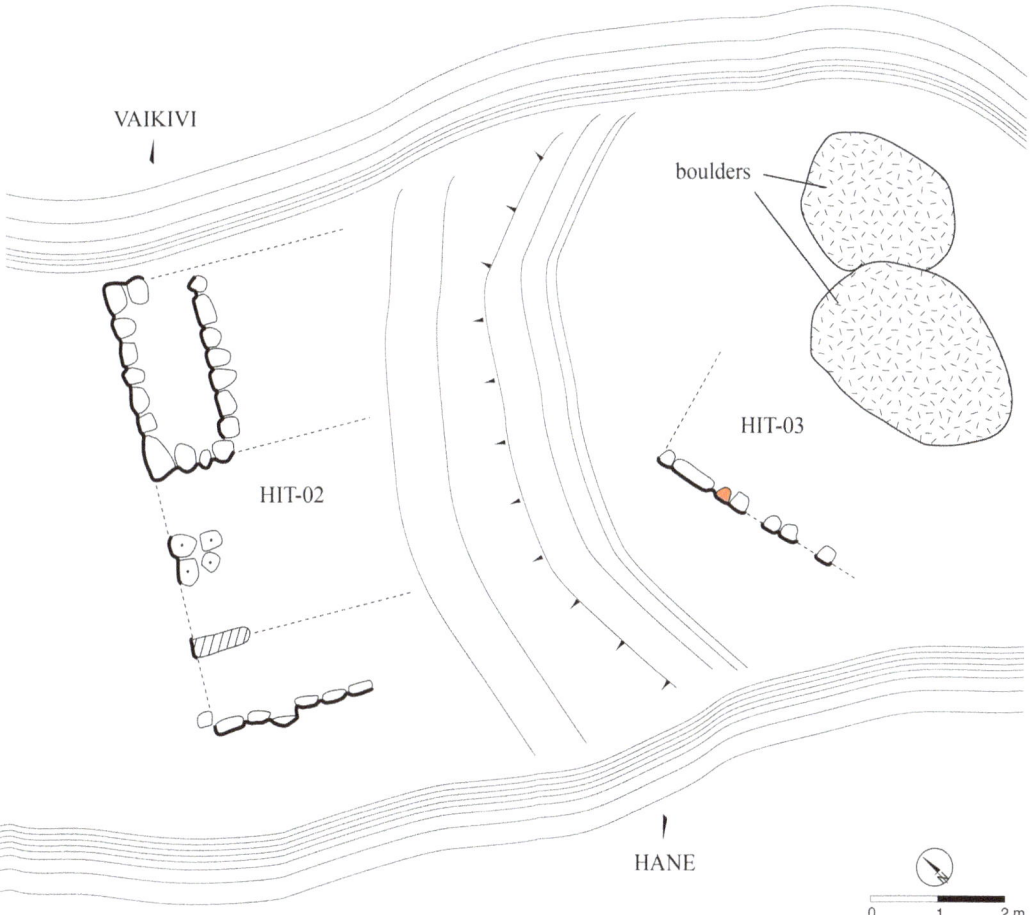

Figure 6.4. Map of observation posts on the Penau ridge, Ua Huka.
Source: Guillaume Molle and Vincent Marolleau, adapted from Molle (2011b).

Stone walls and stockades

Numerous remnant stone walls are visible in Marquesan valleys, with the majority associated with horticultural practices and delineated gardens. In some cases though, stone walls were erected to prevent access to particular areas in the villages while attempting to stop or slow down attackers. Stewart came upon an extended breastwork of this kind in Ho'oumi (Stewart 1833:313).

Whether such stone walls were replaced by wooden fences or not remains uncertain, but stockades were witnessed by Europeans in the early nineteenth century, attesting the advanced fortification techniques. Porter (1822:20) described defensive stockades in Nuku Hiva:

> The manner of fortifying these places is to plant closely on end the bodies of large trees, of forty feet in length, securing them together with pieces of timber, strongly lashed across, presenting on the brow of a hill difficult of access, a breastwork of considerable extent, which would require European artillery to destroy. At the back of this a scaffolding is raised, on which is placed a platform for the warriors, who ascend by the means of ladders, and thence shower down on their assailants spears and stones.

Despite the exaggeration of the height of the poles, this type of structure seems to have been used throughout the archipelago. Linton (1925:20) suggested they became obsolete following the introduction of firearms.

Trenches

Wooden stockades were sometimes used in association with trenches or ditches, a defensive feature commonly described in the archaeological literature. They are often referred to as 'cut ridges' (Linton 1925:21; Suggs 1961:163). On Ua Huka, Sinoto described and mapped a series of three trenches dug across the ridge at the back of Hane valley, once providing favourable access to the high plateau of Mahaki (Sinoto 1970:122). The ditches are 12–15 m deep and about 8 m wide. Between the ditches are long and narrow areas up to 130 m long, one of which includes terraces, which were likely the foundations for houses, as well as two purported breadfruit-storage pits (Figure 6.5). The succession of trenches cut onto this narrow ridge created a series of obstacles for enemies while defenders could easily hold their position to the rear. Similar ditch systems have been reported on Hiva Oa (Chavaillon and Olivier 2007), particularly in Hanaiapa valley, where some are stone-faced (Sinoto 1970:123).

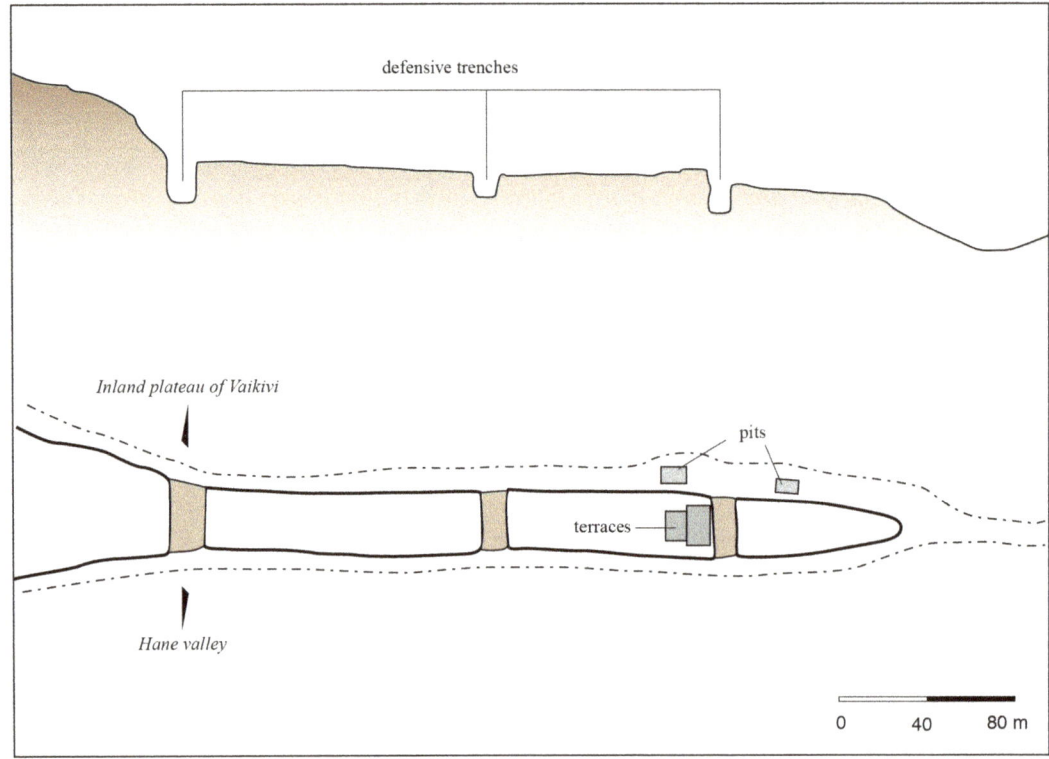

Figure 6.5. Map of the cut-ridge of Penau, Hane valley, Ua Huka.
Source: Guillaume Molle and Vincent Marolleau, adapted from Sinoto (1970).

Fortified complexes and places of refuge

Previous authors have classified *'enata* fortifications into two main categories—the cut-ridge forts and the stone-walled forts (Bellwood 1972; Sinoto 1970; Suggs 1961; see also Green 1967). The latter category includes both pre-European stone enclosures and historical loopholed ones that developed after the introduction of muskets in the early nineteenth century (Linton 1925). This classification of fortified sites was originally based on a very limited number of sites and mostly on surface recording, therefore limiting the understanding of the chronology of these sites. The classification is also problematic as the two types of forts are characterised by supposedly diagnostic features (ditches and stone walls), which can be present across both categories. The plan of the terraced hill fort on the East Ridge of Hanaiapa, Hiva Oa (Sinoto 1970:125) shows a stone-walled enclosure constructed on a levelled area on top of the hill, and immediately south of it, with a deep ditch protecting access to the site. Sinoto suggested that palisades were erected on top of the walls and identified some pits within the enclosure as breadfruit paste storage. At other sites in Hiva Oa, large enclosures also contain stone platforms and paved areas, usually interpreted as foundations for houses, as seen in the neighbouring valley of Hanatekua (Bellwood 1972:33). Such sites should then be described as 'combined settlement units' that aggregate various features—ditches, stone walls with or without palisades, terraces, platforms, pits—within a pattern uniquely adapted to the topography (Bellwood 1979:313). Much of the variability in the layout of fortifications stems from environmental constraints and the need to control higher ground. Forts often took advantage of high hills, uplands, promontories and ridges (Suggs 1961:27). Mobility strategies of the groups were likewise taken into account. On Hiva Oa, Linton described a well-preserved fort built against a high cliff at the western end of Hanamenu beach. This strategic location was likely chosen for resisting attacks from the enemy tribe occupying the upper valley while providing the opportunity to escape by sea if necessary (Linton 1925:21). With regards to the topographic factor, the default position of many authors—that any occupation evidence on high locations attests to a refuge or defensive site—introduces a detrimental bias. *'Enata* visited and occupied so-called 'marginal' areas (or 'hinterlands', following Kahn 2020) for economic, mortuary and ceremonial purposes. For instance, evidence of ritual *me'ae* structures built on high and isolated ridges are reported on all the islands (see Molle 2011a:245). Of course, this does not prevent some high locations traditionally used for non-defensive purposes being turned into refuges when necessary. It thus matters to carefully interpret the archaeological record in these marginal areas within an experienced landscape changing through time, as demonstrated in the case of Mahaki on Ua Huka (Molle and Marolleau, In press).

Such complex sites must also be integrated into larger geographic scales in order to comprehend local defensive systems set up by each community. The example of Hanaiapa illustrates an extensive system, including many sites and clusters on almost all ridges located on the eastern border of the valley, with trenches protecting most access to the main ridge leading to the fort (Sinoto 1970:123; see Figure 6.6). Although these sites may have been built progressively, they eventually contributed to the emergence of large-scale complex defensive systems, which reflects increasing warfare during the century preceding European contact and beyond.

Aside from the formal classification of fortified sites, the question of their function remains. The identification of sites as either defensive or refuge is problematic. Defensive places are defined as fortified areas that could be located both in the valleys in the vicinity of village centres and in marginal remote locations in the mountains. On the other hand, refuges are not always fortified but they are set up in isolated areas, on the valley ridges or in the upper valley in the centre of the island. Remoteness and difficulty of access prove the main criteria to identify a site as a refuge. However, a closer inspection of the archaeological record and European accounts reveal that both functions were closely connected—stone-walled enclosures, even when located in the valley, provided a secure place for members of the group even if standing primarily as a line of defence. Similarly, areas strictly defined as refuges could display defensive features along access pathways. Distinction between defence and refuge thus does not appear relevant. Instead, we argue hereafter that both the number of individuals and the duration of residency defined the nature of occupation at those sites and influenced their layout.

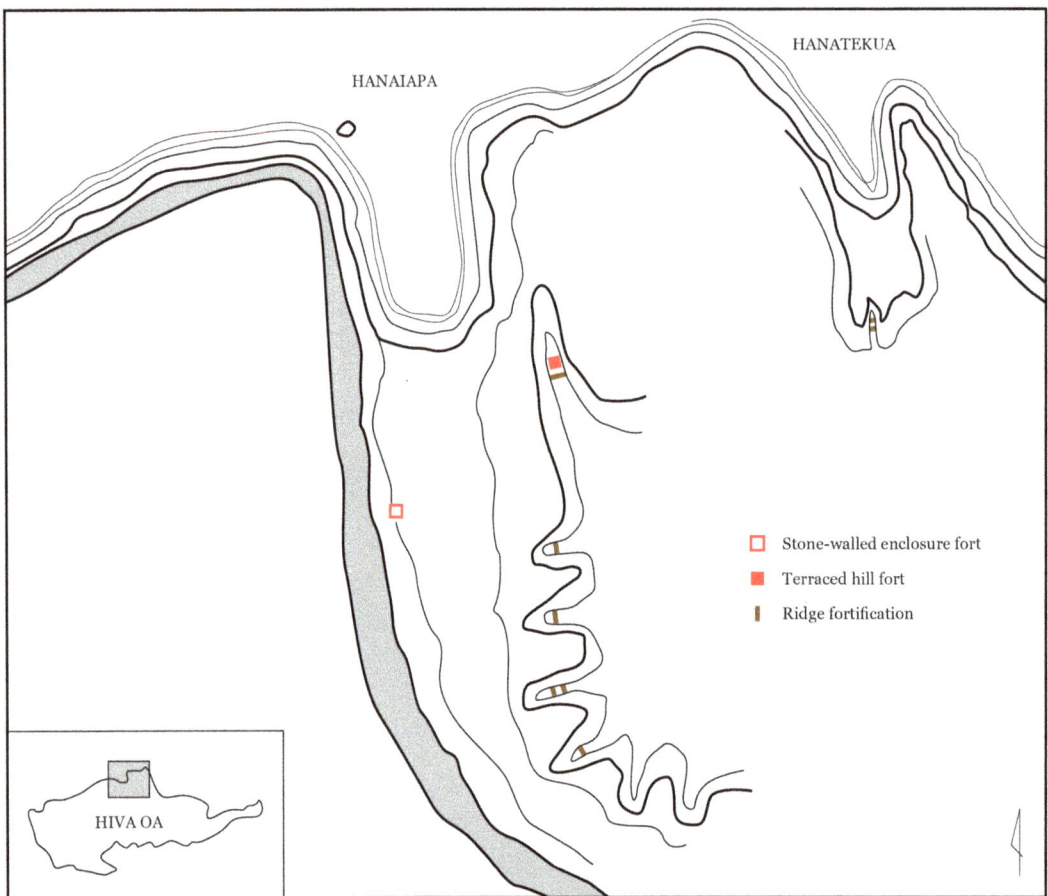

Figure 6.6. Map of Hanaipa defensive system, Hiva Oa.
Source: Guillaume Molle and Vincent Marolleau, adapted from Sinoto (1970).

'Enata sometimes chose to retreat into natural locations in the valleys. The Marquesan word *mouka* refers to a mountain or high peak and also to a natural feature providing protection—Dordillon (1931:272) even translated it as 'refuge place'. On Ua Huka, a traditional story recounts an attack led by the Hokatu warriors on the Hinitaihava tribe, whose chief was Vaiti'ia. He was the single remaining combatant in the village at the time—the rest of the men had gone fishing. In order to defend and protect the women of his group, they took refuge on top of the neighbouring peak. Despite his effort, Vaiti'ia was eventually killed and the women, refusing to be captured alive by the assailants, threw themselves off the cliff. The name given to this peak, *mouka tapu*, commemorates this episode. Archaeological surveys of the steep slopes surrounding the peak, as well as the narrow ridge serving as the unique access to the mountain, revealed the existence of a few stone walls and platforms (Molle 2011a:217).

Von den Steinen visited a narrow gorge called Anaotako located at an altitude of approximately 600 m in Taiohae uplands (1925–1928:Volume II, 34; see also Rollin 1974:235). He was told that people from Hakaui took refuge in this gorge following attacks by sea. In 1847 CE, George Winter, the translator for the Governor Brunet, was sent to negotiate a truce with dissident chief Motane-hitu. The latter was wounded during a fight and found refuge in Anaotako with 200 warriors (a number that could have been exaggerated). Winter (1882) reported that the entrance tunnel was barricaded with the large trunks of breadfruit trees and boulders. Aside from some *ma* pits, these locations display no remains of any huts or shelters, and likely served as short-term refuge. Nevertheless, Gracia (1843) recalled that women and children of Taiohae once hid for 15 months in the mountain caves.

In contrast, other locations have been heavily transformed and converted into temporary residences for longer periods of time. Such places not only display defensive features but also domestic structures, storage units, wells and sometimes religious edifices, providing relative autonomy to the group for a few days or maybe weeks in the case of a longer siege. The site of Teniuaefiti is located in a marginal area of the Hakao'hoka valley on Ua Pou (Ottino and De Bergh 1990:53). It stands on top of a rocky spur, at an altitude of 530 m, and the faces are difficult to climb, with access only through a narrow, easily defendable ridge. Six platforms covered an area of 80 m x 50 m. A stack of sling stones was found on one platform. Other small structures were found in the vicinity, with some containing human remains, suggesting a funerary function. Finally, simple pavements functioned as posts to observe the strategic location of the spur, which overhangs the whole valley and neighbouring bays. Ottino interpreted Teniuaefiti as a refuge for a part of the population or a particular social group, while also being a sacred repository of human remains.

Another complex site has recently been investigated by the authors on Ua Huka (Marolleau 2016; Molle and Marolleau, In press). Mahaki is a high plateau developing at an altitude of 800 m, which offers a complete view of all surrounding valleys. The whole area covers 8 ha^2 (Butaud and Jacq 2010:105). Oral traditions relate that Mahaki was the main refuge place for the Maku-oho tribe of the Hokatu valley, whose population used to retreat during frequent attacks from the Naiki of Vaipaee (Kellum-Ottino 1971). Extensive surveys of the plateau revealed the existence of numerous structures fulfilling various functions. The most impressive feature is the large western trench protecting the only access to the plateau from Vaipaee and Vaikivi. The ridge has been heavily dug into a 15 m vertical cliff, which one can only ascend with ropes (Figure 6.7). At the top of the cliff is a levelled area that may have received a stockade from where warriors could repel assailants. Above, a large stone platform overlooks the trench and the main access. This construction includes some coral slabs and branches at the foundation, as well as petroglyphs and *tiki* figures carved on boulders, attesting to a ritual function. Suggs (1961:27) also reported a *tiki* face petroglyph cut in the wall of a trench at the Mouake site in Taiohae. Further east, in the centre of the plateau, we recorded another small ritual structure, three domestic stone platforms, some paved areas potentially serving for culinary preparations and 50 storage pits for fermented breadfruit paste. Some stone walls are also erected on the main pathways to defend access to the site, as attested by stacks of sling stones. The Mahaki site illustrates a combined settlement unit adapted to longer residency of the Maku-oho during times of war. The site is a combination of highly developed defensive features with more permanent domestic and economic structures that would have afforded a degree of autonomy for the group. The exact purpose of the storage pits remains unclear for they may have provided food to groups of refugees, although the uncommon density of *ma* pits also points to their function as emergency reserves, efficiently protected, in case the main resources located in the valley were destroyed during conflict. A similar situation is documented on a high ridge in the bottom of Atuona valley (Hiva Oa). A series of 15 pits associated with platforms and terraces were interpreted as storage pits (Chavaillon and Olivier 2007:67). This would imply the permanent residency of a few individuals in charge of site maintenance and indicate a long-term management strategy to ensure the survival of the chiefdom. Additionally, the discovery of ritual structures within the fortified area further informs us on the intersection of sociopolitical and religious dynamics in traditional *'enata* warfare. Construction of the ceremonial stone platform overlooking the western trench is especially relevant. It symbolically marks the role of ancestors and deities in protecting the community and the remains of vital territory during times of great fragility.

Figure 6.7. Photo of the western Makahi trench, Ua Huka island.
Source: Guillaume Molle and Vincent Marolleau.

Why does an archaeology of Polynesian warfare matter?

> 'Enata were always violent. Death marked their Land in a very particular way. Their institutions, of course, were intertwined. E ika, tapu, haka'iki, pekio, koina, could not have been changed in part without changing the whole, and violent death was a theme of them all. Violent death sustained their tribal divisions; violent death sustained the social divisions between kikino and tapu; violent death of the heana sustained the lines of descent and the position of the haka'iki; violent death sustained the male as toa. Violent death had its functions in the creation of order, status and identity. (Dening 1980:247)

Dening's (1980) and Thomas's (1990) reassessments of Marquesan ethnographic material have demonstrated the importance of the interweaving of sociopolitical, economic and religious endeavours to the development of intra- and intertribal competition. Resulting warfare became a preeminent feature of *'enata* chiefdoms and varied in both scale and intensity, from raids to wars of conquest. Conflict undoubtedly contributed to shaping the histories of local communities and shed light on some unique characteristics of *'enata* society by the time of Western contact.

Current narratives, which are based on abundant ethnohistorical literature, incorporate conflict as a key factor in the development of chiefdoms, but material evidence to support any hypotheses remains weak. For this reason, an in-depth investigation of warfare is a necessary trajectory for archaeological research in the archipelago.

From a material perspective, warfare did not radically transform the traditional *'enata* lifeway. As the fortified sites were temporarily occupied, they differed from the *pare* on Rapa and the Maori *pa* in Aotearoa/New Zealand. In these latter cases, warfare drove an almost complete restructure of community activities within the fortified villages, which consequently became the main focus of settlement patterns. In the Marquesas, the development of war-related structures described in this chapter demonstrates a dynamic and extensive use of territory, particularly in marginal areas. Mountains, peaks, high ridges, remote and difficult-to-access natural features have often been characterised through their *tapu* mortuary functions. But they were also used and sometimes impressively transformed and integrated into complex defensive systems. Not only does this reveal *'enata* knowledge of their environment and its strategic potential, but also contributes to redefining the notion of *fenua*, or 'traditional territory', beyond the physical boundaries of the valley itself. Including this warfare perspective would greatly enrich our comprehension of ancient settlement and mobility patterns.

Increasing identification of defensive structures in the archaeological landscape will also allow us to revisit previous categories. We here argued that defensive systems should be considered as complex combinations of various features (trenches, walls, platforms and terraces) rather than closed types. Additionally, anchoring the development of the war-related structures in time becomes critical, owing to the current lack of temporality. Efforts need to be focused on the acquisition of radiocarbon dates from these sites, which would further assist in testing our model, which links social competition, feasting cycles, food displays and warfare.

References

Allen, M.S. 2004. Revisiting and revising Marquesan culture history: New archaeological investigation at Anaho Bay, Nuku Hiva Island. *Journal of the Polynesian Society* 113:143–196.

Allen, M.S. 2010. Oscillating climate and social-political process: The case of the Marquesas chiefdom, Polynesia. *Antiquity* 84(323):86–102. doi.org/10.1017/s0003598x00099786.

Anderson, A.J. and D. Kennett 2012. *Taking the high ground: The archaeology of Rapa, a fortified island in remote East Polynesia.* Terra Australis 37. ANU E Press, Canberra. doi.org/10.22459/TA37.11.2012.

Bell, F.L.S. 1931. The place of food in social life of Central Polynesia. *Oceania* 2(2):117–135.

Bellwood, P.S. 1972. *A settlement pattern survey: Hanatekua Valley, Hiva Oa, Marquesas Islands, Pacific anthropological records.* Bernice P. Bishop Museum Press, Honolulu.

Bellwood, P.S. 1979. Settlement pattern. In J. Jennings (ed.), *The prehistory of Polynesia*, pp. 308–322. Australian National University Press, Canberra.

Best, E. 1975. *The Pa Maori.* Government Printer, Wellington.

Boes, E. and S. Sears 1996. Les crânes trophées marquisiens (XVIIIe et XIXe siècles): Interprétation des interventions anthropiques. *Bulletins et Mémoires de la Société d'Anthropologie de Paris* 8(3–4):275–288. doi.org/10.3406/bmsap.1996.2448.

Butaud, J.F. and F. Jacq 2010. Inventaire et cartographie du patrimoine naturel et culturel de l'espace protégé de Vaikivi à Ua Huka, et proposition d'un parcours de découverte du parc du domaine de Vaikivi. Direction de l'environnement de la Polynésie français, Papeete.

Chavaillon, C. and E. Olivier 2007. Le patrimoine archéologique de l'île de Hiva Oa (Archipel des Marquises). Service de la Culture et du Patrimoine de la Polynésie Française, Papeete.

Clavel, C.L. 1885. *Les Marquisiens.* Octave Doin, Paris.

Conte, E. and G. Molle 2014. Reinvestigating a key site for Polynesian prehistory: New results from the Hane dune site, Ua Huka (Marquesas). *Archaeology in Oceania* 49:121–136. doi.org/10.1002/arco.5037.

Conte, E., A. Noury and N. Tartinville 2001. *Recherches ethnoarchéologiques à Ua Huka (Marquises, Polynésie Française)*. Université de la Polynésie Française, Punaauia.

Cordy, R. 1974. Cultural adaptation and evolution in Hawaii: A suggested new sequence. *Journal of the Polynesian Society* 83:180–191.

Crook, W.P. 2007. *Récit aux îles Marquises 1797–1799*. Editions Haere Po, Papeete.

Daugherty, J.S. 1979. Polynesian warfare and fortifications. PhD thesis. University of Auckland, Auckland.

Delmas, S. 1927. *La religion ou le paganisme des îles Marquises, d'après les notes des anciens missionnaires*. University of California Press, Oakland.

Dening, G. 1978. Institutions of violence in the Marquesas. In N. Gunson (ed.), *The changing Pacific: Essays in honour of H.E. Maude*, pp. 134–141. Oxford University Press, Melbourne.

Dening, G. 1980. *Islands and beaches: Discourse on a silent land: Marquesas, 1774–1880*. Dorsey Press, Illinois.

Dordillon, R. 1931. *Grammaire et dictionnaire de la langue des Iles Marquises, travaux et mémoires*. Institut d'Ethnologie de l'Université de Paris, Paris.

Duff, R. 1967. The evolution of Maori warfare. *New Zealand Archaeological Association Newsletter* 10:114–129.

Fanning, E. 1833. *Voyages round the world*. Collins and Hannay, New York.

Goldman, I. 1955. Status rivalry and cultural evolution in Polynesia. *American Anthropologist* 57:680–697. doi.org/10.1525/aa.1955.57.4.02a00030.

Gracia, M. 1843. *Lettres sur les îles Marquises 1838–1842*. Gaume Frères, Paris.

Green, R. 1967. Fortifications in other parts of tropical Polynesia. *New Zealand Archaeological Association Newsletter* 10:96–113.

Handy, E.S.C. 1923. *The native culture in the Marquesas. Volume 9: Bayard Dominick expedition*. Bernice P. Bishop Museum, Honolulu.

Jouan, M. 1858. Archipel des Marquises. *Revue Coloniale* 18:449–479, 19:27–39, 122–141, 308–333.

Kahn, J.G. 2020. The Ma'ohi hinterlands: Regional variability and multi-scalar socio-economic networks in the pre-contact Society Islands. *Journal of Pacific Archaeology* 11(1):41–52.

Kellum-Ottino, M. 1971. *Archéologie d'une vallée des îles Marquises: évolution des structures de l'habitat à Hane*. Société des océanistes, Musée de l'homme, Ua Huka. doi.org/10.4000/books.sdo.355.

Kirch, P.V. 1984. *The evolution of the Polynesian chiefdoms*. New Studies in Archaeology. Cambridge University Press, Cambridge.

Kirch, P.V. 1991. Chiefship and competitive involution: The Marquesas Islands of Eastern Polynesia, In T. Earle (ed.), *Chiefdoms, power, economy and ideology*, pp. 19–145. Cambridge University Press, Cambridge.

Lawson, T.C. 1867. *Ecrits marquisiens 1861–1867*. Bernice P. Bishop Museum, Honolulu.

Linton, R. 1925. *Archaeology of the Marquesas Islands*. Bernice P. Bishop Museum, Honolulu.

Maric, T. and A. Noury 2002. *Prospection Archéologique sur le plateau de Vaikivi à Ua Huka (Marquises, Polynésie Française)*. Service de la Culture et du Patrimoine de la Polynésie Française, Papeete.

Marolleau, V. 2016. Organisation préhistorique de l'Espace du plateau de Mahaki, Ile de Ua Huka, Archipel des Marquises (Polynésie Française). Unpublished MA thesis. Panthéon-Sorbonne, Paris.

Maureille, B. and P. Sellier 1996. Dislocation en ordre paradoxal, momification et décomposition: Observations et hypothèses. *Bulletins et Mémoires de la Société d'Anthropologie de Paris* 8(3–4):313–327. doi.org/10.3406/bmsap.1996.2451.

McCoy, P.C. 1979. Easter Island. In J. Jennings (ed.), *The prehistory of Polynesia*, pp. 135–166. Australian National University Press, Canberra.

Millerstrom, S. 1985. Rock art project in the Marquesas Islands, a preliminary report. *American Rock Art Research Association Newsletter* 12.

Mills, A. 2009. Violent encounters: Historical notes on the curatorial representation of Polynesian weapons. *Journal of Museum Ethnography* 21:186–201.

Molle, G. 2011a. Ua Huka, une île dans l'histoire—histoire pré- et post-Européenne d'une société Marquisienne. Unpublished PhD thesis. Université de la Polynésie Française, Punaauia.

Molle, G. 2011b. *Recherches archéologiques à Ua Huka, Marquises. Rapport final 2008–2009*. CIRAP, Université de la Polynésie Française, Punaauia.

Molle, G. and E. Conte 2011. New perspectives on Hatuana dune site. *Journal of Pacific Archaeology* 2(2):103–108.

Molle, G. and E. Conte 2015. Nuancing the Marquesan post-contact demographic decline: An archaeological and historical case study on Ua Huka Island. *The Journal of Pacific History* 50(3):253–274. doi.org/10.1080/00223344.2015.1078065.

Molle, G. and V. Marolleau In press. You don't have to live like a refugee: New insights on the defensive, economic, and ritual functions of a fortified pā on Ua Huka, Marquesas Islands. *Asian Perspectives*.

Ottino, P. 1996. Archéologie et restauration à Hiva Oa: le 'meʻae' Lipona de Puamau, aux îles Marquises. In M. Julien and C. Orliac (eds), *Mémoire de pierre, mémoire d'homme. Tradition et archéologie en Océanie. Hommage à José Garanger*, pp. 345–376. Publications de la Sorbonne, coll. Homme et société, Paris.

Ottino, P. and M.N. De Bergh. 1990. Hakaoʻhoka: étude d'une vallée Marquisienne. Collection Travaux et Documents Microédités. ORSTOM, Paris.

Pechberty, D. 1995a. Répartition des tribus dans les îles Marquises au XVIIIème siècle d'après W.P. Crook et E. Robarts. *Bulletin de la Société des Etudes Océaniennes* XXIII(5):68–71.

Pechberty, D. 1995b. Parenté et residence à Taiohae aux îles Marquises au XVIIIème siècle. *Bulletin de la Société des Etudes Océaniennes* XXIII(5):72–76.

Peltier, F. 1973. Structures préhistoriques d'une vallée des Marquises. Hanaiapa, Hiva Oa. *Bulletin de la Société des Etudes Océaniennes* XV(183):272–306.

Pietrusewsky, M. 1986. *Prehistoric human skeletal remains from Papua New Guinea and the Marquesas*. Asian and Pacific Archaeology Series Vol. 7. University of Hawaiʻi, Manoa.

Porter, D. 1822. *Journal of a cruise made to the Pacific Ocean*. Wiley and Halsted, New York.

Porter, D. 1834. *Voyages autour du monde: Bibliothèque universelle des voyages*. Aubrée, Paris.

Radiguet, M.R. 1882. *Les derniers Sauvages: La vie et les mœurs aux îles Marquises (1842–1859)*. Calmann Lévy, Paris.

Rallu, J.-L. 1990. *Les populations Océaniennes aux XIXème et XXème siècles*. Travaux et Documents No. 128. INED, Paris.

Robarts, E. 1974. *The Marquesan journal of Ed Robarts, 1797–1824*. Pacific History Series Volume 6. Australian National University Press, Canberra.

Rolett, B.V. 1998. *Hanamiai: Prehistoric colonization and cultural change in the Marquesas Islands (East Polynesia)*. Yale University Publications in Anthropology 81. Yale University Press, New Haven.

Rollin, L. 1974. *Mœurs et coutumes des anciens Maoris des Iles Marquises*. Stepolde Ed, Papeete.

Sahlins, M.D. 1958. *Social stratification in Polynesia*. University of Washington Press, Seattle.

Sand, C., F. Valentin and D. Frimigacci 2006. Sépultures à caveau en Polynésie occidentale: Des traditions orales a l'archéologie. *Journal de la Société des Océanistes* 122–123:13–25. doi.org/10.4000/jso.511.

Saura, B. 2002. *Tinito, la communauté chinoise de Tahiti: installation, structuration, intégration*. Au vent des îles, Papeete.

Scott, R. and H. Buckley 2014. Exploring prehistoric violence in Tonga: Understanding skeletal trauma from a biocultural perspective. *Current Anthropology* 55(3):335–347. doi.org/10.1086/676477.

Sinoto, Y. 1970. An archaeologically based assessment of the Marquesas as a dispersal center in East Polynesia. In R.C. Kelly Green and M. Kelly Green (eds), *Studies in Oceanic culture history*, pp. 105–132. Pacific Anthropological Records.

Stewart, C.S. 1833. *A visit to the South Seas in the United States ship Vincennes during the years 1829 and 1830*. John P. Haven, New York.

Suggs, R. 1961. *The archaeology of Nuku Hiva, Marquesas Islands, French Polynesia*. Anthropological Papers of the American Museum of Natural History 49, Part 1. American Museum of Natural History, New York.

Tautain, L.F. 1896. Sur l'anthropophagie et les sacrifices humains aux îles Marquises. *Anthropologie* 7:443–452.

Thomas, N. 1990. *Marquesan societies: Inequality and political transformation in eastern Polynesia*. Clarendon Press.

Thomas, N. 1991. *Entangled objects: Exchange, material culture and colonialism in the Pacific*. Harvard University Press, Cambridge.

Thomas, N. 1996. *Out of time: History and evolution in anthropological discourse*. The University of Michigan Press, Ann Arbor.

Valentin, F. and N. Rolland 2011. Marquesan trophy skulls: Description, osteological analyses and changing motivations in the South Pacific. In M. Bonogofsky (ed.), *The bioarchaeology of the human head: Decapitation, deformation and decoration*, pp. 97–121. University Press of Florida, Gainesville. doi.org/10.5744/florida/9780813035567.003.0004.

Vancouver, G. 1801. *Voyage of discovery to the north Pacific Ocean and round the world*. John Stockdale, London.

Vayda, A. 1960. *Maori warfare*. Polynesian Society Maori Monograph 2. Polynesian Society, Wellington.

Vayda, A. 1976. *War in ecological perspective: Persistence, change, and adaptive processes in three Oceanian societies*. Plenum Press, New York and London. doi.org/10.1007/978-1-4684-2193-4.

Vigneron, E. 1985. Recherches sur l'histoire des attitudes devant la mort en Polynésie Française. Unpublished PhD thesis. EHESS, France.

Vincendon-Dumoulin, M.M. 1843. *Iles Marquises ou Nouku-Hiva*. Arthus Bertrand, Paris.

von den Steinen, K. 1925–1928. *Les Marquisiens et leur art. L'ornementation primitive des Mers du Sud*. 3 volumes. Musée de Tahiti et des Iles–Te fare iamanaha, Tahiti.

Winter, G.L. 1882. Un vosgien tabou à Nuku Hiva, Souvenirs de voyages d'un soldat d'Infanterie de Marine. *Bulletin de la Société de Géographie de l'Est* 4:291–312, 697–702.

7

Practical defensive features in Palau's earthwork landscape

Jolie Liston

Introduction

The massive earthworks shaped into the volcanic portions of the Palau archipelago in the Western Carolines of Micronesia are considered integral ideological symbols of competition and territoriality between and within the districts they define (Liston 2013; Liston and Tuggle 2006). The spatial patterning of the imposing monumental earth structures suggests that Palau's rival groups may have largely competed by symbolic posturing rather than outright combat, a common tactic in warfare and violence throughout the Caroline Islands (Younger 2009).

During the period of earthwork construction and occupation (c. 2400–1100 cal. BP), there is no direct evidence for conflict in the form of military weapons or human burials showing trauma. Furthermore, there are very limited references in traditional narratives that associate earth structures with warfare. However, earthworks have been considered to contain a practical defensive component since their first documentation by Cheyne (1864 in Parmentier 1987:30), an English trader in Palau in the mid-1800s, who interpreted the square hills, or 'crowns', surrounded by a deep and wide ditch atop the unoccupied terraces, as forts. Most scholars continue to conclude that the primary purpose of the crown and ditch complexes is defence while the function most commonly attributed to the remaining terraces is agricultural (Butler 1984; Gumerman 1986; Lucking 1984; Masse et al. 1984; Osborne 1966, 1979; Snyder et al. 2011).

Disentangling the multifaceted, simultaneous and evolving ideological and practical functions of individual earthwork components is a complex undertaking. While acknowledging that symbolism plays a crucial role in the emergence, construction and use of Palau's earthworks, this chapter examines the structural components most commonly categorised as defensive—crowns and ditches—for their practical use as primarily defensive features. A type of earthwork complex, the Type III, is proposed to play a role in the practical aspects of Palauan competition and warfare. As only a single earth wall, a potential defensive component, is documented in Palauan earthworks, the feature type is not included in this discussion. Also not assessed is the relative height of step-terraces and other earthworks, a likely structural mechanism used in defence.

Earthworks in Palau

Archaeological evidence suggests that earth architecture supported the majority of community activities for more than 1200 years of Palau's history, a period extending from c. 2400 to 1100 cal. BP, labelled the Earthwork Era. An estimated minimum of 64 km² (20.4 per cent) of the volcanic island of Babeldaob, Palau's largest island, was shaped into earth structures.[1] This relict landscape is composed of 10 clusters of contiguous modified terrain with each cluster ranging in size from about 8 to 27 km². Scattered and smaller earthworks are found in the buffer zones separating each cluster.

Within each cluster are morphologically diverse earthwork complexes. These complexes are composed of various combinations of at least 12 structural components, each of which is represented by varied forms and a wide range of sizes. Most apparent in the step-terraces rising up to 5 m high, these structural components are often far larger than needed to perform their primary practical function.

Palau's earthworks appear to have operated as an integrated system (Masse et al. 1984), an engineered landscape that supported the full range of community activities. They held burial grounds and habitations; were used for water management, trails, cultivation and other infrastructure; contained defensive elements; and played ceremonial and ritual roles. Although supporting these practical uses, the distributional patterning, enormity and elaboration of these earth structures suggest that, taken as a unit, they primarily functioned to symbolise the relative status of the hereditary unit or leader that occupied each earthwork complex and district (Liston and Tuggle 2006). The districts, as well as the individual complexes and components, transformed in function, meaning, spatial patterning, morphology and size as Babeldaob's society evolved over the millennium of the Earthwork Era.[2]

Crowns

Palau's most distinctive earthworks are the crowns,[3] small hills whose summits are difficult to access due to some combination of being encircled by a ditch or a precipitous scarp, artificially steep slopes of ≥65 degrees, and heights of up to 10 m. Until recently, a separate type of earthwork feature, the levelled hill, was not differentiated from crowns. The crown and the levelled hill are entirely different categories of earthworks that are distinguished by form, size, distributional patterning, and associated earthwork components, stonework and artefacts (Figure 7.1). These two significant types of earthworks coexisted on the landscape but served different practical functions and were hence likely embedded with distinct meanings. Crowns, rather than levelled hills, are discussed here.

Although some crowns retain an apparently natural rounded appearance, others are sculpted into steep-sided and flat-topped forms. Crown surface area ranges from about 80 to 2000 m². With a surface area of about 3800 m², the potentially minimally shaped hill of Ngerulmud far exceeds the size of other crowns (Kaschko 1998; Liston et al. 1998; Welch 2002). The hill is categorised as a crown due to the ditch encircling its middle slope. Ditches bisect the two ridgeline approaches to Ngerulmud.

Ditches, some of whose outer berms remain, are found separating adjacent crowns, and ring-ditches encircle or partly encircle many crowns to magnify the height of the hill. Where only a partial ring-ditch is present, a steep cliff often forms one or more sides of the crown. A millennium of erosional events have infilled the ditches so a substantial number of ring-ditches are no longer visible on the surface.

---

1   This estimate is low, as about 63 per cent of Babeldaob's volcanic landscape has yet to undergo archaeological survey and was not included in the calculation, which was derived from pedestrian survey and geospatial analysis of historic aerial photographs.

2   Additional research is needed to ascertain the chronological trajectory and temporal relationship of specific structural types, complexes and clusters.

3   The term 'crown' originated with Osborne (1966:150–151), who followed the terminology used by Captain Cheyne (1864). Embankments around ring-ditches at the bases of crowns are called brims, as in the brim of a hat.

Figure 7.1. Aerial view of the Type II Ngermedangeb complex and the Ngermelkii crown and ditch in the Ngatpang (1969-6-2-53).

Source: Jolie Liston, based on 1969 aerial photo.

Recent excavation shows that the summits of many crowns were shaped into one or two deep basins by cutting and adding encircling berms (Liston 2013; Phear 2007). Where not purposefully infilled, most of the surrounding berms have eroded back into the basin so that they are now only identifiable on the surface as shallow depressions. Some crowns support earth knobs or embankments that appear to have been added late in the crown's use-life, after the basin was infilled, and contain burials of high-ranking individuals (Liston 2013; Tuggle 2011). Possibly once supporting more stonework than currently present, the relatively few stone surface features associated with crowns include small pavements, large slabs, edgings and monoliths. Cobbles embedded in the sides of crowns indicate some of them were faced in stone for soil stabilisation and symbolic decoration.

Very few crowns are solitary structures, as most are topographically integrated into an earthwork complex—not imposed or reworked on it—to form the high point overlooking the complex or a portion of the earthwork cluster. Other crowns are lower in the earthwork complex to oversee a specific space. Even low crowns are very prominent on the topography and often dominate other structures in their immediate vicinity.

Crowns have long been considered defensive features due to the difficulty in accessing their summit. What the crowns were defending is difficult to determine, as they are too small to support even a small community and, as yet, there is no evidence of water or food storage. In addition to symbolic roles, crowns have therefore been hypothesised to have served as sentry posts, lookout positions, places of refuge, or communication towers (Lucking 1984; Osborne 1966).

Ditches

Substantially sized ditches are strategically placed within Palauan earthwork complexes.[4] They are found bisecting ridge crests, extending down the length of complexes, circling the base of a crown as a ring-ditch, between adjacent crowns and occasionally splitting a crown (Figures 7.1, 7.2, 7.3 and 7.4). Gullies, a common earthwork component placed to descend the slopes of step-terrace systems and levelled hills, particularly in Type II complexes, are substantially wider and shallower and served a different practical function than ditches (Figure 7.1).

Figure 7.2. A ridge-cut impeding access to the Ngetilai crown, a Type IIIa complex in Ngardmau.
Source: Jolie Liston.

Figure 7.3. Infilled ring-ditch around base of the Oratelruul crown in Ngiwal.
Source: Jolie Liston.

---

4   Not included in the discussion of large ditches are the small field ditch features, now deeply buried by erosion or construction fill. These small ditches were identified during excavations on step-terrace treads at Nkebeduul and in a gully at Ked-era Aranguong (Liston 2013).

Figure 7.4. A ditch bisecting a levelled ridge crest at Ked ra Ikerbeluu in Ngatpang (1976-4-217).

Source: Jolie Liston, based on 1976 aerial photo.

The soil from ditch construction often formed a steep embankment to deepen the ditch. Few of these embankments remain on the landscape as they have eroded back into the ditch. Many of these infilled ditches are now only recognisable as shallow dips in the landscape or by vegetation differences, while others remain apparent at 2 to 10 m deep even with long-term erosion. Excavation has identified that the constructed depth of ditches—without the added height of an embankment—can range from 2 to 6 m. They can be up to 8 m wide although their original width was likely substantially narrower with expansion due to natural degradation processes.

While most ditches are only as long as needed to circle a crown or bisect a ridge crest, some lengthy transverse ditches were cut through level terrain. These features may be World War II–era anti-tank ditches associated with the Japanese Imperial Army's fortification of Babeldaob in preparation for an American invasion of the island that never materialised. Ditches currently measuring roughly 3–6 m wide, 2 m deep, and up to 126 m long are documented in Aimeliik, Ngardmau and Melekeok, where they are interpreted as anti-tank ditches (Butler and Snyder 1991; Grant 2007; Liston 2011). These ditches should be reassessed within a landscape perspective for their potential association with the Earthwork Era, as an over 150 m long ditch at the base of a Ngiwal earthwork complex is decidedly not a Japanese defensive feature and indicates lengthy ditches were an earthwork component.

Universally, ditches are used for defence, water control (irrigation, drainage, aqueducts, moats) and to produce soil for construction (Bayliss-Smith 2007). The defensive aspect of many of Palau's ditches is identified in those blocking passage down a ridgeline or onto a crown. Palauan terms for transverse (*klaidebangel,* 'hole dug as a trap') and lateral (*chomedoilmach, omdok uach,* 'to catch a foot') ditches reflect their defensive function.

Complex and extensive landscape engineering techniques were used in the Earthwork Era for erosion and water management (Liston 2013). Gullies and some ditches controlled and directed water flow and fertile erosional soil away from inhabited areas and more unstable architectural elements and onto step-terraces and basins built as cultivated plots and pondfields (Liston 2008, 2013; Lucking 1984; Lucking and Parmentier 1990:129). Additionally, those ditches that facilitate rather than impede access to specific places may have identified intra-complex boundaries or been long-used parts of the extensive trail system that criss-crossed Babeldaob on levelled ridge crests and artificial earth causeways (Liston 2013; Liston et al. 2002) (Figure 7.5).

Although some of Palau's ditches may have served a single practical purpose, others were likely multifunctional features. For example, a ditch between two adjacent crowns on Toimeduu inhibits access to the steep-sided crown and drains into Tabelmeduu's large cultivation basin located directly below (Liston 2008).

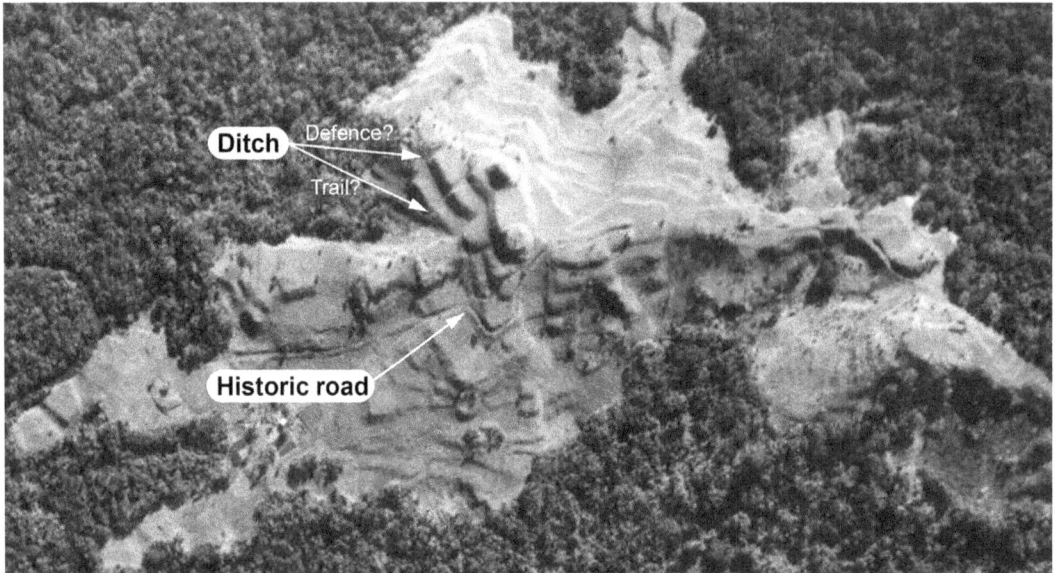

Figure 7.5. Aerial view of a lateral ditch (lower ditch in photo) that may be a trail or water control feature leading to a crown in Aimeliik (1976-6-2).

Source: Jolie Liston, based on 1976 aerial photo.

By comparing the mechanical and geometric characteristics of ditch forms with potential functions, Keeley et al. (2007) maintain that V-sectioned ditches are ineffective for any purpose other than defence. The geometry of triangular ditches makes them challenging obstacles to cross yet comparatively difficult to excavate, inefficient sources of earth for ramparts or revetments, and more prone to erosion when filled with moving water than other ditch forms. It is the steep sides and narrow base, rather than their dimensions, that produce an effective barrier, as ancient Roman army units commonly fortified their encampments with curtained V-sectioned ditches measuring only 1.0 m deep and 1.5 m wide (Keeley et al. 2007:61). This does not preclude ditches with other base forms from serving a defensive function, nor suggest that V-sectioned ditches did not serve a symbolic purpose, but suggests that those triangular ditches of a metre or more deep are inefficient and inappropriate for any purpose other than defence (Keeley et al. 2007:57).

The V-sectioned ditch is a component of an *enceinte*, a barrier preventing access to and generally obscuring vision of a specific place. In addition to the three universal and unambiguous earthwork defensive features of V-sectioned ditches, defended gates, and bastions presented by Keeley et al. (2007),[5] *enceintes* can also contain curtains formed from palisades, ramparts or walls to shield the defenders. However, in contrast to the three features, the primary function of these curtains may not have been defence (Keeley et al. 2007:57). They could serve to monitor channels for goods or people entering and exiting a space, block access to sacred areas or ensure the privacy of those within.

The few Palauan ditches that have been cross-sectioned reveal rounded and occasionally V-shaped bases. The Ngebars and Engol crown and ditch complexes provide examples of ditch forms, sizes, period of use and association with like archaeological features.

---

5   Neither defended gates nor bastions occur as earthworks in Palau.

Engol crown and ditch

Ditches partially enclose the low Engol crown in Melekeok (Kashko 2007:107–127; Welch 2002). The crown rises 3.5 m above the base of the infilled ditches. The surrounding gentle slopes do not appear to have been shaped into earthworks although 36 m from the hill a ditch bisects a north-east extending ridge. A 50 cm high berm crosses the centre of the levelled 750 m² summit.

The Engol crown descends sharply into the ditches on the south and west sides and a scarp on its north edge. To the north-east is the narrow ridge, while to the south-east the hill slopes gently into the forest below. The 4 m wide, 23 m long western ditch forms a T-shaped intersection with the 4.4 m wide, 19 m long southern ditch.

Stratigraphic trenches placed in the ditches reveal that both are triangular in cross-section and are 3–4 m deeper than the present eroded surface. When constructed, there would have been a c. 6–7 m ascent from the base of the ditches to the summit constituting an effective barrier to the top. Excavation also indicates the crown never supported a basin but was simply a levelled surface with a thin cultural deposit.

Three charcoal samples, two from the summit's cultural deposit and one from the infilling sediment layer in the ring-ditch, produced a combined radiocarbon date range of 1870–1330 cal. BP. The assays are almost identical to those indicating ditch use at Ngebars.

Ngebars crown and ditch

A variety of ditches were revealed in the imposing Ngebars earthwork complex in the interior of Ngermeduu Bay in Ngatpang during construction of the Compact Road, which sheared off the west edge of the complex's crown (Liston 2011:217–263) (Figures 7.6 and 7.7).[6] The Ngebars complex is characterised by a series of high, wide step-terraces, capped by a 1600 m² crown that is connected to adjacent earthworks with modified ridges and a gully. The summit of Ngebars does not support knobs or an embankment and the road cut revealed it was never fashioned into a basin.

Figure 7.6. Section where the Compact Road has cut through east side of the Ngebars earthworks in Ngatpang.
Source: Jolie Liston.

---

6 The image shows the profile, which extends from halfway inside the tree line on the left side of the photograph, south across the crown, to halfway across the step-terrace beneath the crown on the right side of the photograph.

Road construction exposed five ditches over a 100 m span, only one of which was identifiable through variations in topography or vegetation prior to construction work. The complexity of interpreting earthwork landscape modification due to reconstruction events during the lengthy extent of their use and subsequent erosion is exemplified in the Ngebars profile.

Visible on the surface 30 m north of the crown is an 80 m long ditch bisecting the low ridge separating Ngebars from the Iksid earthworks to the north. The road cut exposed this ditch (Feature 1) as triangular in profile. The 2–3 m high banks of Feature 1 resulted in an original total ditch depth of c. 6 m, with a width of about 6–7 m. Closer to the crown, a semicircular-based ditch (Feature 2) was exposed in the inner margin of a deep step-terrace. Feature 2 is 10 m wide and had an original depth of at least 2.5 m, although if earth berms formed the feature's upper margins it could have been substantially deeper.

A ring-ditch (Feature 3) circling the base of the crown was only evident in profile. The north side of the ring-ditch (Feature 3a) occupies the entirety of what appears to be the second tier down from the crown and measures 8 m wide at the top and 5 m deep. The south side of the ring-ditch (Feature 3b) is at the base of the 7 m high crown and at the inner edge of a 9 m deep step-terrace that wraps around the west, north and south sides of the crown. Feature 3b is 8.0 m wide, tapering to 2.0 m wide at the base, and is cut 3.1 m deep into basal saprolite. There is no evidence of a berm as it appears to have eroded into the ditch. A burned *Pterocarpus indicus* post, interpreted as a component of a palisade, was revealed in the inner margin of the Feature 3b ditch.

As both Features 3a and 3b are actually on the same step-terrace, and Feature 3a is infilled with homogenous material, it appears the stepped nature of the upper reaches of the north side of the crown could result from partial collapse of the crown or a reconstruction event. Alternatively, Feature 3a and 3b could be two entirely separate ditches, a possibility suggested by the differing geometrics of the two profiles where Feature 3a is an asymmetric V and Feature 3b is semicircular in cross-section.

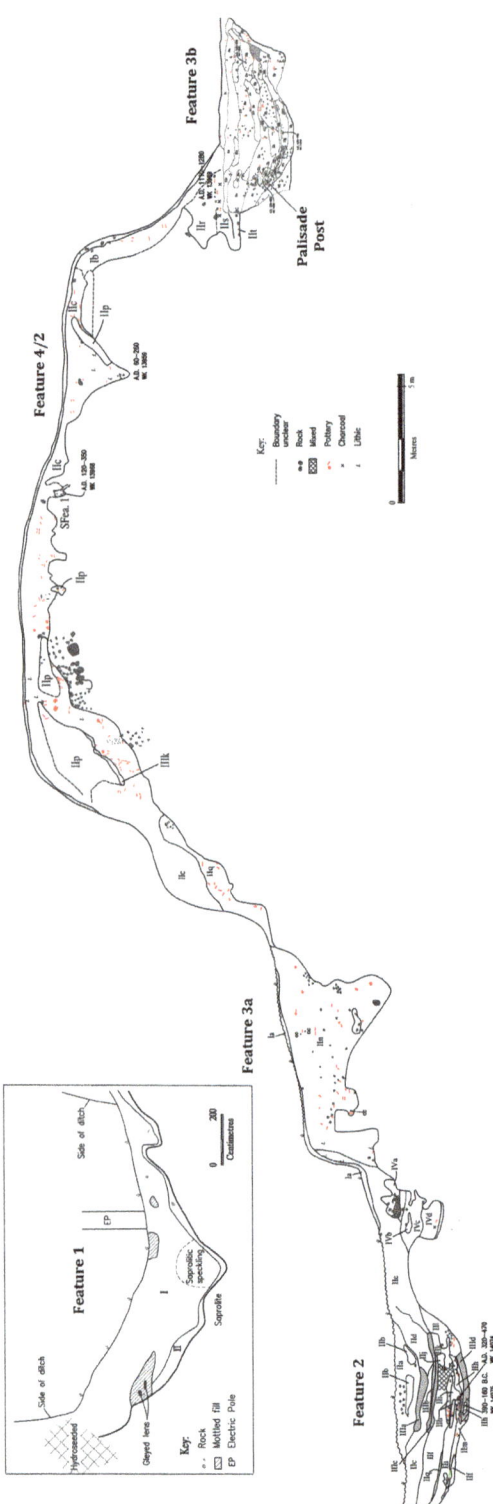

Figure 7.7. Profile of road cut through the Ngebars earthwork complex.
Source: Jolie Liston, adapted from Liston (2011:223, 258, Figures 32–34).

Feature 4/2 is a triangular ditch, or less likely a pit, placed in the inner edge of the summit's gradual slope to the south. The pit is 3.1 m wide at the top, tapering to 0.2 m wide at the base, and is 2.0 m deep. The ditch could have been the last line of defence to an earlier use of the hill, before Ngebars was fully shaped into a levelled and steep-sided crown.

Of the five ditches in the Ngebars profile, two are semicircular, two are triangular and one forms an asymmetric V in cross-section. All five ditches would impede access to the top of Ngebars. The three V-sectioned ditches form a certain ridge-cut (Feature 1), one side of the ring-ditch circling the crown (Feature 3a), and a ditch on the crown next to the summit (Feature 4/2). Ditch geometry and its placement in the landscape suggest the semicircular-based Feature 2 could have served as a water control feature as well as a barrier. The location of the semicircular ditch at the base of the crown and the presence of a palisade post embedded in its inner margin confirms that Feature 3b is primarily defensive.

The majority of the 14 dated charcoal samples from the Ngebars complex originate from redeposited strata (construction fill and erosional material) that of necessity must be interpreted from the perspective of landscape modification. The dates directly associated with the crown and ditches indicate crown use by at least 1900 cal. BP and last use of the ring-ditch by about 1300 cal. BP.

Type III complexes

Of the four morphological types of earthwork complexes identified, Type III complexes invariably contain an arrangement of ditches and a crown[7] whose pattern is suggestive of a defensive function. Type III earthwork complexes are characterised by a ridgeline cut by a ditch whose physical focus is the crown capping the highest point on the ridge (Figure 7.2). It appears that not all capping crowns on Type III complexes contain basins and it remains uncertain whether the occasional associated stonework is a later repurposing of the complex (see Tuggle 2011:218–227).

Type III complexes are found as a simple ridge-cut and crown on a ridgeline (Figure 7.8) and as two subtypes identified by additional earthwork components in a specific pattern. In all cases, the sides of the ridge either fall steeply without any apparent modification or are shaped into high step-terraces. In Type IIIa complexes, transverse ditches are found at the base of each of a series of levelled areas ascending the ridge. The deepest ditches are those located on one or both sides of the small diameter crown, as in the massive Type IIIa Ngulitel complex in Ngaraard.

Figure 7.8. A Type III earthwork complex in Ngardmau.
Source: Jolie Liston.

---

7   Although all Type III complexes contain crowns and ditches, these features are also frequently found separate from Type III complexes.

A Type IIIb complex is characterised by one or two ditches bisecting the ridgeline leading to step-terraces with high risers. The ridge is capped by a slightly larger diameter crown than found in Type IIIa complexes. Perhaps already effectively blocked by the ridge-cuts and height of the step-terraces, the crown on a Type IIIb complex is generally not contained in a ring-ditch. Roisingang in Ngaraard and Ngerkelalk in Aimeliik are typical Type IIIb complexes (Figure 7.9).

Often dominating the surrounding landscape, Type III complexes are found at the inland borders and in the middle of earthwork districts. Although many of these complexes are now heavily forested, the crown's summit would have provided a clear 360-degree view, be prominently displayed to adjacent earthworks, and be seen by distant earthworks. The ditches, high step-terraces, steep ridge slopes and crown served a defensive function by blocking access into or out of areas.

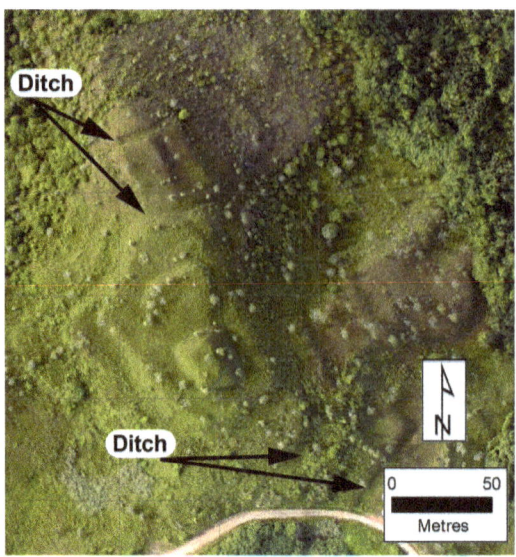

Figure 7.9. Ngerkelalk, a Type IIIb complex with ridge-cuts and high step-terraces leading to a crown in Aimeliik.
Source: Jolie Liston.

Discussion

Ditches, crowns and Type III complexes are evaluated for their use as fortifications. Ditches, as individual features, are more limited in purpose than crowns or Type III complexes of which they are a component part. Defence is expressed in a ditch's capacity as a barrier to obstruct human movement and to demarcate space. Some ditch features were strictly or simultaneously water management features. Others may have been long-used trails eroded below the surrounding topography by centuries of use that assisted rather than impeded movement.

To ascertain whether ditches simultaneously or strictly served as defensive rather than water control features or paths entails examination of each feature within its spatial context, its geometric form and its association with curtains such as palisades or embankments. Examples of strictly defensive ditches include the ridge-cuts bisecting the ancient trail systems. Other potentially strictly defensive ditches include those bisecting the ridge crests in Type III complexes and circling the base of crowns. In both cases, ditches blocked access to the crown site and the complex to fortify the site.

The sheer angle and height of most crowns, and their enclosure within ring-ditches, palisades, and natural barriers, impedes access to the summit to create a confined ritual or social space (Osborne 1966; Phear 2007; Liston and Tuggle 2006). The crown's small surface area ensured limited use by a select few. Effectively isolated from the surrounding landscape, crowns were hence fortified sites, places meant to protect or symbolically emphasise specific activities, resources, high-ranking people or kin groups.

The elements of ditches bisecting a high ridge, significantly steep ridge slopes, high step-terraces and crowns are all meant to block entrance onto the surface of Type III complexes. Type III complexes are thus fortified, where the entire surface of the complex and the crown, rather than just the crown, are being fortified. The practical functions of crowns and Type III complexes almost certainly revolve around identical concepts of power, ritual and use by high-status individuals.

Those crowns containing basins, berms and knobs functioned as a fortified stage for ritual cultivation and burial grounds for likely higher-status individuals (Liston 2014; Tuggle 2011). However, the basins and earth embellishments were not present throughout the crown's long use-life, indicating the crown's practical function changed through time.

As crown summits are too small to shelter a substantial number of people, they are not strictly 'hill forts' but they may have served as temporary residences for healers, priests or rulers to solidify their importance to the community. Or crowns may have been places of refuge (or asylum), sites that play a prominent part in ethnographic accounts of Palauan warfare and are understood by all parties to be havens from attack. Places of refuge on Palau are described as small places (e.g. stone platforms) that serve as a safe space for individuals in conflict or as a boundary (e.g. a stone weir) that one must cross to be protected from attack. The small size of these places of refuge in ethnographic accounts suggests that the small diameter crown summits could have functioned as places of refuge.

Reinforcing their defensive role, both as individual features and within Type III complexes, are the crowns' commanding views over great expanses of the island and lagoon and their strategic placement around the perimeter and within earthwork clusters. With a clear line of sight between them, many crowns could serve as sentry posts for guarding the immediate area from an encroaching enemy, or for alerting distant allies with smoke signal communications. Within an earthwork district, guards on crowns could oversee the population's resource production and other activities. On the seaward edge of the polity, retainers stationed on high earthworks might have monitored fishing and gathering activities on the lagoon and reef. This ensured elite control of the subsistence base as well as reminding the population of their work responsibilities, their subordinate role and elite hegemony. Surveillance is an effective mechanism to both enforce and express the power of the elite (Simpson 2009).

Crowns also contained symbolic significance related to power and ownership to legitimise claims of land and other resources and elite or group posturing to re-enforce chiefly rule. In this capacity, the crown may be a location the enemy would strive to capture for symbolic reasons.

Unravelling the nature of the distributional patterning of these fortified stages on the landscape, within earthwork districts and in relation to the later period stonework villages will lead to a greater understanding of the practical and symbolic role of warfare and competition through symbolic posturing in early Palau. Documentation of Palau's earthworks is in its infancy with identification of the initial four earthwork types a recent development.

Figure 7.10 illustrates the frequency and distribution of currently known crowns and Type III complexes in the Ngaraard Earthwork District.[8] The 20 crowns are dispersed across the entire district with five Type III complexes found along the highest hills in the district's central ridgeline. The summit of the majority of the crowns shown is difficult to access through a combination of steep sides, height and encircling ditches or scarps. Crowns and Type III complexes in other earthwork districts display a very similar frequency and distributional patterning.

For now, there is no discernible direct spatial relationship between the fortified sites and the coastal stonework villages which appeared at roughly 1000 BP. In Figure 7.10, nucleated stonework villages and their associated wetland taro patches are densely interspersed along the sandy shoreline and behind the mangrove forests.

---

8   Ngaraard is the only earthwork district with enough comprehensive data to produce a reasonably accurate map. The majority of the landscape shown on the map is shaped into earthworks.

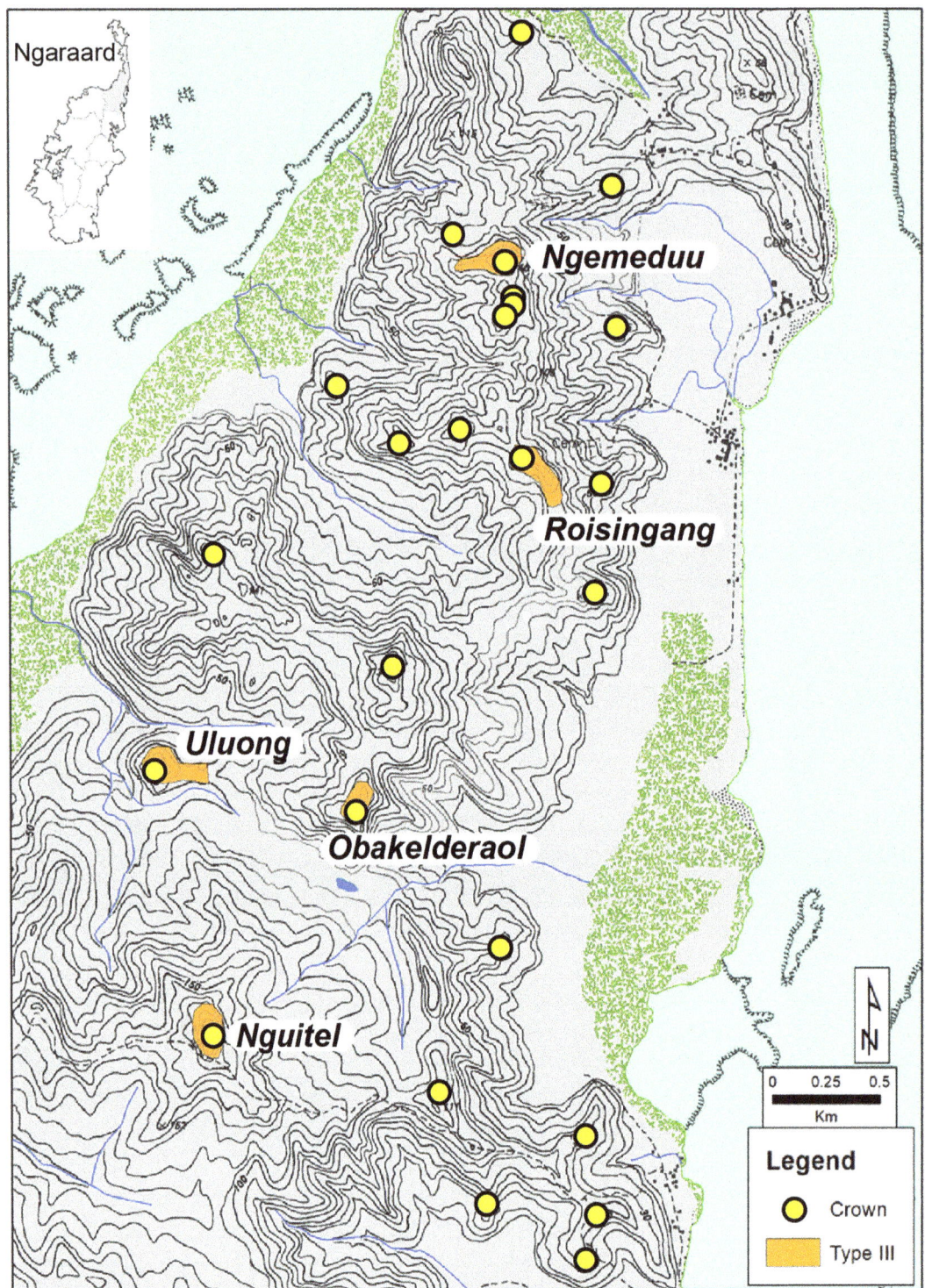

Figure 7.10. Documented crowns and Type III complexes in the Ngaraard Earthwork District.
Source: Jolie Liston.

Conclusion

Examination of crowns, ditches, and the combination of these components within a Type III complex to ascertain their primary practical purpose shows that only those ditches placed solely as barriers to impede access served a predominantly defensive function. Crowns and Type III complexes are fortified sites whose primary practical function was the activity requiring protection.

Those ditches placed to bisect ridge crests and circle the bases of crowns served a primarily defensive function. Other ditches were used for water management and likely trails, and some ditches were multifunctional, serving as barriers and water control features simultaneously. The very definition of a crown and a Type III complex is an incorporation of the defensive elements—steep ridgelines, high step-terraces, crown height and slope angle, ridge-cuts, ring-ditches—that created their fortification. The fortified sites had concurrent practical and symbolic functions, whose purposes evolved over the millennium of the Earthwork Era.

However, the primary practical function of crowns and Type III complexes was not defence but the activity that occurred on the exclusionary space of the complex and crown summit.

Identification of the mechanisms involved, the leadership employed, and the particular players participating in the development of the Earthwork Era's politicised landscape remains a significant research objective. Identifying and interpreting the sequence of transformations in the symbolic and practical functions of Palau's evolving engineered landscape requires a significant amount of additional archaeological investigation. Excavation will illuminate the nature and timing of the various specific activities that occurred on the fortified sites and the chronology of the construction and remodelling events. A thorough geospatial analysis will reveal the distributional patterning of fortified sites within and between the earthwork districts. This landscape perspective, in combination with radiocarbon assays, can assist in developing models of the evolution of leadership strategies in the Earthwork Era.

References

Bayliss-Smith, T. 2007. The meaning of ditches: Interpreting the archaeological record from New Guinea using insights from ethnography. In T. Denham, J. Iriarte and L. Vrydaghs (eds), *Rethinking agriculture: Archaeological and ethnoarchaeological perspectives*, pp. 126–148. Left Coast Press, Walnut Creek.

Butler, B.M. 1984. *A preliminary report on the 1983 archaeological survey of Aimeliik State, Republic of Palau*. Prepared for the Belau National Museum, Inc., Ministry of Social Services Division of Cultural Affairs, Republic of Palau. Center for Archaeological Investigations, Southern Illinois University, Carbondale.

Butler, B.M. and D. Snyder 1991. An archaeological landscape of the Pacific War: The Palau Islands. In W.R. Wood (ed.), *Archaeological studies of World War II*, pp. 48–63. Monograph No. 10. University of Missouri-Columbia Museum of Anthropology, Columbia.

Grant, D. 2007. Historic era: Archival and field investigations. In J. Liston, H.D. Tuggle, T.M. Mangieri, M.W. Kaschko and M. Desilets (eds), *Palau archaeological investigations, Babeldaob Island, Republic of Palau. Phase II: Archaeological data recovery. Volume V: Fieldwork reports*, pp. 277–361. Prepared for the U.S. Army Corps of Engineer District, Honolulu, Fort Shafter, Hawai'i. International Archaeological Research Institute, Inc., Honolulu.

Gumerman, G.J. 1986. The role of competition and cooperation in the evolution of island societies. In P.V. Kirch (ed.), *Island societies: Archaeological approaches to evolution and transformation*, pp. 42–49. Cambridge University Press, New York.

Kaschko, M.W. 1998. Fortified hilltops, black pottery, and early settlement in Palau. Paper presented at the Society for American Archaeology 63rd annual meeting, 25–29 March. Seattle, Washington.

Kaschko, M.W. 2007. Melekeok field report. In Liston, J., T.M. Mangieri, D. Grant, M.W. Kaschko, H.D. Tuggle and M. Desilets (eds), *Archaeological data recovery for the Compact Road, Babeldaob Island, Republic of Palau. Historic preservation investigations Phase II. Volume VI: Fieldwork reports*, pp. 134–150. Prepared for the U.S. Army Corps of Engineers, Pacific Ocean Division, Hawai'i. International Archaeological Research Institute, Inc., Honolulu.

Keeley, L.H., M. Fontana and R. Quick 2007. Baffles and bastions: The universal features of fortifications. *Journal of Archaeological Research* 15(1):55–95. doi.org/10.1007/s10814-006-9009-0.

Liston, J. 2008. *Archaeological data recovery at Tabelmeduu, Ngaraard Earthwork District, Republic of Palau*. Prepared for Ngaraard State, Republic of Palau. Garcia and Associates, Kailua, Hawai'i.

Liston, J. 2011. *Archaeological monitoring for the Compact Road, Babeldaob Island, Republic of Palau. Historic preservation investigations Phase III. Volume XI: Monitoring: Fieldwork reports*. Prepared for the U.S. Army Corps of Engineers, Pacific Ocean Division, Hawai'i. International Archaeological Research Institute, Inc., Honolulu.

Liston, J. 2013. Sociopolitical development and a monumental earthwork landscape on Babeldaob Island, Palau. Unpublished PhD thesis. The Australian National University, Canberra.

Liston, J. 2014. Ritual use of Palau's monumental earthworks and leadership strategies. In H. Martinsson-Wallin and T. Thomas (eds), *Monuments and people in the Pacific*, pp. 101–128. Studies in Global Archaeology No. 20. Uppsala University, Sweden.

Liston, J. and H.D. Tuggle 2006. Prehistoric warfare in Palau. In E. Arkush and M.W. Allen (eds), *The archaeology of warfare: Prehistories of raiding and conquest*, pp. 148–183. University Press of Florida, Florida.

Liston, J., M.W. Kaschko and D. J. Welch 1998. *Archaeological inventory survey of the Capitol relocation project, Melekeok, Republic of Palau*. Prepared for Architects Hawai'i, Inc., Honolulu. International Archaeological Research Institute, Inc., Honolulu.

Liston, J., J. Tellei, U. Basilius and F.K. Rehuher 2002. *Archaeological survey, monitoring, and oral history of bore holes, rock quarries, and coral dredging locations for the Compact Road, Babeldaob Island, Republic of Palau*. Prepared for the U.S. Army Corps of Engineers, Pacific Ocean Division, Hawai'i. International Archaeological Research Institute, Inc., Honolulu.

Lucking, L.J. 1984. An archaeological investigation of prehistoric Palauan terraces. Unpublished PhD thesis. University of Minnesota, Minneapolis.

Lucking, L.J. and R.J. Parmentier 1990. Terraces and traditions of Uluang: Ethnographic and archaeological perspectives on a prehistoric Belauan site. *Micronesica* Supplement 2:125–136.

Masse, W.B., D. Snyder and G.J. Gumerman 1984. Prehistoric and historic settlement in the Palau Islands, Micronesia. *New Zealand Journal of Archaeology* 6:107–127.

Osborne, D. 1966. *The archaeology of the Palau Islands, An intensive survey*. Bernice P. Bishop Museum Bulletin 230. Bishop Museum Press, Honolulu.

Osborne, D. 1979. Archaeological test excavations, Palau Islands, 1968–1969. *Micronesica* Supplement 1.

Parmentier, R.J. 1987. *The sacred remains: Myth, history, and polity in Belau*. The University of Chicago Press, Chicago.

Phear, S. 2007. *The monumental earthworks of Palau, Micronesia: A landscape perspective*. British Archaeological Reports International Series 1626. British Archaeological Reports, Oxford.

Simpson, D. 2009. Rapa Nui's political economy and the visibility of its monumental architecture. *Rapa Nui Journal* 23(2):131–148.

Snyder, D., W.B. Masse and J. Carucci 2011. Dynamic settlement, landscape modification, resource utilisation and the value of oral traditions in Palauan archaeology. In J. Liston, G. Clark and D. Alexander (eds), *Pacific Island heritage: Archaeology, community & identity*, pp. 155–180. Terra Australis 35. ANU E Press, Canberra. doi.org/10.22459/ta35.11.2011.12.

Tuggle, H.D. 2011. Ngaraard ridge: Data recovery. In H.D. Tuggle, T.M. Mangieri and J. Liston (eds), *Archaeological monitoring and emergency data recovery for the Compact Road, Babeldaob Island, Republic of Palau. Historic preservation investigations Phase III. Volume IX: Planned data recovery field reports*. pp. 143–240. Prepared for the U.S. Army Corps of Engineers, Pacific Ocean Division, Hawai'i. International Archaeological Research Institute, Inc., Honolulu.

Welch, D.J. 2002. Archaeological and paleoenvironmental evidence of early settlement in Palau. *Bulletin of the Indo-Pacific Prehistory Association* 22:161–173.

Younger, S.M. 2009. Violence and warfare in the pre-contact Caroline Islands. *Journal of the Polynesian Society* 118(2):135–164.

8

High-resolution lidar analysis of the Fisi Tea defensive earthwork at Lapaha, Kingdom of Tonga

Phillip Parton, Geoffrey Clark and Christian Reepmeyer

Introduction

In many prehistoric societies, earthwork defences were among the costliest and largest built structures and required a significant investment in resources, particularly labour, land and materials. Consequently, the construction of major defences was not undertaken lightly and they were frequently built in response to an imminent threat of intense violence (Keeley 1996). Earthwork defences often enclosed residential communities and elite centres, whereas others were larger and included hinterlands and appear to have defended a regional area (Connah 2000; Fox 1976; Scherer and Golden 2006; Webster et al. 2007). In both cases, defences protected the areas most important to the community and represent emic statements of group territory (Webster et al. 2008:349).

Long defensive systems and 'great walls' that protect settlements and their hinterlands have been something of a puzzle to archaeologists (Arkush and Stanish 2005:10). While the perceived logistical challenge of occupying long defensive systems may be the primary source of confusion, traditional archaeological and survey methodologies often limit the amount of spatial data that can be gathered. Long defensive systems require considerable resources to map and to record in detail the various defensive elaborations, in addition to the regional geography of the areas on both side of the defences.

Remote sensing technologies, in particular lidar, have potential to provide the high-resolution data necessary to analyse earthworks at both local and landscape levels. The adoption of lidar technology by archaeologists for site prospection has been swift and profound, and has been likened to a 'paradigm shift' by some (Chase et al. 2012). Despite calls for archaeologists to better engage with the full value of lidar data (Opitz et al. 2015), applications beyond site prospection are still limited (Hannon et al. 2017; Lustig et al. 2018).

The high accuracy and vegetation-penetrating properties that make lidar so useful for site prospection also allow lidar to be used in lieu of traditional archaeological and survey methodologies. Lidar is particularly well suited to the analysis of structurally simple monumental earthworks such as ditches, ramparts, mounds and quarries/excavations. However, when using lidar data, it is important to understand the sources of error present in the survey system and to implement a methodology to evaluate measurement error throughout an analysis to ensure that results are accurate and defensible.

In this chapter, lidar data are analysed to examine a large and newly reported earthwork defending the elite centre of Lapaha and eastern hinterlands on the island of Tongatapu in the Kingdom of Tonga. The analysis demonstrates how a thorough investigation of lidar datasets, in conjunction with targeted field excavations, contributes new knowledge about the earthwork—including its defensive features and method of construction—and inferences about labour organisation and workforce size. In addition, our study suggests that Fisi Tea represents a schism between two or more groups on Tongatapu at the time it was built that is only hinted at in traditional history. The age and location of the defensive boundary highlights the key role that warfare played in the development of Tonga's prehistoric political system, arguably one of the few archaic states to develop in Oceania.

Materials and methods

Site description

The island of Tongatapu is the largest in the Tongan archipelago and is the location of the present-day capital of Nukuʻalofa. Prior to the establishment of the nation state of Tonga in the nineteenth century, Tongatapu was also the seat of power of the paramount chiefly lineage known as the Tuʻi Tonga, who was a descendant of the god Tangaloa Eitumatāpuʻa. The influence of the Tuʻi Tonga chiefly system extended to eastern Fiji, ʻUvea and Samoa in addition to the Tongan archipelago c. 1200–1800 CE. Monumental architecture is associated with the principal places of the Tuʻi Tonga, first at Heketā in the north-east of Tongatapu (1200–1300 CE), and shortly after at Lapaha some 8 km south-west of Heketā, on the sheltered shores of the Fanga ʻUta lagoon (Clark and Reepmeyer 2014). Lapaha is remarkable in Tonga as the site of the monumental tombs of the Tuʻi Tonga as well as other large engineering projects such as a c. 20 ha area of reclaimed land, wharf infrastructure, and a series of fortifications that enclosed the administrative and religious core of the ancient Tongan state (Figure 8.1) (Clark et al. 2008).

The fortification of Fisi Tea (Figure 8.1) was first identified by Parton et al. (2018) in an inventory of defensive sites on Tongatapu located with lidar. Defensive sites on Tongatapu are predominantly ring-ditch fortifications enclosing areas of up 315 000 m^2, but more commonly are between 10 000 m^2 and 50 000 m^2. The inventory also identified a subset of defensive earthworks termed linear fortifications with different characteristics from enclosure fortifications. Linear fortifications often begin at natural barriers/terrain edges and appear to have been regionally focused compared with enclosed fortifications that protected community groups. Of the seven linear fortifications identified with lidar, Fisi Tea was the most enigmatic due to its imposing dimensions and association with the Tuʻi Tonga centre at Lapaha. We examined Fisi Tea through an analysis of lidar data, archaeological investigation, radiocarbon dating and traditional history.

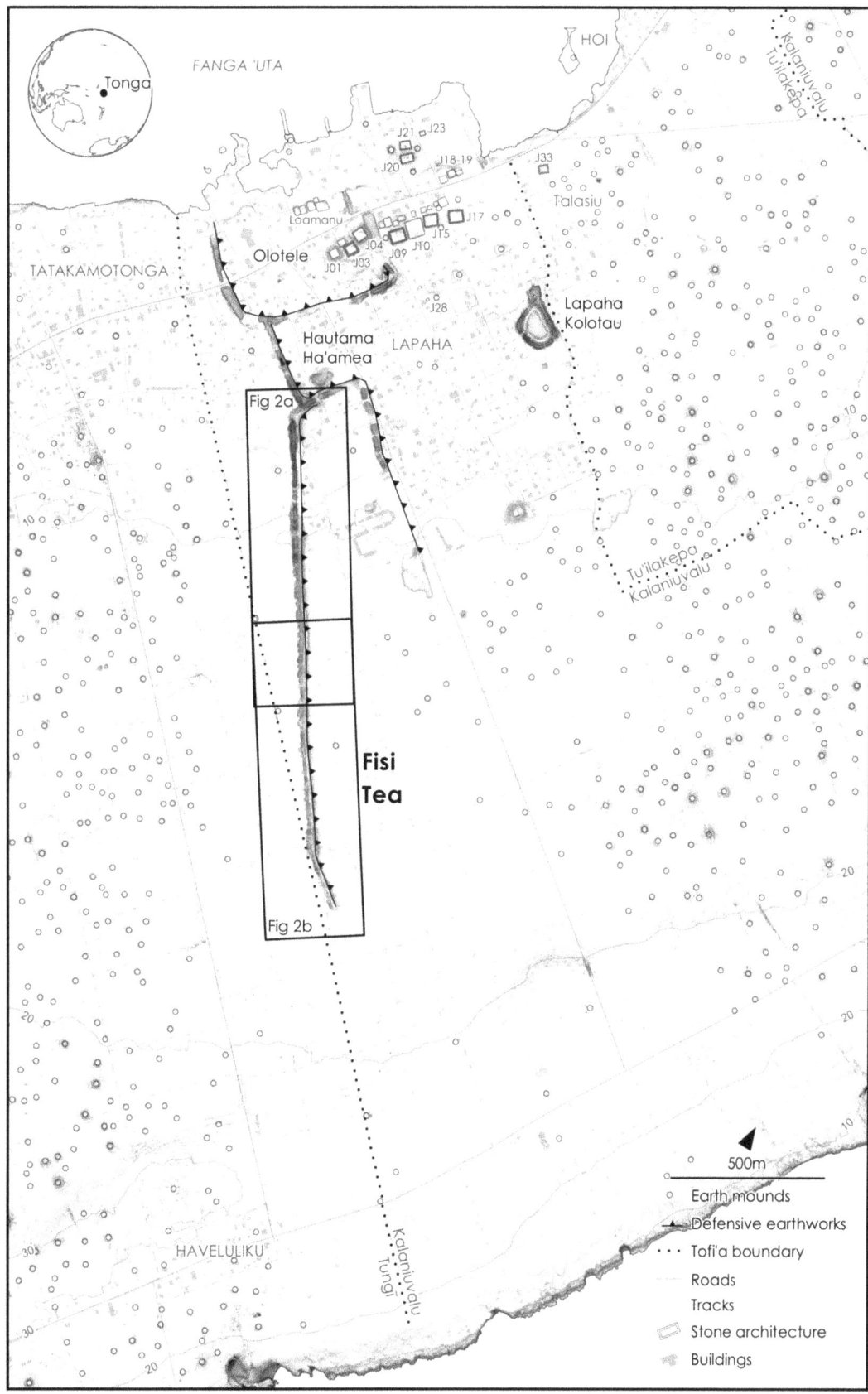

Figure 8.1. Map of Lapaha and hinterlands with location of Fisi Tea and other defensive earthworks highlighted.

Source: Phillip Parton, Geoffrey Clark and Christian Reepmeyer.

Lidar data

Aerial topographic lidar and aerial photography were acquired by the Tongan Government as a component of the AusAid (currently Australian Aid) funded Pacific Adaptation Strategies Assistance Program over the islands of Tongatapu, Lifuka and Foa to inform coastal and planning management and climate change. The lidar was captured on six flights carried out from 3 to 24 October 2011 with 104 runs, and eight cross runs flown at 750 m above ground level. The Optech ALTM-Orion sensor collected four discrete returns and intensity. The swath width of the lidar was 578 m and overlap between flight lines was 20 per cent. The project was designed to meet project specifications of 4 pt/m^2; however, post survey checks indicate that 7.87 pt/m^2 was achieved with all returns and a 5.67 pt/m^2 density with only first returns (a pseudo pulse density). The survey was conducted on the WGS84 horizontal datum and projected to the Tonga Map Grid 2005. Vertical datum for the survey was the EGM2008 geoid and a local adjustment of 0.77 m was made by the contractor to adjust the vertical datum of the project to mean sea level at the benchmark TON1 as set by the 'Nuku'alofa SEAFRAME tide gauge. The GPS base station was located at the Fua'amotu International Airport and the entirety of the survey area was within 50 km of the base station (Anderson 2011).

Raw laser data was classified by the contractor into ground or non-ground classifications, according to the Intergovernmental Committee on Surveying and Mapping (ICSM) Classification Level 2 Ground Surface Improvement standards. Independent survey checks indicate that the vertical accuracy of the project in Tongatapu is 0.15 m at 95 per cent confidence level. The density of points classified as 'ground' was calculated at 1.04 pt/m^2. Point cloud data was stored in the binary LAS format where derivative products, such as digital elevation models (DEM), intensity imagery and foliage models, were created by the contractor and delivered to the Tongan Government. Approval to use the lidar dataset for archaeological research was granted to the authors by the Tongan Government and Geosciences Australia.

Sources of lidar error

Error is inherent in all measurement systems. If we are to unlock the potential of lidar as a survey tool to investigate prehistoric earthworks, the sources of lidar error need to be understood and quantified, and propagated through an analysis so that reliable results are obtained (see Fernandez-Diaz et al. 2014 for description of components of lidar for archaeologists). Error in lidar is complex, but sources can be summarised as coming from positioning and altitude of the aircraft, sensor errors, and point cloud classification errors (Hodgson and Bresnahan 2004:333). These sources of error can be minimised thorough survey design, and although archaeologists may have little control over the survey design, awareness of error sources is important for understanding measurement accuracy.

Lidar manipulation

DEM creation

A primary deliverable from the contractor were pre-processed raster DEMs. Survey documentation describing the processing methodologies to create the DEMs from the point cloud data was not sufficient to recreate the methodology. This is important as different methods of point cloud rasterisation propagate error in different ways (Hartzell et al. 2015:1150–1151). Point clouds were rasterised using a binning approach, where elevation points are placed into raster bins (or cells) and a single elevation value is returned for each bin by averaging all the points that fall within the raster bin. The binning approach was used as it simplifies the propagation of error through to the final volume determinations.

DEM error

Modelling of error in the lidar elevation model follows the methodology of Hodgson and Bresnahan (2004), where a reference dataset collected from a source of higher accuracy is compared to the elevation model and a root mean square (RMS) value calculated. Different types of vegetation cover affect the accuracy of ground point determination and subsequent DEM creation, therefore error needed to be calculated and applied based on vegetation type. Because the lidar dataset is being reprocessed several years after initial capture, it was difficult to identify with confidence vegetation types based on the supplied information, therefore reference data was amalgamated into two vegetation types: 'trees' and 'long grass', capturing the main variation in vegetation on Tongatapu. An additional category of 'bare earth' includes areas with little or no vegetation cover. RMS was calculated for each of the vegetation types (Table 8.1).

It should be noted that the check measurements also contain error, and ideally these errors too would be propagated through the calculations. The survey report did not contain information on how these points were acquired so it is not possible to account for these errors. In practice, these errors are likely to be very small and contribute minimally to the overall error budget.

Vegetation cover was mapped by combining the supplied canopy height model (CHM) and foliage cover model (FCM). The CHM measures the height of the canopy above ground surface whereas the FCM measures foliage density. While not a rigorous vegetation classification, an overall accuracy of 91 per cent (Table 8.2) following evaluation and the results of the classification were suitable for assigning error to different vegetation types (Congalton and Green 2009:57).

Table 8.1. Root mean square (RMS) values calculated per vegetation type used in error analysis.

Vegetation type	Number of points in class	RMS (mm)
Trees	92	0.094
Long grass	54	0.175
Bare earth	1128	0.061

Source: Authors' data.

Table 8.2. Error matrix and accuracy assessment of vegetation classification for determination of digital elevation model (DEM) error zones.

		Reference data			Row total
		1	2	3	
Classified data	1	1042	3	7	1052
	2	78	46	19	143
	3	8	5	66	79
	Column total	1128	54	92	1274

Overall accuracy = 91%	
Producer's accuracy	User's accuracy
1 = 92%	1 = 99%
2 = 85%	2 = 32%
3 = 71%	3 = 84%

1 = bare earth, 2 = long grass and 3 = trees. Producer accuracy describes the accuracy of the classifier to correctly place the reference data in the right class, and User accuracy describes the reliability of each class.
Source: Authors' data.

Calculation of earthwork volumes

The volume under the binned raster surface can be defined mathematically as:

$$V = A \sum_{i=1}^{n} z_i$$

Where A is the size of the raster bins used to create the DEM and z is the binned elevation value.

The global propagation of variance (GLOPOV) (Ghilani 2010) defines the variance of the volume under the binned raster surface:

$$\sigma_V^2 = A^2 \sum_{i=1}^{n} z_i^2$$

Finally, to calculate the volume of the earthwork, the DEM is subtracted from a DEM without the earthwork. Variance of the volume of the earthwork is defined as:

$$\sigma_{V\,earth\,work}^2 = \sigma_{V\,with\,earth\,work}^2 + \sigma_{V\,without\,earth\,work}^2$$

Creation of pre-earthworks DEM

To create a surface showing the original ground surface before Fisi Tea construction, Fisi Tea needed to be digitally 'erased' from the DEM. Since the construction area of Fisi Tea is well defined by changes in surface slope, a slope threshold of five degrees was applied to define the construction area. The slope threshold raster was then used to mask the construction area and a plane fitting/inverse distance weighting (IDW) interpolation was used in ArcMap to fill the created void. DEM visualisation techniques were applied to the new DEM to highlight boundary or interpolation errors and the slope threshold boundary was manually altered as necessary. The error model of the original DEM was adopted as the error model for the pre-earthworks DEM.

Extraction of morphological attributes

A series of morphological attributes were extracted from the DEM for survey analysis. The overall limits of Fisi Tea were previously defined by the slope threshold raster, and additional earthwork morphological variables defined include: the centre or highest point of the rampart, the centre or lowest point of the ditch, and the transition between the cut and fill.

The position of the rampart centre was defined by the line of the watershed between the northern and southern parts of the rampart. Hydrology tools in ArcMap were used to identify the watershed and the line extracted. Similarly, the centre of the ditch was defined in the same manner; however, the ditch only becomes the watershed when the DEM is inverted. The $DEM_{inverse}$ is calculated by:

$$DEM_{inverse} = (-1 \times (DEM - MaxHgt)) + MinHgt$$

The watershed is then calculated in the same manner and digitised. Finally, the cut/fill transition is defined by calculating the zero elevation contour when the pre-earthworks DEM is subtracted from the DEM including the earthwork.

Creation of analysis units

To analyse the morphology of Fisi Tea, analysis units in the form of regularly spaced elevation profiles, called chainages, were used. A reference line from which the profiles were based was created as a 'best fit' line separately through the cut/fill transition of both the main length and bend portion of Fisi Tea. Elevation profiles were created at one metre intervals perpendicular to the line of best fit (Figure 8.2).

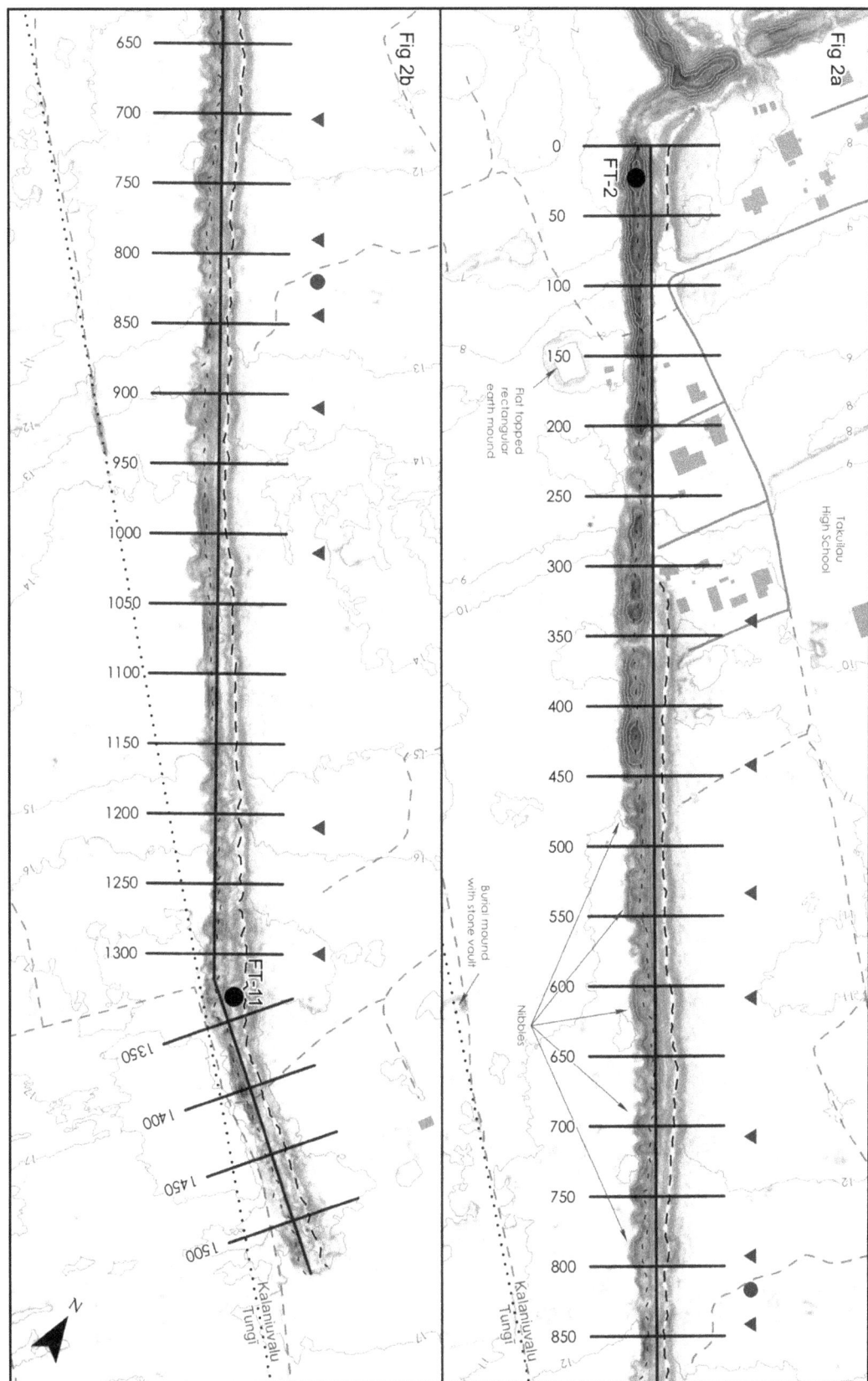

Figure 8.2. Detail of Fisi Tea.

Location of radiocarbon samples highlighted. Triangles are placed at high point lookouts and the circle locates the possible minor gate feature.

Source: Phillip Parton, Geoffrey Clark and Christian Reepmeyer.

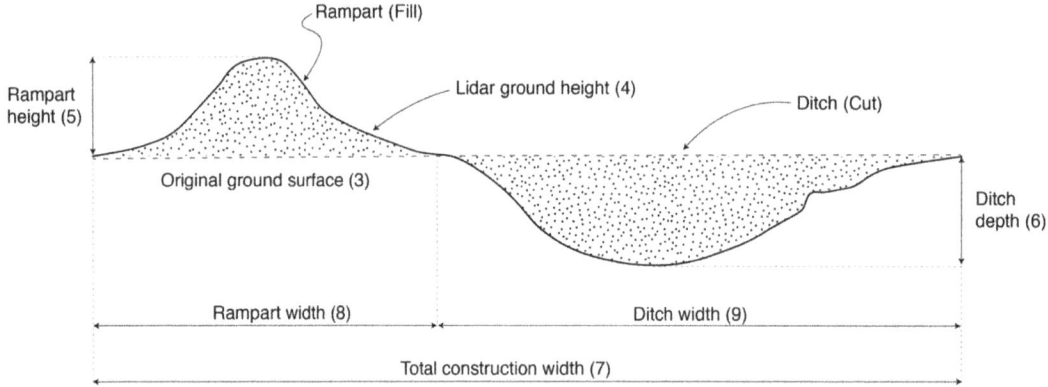

Figure 8.3. Pictorial overview of morphological attributes calculated at each elevation profile.
Source: Phillip Parton, Geoffrey Clark and Christian Reepmeyer.

For each of the elevation profiles, nine attributes were extracted totalling over 474 000 individual observations of rampart and ditch morphology. The attributes were: (1) elevation profile chainage; (2) variance; (3) original ground height; (4) lidar ground height; (5) maximum rampart height; (6) maximum ditch depth; (7) total construction width; (8) rampart width and (9) ditch width (Figure 8.3).

The attribute data were exported from ArcMap and were summarised using R scripts (3.5.0) and Tidyverse (1.2.1) packages to group attributes by chainage and calculate cut and fill volumes at each chainage.

Radiocarbon dating Fisi Tea

Five radiocarbon ages from Fisi Tea were obtained on charcoal samples excavated at two locations. The FT–2 excavation was located in the centre of the ditch toward the start of Fisi Tea to examine the depth of ditch fill from rampart erosion. FT–11 was on the inner (ditch side) of the rampart, inland and near to where the earthwork changes direction (Figure 8.2). Two charcoal samples of unidentified wood charcoal were collected from limestone debris at the ditch base c. 70 cm below the surface. Ditches are notorious for capturing material unrelated to the age of construction (Bell et al. 1996:79), and unidentified wood charcoal can contain significant in-built age. The FT–2 charcoal samples were discrete charcoal fragments in quarried limestone that may have been deposited during ditch construction, but the charcoal could be from burning old wood. From the FT–11 excavation, three charcoal endocarp samples were collected from the interface between the rampart fill and the buried topsoil horizon (O Horizon). Endocarp has a small amount of in-built age, but carbonised nut shell can exist in upper soils for long periods.

All charcoals were dated with AMS (accelerator mass spectrometry) at the ANU Radiocarbon Laboratory and calibrated with Calib 8.1 using the SHcal13 dataset.

Energetics

The calculation of energetics estimates the energy and labour investments for earthwork features and the results can encode many of the social decisions made at the time of construction (Clark and Martinsson-Wallin 2007; Kim 2013). Energetics are calculated by accounting for the materials used in the construction of the feature that in the case of Fisi Tea is the volume of the ditch excavation and related volume of the associated rampart 'fill'.

These volume measurements are converted to labour estimates to determine how long construction activity might have taken using a larger or smaller workforce. The high resolution of lidar-based volume determinations allows accurate and defensible estimates of the amount of energy invested in the construction of large archaeological features that are otherwise difficult to obtain with ground-based mapping techniques.

While the energetics calculations are simple mathematically, the energetics approach is not without its limitations and caveats. Firstly, the presence of a large and monumental scale earthwork does not necessarily indicate social complexity nor the use of corvée labour in construction. If an earthwork is being used to argue for these aspects, then Rosenswig and Burger (2012) argue that they need to be demonstrated by additional lines of evidence. Corvée labour in prehistoric Tonga was called *fatongia*. *Fatongia* is defined as: 'a tax, work done for the government; compulsion, necessity' (Rabone 1845:90), and 'a tax, impost' (Martin 1991). A broader definition of *fatongia* is given by Lātūkefu (1980:65–66), where it forms part of the 'traditional values' of Tongan society consisting of *fakaʻapaʻapa* (respect), *mateaki* (loyalty) and *fatongia* (duty). Lātūkefu expands on the definition of *fatongia* by describing it as the governing principle of relationships between classes. The chief's *fatongia* to their people was to protect them, settle disputes and provide them with good living conditions. The *fatongia* of the people to their chiefs was to give both their labour and the best of their produce and crafts to the chief when called upon through a *fono* or town meeting. Traditionally, *fatongia* is linked to the transformations introduced by the chief Loʻau when the kava ceremony was introduced by the tenth Tuʻi Tonga, Momo, around 1200 CE (Gifford 1929:131).

Secondly, the interpretation of energetics calculations will be different if the earthwork feature was constructed over a long period of time or in multiple stages (Blitz and Livingood 2004). The proposed defensive function of Fisi Tea makes it unlikely that it was built incrementally over a long period of time due to the imminent threat of intense violence that likely prompted its construction. While differing construction strategies were employed along the length of Fisi Tea, the archaeological data supports the view that Fisi Tea is a single-event construction (see below).

Finally, it is important to note that energetics calculations do not account for the construction of structures built using perishable materials (Kolb 1997). Nineteenth-century fortifications in Tonga were made with palisades on the rampart and included additional elaborations such as fighting stages and observation posts, all of which are unaccounted for in the calculations. Additionally, the calculations do not record the energy invested in the workforce such as in additional food production and tool use and maintenance. For these reasons, the estimates should be treated as conservative 'minimum' values.

Accounts of the digging technology used by Tongans by early European visitors describe the ground being dug 'with an instrument of hardwood, about five feet long, narrow, with sharp edges, and pointed', called *huo* in Tongan (Anderson in Beaglehole 1967:934; Wilson 1799:245). The description of the *huo* is similar to those of digging sticks in Mesoamerica and the labour estimates of Erasmus (1965) and Abrams (1989) were therefore used to calculate the amount of labour required to excavate material necessary to construct Fisi Tea (2.6 m^3/day (Abrams 1989:70; Erasmus 1965:285)). Data from Abrams provides the additional information of the labour required to shape and compact the fill layers of the earthwork (4.8 m^3/day (Abrams 1989:70)). The Erasmus values are a widely used standard for labour calculations, allowing cross-referencing to other projects (e.g. Kolb 1997; Ortmann and Kidder 2013; Pickett et al. 2016; Sherwood and Kidder 2011). The figures of Erasmus and Abrams lack standard deviations and a nominal standard deviation of 1 m^3 was applied to both the excavation rate and the fill rate. Based on modern field observations, including our observations of manual earth moving in Tonga, these estimates appear to be appropriate.

Results

Fisi Tea morphology

Analysis of rampart and ditch height above and below the original ground surface along the length of Fisi Tea indicate little variation in rampart height. The average height of the rampart was 1.8 ± 0.4 m. In contrast, ditch depth was more variable, with deeper excavations for approximately the first third of the earthwork and shallower excavations over the remaining two thirds. A large change in depth occurs at c. CH450.00 with another smaller change at c. CH800.00. The results match field observations where rampart height appeared consistent whereas ditch depth became shallower as the excavation moved inland from Lapaha (Figure 8.4a).

The cut and fill analysis mirrors that of rampart height. Fill volumes used in rampart construction remain consistent along Fisi Tea and ditch-cut volumes (and ditch depth) are largest to c. CH450.00, then become smaller, but are variable through to approximately CH800.00, and then excavation volume decreases toward the inland end of Fisi Tea (Figure 8.4b).

The average width of the Fisi Tea construction limits (ditch and width) was 37 ± 6 m, with width ranging from 52 m to 21 m. Average rampart width was 9 ± 2 m and again the limited variation of the rampart is notable (Figure 8.4c). Ditch widths begin large and a decrease in ditch width is recorded at CH450.00. Further changes to the end of Fisi Tea are obscured by highly variable ditch widths that are likely related to the decreasing depth of sediment on the inland slopes of Tongatapu (Gibbs 1976).

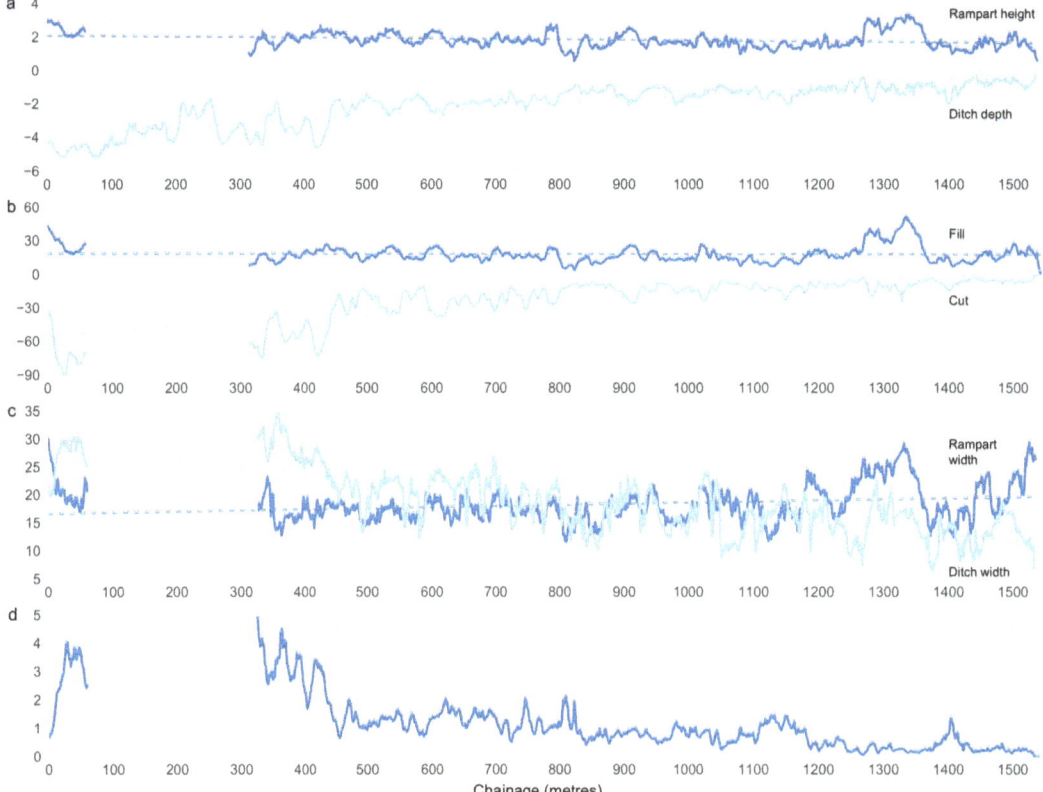

Figure 8.4. Plots of morphological variables.

A. Rampart height and ditch depth above and below original ground surface (metres). B. Cut and fill volumes (metres^3). C. Width of construction limits (metres). D. Cut and fill ratio (unitless).

Source: Phillip Parton, Geoffrey Clark and Christian Reepmeyer.

Defensive features

Identifying breaks in the rampart that might be gates is difficult with the current data and no evidence exists for the elaboration of gates such as baffles or screens that are found at some enclosure forts. A small depression in the rampart height data at c. CH825.00 may represent a gate as the rampart is low and the ditch shallow at this location (Figure 8.4a). The location could postdate construction where a section of eroded and slumped rampart was used to make a causeway to cross the ditch. However, either side of the low point are two high rampart points that potentially flanked the defending gate. At the time of the lidar survey in 2011, the area was covered in long grass with no indication of vehicle tracks in the area. In 2018 aerial photography a vehicle track is present. At other fortifications in Tonga, entrance causeways have been adapted to vehicle use. Excavation and additional historical datasets will be necessary to determine whether the location is an original gate and causeway or was formed more recently by vehicle traffic.

A series of regularly spaced high points are visible in the rampart height data (Figure 8.4a). The high points are approximately 1 m higher than the surrounding rampart and might represent observation or signalling outposts which are critical for the effective use of linear defences (Arkush and Stanish 2005:10). At the bend point of Fisi Tea (Figures 8.1 and 8.2), an enlarged high point, approximately 70 m long, is present accompanied by significant widening of the rampart. The position close to the end of Fisi Tea appears a likely spot for a major observation or signalling outpost that was built to observe the hinterland. Fully occupying a large linear structure, like Fisi Tea, would require prohibitively high numbers of personnel and signalling or observation outposts are needed for the early identification of an incoming threat and to allow defenders to concentrate forces against attackers along the wall (Connah 2000; LeBlanc 2006).

Volume of Fisi Tea

The rampart construction attributes observed in the analysis of height, width and volume are strong evidence for the standardisation of the Fisi Tea rampart. Because the rampart construction is relatively uniform, and the destroyed section of rampart (CH61.00–CH313.00) was pushed into the ditch with a bulldozer, it is possible to interpolate the volume of the rampart in this section and to remove it from the ditch to calculate final cut and fill values for the Fisi Tea earthwork. The average rampart volume was used to interpolate the missing values and these values were removed from the excavation volumes to undo the effects of rampart destruction.

The total amount of material used for the construction of the rampart component of Fisi Tea is $28\ 460 \pm 30\ m^3$ and the volume of material excavated for the ditch component is $43\ 330 \pm 42\ m^3$ leaving a total of $14\ 870\ m^3$ of material excess to requirements for rampart construction that was removed from the site. The propagated volume errors are c. 0.1 per cent of the cut and fill volumes, highlighting the high accuracy of lidar-based volume determinations.

Construction sequence

To investigate the observed changes in rampart/ditch morphology in more detail, the ratio between cut and fill volumes was calculated. Due to the apparent standardisation of the rampart, variation in the cut/fill ratio should largely reflect changes in the excavation strategy. A cut/fill ratio close to 1 indicates that all the material excavated from the ditch was used to construct the immediately adjacent rampart. A ratio larger than 1 indicates that surplus material was excavated and conversely a ratio below 1 indicates the excavation was unable to provide enough material for rampart construction.

The ratio of cut and fill at Fisi Tea suggests that three possible construction strategies were employed. First, in the locations closest to Lapaha (CH0.00 to CH450.00), between 2.5 and 4 times more material was excavated from the ditch than was necessary for rampart construction (Figure 8.4d). Field survey indicates that in the lower sections of Fisi Tea, excavation reached into the limestone bedrock while large boulders were left in place. Other early defensive earthworks in Lapaha follow a similar pattern of excessive ditch excavation relative to rampart volume (Olotele 3.1:1, Hautama/Haʻamea 3.6:1, Lapaha Kolotau 2.6:1).

Between CH450.00 and CH825.00 the cut/fill ratio stabilises and varies between 1 and 2. Field survey through this section showed that excavation into the fractured limestone base ceased and the ditch tracked the bedrock surface. From CH825.00 to the end of Fisi Tea, the cut/fill ratio rarely exceeds 1. Ditch depths become shallower while still tracking the top of the limestone bedrock while the soil–clay layers become thinner as elevation increases on Tongatapu (Gibbs 1976).

The decreasing cut/fill ratios highlight the challenges faced by the builders of Fisi Tea as they worked to build a standardised rampart while excavating less and less material from the ditch. During excavation of the rampart in the upper reaches of Fisi Tea, where the ditch depth is only c. 1 m, the rampart contained a thick redeposited topsoil lens (Figures 8.5a and 8.5b). The topsoil sediment is unlikely to derive from the adjacent shallow ditch and the material likely represents non-local procurement from a series of excavation 'nibbles' or small quarries made into the southern edge of the ditch predominantly between CH450.00 and CH825.00 (Figure 8.2). Calculation of the volume of material removed from the 'nibble' excavations of the south-eastern bank was calculated as 3900 m^3, compared with the total amount of unaccounted rampart material from CH825.00 onwards which is c. 6000 m^3. Additional ditch edge nibbling is possible closer to the disturbed rampart area, but the disturbance prohibits the inclusion of these volumes in the calculation. It is feasible that the nibbles were capable of providing enough material to offset the shortfall of material available locally for rampart construction. The extra distance to transport rampart construction material may have increased the costs of Fisi Tea construction such that it was no longer viable to continue to build the defences in the same manner.

As the ditch became shallower it also became less effective as a defensive structure and Keeley et al. (2007:79) suggest a minimum ditch depth of 1 m or more as necessary to defend against human attackers. Between CH1200.00 and CH1250.00 the Fisi Tea ditch crossed this threshold. The combination of an increasingly costly rampart construction and ineffective defensive ditch likely prompted a rethink of how to defend Lapaha and the hinterland. As the earthwork component of the defence concluded, it is possible that the defence continued to the sea as a palisade or similar barrier made from perishable materials. This can be tested by area excavation of the terminal part of Fisi Tea.

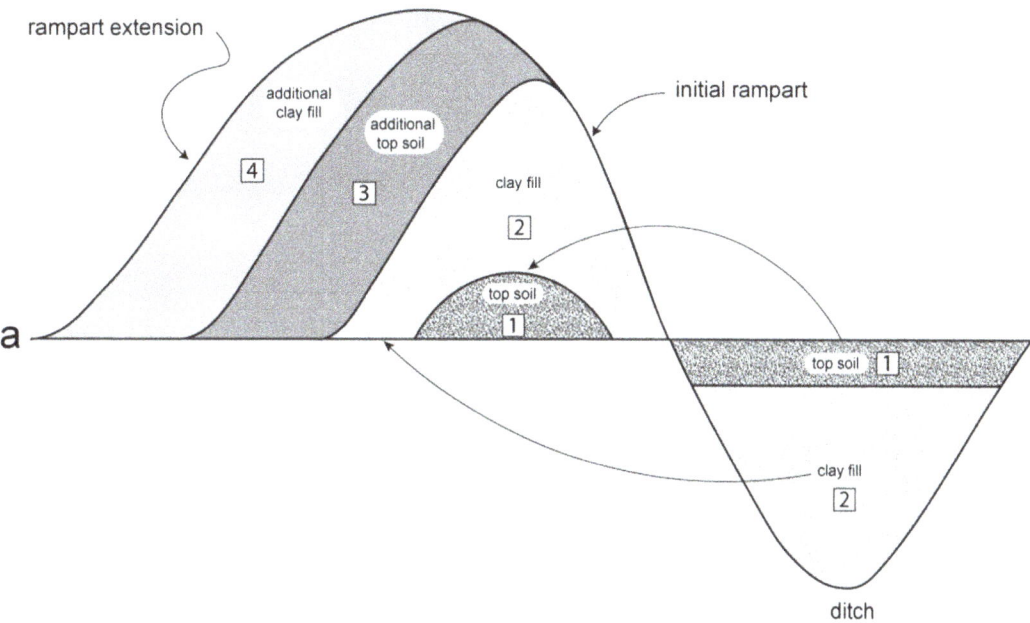

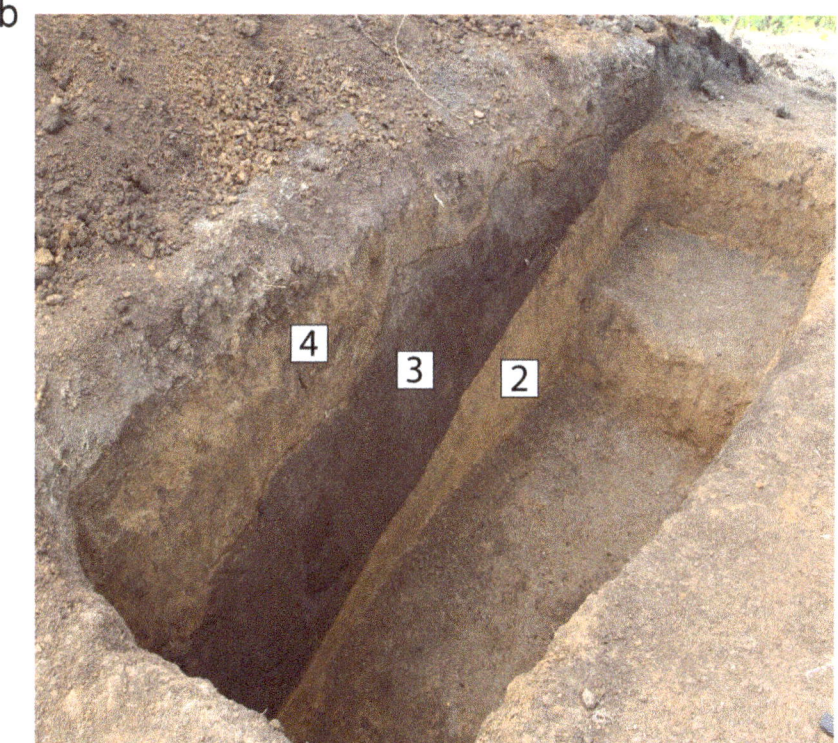

Figure 8.5. Idealised rampart construction sequence.

A. Local topsoil is removed and placed near to the centre of the rampart forming a 'topsoil core' [1]. Local clay fill is removed and the rampart is formed and shaped [2]. If enough local material is available to build the rampart to design then construction continues; otherwise, non-local topsoil is placed on the rampart as quarries for additional material are dug [3]. Non-local clay fill is added to complete the rampart to design [4]. B. Rampart cross-section near to FT-11 excavation showing fill layers 2, 3 and 4. While fill layer 1 is not shown, fill layer 1 is observed in other rampart excavations where the central core has been penetrated.

Source: Phillip Parton, Geoffrey Clark and Christian Reepmeyer.

Age of Fisi Tea

Establishing the age of the Fisi Tea earthwork with radiocarbon is difficult as the concentrated charcoal deposits that are often found beneath the ramparts of enclosed forts were rare, and this paucity has also been noted at other linear defences in Tongatapu that we have examined. At enclosed forts, ditch and rampart construction was preceded by clearing and burning of vegetation presumably to ensure the fortification was of a suitable size to protect a community/group and the earthworks were properly situated for defence. In addition, some enclosed forts were built in already occupied areas. Ditch construction and deposition of excavated sediment to build a fort rampart frequently protected the rich charcoal deposits left by occupation and vegetation clearance. Linear fortifications are different from enclosed forts in that they appear to mark territory boundaries in the hinterland that were located in zones of low-density occupation, and particular field systems where vegetation clearance and burning was sporadic and charcoal was dispersed rather than concentrated. While all charcoal samples from beneath earthworks are necessarily maximum ages those from linear defences appear most likely to contain environmental charcoal that could significantly pre-date earthwork construction.

Age results from the FT–2 ditch excavation are younger than those from FT–11, which date to 1300–1400 CE when a number of large construction projects were undertaken at Lapaha (Table 8.3) (Clark et al. 2016). There are two reasons for suggesting the endocarp results are too old. First, a relative chronology for the defensive earthworks of Lapaha based on rampart position indicate that the Olotele earthwork near the lagoon was built first, followed by the Ha'amea section, and Fisi Tea was made last. Unpublished ^{14}C ages from Olotele indicate probable construction c. 1400–1500 CE. The two charcoal ages from the FT–2 ditch excavation span 1420–1620 CE and are consistent with the inferred construction sequence compared with the older FT–11 determinations. Second, in Tongan traditions the Olotele fortification was built or rebuilt by the 23rd Tu'i Tonga Takalaua (McKern 1929:93). Allowing a generation interval of 20 and 25 years suggests that Takalaua governed c. 1450–1550 CE and Fisi Tea was likely built c. 1400–1600 CE.

Table 8.3. Fisi Tea radiocarbon ages from FT–2 and FT–11 excavations.

S-ANU number	Context	Sample	CRA	^{13}C	Calibrated 95.4%
53907	FT–2; 75 cm bs	unidentified wood charcoal	506 ± 25	-23	1420–1460 CE
53909	FT–2; 76 cm bs	unidentified wood charcoal	429 ± 25	-20	1450–1620 CE
53825	FT–11; 120 cm bs	nut endocarp	656 ± 30	-18	1300–1400 CE
53828	FT–11; 123 cm bs	nut endocarp	664 ± 29	-17	1300–1400 CE
53826	FT–11; 118 cm bs	nut endocarp	641 ± 34	-18	1300–1410 CE

Source: Authors' data.

Energetics

Energetics estimates indicate that a likely number of people required to construct the ditch and rampart component of Fisi Tea lies in the range of 750 to 1000 people (Figure 8.6). It is possible that more people were used to speed up the construction process, but this would also have come with additional costs to maintain a larger work crew and greater supervision and management of the labour force. Similarly, a smaller number of people is unlikely due to the imminent threat of violence that likely necessitated the construction of Fisi Tea. The missionary George Vason observed 500 people performing *fatongia* to the Tu'i Kanokupolu Tuku'aho by working in the chief's fields (Orange 1840:140) and this is likely the lower limit to the size of the Fisi Tea workforce. While the presence of a palisade at Fisi Tea has not been confirmed, the nineteenth-century civil war–era fortification at Neiafu in Vava'u took three days to dig the earthworks and a day and a half to construct the palisade (Martin 1991:126), suggesting the Fisi Tea palisade may have taken 10–15 days to complete. A construction period of 30–50 days for the construction of Fisi Tea is likely given that traditional conflict in Tonga involved a period of time for chiefs to agree to an attack, and for different leaders to assemble, supply and coordinate their warriors.

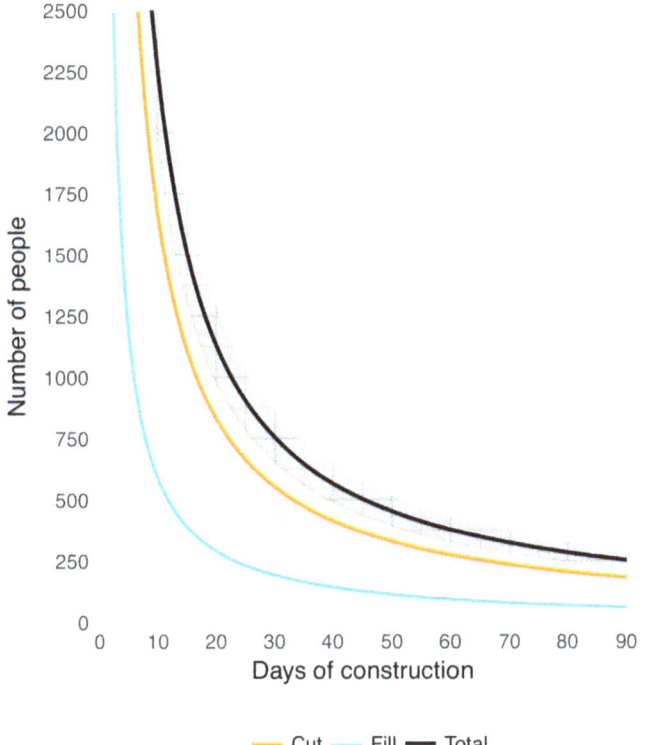

Figure 8.6. Energetics calculation for construction of Fisi Tea.
Uncertainties shown with shaded area surrounding the line.
Source: Phillip Parton, Geoffrey Clark and Christian Reepmeyer.

Discussion

Of the numerous potential functions that a large earthwork like Fisi Tea could have had, the single most important function was to protect the community and the eastern region of Tongatapu from a significant and imminent threat of violence. Of the criteria proposed by Keeley et al. (2007:79) and adopted by Parton et al. (2018) to define the defensive function of an earthwork, the V-sectioned ditch backed by a rampart is the most diagnostic, having no other rational or practical function. Extraction of elevation profiles from Fisi Tea highlights a predominantly V-sectioned ditch (Figure 8.7). A water-carrying function for Fisi Tea can be ruled out as the V-sectioned ditch is inefficient at transporting water (Keeley et al. 2007:58). Most telling is that there is no standing source of fresh water in the vicinity of Fisi Tea (nor elsewhere on the limestone island) that could be directed by the Fisi Tea ditch toward Lapaha, the field systems and settlement; and the position of the rampart prevents overland flow of water into the ditch. In addition to a V-sectioned ditch, probable, lookouts and a defended gate were likely important components of Fisi Tea. Placing warriors along an entire rampart wall is impractical and dilutes the strength of the defenders. To overcome this problem, lookouts are a predictable component of defensive walls and are placed at regular intervals to observe and communicate potential threats so that defenders can move directly to the point of attack.

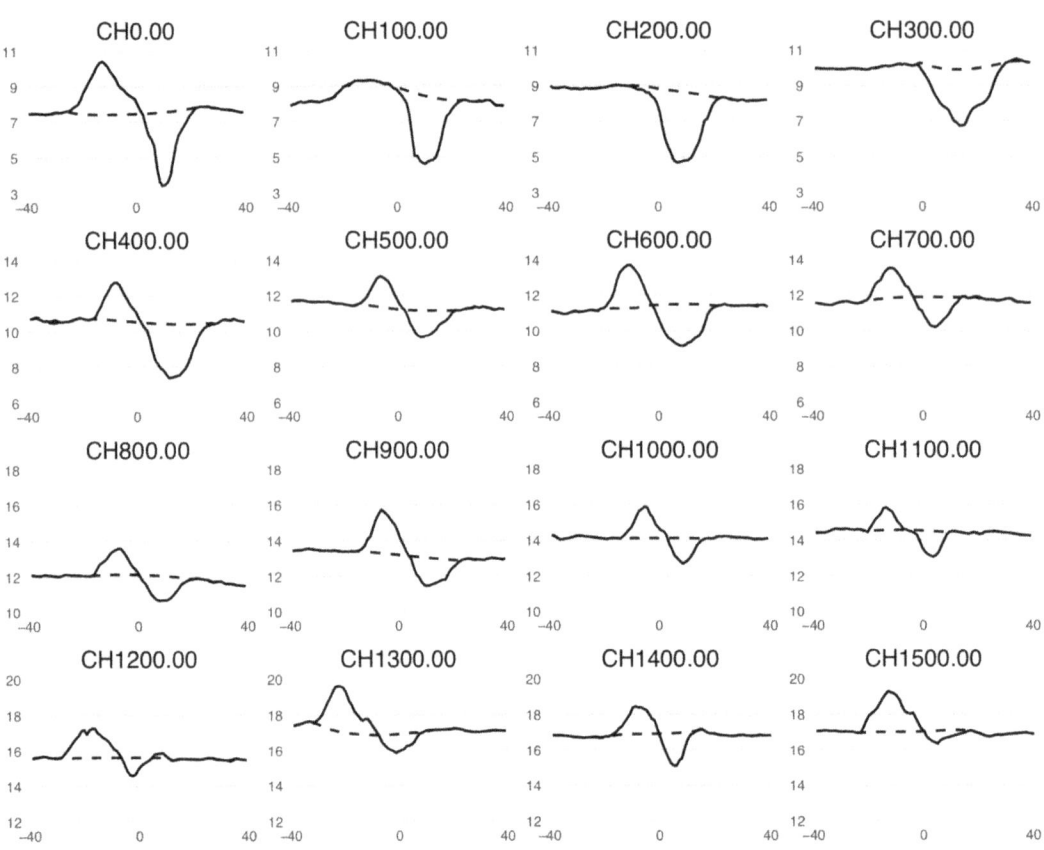

Figure 8.7. Selected elevation profiles extracted from the length of Fisi Tea.
Note the predominantly V-sectioned ditch. CH100.00, CH200.00 and CH300.00 are all situated in the destroyed section of the rampart. Interpolated original ground surface is shown with a dashed line.
Source: Phillip Parton, Geoffrey Clark and Christian Reepmeyer.

With an incoming force being monitored by a series of lookouts, attackers are forced to identify and direct their attacks towards weak points in the defensive wall, particularly gates, or try to bypass the defensive structure. Directing attacks towards gates has advantages for the attackers, but can also help defenders as the concentration of forces on a small section of wall mitigates any numerical superiority the attacking force may hold, buying time for extra defenders to arrive and mount a counterattack (Keeley 1996:56). Thus, gates become key locations that contain additional defensive features designed to strengthen the entrance. In Tonga, several visitors who described the civil war-era fortifications noted carefully designed gates (Martin 1991:79; Wilkes 1985:14, 22). At Fisi Tea, the only potential gate site is flanked by raised areas that may have supported defensive platform structures overlooking the entrance like those recorded in the nineteenth century. Vason described the effectiveness of gate elaborations in an attack on the Maʻufanga sanctuary by the chief ʻUlukālala ʻi Feletoa in 1799 CE, when their 'grand push at the entrance' was thwarted when 'the enemy stood immovable' as 'only a few of our troops could engage them' (Orange 1840:187). The gate then became an important position from which the defenders could counterattack and drive off the attackers.

The landscape immediately adjacent to Fisi Tea is characterised by a conspicuous absence of earth mounds, in an otherwise densely populated mound landscape (Figure 8.1) (Freeland et al. 2016). Despite mounds being largely unexplored, both archaeological and ethnographic sources indicate mounds were mainly built in the past 1000 years (Burley 1998:365; Davidson 1979), and functioned as house platforms, burial sites or a combination of both (Davidson 1969; Spenneman 1990). The important point is that the density of mounds at a location is likely to reflect the intensity of human occupation. Open areas or buffer zones can develop between two competing territories as a defensive measure to identify and repel attacks (LeBlanc 2006:443–444), or arise passively to avoid possible conflict with neighbouring groups along a sensitive border. If mounds were built from c. 1000 years ago the buffer zone must pre-date the Fisi Tea construction and likely represents an undefended, or palisaded, territorial boundary.

At some point, additional defensive measures were necessary to protect the Lapaha hinterlands and the boundary was fortified with an earthwork. Fisi Tea's size, orientation and relationship with other defensive earthworks in Lapaha suggests an increase in the scale and intensity of territorial warfare. In Samoa, where Tongans were reputed to have built many fortifications, Krämer (1995:392) described the importance of territorial boundaries in traditional conflict:

> Battles were in general fought at the border of both territories … Only after a party had lost a battle, or at least after its retreat, did the other party penetrate into enemy territory.

Fisi Tea appears to be an ancient territorial boundary, as noted in a description of the *tofi'a*, or chiefly estate boundary between Lapaha (chiefly title 'Kalaniuvalu') and Tatakamotonga (chiefly title 'Tungī') made by Gifford (1929:172), which has the boundary 'following the road **(or trench)** [emphasis added] straight to the weather shore', highlighting the importance of the Fisi Tea ditch in the late nineteenth and early twentieth centuries. The boundary retains modern importance and despite slight alterations following cadastral survey in the 1960s, the modern chiefly boundaries are anchored to the bend point of Fisi Tea (Figure 8.1).

Two unresolved issues raised by Fisi Tea are the cause and timing of regional conflict within the Tongan state. Traditions mention several episodes of external warfare involving 'Uvea, Futuna and Samoa as well as conflict in other parts of Tonga (Ella 1899; Sand 2008; Thomas 2013). However, it was not until after European arrival that Tongatapu fell into civil war and many fortifications were built, leading to an assumption that almost all earthworks on Tongatapu were of recent age (Spennemann 1990:483). Prehistoric fortifications were certainly built earlier (Clark et al. 2018), but there is no detailed traditional history about many structures such as Fisi Tea, which, despite its imposing dimensions and location near the monumental core of Lapaha, was not recorded in previous archaeological studies of defensive earthworks (e.g. Spennemann 1990:483). One of the defining moments of the Tongan state in traditional history was the assassination of the 23rd Tu'i Tonga Takalaua, which had been preceded by the assassination of the 19th and 22nd Tu'i Tongas, indicating a period of significant political instability (Clark 2016).

Traditions contribute the important details that Takalaua's killers came from Ha'atalafale, a locality south of Lapaha, and the reason for regicide was the impost of labour to build a royal tomb during the yam planting season (Thomson 1968:301–302), or the alteration of traditional marriage arrangements (Thomas 2013:29). The immediate impact of Takalaua's death was a vigorous military campaign by his son, the 24th Tu'i Tonga Kau'ulufonuafekai, that extended through Tonga and into adjacent islands (Thomas 2013:29–30). Clearly, the geographic extent of warfare indicates the assassination involved more than two people and must have included a number of chiefs and long-running dissatisfaction with the Tu'i Tonga system. This is shown by the creation, after Kau'ulufonuafekai's return to Tongatapu, of a new chiefly lineage known as the Tu'i Ha'atakalaua. The lineage had a focus on administrative and practical governance, which distanced the Tu'i Tonga from unpopular decisions that had previously led to political assassination and conflict while maintaining, at least initially, the paramount's status and influence. The creation of a diarchy at Lapaha was manifested spatially by the Tu'i Ha'atakalaua line occupying the reclaimed land in front of the old shoreline, while the Tu'i Tonga held the landward area. The division led to the term *Kauhala'uta* to refer to the Tu'i Tonga's followers and *Kauhalalalo* to describe people under junior chiefly titles (Bott 1982:156). We suggest that Fisi Tea represents another political axis that is not recorded in traditional history, with the fortified boundary between Lapaha and the rest of Tongatapu built to defend Lapaha and parts of the greater Hahake region against a coalition of chiefs based elsewhere on Tongatapu who organised or supported the assassination of Takalaua (and previous Tuʻi Tonga).

At Fisi Tea, a secondary function in building the earthwork was likely the construction of large and deep ditches close to Lapaha. The size of the ditches in this area matches those of Olotele and Hautama/Haʻamea, which surround the political core of monumental architecture and represents what Trigger (1990:124) calls 'conspicuous consumption'. Building the defences closest to Lapaha at a monumental scale communicates the power and prestige of the polity to both internal and external groups (Rapoport 2006; Trigger 1990). Successfully repelling enemy attacks would also increase the prestige and symbolic value of the defence (Keeley 1996:57). Ultimately, 'fortifications are most symbolically useful when they are militarily functional' (Keeley et al. 2007:81), and advances in military technology can quickly make the secondary functions of the defence a liability—as seen in fifteenth-century Europe, where impressive city walls were destroyed following the introduction of the cannon (de la Croix 1972:39–41; Parker 2000).

As the weakest points of the overall construction of the wall and focal points of enemy attack, gates receive elaborations to prevent attackers penetrating the territory. In peacetime, leaders quickly realised that gates continue to restrict the movement of people and goods through the region and with small alterations, can be redesigned or adapted to collect customs, taxes and information as people are funnelled through them (Connah 2000:41; Richmond 2013:247–248; Russell 2013; Turner 1970). McKern (1929:95) identified a single gate from the south into Olotele and survey analysis suggests a second gate in the hinterland. In contrast, an approximately 350 m portion of the Huʻatolitoli linear fortification (Number 54 in Parton et al. 2018:Table 1) visited in the field has a series of major and minor gates at 70–80 m intervals that would permit the regular movement of people and goods through the defence. The small number of major gates and absence of minor gates on Fisi Tea indicate that control over the movement of goods and people entering the eastern region remained important long after the initial requirement for the construction of Fisi Tea had passed, with supporting evidence in local traditions and historical accounts. First, Lapaha traditions state that visitors to Olotele were required to wait by the gate on the Tatakamotonga side before being escorted into the compound and failure to wait for an escort resulted in death. Second, in 1799 CE while waging war after the assassination of Tuʻi Kanokupolu Tukuʻaho, the chief Vahaʻi was advancing from Hihifo to the stronghold of Poha located in north-east Hahake. The army of Vahaʻi was only allowed to pass through the area after hiding their weapons and pretending to be on a visit to relatives (Collocott 1928:91).

Large defensive earthworks like Fisi Tea differ from other types of monumental architecture built in Tonga, and consequently illuminate different aspects of social organisation. Where the elite chiefly class were able to levy labour for stone-faced tombs, sporting venues and ocean-going vessels through *fatongia* (Burley 1993), the construction of defensive earthworks by a group as a response to an imminent threat of intense violence suggests that labour procurement was through cooperation rather than coercion (i.e. Roscoe 2012:75).

Energetics calculations provide an empirical estimate of community participation in the Fisi Tea earthwork. The most recent estimates of prehistoric population size of Tongatapu are approximately 18 000 people (Burley 2007:185). Using mound number and land area of the total eastern region enclosed by Fisi Tea as a proxy for population distribution, the Hahake region would have been home to approximately 4500 people. With 750–1000 people working on the construction of Fisi Tea over a period of 30–50 days, a significant proportion of the population would have had a direct role in the construction and many others would have been involved indirectly in supporting the work.

Managing the large number of people present during construction requires a level of managerial expertise to coordinate their movements and activities, and to ensure construction is completed on time and to specification (Webster et al. 2007). Additional interrelated tasks such as vegetation clearing, surveying the route and preparing construction surfaces all contribute to the construction of Fisi Tea. The standardised rampart construction observed in the survey analysis indicates that the designers had clear ideas of how Fisi Tea should look and they were able to communicate the plan to the workers with remarkable precision, and when problems were encountered adjustments were devised to solve them. The regular placement of probable lookouts and the incorporation of the adjacent buffer zones into the overall defences shows that the architects of Fisi Tea had strong strategic and tactical knowledge, which might indicate a long history of conflict at territory borders.

High community participation combined with project supervision by elites in the construction of defensive walls is recorded historically in Tonga and in other parts of the world. The Aurelian walls of Rome were constructed by community level *collegia* with oversight and coordination coming directly from Emperor Aurelian (Richmond 2013:244). In Tonga, the chief 'Ulukālala 'i Feletoa (Mariner's 'Finow', in Martin 1991) was actively involved in fort-building by coordinating work parties and procuring the necessary materials, and while the workers were performing these activities, 'Finow and his principal chiefs remained to lay out the plan' (Martin 1991:126).

Conclusion

This study of the Fisi Tea earthwork has demonstrated the power of lidar data to examine the archaeological landscape at a level well beyond its more common use in site prospection. By employing a high-resolution spatial analysis incorporating multiple earthwork morphology variables, and associated error estimates, the lidar data informed our knowledge of defensive features. These included subtle changes to the landscape that challenged the builders of Fisi Tea and the innovative solutions they used to overcome construction problems. The methodology can be applied to other defensive earthworks in Tonga, and extended to a variety of prehistoric sites such as earth mounds to examine the size, distribution and density of built structures throughout the landscape (e.g. Freeland et al. 2016).

Fisi Tea shows the growing capacity of the Tongan state to respond to significant threats to the government of the Tu'i Tonga, potentially during a time of major political upheaval within the Tonga Group. The landscape surrounding Fisi Tea is characterised by a marked absence of residential structures in the vicinity of the earthwork, suggesting that Fisi Tea was located on a pre-existing boundary between groups that may have been palisaded before the earthwork was built. In addition to earlier fortifications in the Lapaha area (Lapaha Kolotau and Olotele), Fisi Tea supports a view that political centralisation in Tonga was contested (Clark et al. 2018:416), and the monumental core of the paramount Tu'i Tonga was exposed to the threat of serial conflict. On Tongatapu, many of the traditional land boundaries associated with chiefly titles traversed the island from one coastline to another (e.g. Gifford 1929:Figure 4). During episodes of conflict these boundaries were probably controlled and, at times, defended by linear earthworks like Fisi Tea that defined the political territory of a social group. Following hostilities a new kind of chiefly structure and landscape emerged that spread Tongan influence to many parts of the Pacific, demonstrating the role of warfare in forging strong political systems. It is notable that warfare within Tongatapu prior to the nineteenth century is poorly attested in traditional history and lidar analysis in conjunction with archaeological excavation of defensive systems can provide insight to the 'hidden' history of conflict in Tonga.

References

Abrams, E.M. 1989. Architecture and energy: An evolutionary perspective. *Archaeological Method and Theory* 1:47–87.

Anderson, H. 2011. Tongatapu and Lifuka Islands, topographic and bathymetric LIDAR, data capture project. Final Project Report 18924A. AAM Group, Melbourne.

Arkush, E. and C. Stanish 2005. Interpreting conflict in the ancient Andes. *Current Anthropology* 46:3–28. doi.org/10.1086/425660.

Beaglehole, J.C. (ed.) 1967. *The journals of Captain James Cook on his voyages of discovery. Volume III: The voyage of the* Resolution *and* Discovery *1776–1780*. Cambridge University Press, London.

Bell, M., P.J. Fowler and S.W. Hillson 1996. *The experimental earthworks project: 1960–1992*. Research Report 100. Council for British Archaeology, York.

Blitz, J.H. and P. Livingood 2004. Sociopolitical implications of Mississippian mound volume. *American Antiquity* 69:291–301.

Bott, E. 1982. *Tongan society at the time of Cook's visit: Discussions with Her Majesty Queen Sālote Tupou*. Memoir No. 44. The Polynesian Society, Wellington.

Burley, D.V. 1993. Chiefly prerogatives over critical resources: Archaeology, oral traditions and symbolic landscapes in the Ha'apai Islands, Kingdom of Tonga. In R. Jamieson, S. Abonyi and N. Mirau (eds), *Culture and environment: A fragile co-existence*, pp. 437–443. University of Calgary, Calgary.

Burley, D.V. 1998. Tongan archaeology and the Tongan past, 2850–150 B.P. *Journal of World Prehistory* 12:337–392.

Burley, D.V. 2007. Archaeological demography and population growth in the Kingdom of Tonga. In P.V. Kirch and J.-L. Rallu (eds), *The growth and collapse of Pacific island societies*, pp. 177–202. University of Hawai'i Press, Honolulu. doi.org/10.1515/9780824864767-013.

Chase, A.F., D.Z. Chase, C.T. Fisher, S.J. Leisz and J.F. Weishampel 2012. Geospatial revolution and remote sensing LiDAR in Mesoamerican archaeology. *Proceedings of the National Academy of Sciences USA* 109:12916–12921. doi.org/10.1073/pnas.1205198109.

Clark, G. 2016. Chiefly tombs, lineage history, and the ancient Tongan state. *Journal of Island and Coastal Archaeology* 11(3):326–343. doi.org/10.1080/15564894.2015.1098754.

Clark, G. and C. Reepmeyer 2014. Stone architecture, monumentality and the rise of the early Tongan chiefdom. *Antiquity* 88:1244–1260. doi.org/10.1017/s0003598x00115431.

Clark, G. and H. Martinsson-Wallin 2007. Monumental architecture in West Polynesia: Origins, chiefs and archaeological approaches. *Archaeology of Oceania Supplement* 42:28–40. doi.org/10.1002/j.1834-4453.2007.tb00006.x.

Clark, G., D. Burley and T. Murray 2008. Monumentality and the development of the Tongan maritime chiefdom. *Antiquity* 82:994–1008. doi.org/10.1017/s0003598x00097738.

Clark, G., C. Reepmeyer and N. Melekiola 2016. The rapid emergence of the archaic Tongan state: The royal tomb of Paepaeotelea. *Antiquity* 90:1038–1053. doi.org/10.15184/aqy.2016.114.

Clark, G., P. Parton, C. Reepmeyer, N. Melekiola and D. Burley 2018. Conflict and state development in ancient Tonga: The Lapaha earth fort. *Journal of Island and Coastal Archaeology* 13(3):405–419. doi.org/10.1080/15564894.2017.1337658.

Collocott, E.E.V. 1928. *Tales and poems of Tonga*. Bernice P. Bishop Museum Bulletin 46. Bernice P. Bishop Museum, Honolulu.

Congalton, R. and K. Green 2009. *Assessing the accuracy of remotely sensed data: Principles and practices*. 2nd edition. CRC Press, Boca Raton. doi.org/10.1201/9781420055139.

Connah, G. 2000. Contained communities in tropical Africa. In J. Tracey (ed.), *City walls: The urban enciente in global perspective*, pp. 19–45. Cambridge University Press, Cambridge.

Davidson, J.M. 1969. Archaeological excavations in two burial mounds at 'Atele, Tongatapu. *Records of the Auckland Institute and Museum* 6:251–286.

Davidson, J.M. 1979. Samoa and Tonga. In J.D. Jennings (ed.), *The prehistory of Polynesia*, pp. 82–109. Harvard University Press, Harvard and Cambridge.

de la Croix, H. 1972. *Military considerations in city planning: Fortifications*. George Braziller, New York.

Ella, S. 1899. The war of Tonga and Samoa and the origin of the name Malietoa. *Journal of the Polynesian Society* 8(4):231–234.

Erasmus, C.J. 1965. Monument building: Some field experiments. *Southwestern Journal of Anthropology* 21:277–301. doi.org/10.1086/soutjanth.21.4.3629433.

Fernandez-Diaz, J.C., W.E. Carter, R.L. Shrestha and C.L. Glennie 2014. Now you see it … Now you don't: Understanding airborne mapping LiDAR collection and data product generation for archaeological research in Mesoamerica. *Remote Sensing* 6:9951–10001. doi.org/10.3390/rs6109951.

Fox, A. 1976. *Prehistoric Maori fortifications in the North Island of New Zealand*. Longman Paul Limited, Auckland.

Freeland, T., B. Heung, D.V. Burley, G. Clark and A. Knudby 2016. Automated feature extraction for prospection and analysis of monumental earthworks from aerial LiDAR in the Kingdom of Tonga. *Journal of Archaeological Science*. 69:64–74. doi.org/10.1016/j.jas.2016.04.011.

Ghilani, C. 2010. *Adjustment computations: Spatial data analysis*. 5th edition. Wiley, Hoboken.

Gibbs, H. 1976. *Soils of Tongatapu, Tonga*. New Zealand Soil Survey Report 35. Department of Scientific and Industrial Research, Wellington.

Gifford, E.W. 1929. *Tongan society*. Bernice P. Bishop Museum Bulletin 61. Bernice P. Bishop Museum, Honolulu.

Hannon, N., D.J. Rohl and L. Wilson 2017. The Antonine Wall's distance-slabs: LiDAR as metric survey. *Journal of Roman Archaeology* 30:447–468. doi.org/10.1017/s1047759400074201.

Hartzell, P.J., P.J. Gadomski, C.L. Glennie, D.C. Finnegan and J.S. Deems 2015. Rigorous error propagation for terrestrial laser scanning with application to snow volume uncertainty. *Journal of Glaciology* 61:1147–1158. doi.org/10.3189/2015jog15j031.

Hodgson, M.E. and P. Bresnahan 2004. Accuracy of airborne Lidar-derived elevation. *Photogrammetric engineering and remote sensing* 70:331–339. doi.org/10.14358/pers.70.3.331.

Keeley, L.H. 1996. *War before civilization: The myth of the peaceful savage*. Oxford University Press, New York.

Keeley, L.H., M. Fontana and R. Quick 2007. Baffles and bastions: The universal features of fortifications. *Journal of Archaeological Research* 15(1):55–95. doi.org/10.1007/s10814-006-9009-0.

Kim, N.C. 2013. Lasting monuments and durable institutions: Labor, urbanism, and statehood in Northern Vietnam and beyond. *Journal of Archaeological Research* 21:217–267. doi.org/10.1007/s10814-012-9064-7.

Kolb, M.J. 1997. Labor mobilization, ethnohistory, and the archaeology of community in Hawaiʻi. *Journal of Archaeological Method and Theory* 4:265–285. doi.org/10.1007/bf02428064.

Krämer, A. 1995. *The Samoa Islands. Volume II: Material culture*. Translated by Dr Theodore Verhaaren. University of Hawaiʻi Press, Honolulu.

Lātūkefu, S. 1980. The definition of authentic Oceanic cultures with particular reference to Tongan culture. *Pacific Studies* 4:60–81.

LeBlanc, S. 2006. Warfare and the development of social complexity. In E. Arkush and M. Allen (eds), *The archaeology of warfare: Prehistories of raiding and conquest*, pp. 437–468. University Press of Florida, Florida.

Lustig, T., S. Klassen, D. Evans, R. French and I. Mo 2018. Evidence for the breakdown of an Angkorian hydraulic system, and its historical implications for understanding the Khmer Empire. *Journal of Archaeological Science: Reports* 17:195–211. doi.org/10.1016/j.jasrep.2017.11.014.

Martin, J. 1991. *Tonga islands: William Mariner's account.* 5th edition. Vavaʻu Press, Nukuʻalofa.

McKern, W.C. 1929. *Archaeology of Tonga.* Bernice P. Bishop Museum Bulletin 60. Bernice P. Bishop Museum, Honolulu.

Opitz, R.S., K. Ryzewski, J.F. Cherry and B. Moloney 2015. Using airborne LiDAR survey to explore historic-era archaeological landscapes of Montserrat in the Eastern Caribbean. *Journal of Field Archaeology* 40(5):523–541. doi.org/10.1179/2042458215y.0000000016.

Orange, J. 1840. *Life of the late George Vason of Nottingham.* Henry Mozley and Sons, Derby.

Ortmann, A.L. and T.R. Kidder 2013. Building Mound A at Poverty Point, Louisiana: Monumental public architecture, ritual practice, and implications for hunter-gatherer complexity. *Geoarchaeology* 28:66–86. doi.org/10.1002/gea.21430.

Parker, G. 2000. The artillery fortress as an engine of European overseas expansion, 1480–1750. In J. Tracey (ed.), *City walls: The urban enciente in global perspective*, pp. 386–418. Cambridge University Press, Cambridge.

Parton, P., G. Clark, C. Reepmeyer and D. Burley 2018. The field of war: LiDAR identification of earthwork defences on Tongatapu Island, Kingdom of Tonga. *Journal of Pacific Archaeology* 9(1):11–24.

Pickett, J., J.S. Schreck, R. Holod, Y. Rassamakin, O. Halenko and W. Wood 2016. Architectural energetics for tumuli construction: The case of the medieval Chungul Kurgan on the Eurasian steppe. *Journal of Archaeological Science* 75:101–114. doi.org/10.1016/j.jas.2016.09.006.

Rabone, S. 1845. *Vocabulary of the Tonga language.* Wesleyan Mission Press, Vavaʻu.

Rapoport, A. 2006. Archaeology and environment–behavior studies. In W. Ashmore, M. Dobres, S. Nelson and A. Rosen (eds), *Integrating the diversity of twenty-first-century anthropology: The life and intellectual legacies of Susan Kent*, pp. 59–70. American Anthropological Association, Washington.

Richmond, I. 2013. *The city wall of Imperial Rome: An account of its architectural development from Aurelian to Narses.* Westholme Publishing, Yardley.

Roscoe, P. 2012. War, collective action, and the 'evolution' of human polities. In D.M. Carballo (ed.), *Cooperation and collective action: Archaeological perspectives*, pp. 70–96. University Press of Colorado, Boulder.

Rosenswig, R.M. and R. Burger 2012. Considering early New World monumentality. In R. Burger (ed.), *Early New World monumentality*, pp. 3–22. University Press of Florida. Gainesville. doi.org/10.5744/florida/9780813038087.003.0001.

Russell, B.W. 2013. Fortress Mayapan: Defensive features and secondary functions of a postclassic Maya fortification. *Ancient Mesoamerica* 24:275–294. doi.org/10.1017/s0956536113000217.

Sand, C. 2008. Prehistoric maritime empires in the Pacific: Ga'asialili ('Elili) and the establishment of a Tongan colony on 'Uvea (Wallis, Western Polynesia). In A. Di Piazza, E. Pearthree and C. Sand (eds), *At the heart of ancient societies: French contributions to Pacific archaeology*, pp. 73–105. Cahiers de l'Archeologie en Nouvelle Caledonie, Noumea.

Scherer, A.K. and C. Golden 2006. Tecolote, Guatemala: Archaeological evidence for a fortified Late Classic Maya political border. *Journal of Field Archaeology* 34(3):285–305. doi.org/10.1179/009346909791070907.

Sherwood, S.C. and T.R. Kidder 2011. The DaVincis of dirt: Geoarchaeological perspectives on Native American mound building in the Mississippi River basin. *Journal of Anthropological Archaeology* 30:69–87. doi.org/10.1016/j.jaa.2010.11.001.

Spenneman, D.H.R. 1990. 'ata 'a Tonga mo 'ata 'o Tonga: Early and later prehistory of the Tongan Islands. Volumes I and II. Unpublished PhD thesis. The Australian National University, Canberra.

Thomas, J. 2013. *A history of Tonga*. Bible Society in Korea, Seoul.

Thomson, B. 1968. *The diversions of a Prime Minister*. Dawsons of Pall Mall, London.

Trigger, B.G. 1990. Monumental architecture: A thermodynamic explanation of symbolic behaviour. *World Archaeology* 22:119–132. doi.org/10.1080/00438243.1990.9980135.

Turner, H. 1970. *Town defences in England and Wales: An architectural and documentary study, AD 900–1500*. John Baker, London.

Webster, D., T. Murtha, K.D. Straight, J. Silverstein, H. Martinez, R.E. Terry and R. Burnett 2007. The Great Tikal earthwork revisited. *Journal of Field Archaeology* 32:41–64. doi.org/10.1179/009346907791071700.

Webster, D., J. Silverstein, T. Murtha, H. Martinez and K. Straight 2008. Political ecology of the Tikal earthworks: A Maya Altepetl boundary? *Urbanism in Mesoamerica* 1:349–376.

Wilkes, C. 1985. *United States Exploring Expedition. Volume III: Tongataboo, Feejee group, Honolulu*. Fiji Museum, Suva.

Wilson, J. 1799. *A missionary voyage to the Southern Pacific Ocean, performed in the years 1796, 1796, 1798, in the ship* Duff, *commanded by Captain James Wilson*. Frederick A. Praeger, New York.

9

Geospatial analysis of fortification locations on the island of Tongatapu, Tonga

Christian Reepmeyer, Geoffrey Clark, Phillip Parton, Malia Melekiola and David Burley

Introduction

Recent research investigating earthwork fortifications on Tongatapu, Kingdom of Tonga, using lidar data identified numerous defensive sites on the island (Parton et al. 2018), with the antiquity of the earliest building phase dating to at least 1300 CE (Clark et al. 2018; Spennemann 1989). This corresponds well with the hypothesis that fortifications appear in the Pacific at 1300–1800 CE (Field 2008). However, it is widely held that most fortifications on Tongatapu were constructed during the civil war era, from 1799 to 1852 CE (McKern 1929; Spennemann 1986; Wood 1975). Beyond questions about the exact timing of initial fortification construction, there is considerable debate about the reasons populations need to defend their land. This debate is not limited to Tonga, as it has been suggested that environmental factors and climate shifts played a significant role in the emergence of social conflict in the Pacific in general (Field 2004; Field and Lape 2010).

The selection of natural defensive locations on islands has been reported from numerous parts of Oceania (Field 2008). Hill fort/ridgeline location is a common occurrence on well-researched island groups, such as Fiji (Best 1993) and Samoa (Golson 1969). This argument is also reflected in previous descriptions of fort construction under Tongan influence, such as Spennemann's (1989:481, see also Best 1993) assertion that Tongans constructed a large upland fort on the island of Lakeba in east Fiji:

> Tongans were actually responsible for the erection of the Ulunikoro fortification, and Best's argument appears convincing in the light of present evidence, it is a good example to show that fortification types are predominantly governed by topographical conditions rather than by 'cultural' traits.

In this chapter, we report geospatial analyses of earthwork fortifications on Tongatapu (Figure 9.1). Our primary concern is the location of forts in the landscape rather than the age of defensive sites as the majority of Tongatapu forts are currently undated. In addition, we focus on enclosed/partially enclosed earthwork fortifications that are the dominant type of defensive site on Tongatapu compared with the small number of linear earthworks (Parton et al. 2018). Tongatapu is a low-lying limestone island with few natural defences. There are no steep escarpments on the lagoon side of the island, and few inland high points or vertical ridges.

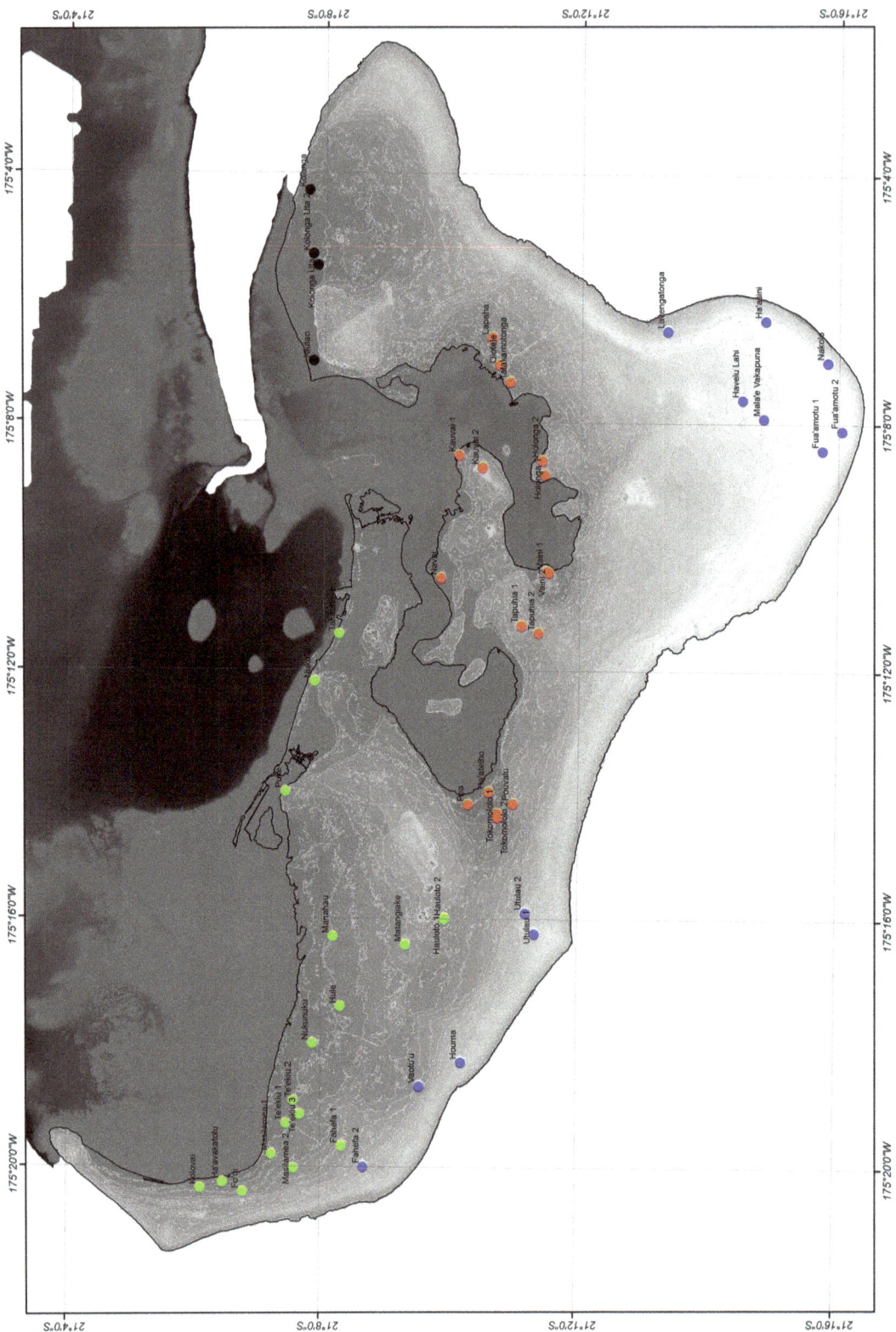

Figure 9.1. Topographic map (2 m isoclines) of Tongatapu with lidar digital elevation model (DEM) and site location of fortifications.

Locations in blue are on limestone ridges, green are low-lying coastal areas, red associated with the Fanga 'Uta Lagoon and black are sites on the north-east coast.

Source: Christian Reepmeyer, Geoffrey Clark, Phillip Parton, Malia Melekiola and David Burley.

Using the lidar dataset of enclosed forts identified (Parton et al. 2018), we examine the association of forts with natural features. The currently dominant hypothesis about the location of forts in the Pacific is that they are placed on high points/defendable areas in close proximity to a group's agricultural land (Field 2008). This is the proposed explanation for the focus of many Maori *pa* (earthwork defences) in New Zealand on high points along the coast and river systems of the North Island (e.g. Anderson 2016). Similarly, in the Sigatoka Valley, Fijian forts were established overlooking gardens (wetland *vuci* or dryland *were*) or were defended settlements located within field systems (Best 1984; Parry 1987). As Field (1998:33) notes, the association between defences and tuber cultivation aligns with the tenets of evolutionary ecology, which have increasing competition for resources as a catalyst for group formation, territorial defence and the intensification of cultivation.

There are also forts in west and east Fiji positioned in often inaccessible and high areas away from main gardens that likely functioned as territorial refuges. These forts are built and traditionally occupied by non-locals, particularly Tongans, in Fiji, Samoa and 'Uvea (Best 1993; Sand 2008). There is a high likelihood that some defensive sites were made to control strategic locations and non-agricultural resources (Best 1984; Clark et al. 2018). The topographic features of Tongatapu forts examined here were elevation, elevation difference to surrounding landscapes (peaks), slope, distance to coast, distance to potential freshwater sources and soil quality. Visibility has been considered important for site location on Fiji (Field 1998; Smith and Cochrane 2011) and we conducted an initial intervisibility analysis to examine geospatial relationships between sites.

Geographical aspects of fortification location

The analysis is based on high-resolution contours interpolated from a lidar digital elevation model (DEM; for a detailed description of the methods used, see Parton et al. 2018) combined with information from the Tonga Government Ministry of Land, Survey and Natural Resources geospatial database. The low relief and generally gentle topography of Tongatapu, in addition to the intensive agricultural usage of most of the land, allowed standard lidar visualisation techniques to view and interpret archaeological features. In some areas, however, urban development had severely degraded or even destroyed portions of earthworks. All lidar visualisations used the contractor-supplied 1 m DEM as a base from which additional visualisations were prepared. Examination of the DEM was conducted using 'default' hillshade algorithms that are standard in ArcGIS packages (ESRI 2011). The basic visualisation revealed a number of archaeological features present in the lidar data, including mounds, chiefly tombs, sunken roads and defensive structures.

Physical geography of Tongatapu

Tongatapu is a low-lying raised limestone island overlain by andesitic tephras of variable depth (Cowie 1980; Gibbs 1976). Its current geomorphology originates from six phases of volcanic activity, which uplifted the island to 65 m above sea level in the south-east (Taylor 1978). From this high point the island slopes gently to the north and north-west, and to the coast. Most of the island has a flat relief, with slopes less than five degrees. There are a few areas with rolling slopes, particularly on the southern side of the island. These have developed on undulating reef platforms and reflect relict reef outcrops within the original lagoon and barrier reefs along the coastal margins. Low scarps can be seen across the island, but are commonly covered by thinner overlain tephras, which are deeper in the depressions in between. There is a general trend in soil thickness from west to east, with soils reaching 2 m deep in the western end decreasing to around 0.4 m in the eastern end of the island (Cowie 1980).

On the south side of the island, the rocky *liku* coastlines are mostly steep, rising to 35 m above sea level. These steep coasts are interrupted by small pocket beaches, most likely originating from erosion of sinkholes and coastal limestone. No reef passages exist on the south side of the island (Taylor 1978) but there are rare deep water channels to the north. The south coast of the island is highly dynamic, whereas the northern leeward side of the island receives little wave action and is sheltered from tidal action by a lagoon fronted by a series of outer islands. The Fanga 'Uta Lagoon is the main feature of central–north Tongatapu and has large areas of mangrove. The lagoon is shallow and the western part is now enclosed by land and is connected to the sea by tidal channels.

Spatial patterning of fort distribution

Forts on Tongatapu occur in four different geospatial locations: (1) uplifted limestone ridges on the south coast; (2) low-lying coastal areas in the north, and particularly in the western part of the island; (3) coastal areas around the Fanga 'Uta lagoon; (4) along, or close to, the uplifted, low-elevation limestone coast in the north-east.

1. Uplifted limestone ridges. These are areas close to the rocky *liku* coast, at an elevation of >16 m above sea level. Seven forts are located on raised limestone platforms, particularly in the south and south-eastern part of the island along the coast to the east. These forts are: 38–Havelu Lahi, 39–Mala'e Vakapuna, 40–Fua'amatu and 41–Fua'amatu, 42–Nakolo, 43–Ha'asini and 44–Lavengatonga (Figure 9.1). Similar locations in the west of the island are occupied by the forts of: 9–Fahefa, 10–Fahefa, 13–Vaotu'u, 14–Houma and 19–'Utulau and 20–'Utulau.

2. Low-lying coastal. The second group of fortifications are located on low-lying areas mainly in the west. These include: 1–Kolovai, 2–Ha'avakatolu, 3–Fo'ui, 4–Masilamea and 5–Masilamea, 6–Te'ekiu, 7–Te'ekiu and 8–Te'ekiu, 11–Nukunuku, 12–Hule and 15–Manahau. Two forts (27–Nuku'alofa and 28–Takaunove) are directly associated with coastal areas that are now incorporated within the capital of Nuku'alofa with 21–Puke further west. Three forts not associated with the coastline, but still located on low-lying near-coast areas are: 16–Matangiake, 17–Hauloto and 18–Hauloto.

3. Fanga 'Uta Lagoon. Forts directly associated with the Fanga 'Uta Lagoon in the centre of the island are located in two distinct groups. The western group consists of 22–Pea, 23–Ha'ateiho, 24–Tokomololo and 25–Tokomololo and 26–Pouvalu; the eastern group comprises 36–Holonga and 37–Holonga, 45–Tatakamotonga, 46–Olotele and 47–Lapaha, and on the opposite site of the lagoon, 29–Navai, 30–Tapuhia, 31–Tapuhia, 32–Kauvai and 33–Kauvai and 34–Vainī and 35–Vainī.

4. North-east coast. Finally, 48–Niutao, 49–Kolonga'Uta 1 and 50–Kolonga'Uta 2, and 51–Kolonga are situated on the north-east coast. Two of these forts are low-lying, with 48–Niutao in a coastal swamp and parts of the ditches made at 49–Kolonga'Uta 1 and 50–Kolonga'Uta 2 carrying water after heavy rainfall and high tide events.

Elevation

Fortifications on Tongatapu can be found on all elevations; however, they tend to be more common at lower elevations (Table 9.1). Twenty-six forts are located at an elevation of <6 m, 13 forts are at an elevation of 7–15 m and only 12 forts are at an elevation of 18 m or higher, with the highest elevation recorded at 62 m (41–Fua'amotu). This reflects the overall landforms of Tongatapu, which gently rise from the low-lying areas in the north and north-west to the higher elevations of the south and east.

In general, there is little evidence that forts were concentrated along certain elevations; rather, they were built on all landforms. The prevalence of forts at lower elevations indicates that elevation by itself was not a determining factor. In some areas, raised elevations have been actively avoided, such as at the forts of 49–Kolonga'Uta and 48–Niutao on the east side of the island, 1–Kolovai in the west and 17–Hauloto and 18–Hauloto in the centre of the island. The topography of Tongatapu only rarely has slopes with a gradient of more than 5 per cent. There are a few locations in the west, such as 19–'Utulau and 20–'Utulau, 14–Houma or 10–Fahefa that are on elevated areas on the uplifted southern border of the island. These, however, are not located backing toward the shoreline but several hundred metres away from any steep slope or cliff edge. Even at the highest elevation, such as the cluster of sites in the south-east corner of the island, namely 40–Fua'amotu and 41–Fua'amotu, 42–Nakolo and 43–Ha'asini, forts are not located in close vicinity to what might be assumed to be the 'best' naturally defended location. The forts 42–Nakolo, 43–Ha'asini and 44–Lavengatonga are not placed on top of the ridgeline itself, but rather on the down-sloping area that leads to the south coast, where there are steep cliffs that would provide difficult access if the cliff top was defended.

Table 9.1. Site names/locations for fortified sites on Tongatapu with basic geographic data for elevation, slope, distance to coast, distance to water sources and soil types.

	Name	Elevation (m)	Peaks and ridges	Slope (%)	Distance to coast (m)	Distance to fresh water (m)	Soil type
1	Kolovai	2.7	No	2.52	220	447	Fatai
2	Ha'avakatolu	2.4	No	0.92	119	312	Sandy loam
3	Fo'ui	6.3	No	0.28	524	325	Fatai
4	Masilamea	4.7	No	0.8	271	197	Fatai
5	Masilamea	8.3	No	1.54	1020	343	Fatai
6	Te'ekiu	3.8	No	0.46	561	673	Fatai
7	Te'ekiu	2.8	No	0.36	744	419	Fatai
8	Te'ekiu	4.8	No	0.93	965	462	Fatai
9	Fahefa	10.2	No	0.24	1664	334	Fatai
10	Fahefa	18.5	No	8.75	1008	450	Fatai
11	Nukunuku	3.8	No	1.23	770	83	Fatai
12	Hule	4.4	No	0.71	1214	146	Fatai
13	Vaotu'u	11.0	No	1.05	965	202	Fatai
14	Houma	23.2	Possible	1.92	560	812	Fatai
15	Manahau	4.6	No	0.22	754	210	Fatai
16	Matangiake	9.6	No	0.42	2895	515	Fatai
17	Hauloto	9.6	No	0.23	3234	72	Fatai
18	Hauloto	9.8	No	0.6	3235	83	Fatai
19	'Utulau	26.0	Possible	0.46	1002	447	Fatai
20	'Utulau	22.3	Possible	0.43	1298	264	Fatai
21	Puke	4.4	No	0.81	67	250	Fatai
22	Pea	2.4	No	4.03	276	374	Fatai
23	Ha'ateiho	1.4	No	0.98	279	609	Fatai
24	Tokomololo	3.2	No	0.97	945	60	Fatai
25	Tokomololo	2.6	No	0.88	854	73	Fatai
26	Pouvalu	10.1	No	2.42	1032	161	Fatai

	Name	Elevation (m)	Peaks and ridges	Slope (%)	Distance to coast (m)	Distance to fresh water (m)	Soil type
27	Nuku'alofa	15.2	No	1.44	190	545	Sandy loam
28	Takaunove	1.3	No	0.28	83	1129	Sandy loam
29	Navai	0.9	No	0.35	214	368	Vaini
30	Tapuhia	1.7	No	2.83	927	243	Vaini
31	Tapuhia	13.5	No	1.36	1100	87	Vaini
32	Kauvai	0.8	No	1.71	69	44	Vaini
33	Kauvai	26.6	Yes	2.8	420	289	Lapaha
34	Vainī	10.3	Possible	2.87	167	307	Vaini
35	Vainī	10.5	Possible	2.55	134	327	Vaini
36	Holonga	8.6	No	1.06	179	169	Vaini
37	Holonga	9.0	No	1.86	118	28	Vaini
38	Havelu Lahi	34.2	No	0.47	2804	254	Vaini
39	Mala'e Vakapuna	52.6	Possible	0.98	2759	117	Vaini
40	Fua'amotu	60.9	No	0.06	898	429	Lapaha
41	Fua'amotu	62.3	No	0.73	530	143	Lapaha
42	Nakolo	35.3	No	12.72	380	4	Sandy loam
43	Ha'asini	34.8	No	0.64	535	184	Lapaha
44	Lavengatonga	21.7	No	1.35	460	114	Lapaha
45	Tatakamotonga	5.5	No	0.72	186	330	Lapaha
46	Olotele	5.3	No	0.97	264	276	Lapaha
47	Lapaha	6.7	No	0.75	555	130	Lapaha
48	Niutao	0.3	No	0.6	210	286	Lapaha
49	Kolonga 'Uta	1.7	No	3.18	1175	192	Lapaha
50	Kolonga 'Uta	1.3	No	0.83	926	120	Lapaha
51	Kolonga	2.6	No	0.52	348	203	Lapaha

Source: Authors' data.

Peaks and ridges

Isolated peaks are scarce in the landscape and therefore fortifications on Tongatapu are rarely associated with high points. Only one fort, 33–Kauvai, is located on a defined peak or hill in order to utilise the natural defences of the area. 39–Mala'e Vakapuna in the south-east is located on a slight rise with an artificial central mound built on top of the rise. 27–Nuku'alofa, 34–Vainī and 35–Vainī are located on hillocks backing on to the lagoon. On the west side of the island the 14–Houma fort is located on a high point, with gentle slopes to the north and north-east, and a plateau extending to the south and west. Similarly, the forts of 19–'Utulau and 20–'Utulau are located on high points, with the terrain sloping to the north and a plateau to the south.

Slope

Slopes were calculated from the lidar DEM using the '3D analyst slope' function in ArcGIS and values were extracted for each point (Table 9.1). Sloping terrains might have been selected for defence in several cases as indicated by Firth (1927:68) in his description of Maori *pa*: 'Sloping ground, even if only of gentle gradient, confers a great advantage both in the construction of defensive works and the repelling of an assault'. The sites of 42–Nakolo (12 per cent slope) and

10–Fahefa (8 per cent) are unambiguously associated with relatively steep slopes. The 42–Nakolo fort is located on a high elevation on the south-eastern side of the island, and 10–Fahefa is situated in the west on a slope facing the interior of the island. Both 22–Pea, in the centre of the island, and 49–Kolonga 'Uta, on the north-east coast, are constructed on slopes in excess of 3 per cent. In the south-east, other forts on relatively steep slopes are 44–Lavengatonga and 43–Ha'asini. Six sites located on slopes in excess of 2–3 per cent are predominantly on the west side of the island; none is further east than 34–Vainī and 35–Vainī. All remaining sites are located on slopes less than 2 per cent.

Distance from coast

Distance from the coast was calculated by the 'Near 3D' algorithm in ArcGIS to the centre point of each fort (Table 9.1). Fortifications appear to be primarily located relatively close to the coast, particularly the accessible coast to the north of the island, with a median distance of 550 m. Exceptions to this are the forts of 16–Matangiake (2894 m), 17–Hauloto (3233 m) and 18–Hauloto (3234 m) in the centre of the island, and the sites of 38–Havelu Lahi (2803 m) and 39–Mala'e Vakapuna (2758 m) in the south-east. Fortifications close to the shore are found only on the north side of the island where access to land is readily available. Ten sites are located at a distance of less than 200 m from the coast, 7 sites at a distance of less than 300 m, 10 sites are less than 600 m, 17 sites less than 1300 m and only 6 sites are inland and more than 1300 m away from the coast. Thirteen sites are directly bordering the coastline or have sites open to the coast: 1–Kolovai (220 m), 2–Ha'avakatolu (119 m), 21–Puke (67 m), 27–Nuku'alofa (190 m), 28–Takaunove (83 m), 22–Pea (276 m), 23–Ha'atehio (279 m), 32–Kauvai (69 m), 34–Vainī (167 m) and 35–Vainī (134 m), 37–Holonga (118 m), 46–Olotele (271 m) and 48–Niutao (210 m).

According to historical records, Tongatapu was densely settled with population centres stretching from the northern coast about 1500 m into the interior (Beaglehole 1969; Martin 1820; Spennemann 2002). This was followed by an area of intensive arable land up to 4500 m from the north coast. The remaining land to the south coast was described as having only had limited cultivation and occasional settlement.

Comparing location selection to the two boundaries (Figure 9.2), only 18 (35 per cent) of the 51 identified fortifications fall outside the historically recorded intensively occupied zone close to the north coast. Seven fortifications (14 per cent), almost all on the west side of the island, are located in the zone of intensive agriculture, less than 4.5 km distance from the north coast. Almost all fortifications, with the exception of 14–Houma in the west and the south-east cluster at high elevations, fall in the first two zones and are either associated with the residential high population density zone or with the zone of intensive agricultural activity. The south-east cluster of sites is not associated with either of these zones, and forts there are located in areas that could have been pockets of intensive inhabitation or agriculture (note: there is a high mound density in the south-east area).

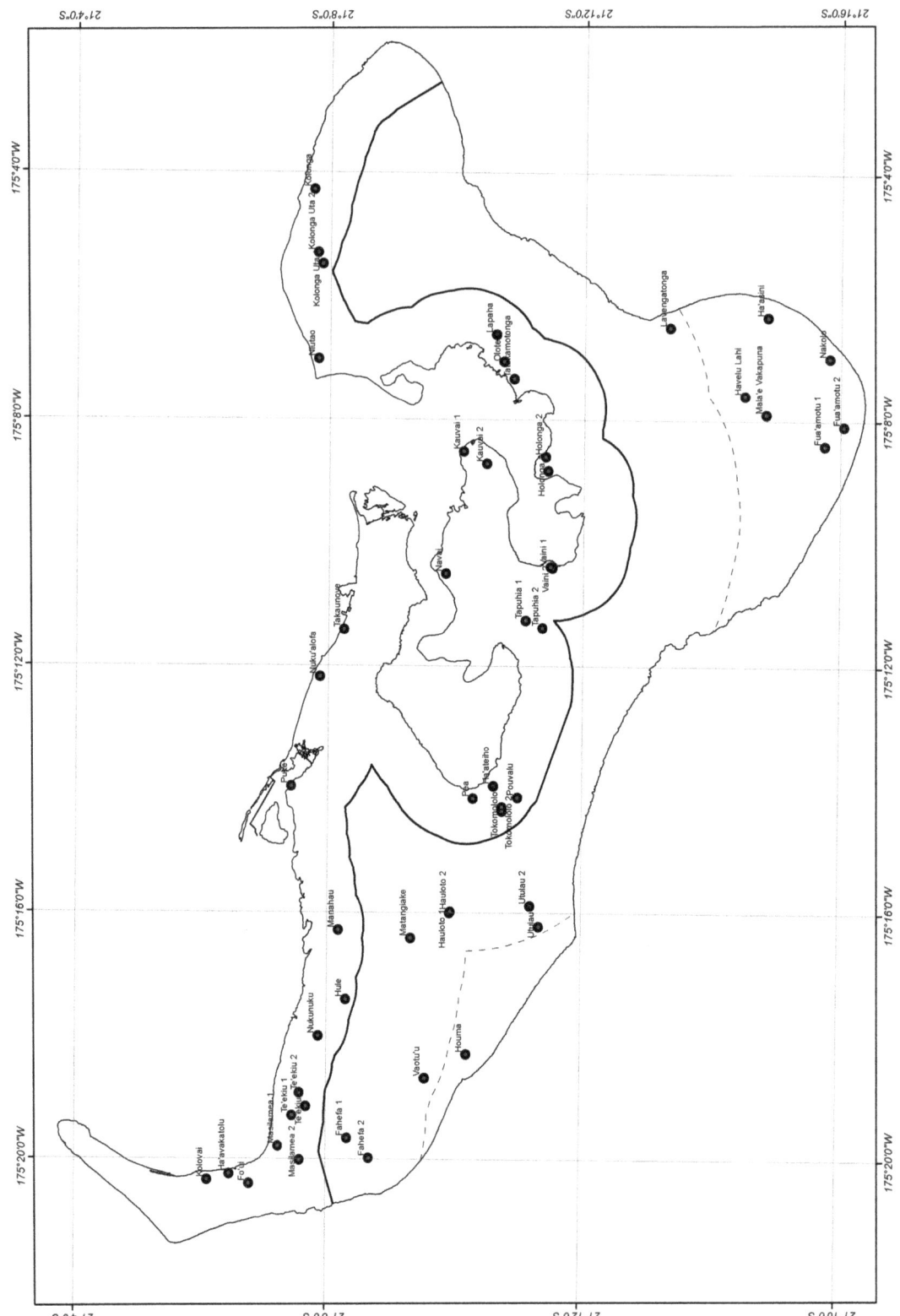

Figure 9.2. Map of Tongatapu with boundaries of 1500 m (solid black line) and 4500 m (dashed line) from the north shore showing area of intensive inhabitation and extent of intensive agriculture.

Source: Christian Reepmeyer, Geoffrey Clark, Phillip Parton, Malia Melekiola and David Burley.

Distance to water sources

Access to freshwater is a persistent problem on Tongatapu as there are no surface water sources, such as lakes or rivers, on the island. The underlying karst limestone is highly permeable, which results in freshwater discharges in coastal environments. A rain-fed freshwater lens (Ghyben-Herzberg lens) with a thickness of about 20 m exists in the centre of the island (Spennemann 1989:11). However, this lens is substantially impacted by significant evapotranspiration. Surface run-off is extremely rare even during wet seasons. It has been suggested that only 25–30 per cent of annual rainfall reaches the freshwater lens (Hunt 1979). Freshwater springs in the uplifted karst environment of the *liku* coast in the south are not recorded, but there are freshwater pools inside a number of cave systems (Iliffe and Sarbu 1990; Lowe and Gunn 1986).

Freshwater wells in coastal locations have been discussed by Spriggs (1997) and Hunt and Kirch (1988) as being abundant on Pacific Islands today. However, it is unclear whether this abundance of wells was also evident in earlier time periods. Early European explorers in the Pacific frequently discuss the difficulty of accessing potable water, particularly in the Pacific's eastern region. On Tongatapu, James Cook on his second voyage mentions the problem of accessing freshwater:

> If nature has been wanting in any thing, it is in the article of fresh water, which as it is shut up in the bowels of the earth and for which they are obliged to dig wells, of these we saw only one, so that it is probable there are but few. (Beaglehole 1969:273)

There are only limited records of premodern wells on Tongatapu, although nine freshwater solution channels/springs have been identified exiting the northern palaeoshoreline (Spennemann 1989:201). There is a rich oral history about the importance of wells and access to freshwater on Tongatapu (McKern 1929); however, site location of these wells is not clear. Here we use the occurrence of depressions in the landscape as a potential indicator for the collection of rainwater. Depressions likely consist of collapsed karst features including sinkholes, caves and excavated wells, including areas where soil was quarried for earthwork structures. Based on lidar topography there is an abundance of depression features (Figure 9.3). The distance of depression features to the centroid of fortifications was calculated by the 'Near' function in ArcGIS.

It can be seen that most fortifications are located in relatively close vicinity (<500 m) to possible freshwater sources. However, six fortifications (6–Te'ekiu, 14–Houma, 16–Matangiake, 23–Ha'ateiho, 27–Nuku'alofa, and 28–Takaunove) were located at distances of >500 m, and 28–Takaunove most likely had no freshwater access at 1100 m distance (Table 9.1). Density maps of depression features using the 'Point density' function in ArcGIS (Figure 9.3) show that only a small number of fortifications are located in areas with a high density of depressions.

Increased freshwater access can explain the site location of defences at 12–Hule, 15–Manahau, 17–Hauloto and 18–Hauloto, 24–Tokomololo and 25–Tokomololo, 26–Pouvalu, 30–Tapuhia and 46–Olotele. On the other hand, sites such as 1–Kolovai, 2–Ha'avakatolu, 10–Fahefa, 19–'Utulau, 45–Tatakamotonga and 48–Niutao appear to be associated with areas that have some access to freshwater. Further, at least one fort, 42–Nakolo, has a cave with freshwater within the fortification, and at both 46–Olotele and 47–Lapaha forts the ditch excavations exposed areas where freshwater can be collected.

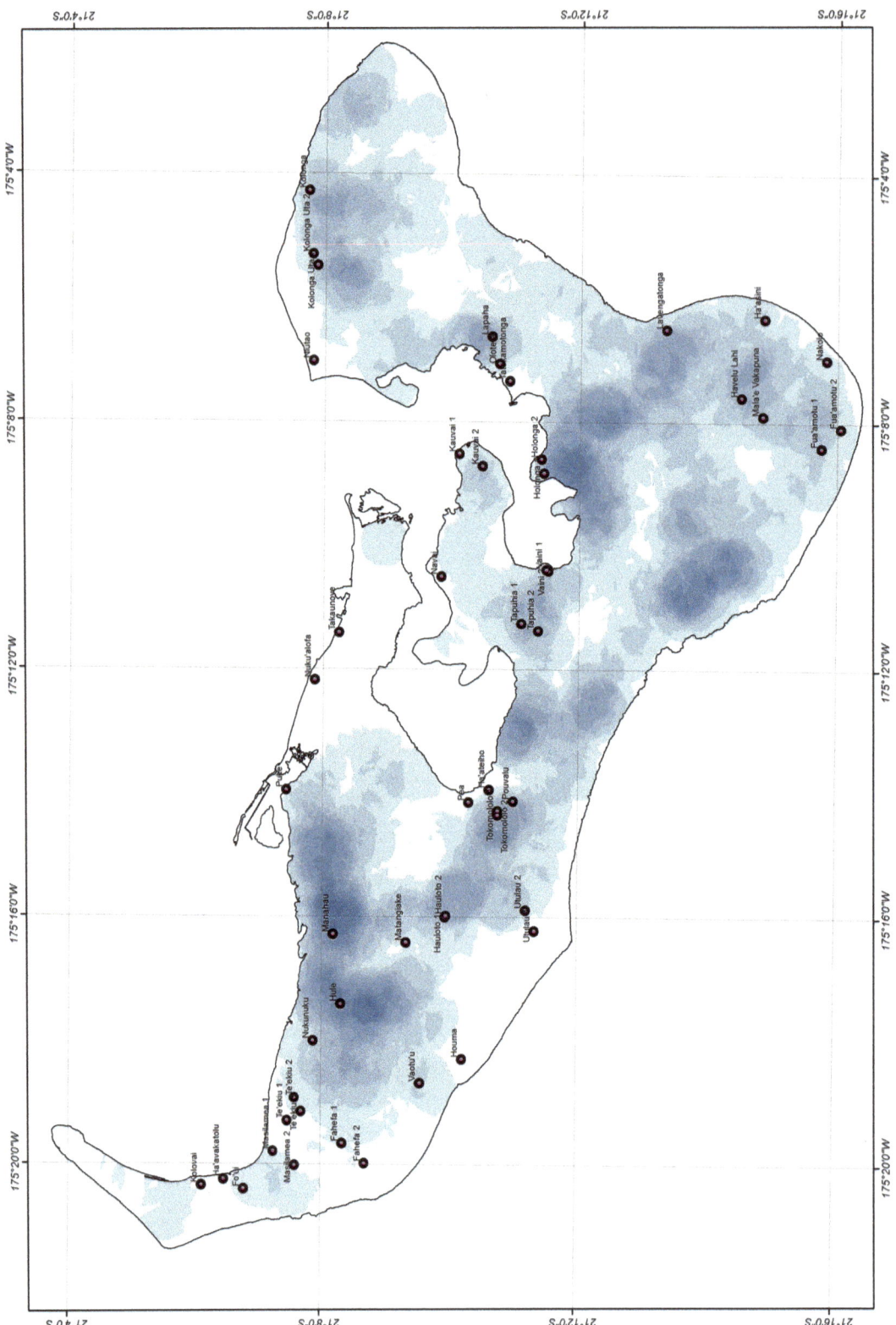

Figure 9.3. Density map of depressions indicating potential freshwater resources.
Darker shaded areas represent zones of higher depression density.
Source: Christian Reepmeyer, Geoffrey Clark, Phillip Parton, Malia Melekiola and David Burley.

9. Geospatial analysis of fortification locations on the island of Tongatapu, Tonga   181

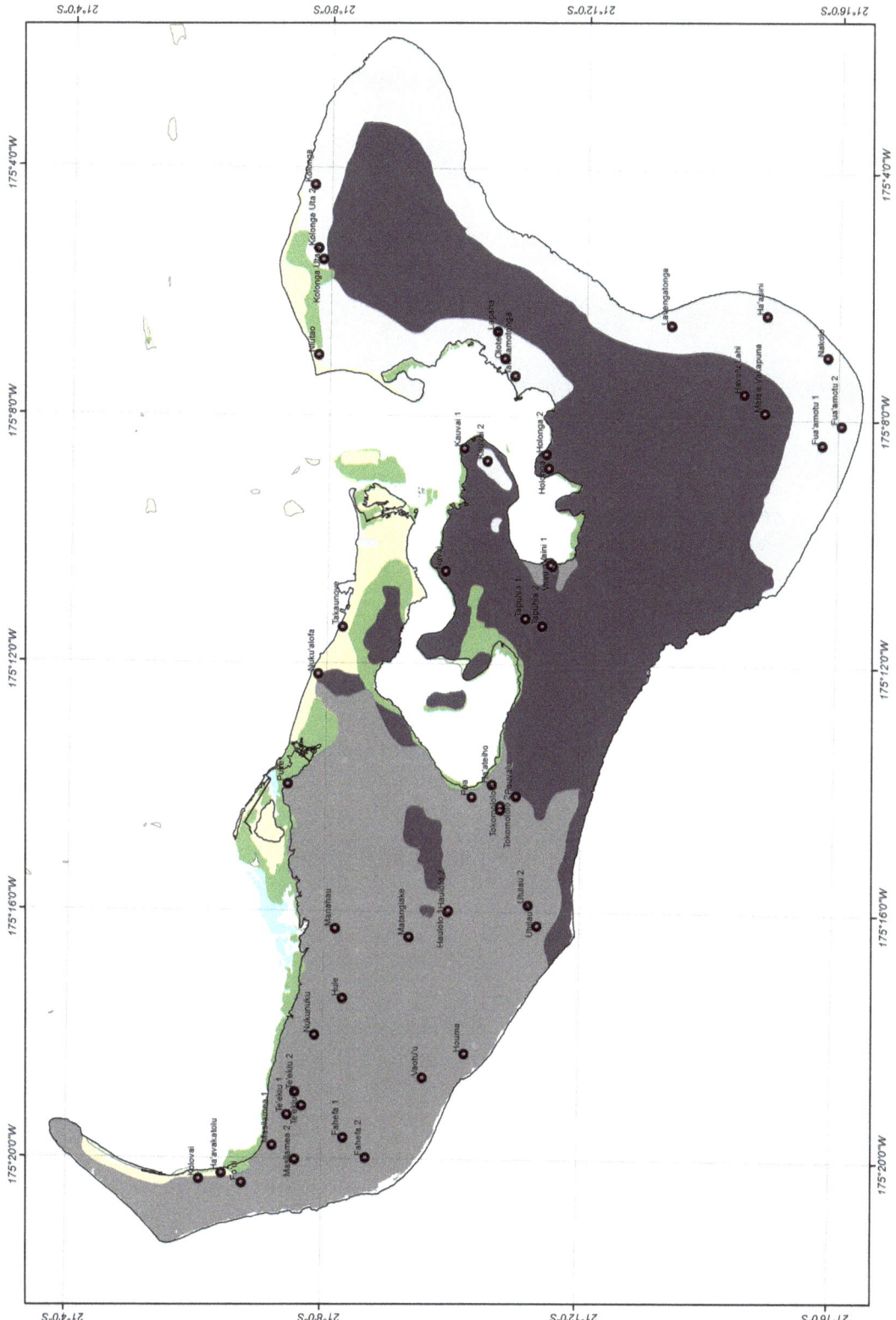

Figure 9.4. Map of Tongatapu with soil types based on the geospatial database from the Tongan Ministry Department for Land, Survey and Natural Resources.

Light-shaded areas around the coast in the east are Lapaha series soils, dark-shaded areas in the centre are Vaini series soils and grey areas in the west are Fatai series soils. Green area is mangrove and swamps; yellow is sandy loams and beach deposits.

Source: Christian Reepmeyer, Geoffrey Clark, Phillip Parton, Malia Melekiola and David Burley.

Soil

Soils on Tongatapu are subdivided into three phases associated with tephra depositions on the island (Figure 9.4). The oldest phase are Lapaha series tephras mainly distributed on the east side of the island close to the coast. Vaini series clays are mainly situated in the centre–east area, and the Fatai series covers most of the west side of the island. All soils are acidic and highly fertile in the A–horizon, which ranges from around 30–40 cm thickness in the Lapaha series to >100 cm in the Fatai series. Underlying older tephras are usually highly compacted and are not suitable for agriculture.

Forts can be found on all tephra soils. On the east side of the island, there seems to be a preference to construct fortifications on Lapaha soils overlying Vaini soils, with the exception of 38–Havelu Lahi and 39–Mala'e Vakapuna. Around the Fanga 'Uta Lagoon, all three soil series have been used to construct fortifications. The western side of the island is dominated by Fatai series soils and we do not see any preference for soil type in relation to fort location.

Intervisibility

Sightline analysis of fort location, using the 'Line of sight' algorithm in ArcGIS, which identifies visibility of two points if view is unimpeded, identified five clusters of forts in a 5 km radius (Figure 9.5). A north-east cluster includes 48–Niutao, 49–Kolonga'Uta and 50–Kolonga'Uta and 51–Kolonga; a south-east cluster of 38–Havelu Lahi, 39–Mala'e Vakapuna, 40–Fua'amotu and 41–Fua'amotu, 42–Nakolo, 43–Ha'asini and 44–Lavengatonga. These two clusters encompass all forts on the east side of the island. There is a central cluster of forts on the eastern shore of the Fanga 'Uta Lagoon that consists of 29–Navai, 30–Tapuhia, 32–Kauvai and 33–Kauvai, 34–Vainī and 35–Vainī, 36–Holonga and 37–Holonga, 47–Lapaha, 45–Tatakamotonga and 46–Olotele. Three sites on the north shore are located in the urban area of Nuku'alofa and form a fourth cluster with 21–Puke, 27–Nuku'alofa and 28–Takaunove. The last cluster comprises all sites in the west of the island, including those in the western part of the Fanga 'Uta Lagoon (Fanga Kakau sector) and sites on low-lying areas and uplifted limestone ridges.

For intervisibility analysis, the ArcGIS package 'Intervisibility' has been used, assuming that the visual height of a person is 1.8 m (Figure 9.6). The results replicate to a certain extent the sightline analysis as they show similar site clusters. However, several inconsistencies with the sightline model can be detected. Intervisibility of sites in the western lowlands shows that most possible sightlines are intervisible from each fort within a 5 km radius, including sites on high ground. We can separate the sites on the west side of the Fanga 'Uta Lagoon from this cluster as these are only visible from 19–'Utulau and 20–'Utulau on higher ground. There is no visibility between the Hauloto sites and the lagoon forts. The area between 15–Manahau, 16–Matangiake and the coastal sites of 21–Puke, 27–Nuku'alofa and 28–Takaunove represents a visual barrier; only 21–Puke is intervisible from the 15–Manahau fort.

Sites on the west and east side of the lagoon can also be separated into clusters. 26–Pouvalu is the only site visible from the east cluster and intervisibility is limited to the site of 31–Tapuhia. Sites in the east cluster are all intervisible, with the exception of 29–Navai, which is isolated and only visible from site 33–Kauvai, which is situated on a peak as described above. It appears that although there are sites located on the coast, such as 33–Vainī and 34–Vainī, these sites are not intervisible with the east end of the cluster that includes the 46–Olotele and 47–Lapaha forts.

In the north-east, the site of 48–Niutao is completely isolated; the three sites of 49–Kolonga'Uta and 50–Kolonga'Uta and 51–Kolonga are intervisible from each other, but are not visible from any other fort. Finally, the sites in the south-east are not visible from any of the other clusters. Interestingly, these sites are also not visible from each other, with the exception of 38–Havelu Lahi and 39–Mala'e Vakapuna, and 40–Fua'amotu and 41–Fua'amotu. 42–Nakola, 43–Ha'asini and 44–Lavengatonga are completely isolated from all sites.

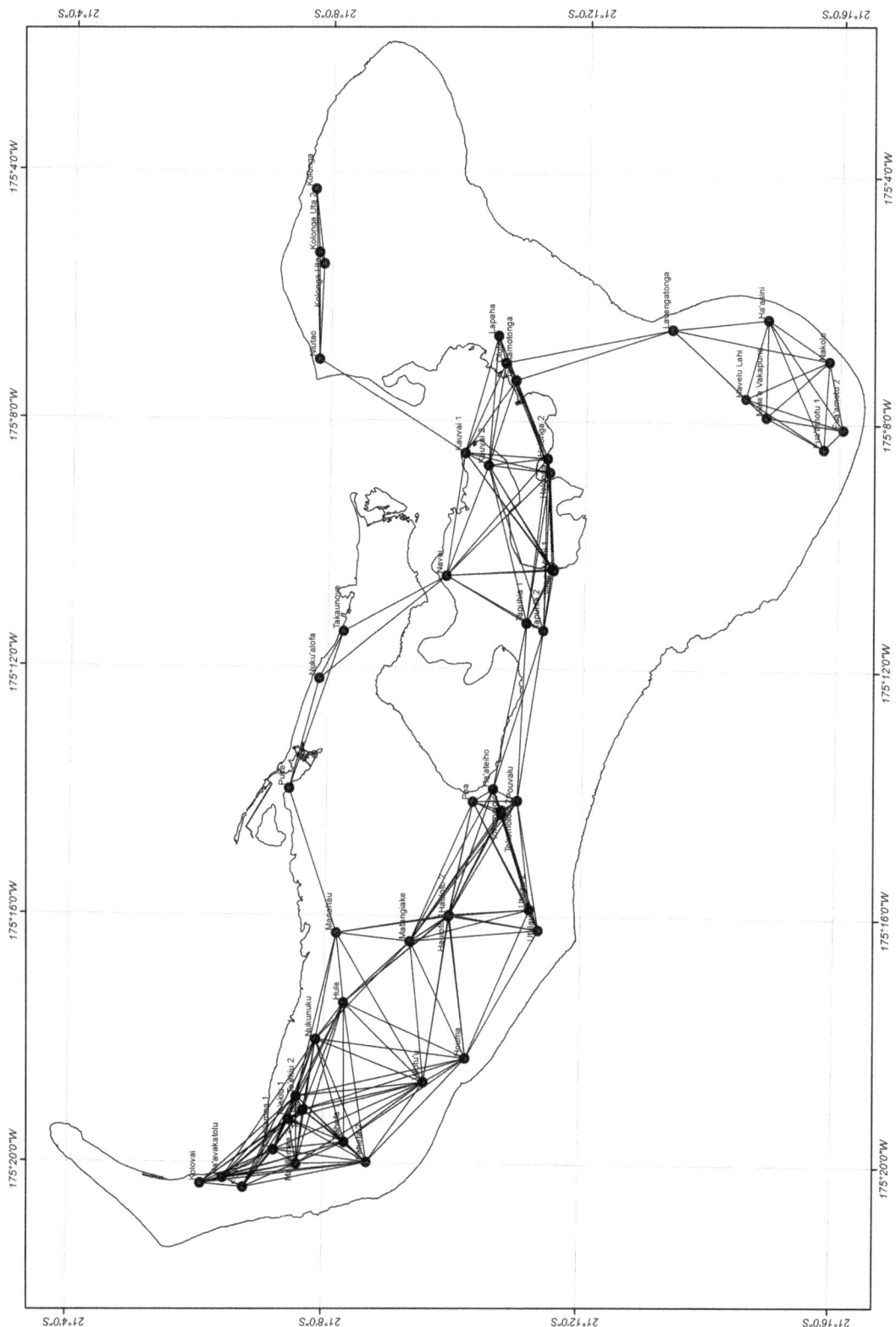

Figure 9.5. Sightline analysis of fort locations 5 km in distance from each other.
Source: Christian Reepmeyer, Geoffrey Clark, Phillip Parton, Malia Melekiola and David Burley.

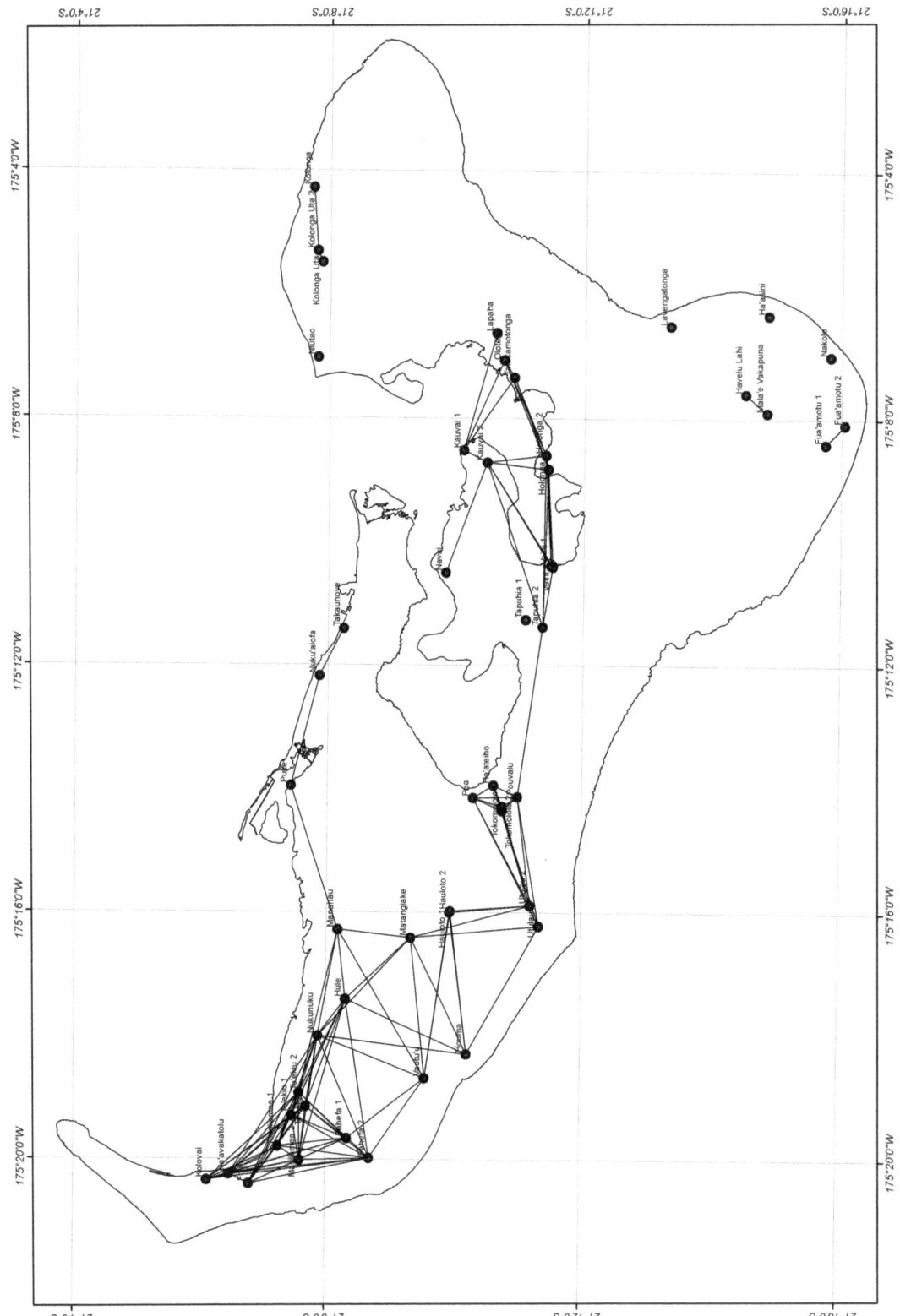

Figure 9.6. Intervisibility analysis of fort location.
Source: Christian Reepmeyer, Geoffrey Clark, Phillip Parton, Malia Melekiola and David Burley.

Discussion and conclusion

There are few historical accounts that describe why forts were located in a particular place. In his account, William Mariner, who was in Tonga during the early nineteenth century, noted that:

> thus was a violent civil contention induced, and the island was soon divided into several petty states. In the course of a little time, each party had built a fort for itself, so that there were at least twelve or thirteen different garrisoned places upon the island; each, in a state of warfare with all the rest, was determined to maintain its claims as long as it had strength to do so … Besides their domestic troubles, every year they were disturbed by attacks from Finow, who made it his annual custom to make a descent upon one or other of their fortresses, and sometimes upon several of them in the same season; but they were all so well fortified and entrenched, that their enemy, however powerful, consisting of the Hapai people, under the command of Finow, and the Vavaoo people, under that of Toobó Nuha, had never succeeded, at the time of Mr. Mariner's first arrival, in taking or destroying a single fort; that is to say, during the space of seven or eight years. (Martin 1820:77)

This situation reflects the settlement pattern of the Tongan population soon after European contact when fortifications had proliferated as a consequence of chiefly competition and the breakdown of traditional society. It appears that at the time of Cook's visits to Tonga (1773–1777 CE) the densest population was located at the northern shore for about 1 to 1.5 km inland, with houses being built directly on the coast (Anderson in Beaglehole 1969; Ledyard 2005). Beyond this, plantations became bigger, but were more dispersed and the population became sparser. According to Anderson in 1777 CE (in Beaglehole 1969), closely packed plantations stretched inland for about up to 3 km. The remaining area was described as uncultivated country covered with high grass. Occasional coconut trees could be seen, which Anderson took as evidence of cultivation. The steep *liku* coast in the south did not have any plantations and it was apparently uninhabited (Martin 1820; Spennemann 2002), although it is unclear whether any visits were made by European visitors to this area in the eighteenth century.

The low-lying relief of the island of Tongatapu means that hilltop fortifications, which are common in other parts of the Pacific, are almost absent from Tongatapu, with the exception of 27–Nuku'alofa, 33–Kauvai and 39–Mala'e Vakapuna. Overall, there is an unusual pattern where areas of raised elevation have not been used and fortifications were built nearby at lower elevations. For example, at the site of 18–Hauloto, a raised ridgeline is located approximately 2 km away, and at 1–Kolovai a ridgeline of around 12 m height is about 700 m away. This pattern is hard to explain, but might reflect a necessity to build forts close to community settlements and gardens rather than to take advantage of high areas.

The distribution of fortifications on Tongatapu indicates that all landforms were used, but forts are not distributed randomly through the landscape and can be grouped into five discrete clusters. Sightline analysis shows that these clusters are separated from each other by areas of limited visibility. Unfortunately, a detailed record of the placement of prehistoric population centres on Tongatapu is difficult to reconstruct, but there appears to be a correlation between modern villages and the presence of fortifications (Figure 9.7). The two main population centres of Nuku'alofa and Lapaha certainly have fortifications associated with them. It has been argued that beyond the defence of population centres, the protection of arable land is a priority for the placement of defensive structures (Field 2008; Sutton 1990), caused by the desire to maintain control over subsistence resources. In the west of Tongatapu, this premise appears to be fulfilled, as there are several forts located outside of dense population zones. In the east, however, fortifications do not occur at any distance from the coast, with the exception of two fortifications on high elevations in the south-east. The whole of Tongatapu is covered with fertile volcanic clays of different thickness that are suitable for intensive agriculture, and historical records show that all fertile arable land was farmed (Martin 1820). There is no marked difference between the soil fertility of Lapaha and Vaini soils in the centre and east, or from the Fatai soils of the west besides an overall increase of the fertile A–horizons (Cowie 1980). Apart from a correlation of A–horizon thickness, which increases from east to west, there is no indication that certain soil types increase the likelihood of fort construction.

Figure 9.7. Ortho-image of Tongatapu showing modern settlements in relation to fort location.
Source: Christian Reepmeyer, Geoffrey Clark, Phillip Parton, Malia Melekiola and David Burley.

The importance of environmental factors, such as precipitation decline during the 'Little Ice Age' (Field 2004), an increase in ENSO (El Niño–Southern Oscillation) variability (Kennett et al. 2006) and an associated decline in the carrying capacity of islands has been argued as the cause of fortification construction in the Late Holocene (Field and Lape 2010). There are no high-resolution climate records available for Tongatapu, and we used the placement of forts in relation to possible freshwater sources as a proxy for investigating on Tongatapu the significance of a scarce but essential resource. Under drought conditions the main source of freshwater would likely be depressions (natural and artificial) that tapped the water table; control of potable water is expected to lead to a higher density of defensive sites in the vicinity of wells, caves and springs (Field 2004; Lape and Chin-Yung 2008). Although it is unclear whether a climate-induced decline in subsistence yields was accompanied by the construction of fortifications on Tonga, the location of defensive earthworks does not correlate closely with potential freshwater sources. This might derive from the age of some fortifications, many of which are assumed to date to 1799–1852 CE (McKern 1929; Spennemann 1986; Wood 1975), a time when regional climate records show relatively low ENSO frequencies and high precipitation (Moy et al. 2002).

It appears that a key to understanding fortification placement in the Tongatapu landscape is the purpose of defensive sites. As noted above (Martin 1820; Parton et al. 2018), forts were not designed to withstand long-term sieges, but rather to give protection from short-term conflicts such as episodic skirmishes and raids. In this situation, an ideal defensive placement that maximally employed the available topographic and environmental variables appears to have been secondary to the construction of forts close to, or located in, cultivated and, especially, residential zones. The construction of early fortifications in the chiefly centre of Lapaha suggests that defence of the political core and supporting agricultural land was the primary purpose (Parton et al. this volume), and in Tongatapu some forts were likely fenced chiefly compounds that were extended in times of war by the addition of earthworks, while other forts were new constructions made at a strategic location in a chief's territory. Thus, reconstruction of the broader settlement pattern from the density of earth mounds (e.g. Freeland et al. 2016), the identification of land and sea transportation routes, and archaeological and historical data on settlements, forts and warfare is needed to refine our understanding as protection of arable land is unlikely to explain the position of all defensive earthworks on Tongatapu.

References

Anderson, A.J. 2016. The making of the Maori middle ages. *Journal of New Zealand Studies* NS23:2–18.

Beaglehole, J.C. (ed.) 1969. *The voyage of the* Resolution *and* Adventure *1772–1775*. Cambridge University Press, Cambridge.

Best, S. 1984. Lakeba: The prehistory of a Fijian Island. Unpublished PhD thesis. University of Auckland, Auckland.

Best, S. 1993. At the halls of the mountain kings. Fijian and Samoan fortifications: Comparison and analysis. *Journal of the Polynesian Society* 102(4):385–447.

Clark, G., P. Parton, C. Reepmeyer, N. Melekiola and D. Burley 2018. Conflict and state development in ancient Tonga: The Lapaha earth fort. *Journal of Island and Coastal Archaeology* 13(3):405–419. doi.org/10.1080/15564894.2017.1337658.

Cowie, J. 1980. Soils from andesitic tephra and their variability, Tongatapu, Kingdom of Tonga. *Soil Research* 18:273–284. doi.org/10.1071/sr9800273.

ESRI 2011. ArcGIS Desktop: Release 10. Redlands. Environmental Systems Research Institute, California.

Field, J.S. 1998. Natural and constructed defenses in Fijian fortifications. *Asian Perspectives* 37:32–58.

Field, J.S. 2004. Environmental and climatic considerations: A hypothesis for conflict and the emergence of social complexity in Fijian prehistory. *Journal of Anthropological Archaeology* 23:79–99. doi.org/10.1016/j.jaa.2003.12.004.

Field, J.S. 2008. Explaining fortifications in Indo-Pacific prehistory. *Archaeology in Oceania* 43:1–10. doi.org/10.1002/j.1834-4453.2008.tb00025.x.

Field, J.S. and P.V. Lape 2010. Paleoclimates and the emergence of fortifications in the tropical Pacific Islands. *Journal of Anthropological Archaeology* 29:113–124. doi.org/10.1016/j.jaa.2009.11.001.

Firth, R. 1927. Maori hill-forts. *Antiquity* 1:66–78. doi.org/10.1017/s0003598x00000077.

Freeland, T., B. Heung, D.V. Burley, G. Clark and A. Knudby 2016. Automated feature extraction for prospection and analysis of monumental earthworks from aerial LiDAR in the Kingdom of Tonga. *Journal of Archaeological Science* 69:64–74. doi.org/10.1016/j.jas.2016.04.011.

Gibbs, H.S. 1976. *Soils of Tongatapu Island, Tonga.* Department of Scientific and Industrial Research, Wellington.

Golson, J. 1969. Preliminary research: Archaeology in Western Samoa, 1957. In R.C. Green and J. Davidson (eds), *Archaeology in Western Samoa,* Volume 1, pp. 4–20. Bulletin of the Auckland Institute and Museum, Auckland.

Hunt, B. 1979. An analysis of the groundwater resources of Tongatapu Island, Kingdom of Tonga. *Journal of Hydrology* 40:185–196. doi.org/10.1016/0022-1694(79)90097-0.

Hunt, T.L. and P.V. Kirch 1988. An archaeological survey of the 'Manu'a islands, American Samoa. *Journal of the Polynesian Society* 97:153–183.

Iliffe, T.M. and S. Sarbu 1990. Anchialine caves and cave fauna of the South Pacific. *National Speleological Society (NSS) News* 48:88–96.

Kennett, D., A. Anderson, M. Prebble, E. Conte and J. Southon 2006. Prehistoric human impacts on Rapa, French Polynesia. *Antiquity* 80:340–354. doi.org/10.1017/s0003598x00093662.

Lape, P.V. and C. Chin-Yung 2008. Fortification as a human response to late Holocene climate change in East Timor. *Archaeology in Oceania* 43:11–21. doi.org/10.1002/j.1834-4453.2008.tb00026.x.

Ledyard, J. 2005. *The last voyage of Captain Cook: The collected writings of John Ledyard.* National Geographic Society, Washington.

Lowe, D. and J. Gunn 1986. Caves and limestones of the islands of Tongatapu and 'Eua, Kingdom of Tonga. *Cave Science* 13:105–130.

Martin, J. 1820. *An account of the natives of the Tonga Islands in the South Pacific Ocean.* Charles Ewer, Boston.

McKern, W.C. 1929. *Archaeology of Tonga.* Bernice P. Bishop Museum Bulletin 60. Bernice P. Bishop Museum, Honolulu.

Moy, C.M., G.O. Seltzer, D.T. Rodbell and D.M. Anderson 2002. Variability of El Niño/Southern Oscillation activity at millennial timescales during the Holocene epoch. *Nature* 420:162–165. doi.org/10.1038/nature01194.

Parry, J.T. 1987. The Sigatoka Valley pathway into prehistory. *Bulletin of the Fiji Museum* 9:1–134.

Parton, P.A., G. Clark, C. Reepmeyer and D. Burley 2018. The field of war: LiDAR identification of earthwork defences on Tongatapu Island, Kingdom of Tonga. *Journal of Pacific Archaeology* 9(1):11–24.

Sand, C. 2008. Prehistoric maritime empires in the Pacific: Ga'asialili ('Elili) and the establishment of a Tongan colony on 'Uvea (Wallis, Western Polynesia). In A. Di Piazza, E. Pearthree and C. Sand (eds), *At the heart of ancient societies: French contributions to Pacific archaeology*, pp. 73–105. Cahiers de l'Archeologie en Nouvelle Caledonie, Noumea.

Smith, C. and E. Cochrane 2011. How is visibility important for defence? A GIS analysis of sites in the western Fijian Islands. *Archaeology in Oceania* 46:76–84. doi.org/10.1002/j.1834-4453.2011.tb00101.x.

Spennemann, D.H.R 1986. Zum gegenwärtigen Stand der archäologischen Forschung auf den Tonga–Inseln–Ergebnisse und Perspektiven–TDARP Report 1. *Anthropos* 81:469–495.

Spennemann, D.H.R. 1989. 'ata 'a Tonga mo 'ata 'o Tonga: Early and later prehistory of the Tongan Islands. Volumes I and II. Unpublished PhD thesis. The Australian National University, Canberra.

Spennemann, D.H.R. 2002. Urbanisation in Tonga: Expansion and contraction of political centres in a tropical chiefdom. In P. Sinclair, W. Mutoro and G. Abung (eds), *The development of urbanism from a global perspective: Proceedings of the Second World Archaeological Congress Intercongress, Mombasa, 1993*. Swedish Central Board of National Antiquities, Stockholm.

Spriggs, M. 1997. *The Island Melanesians*. Blackwell, Oxford.

Sutton, D.G. 1990. *The archaeology of the kainga: A study of precontact Maori undefended settlements at Pouerua, Northland, New Zealand*. Oxford University Press.

Taylor, F.W. 1978. Quaternary tectonic and sea-level history, Tonga and Fiji, southwest Pacific. Unpublished PhD thesis. Cornell University, New York.

Wood, A.H. 1975. *Overseas missions of the Australian Methodist Church. Volume 1: Tonga and Samoa*. Aldersgate Press, Melbourne.

10

The fortified homestead of the Australian frontier

Nic Grguric

Introduction

As the Australian frontier advanced inland across the country from its coastal bridgeheads, violent collisions broke out between European settlers and Aboriginal groups. The frequency and scale of the violence varied from place to place and time to time, but one never has to look far to find examples of violence and fear between European colonists and Indigenous communities in most—if not all—geographic areas of Australia (Reynolds 2013). One of the physical traces of this frontier violence and fear can be seen in the form of what can be termed 'fortified homesteads', buildings constructed by European settlers incorporating provisions for defence against potential Aboriginal attack. Fortified homesteads represent both a real and perceived conflict between the invaders and the invaded. They are significant and unique as artefacts of the hundreds of individual wars of resistance fought by Australia's Aboriginal peoples throughout the colonial period. In 2007, the author completed doctoral research during which he explored the design, role and meaning of these structures and how these buildings can contribute to our understanding of frontier relations between European colonists and Indigenous peoples (Grguric 2007). The findings were based on four sites dating between c. 1847 and 1885, three of which are located in South Australia and one in the Northern Territory. Each of these sites had a documented story associated with them, describing them as having been built with defence against Aboriginal attack in mind. This chapter explores the association of fortified homesteads with Australian frontier conflict, both in terms of their function at the time they were built and their ongoing meaning.

Frontier conflict in Australia

The primary cause of conflict between European colonists and Aboriginal people at a grassroots level was arguably the unwitting refusal of colonists to engage in Aboriginal principles of reciprocity and, in particular, 'demand sharing', a concept introduced into the anthropological lexicon by Nicolas Peterson (1997:171–190). Demand sharing is a practice in which it is socially acceptable to demand food or items from another, as opposed to unsolicited generosity (Altman 2011:188). Peterson believes that demand sharing was widespread throughout Aboriginal society, as well as among hunter-gatherers more generally (Altman 2011:188; Peterson 1997:173). In its most simplistic form, it has a resemblance to what Nicholas Blurton Jones called 'tolerated theft' (Peterson 1997:173).

The problem with the attempts of Aboriginal people to impart the concept of demand sharing upon European settlers was how fundamentally it conflicted with the Western view of generosity. In Aboriginal/European interactions, Aboriginal people commonly expressed it by demanding food and property from colonists and taking their seemingly plentiful livestock at will, such as when in the 1840s the house of Adelaide farmer Thomas Dyke was 'besieged' by Aboriginal people demanding flour and other goods, or when a party of 30 to 40 Aboriginal people en route to Encounter Bay in South Australia 'threatened' women in a farmhouse if they did not hand over flour (Dolling 1981:5, 33). Aboriginal people naturally felt entitled to demand such things in return for the settlers occupying their land, hunting the native game, exploiting their water sources and, all too frequently, their women (Conor 2016:14). To the settler, however, this behaviour was seen as brazen and considered pure theft.

When the colonists inevitably refused to yield their food and property, the breakdown in relations generally turned to violence in one of two ways: either the colonists, full of indignation, threatened or became violent towards the demanders, such as when young Frank Hawson flourished a gun at a group of Aboriginal people demanding food from his father's hut (for which he was speared in retaliation) (Eyre 1964 (1845):163–165), or the latter, irked by the settlers' rudeness in their refusal to conform with the laws of reciprocity, sought vengeance upon the settlers, often by plundering settler's huts, taking large numbers of their sheep by force and spearing the defenders if they resisted, such as happened on South Australia's Eyre Peninsula in the late 1840s (Police Commissioner 1848a, 1848b). Then erupted a state of animosity between the settlers and the Aboriginal people, which was expressed in wariness and tit for tat acts of violence between the two. The two sides were at war. These violent acts then escalated, with spearings of settlers becoming more frequent and economic warfare waged upon the settlers by the driving off and wholesale killing of livestock (such as when South Australian squatter John Gifford had 40 head of cattle speared in one raid in 1847) (Police Commissioner 1848c).

Settlers often dealt with the financial threat caused by this economic warfare with violence, such as when John Cox of Port Fairy in Victoria tracked down his stolen flock and found 100 ewes with their legs dislocated (a traditional Aboriginal method of keeping captured game alive and 'fresh', yet immobile). In a rage he opened fire:

> It was the first time I had ever levelled my gun at my fellow man. I did so with no regret or hesitation in this instance … I distinctly remember knocking over three … two men and a boy, with one discharge of my double barrel. (McKernan and Browne 1988:103)

All-consuming fear and anger brought about by commercial loss of livestock and other property gave rise to that characteristic of the Australian frontier: the punitive raid. The mounting of such a raid usually marked the end of Aboriginal resistance in that particular locality, which speaks volumes for the devastating effect such raids had on the local Aboriginal population. The following excerpt from the letters of early Port Phillip squatter David Henry Wilsone provides a rarely written insight into the typical attitude and thought process of someone premeditating a punitive raid, in order to put an end to Aboriginal resistance once and for all via violent decimation of the local community:

> I expect that we will have a regular fight with the natives as they are becoming very troublesome & bold; the fools of protectors have informed them that we dare not meddle with them, or if we did we would be hanged, they stole from us five fine ewe lambs & since then all our servants are armed and are advised to shoot any one [sic] they see attempt it again or touch them, we are well off by many around us, & soon a regular affair will settle the business and clear our part of the country of these *regular cannibals* [emphasis from original document]. (Serle 1977:57)

In the harsh environment of the Australian frontier, humanitarian ideals usually gave way to self-interest. Far from the eyes of police, wives, teachers or missionaries, the station men were answerable only to themselves and the speculator back in town. This 'freedom' from the moderating influences of 'civilised' society gave vent to attitudes and acts that would have been considered unacceptable away from the frontier. And yet, those same settlers who perpetrated violent acts upon the Aboriginal inhabitants hypocritically considered themselves racially and morally superior to their victims (Serle 1977:57). This is evident in the fact that over and over again, settlers were prepared to kill Aboriginal people for stealing livestock.

Distrust of the Aboriginal inhabitants around them was a common feeling among Australian frontier settlers throughout the colonial period. This was to a large extent caused by the very different ideas of how to carry out warfare on the part of Europeans and Aboriginal peoples. The style of frontier warfare in Australia represented a greater break with tradition for the European than the Aboriginal warrior. The British notion of colonial warfare at this time was one of large forces of 'native' warriors who would attack en masse, generally dashing themselves against firearms. However, Australian frontier warfare involved fast-moving raids and ambushes. The tactics used by Aboriginal warriors was a cause of acute frustration to the settlers, essentially guerrilla warfare, naturally suited to the relatively small, independent tribal group. Traditional Aboriginal warfare was highly localised and ritualised. Its tactics consisted of ambushes and night raids, as well as pitched battles (McKernan and Browne 1988:109–110). In Aboriginal culture, these tactics were an acceptable and traditional form of fighting. To the Europeans, however, ambushes and night raids were viewed as 'treacherous' and created a sense of baffled deflation and anger at an elusive target that would not stand still for the firearm to do its work (Denholm 1979:35; McKernan and Browne 1988:110). Tactics such as these would no doubt have imposed a great psychological strain upon the minds of Europeans unaccustomed to them, especially since the brunt of frontier conflict was overwhelmingly borne by civilian settlers unused to war, rather than police or soldiers (Kerkhove 2015:9–11). Frustration at Aboriginal tactics led to the accumulation of a suppressed rage, stirring a desire to reassert superiority and self-respect by whatever means necessary (Denholm 1979:35). Settler fear was heightened in this oppressive atmosphere of distrust and misunderstanding, where one never knew when a spear might come silently flying through a window or doorway, or from the bushes (McKernan and Browne 1988:113).

Enter the fortified homestead

One of the methods settlers adopted in response to fear of Aboriginal attacks and to protect their lives and property was to fortify their buildings. This is not a purely Australian frontier phenomenon, and examples can be found in most, if not all, frontier contexts, from seventeenth-century Ireland and the United States (Blair St George 1990) to nineteenth-century South Africa (Winer 2001) and Australia (Grguric 2008:60). More recently, Burke et al. and Kerkhove have explored the design and use of fortified buildings on the Queensland frontiers (Burke et al. 2017:151–176; Kerkhove 2015:2–3).

As to the need for such fortification, there is ample evidence for Aboriginal attacks against buildings on the Australian frontier, even featuring in that classic of Australian literature, Mary Durack's *Kings in grass castles,* where following an Aboriginal raid on a hut, Cobby, 'Mr Durack's boy', 'insisted on firing at intervals through a hole in the wall' every night until Mr Durack returned (Durack 1997:87, 115). By way of example, in South Australia and the Northern Territory alone, the Police Commissioner's reports and the Adelaide press contained at least 27 separate cases of rural settlers being attacked, or directly threatened with attack, in their dwellings between 1842 and 1851 (Grguric 2008:78–79). References to fortified buildings on the Australian frontier are also plentiful in the historical literature, as shown in the by no means exhaustive table below, to which many more examples could no doubt be added (Table 10.1). Writing of the Queensland frontier, Kerkhove argues that defensive architecture was in fact the norm rather than the exception (Kerkhove 2015:8).

Figure 10.1. Attack on a settler's hut.
Source: James Bonwick (186-). nla.gov.au/nla.obj-135224743.

Table 10.1. Textual references to the use of defensive architecture on the Australian frontier.

Summary of reference	Site date	Source
(QLD) Huts built in square formation with windows facing inwards, outer walls with 'portholes'.	1839	Reynolds 1987:13–14.
(VIC) Hut loopholed for musketry.	?	Reynolds 1987:15.
(QLD) Twelve square 'portholes' cut into building's walls and a gun and ammunition hung by each one.	?	Reynolds 1987:15.
(TAS) Hut built with 'portholes' to fire out of. Roof barked and covered with turf so as not to ignite.	c. 1824–1831	Connor 2002:90.
(QLD) Description of loopholed huts.	Late 1840s	Lack and Stafford 1964:72.
(QLD) Homesteads built with loopholes for rifles.	?	Lack and Stafford 1964:209.
(QLD) Log grog shanties with loopholes to withstand a siege.	Mid-1870s	Holthouse 1967:101.
(VIC) Dwellings built with loopholes out of fear of Aboriginal attacks.	Late 1830s–1840s	Clark 1995:2.
(TAS) House with two towers loopholed for gunfire against bushrangers or Aboriginal attack.	c. 1818	Halls 1997:87–88.
(SA) Two-storeyed building of South Australia Company, its walls with loopholes against Aboriginal attack.	c. 1840s–1850s	Dolling 1981:213.
(SA) Coach-house refuge, loopholed as a precaution against Aboriginal attack.	c. 1852	Dolling 1981:323.
(VIC) Huts loopholed to enfilade each other.	1842	Robinson and York 1977:36.
(QLD) Mentions that homesteads contained loopholes in walls for rifles.	1850s–1860s	Robinson and York 1977:43.
(NT) Telegraph stations built as forts with loopholes.	Early 1870s	Robinson and York 1977:96.
(NT) Telegraph stations with barred windows and loopholes.	Early 1870s	Mulvaney 1989:119.

Summary of reference	Site date	Source
(QLD) Description of 'Rainworth Fort' as defensively constructed.	1862	Mulvaney 1989:103.
(QLD) Description of a home being made more secure against attack.	?	Fysh 1933:99.
(QLD) Homestead's doors loopholed to accommodate rifles in case of Aboriginal raids.	?	Fysh 1933:126.
(QLD) Log hut with loopholes.	1888	Fysh 1933:191.
(NSW) Angled slit in a dwelling's wall thought to be an embrasure for dealing with intruders.	1840s (?)	Cantlon 1981:46.
(NSW) Hut with embrasures in corners and sides of walls, with hinged wooden shutters which could be opened to fire through.	1845	Cantlon 1981:124.
(NSW) Homestead with large flat-roofed tower with 'portholes' was used as a lookout. Sentry posted to warn of approach. Building also had an armoury.	1888–1891	Croft 1965:29, 31.
(NT) Outbuilding's upper-level apertures in walls thought to be embrasures for defence against attack.	1885	Norris 1976:78–79.
(NT) Telegraph station with enclosed courtyard and embrasures.	1873 (?)	Norris 1976:80–81.
(NT) Telegraph station with enclosed courtyard and embrasures.	1871	Norris 1976:82–83.
(TAS) Homestead with high brick enclosing wall with firing positions.	Late 1820s–1830s	Ryan 1996:104.
(SA) Homestead dwelling with rifle 'porthole'.	Late 1840s	Barrowman 1971:52.
(SA) Door from station outbuilding with aperture to permit use of a rifle.	Late 1840s (?)	Barrowman 1971:52.
(SA) Door from station outbuilding with embrasure for discharge of firearm.	Late 1840s (?)	Banks 1970:8.
(SA) Rifle 'loophole' in men's hut on station.	?	Baillie 1978:134.
(SA) Building's tiny 'windows' built as protection against attack.	Late 1840s	Baillie 1978:134.
(SA) Dwelling with 'attic retreat' with apertures for rifle fire against attack.	1840s (?)	Baillie 1972:20.
(QLD) Log homestead built like a fort with loopholes.	c. 1860	Pike 1978:104–105.
(VIC) Huts built with loopholes.	c. 1840s	McKernan and Browne 1988:103.
(VIC) Huts built like forts with slotted windows for firing through. Settlers using cannon.	1840s (?)	Broome 2005:72.
(QLD & VIC) Homesteads built with shutters rather than windows for defence and inward facing homestead layouts.	?	Cannon 1973:30.
(QLD) Loopholed civilian fort at Bertiehaugh station fitted with a swivel gun.	1887	Pike 1978:165.
(General) Settlers preferred to build atop high creek banks as defence against Aboriginal attack.	?	Taylor 1988:24.
(VIC) Contemporary squatter describes huts as loopholed to enfilade each other.	1830s	Taylor 1988:65.
(WA) Lillimooloora station described as fortified.	1884	Pedersen and Woorunmurra 1995:155.
(WA) Makeshift barricades erected at Noonkanbah station.	1896	Pedersen and Woorunmurra 1995:159.
(WA) Fortress-style construction of Oscar Range station.	1896	Pedersen and Woorunmurra 1995:182.
(VIC) Log hut with loopholes to defend against superior numbers of Aboriginal attackers.	1840	Gardner 1993:13, 44–46.
(QLD) Huts built in square formation with windows facing inwards, outer walls with 'portholes'.	1839	Armstrong 1980: 120.
(TAS) Dwelling with two square towers with musket slots for defence.	1820	Smolicz and Sharp 1983:66.
(General) Homesteads sited on high ground, wooden shutters instead of glass windows and 'gun holes' in walls for defence.	?	Cox and Stacey 1972:9,14.

Source: From Grguric (2007:76).

Identifying fortified homesteads

When it comes to extant buildings, actually differentiating between those architectural features associated with defence and those of a peaceful function can be difficult. It is important that one turns a very measured eye on such features in order to avoid forming a false association between a structure and the sensitive topic of frontier conflict. One can go too far in either direction: on the one hand, being too quick to dismiss the possibility of fortification, thereby (unwittingly or not) playing into the 'empty frontier' narrative and denying Aboriginal resistance its agency. On the other hand, if one is too ready to ascribe a defensive function to buildings, one has the potential to create false evidence of frontier conflict, or at least the fear of European colonists, thereby providing ammunition for frontier conflict deniers to level charges of fabricating data upon researchers of frontier conflict.

A limiting factor for the identification and study of extant fortified homesteads is they need to be in a suitably good state of preservation so that any defensive features are still in situ. In most cases, the key diagnostic feature is the presence of one or more embrasures. The word 'embrasure' is taken from military engineering and can be defined as a small aperture in a wall, sometimes splayed out on the interior, and generally square or rectangular, although they can also be round. It is designed to allow a defender to fire weapons through while its small size renders the defender practically invulnerable to the attacker's missile weapons.

In practical terms, this generally means their walls need to be standing to a sufficient height for any embrasures to be visible. The fortified structures studied as part of the author's research into this phenomenon were generally in a good to very good state of preservation, partially attributable to the fact that they were all constructed of stone. They consisted of a squatter's dwelling built c. 1847 in the south-east of South Australia; a farmer's coach-house in what is now Adelaide's southern suburbs, built c. 1851; an accommodation building for workers on a sheep run on the Eyre Peninsula of South Australia built c. 1856; and a dwelling built c. 1879 and store built c. 1885 at a pastoral station near Katherine, in the Northern Territory.

Vernacular architecture in frontier Australia

The confusion that surrounds civilian use of defensive architecture stems from the dual purpose nature of these sites. Such buildings were not usually purely defensive structures like a fort (although a notable exception in Australia are the civilian-built 'shielans' of Queensland, which were structures built deliberately as defensible refuges in event of an Aboriginal attack), but instead they served primarily as dwellings or outbuildings and secondarily as defensive structures. Sometimes even the non-defensive functions of these structures are unclear or unknown. Therefore, what would usually be a typical diagnostic element of fortification, such as a narrow slit in a wall, may have served an entirely different purpose, such as for ventilation. This issue is not restricted to the Australian context; studies of civilian defensive architecture elsewhere have grappled with the same problem. For example, Blair St George, in his investigation of the Whitfield House, a seventeenth-century house in Connecticut, USA, found that there was disagreement over the existence and function of what he argues was a cannon embrasure—a small opening designed to discharge weapons—located in an upper wall of the house (Blair St George 1990:265). Blair St George convincingly argued that it was in fact a cannon embrasure. One of the ways he supported his interpretation was by comparing it to several surviving seventeenth-century houses in England and France that have well-documented cannon and pistol embrasures (Blair St George 1990:265–266, 276–277). While there is no debate as to whether military-built forts (e.g. Crosby 1978) and civilian-built blockhouses (Roos 1953:4) are what they are (that is, functionally built defensive structures), this is not the case with Australian fortified homesteads.

Some versions of history describe particular sites as having been built for defence, whereas others do not. By comparing the design of the structures that may have defensive features with the 'typical' (i.e. non-defensive) design of the vernacular rural architecture of the period, it is possible to observe the ways in which defensive sites were modified from the typical design.

Nineteenth-century vernacular architecture in Australia was heavily influenced by conventions that had been long established in Britain. The basic type of two-roomed country cottage (Boyd's 'primitive cottage') that influenced the colonial builders, both in town and in rural areas, dates back to the late eighteenth century, with those cottages found in the Scottish highlands and the west coast of Wales being particularly influential to the Australian vernacular styles (Boyd 1961:1; Pikusa 1986:19). The primitive cottage, in its most basic form, was characterised by one room, the living room/kitchen, being slightly longer than the other. One small window was placed either side of the door and a fireplace and chimney stood at the far end of the living room/kitchen. The side and rear walls were nearly always blind (i.e. they had no openings) (Boyd 1961:8). This is a feature of Australian vernacular cottages that comes from their British antecedents and is not a defensive feature. The reason for the lack of windows in the rear wall has its origins in the cottages of the northern hemisphere, which were generally sited so that the openings were on the southern side, protected from the prevailing northerly winds (Pikusa 1986:19–20). The same procedure for siting was followed in Australia, although the building's orientation was often altered depending on the particular direction of the prevailing wind. It appears that, both in the British and Australian cottages, the only time a rear door *was* included in the plan was if there were buildings at the rear of the dwelling such as a washhouse, storage shed, privy or chicken house (Pikusa 1986:23). Otherwise they were not considered necessary. Although superseded by larger houses during the second half of the nineteenth century, in rural areas the simple cellular cottage of two rooms continued to be popular well into the twentieth century (Pikusa 1986:22). This type of plan is also characterised by its additive quality. That is, its open-endedness allowed additional cells to be added to the sides or rear to suit the particular circumstances (Cox and Lucas 1978:14). Incidentally, all three of the fortified dwellings that served as case studies in the author's original research project were based on the primitive cottage plan, though in the more elaborate form of a complex of cells.

The key difference between the typical design and the examples of fortified homesteads that formed the author's case studies was the existence of one or more small embrasures located in the rear walls of the dwellings. As mentioned above, the rear walls of vernacular primitive cottages were typically blind, sometimes with the exception of a doorway. Architectural literature dealing with the design of British and Australian rural dwellings is almost always silent on the function of these apertures. One exception is *The Australian homestead*, which mentions that when defence against bushrangers or Indigenous peoples was needed, wooden shutters were used instead of window panes, and 'gun holes' were incorporated into the walls (Cox and Stacey 1972:14). Their absence from nearly all of the architectural literature suggests that such embrasures were evidently not a part of the usual cottage plan, either in Europe or Australia. Rather, they appear to have been incorporated if, and when, deemed necessary in response to local situations. Therefore, these embrasures would represent a key diagnostic feature of frontier defensive architecture.

The role of fortified homesteads—*then*

The location of embrasures suggests how these structures were designed to function in a defensive capacity. Being primarily places where people lived, it would have been undesirable and impractical to do away with conventional windows all together, and to construct conventional windows in the usually blind rear walls of the dwellings was evidently too far a departure from the vernacular. The construction of one or more embrasures in the usually blind rear wall was a very practical solution. It was cheap, easy to do and relatively unobtrusive, yet it allowed the occupants to observe any threats approaching from that side of the building, and to respond with firearms without exposing themselves.

A classic example of this practice can be seen in the 'men's hut' at Central Outstation in the western Eyre Peninsula, South Australia. Constructed in the 1850s, its façade bears the standard, practical vernacular arrangement of doors and windows, with a fireplace at both ends. The interior is divided into three rooms, one small room in the centre and a larger room to either side. However, its rear is where it departs from the vernacular and into frontier architecture. The rear wall is pierced by three embrasures, the surviving example being approximately 30 cm^2. These embrasures were arranged so that one served each of the three rooms, and provided a means of observation and protection for the rear of the building.

Figure 10.2. Rear view of the 'men's hut', once part of Central Outstation, a sheep run on the western Eyre Peninsula of South Australia.

There were originally three embrasures positioned along this wall, one per internal room. However, due to collapse, only one is still in situ (on the left).

Source: Nic Grguric.

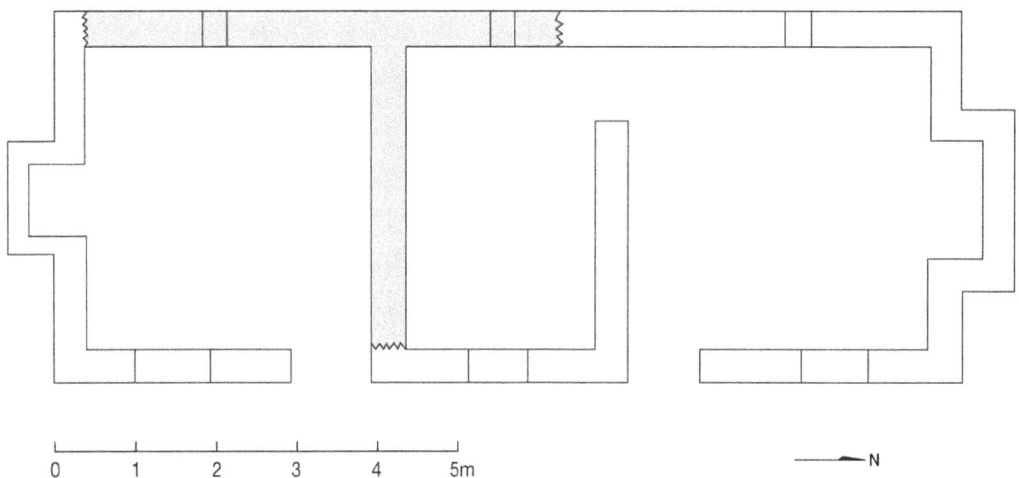

Figure 10.3. Plan view of the 'men's hut' at Central Outstation, with collapsed portions reconstructed based on physical evidence and a historical photograph.

Source: Nic Grguric; ANU CartoGIS (digitisation of plan).

Figure 10.4. Exterior of extant embrasure in the 'men's hut' at Central Outstation, subsequently blocked up.
Source: Nic Grguric.

Figure 10.5. Interior of extant embrasure in the 'men's hut' at Central Outstation, subsequently blocked up.
It is positioned approximately 1.1 m from the floor, a convenient height for a shooting stance.
Source: Nic Grguric.

The retention of conventional windows elsewhere in the building may at first glance appear to defeat the purpose of embrasures in the rear wall—after all, it would have been just as likely that attackers would approach from the front of a building—however, it was common for frontier dwellings to have sturdy wooden shutters, sometimes pierced with an embrasure (Cannon 1973:30; Cox and Stacey 1972:14). When closed and locked, they would render a dwelling very secure from ingress of attackers and their weapons.

There is evidence that doors were also fitted with embrasures. A very rare surviving example from Keilira (originally 'Avenue Range') station in the south-east of South Australia, dating from the 1840s or 1850s, has a small square cut out of it at chest level with a wooden slide. The old, handwritten label attached to the door reads, '[d]oor from old "Keilira", opening specially made by James Brown for the use in many raids on the Aboriginals of his day' (from the text accompanying the door at the Kingston SE National Trust Museum, South Australia).

When it comes to outbuildings, it is even more challenging to differentiate between those apertures that were built for defence and those that were built for ventilation or other purposes. This is because the presence of apertures in outbuildings such as stables and barns are common, and in most cases not intended to serve a defensive function. In these cases, the only way to determine an outbuilding's defensive construction is through supporting evidence and/or a detailed understanding of the building's original function.

It is possible that the apertures of some outbuildings were designed to have a dual function for ventilation and defence should the need arise. Where this is the case it becomes almost impossible to determine with confidence whether the structure was built to serve a defensive role, even as a secondary function. In such cases, all one can do is refer back to the primary documentary evidence, which may, or may not, be considered strong enough to support the interpretation of such a structure as defensive.

Such were the challenges when it came to investigating the defensive functionality of the coach-house and store building that featured in the original research project. The following case studies are discussed below by way of examples as to the analytical process that is required to assess the defensive functionality of outbuildings.

Figure 10.6. Door from 'Avenue Range' (later 'Keilira') pastoral station.

The note attached reads, 'Door from old "Keilira", opening specially made by James Brown for the use in many raids on the Aboriginals of his day'. Although poorly worded, the label identifies the aperture as having been constructed specifically for defensive purposes.

Source: Nic Grguric.

Turning to the 'coach-house', assertions that it was simply a typical English-style bank barn (Bell 1997:10) were refuted partly on the basis that the room with the apertures, which would then have been where grain was stored if it was a bank barn, contained an open fireplace and a conventional casement window. These are features much more indicative of human habitation than crops or livestock. Documentary evidence suggests that this room may have functioned as an office for the running of the farm, with the vehicles that give the building its name being stored below in a lean-to (Grguric 2007:211–212). Further to this, the property already had a much larger barn building (and stables) at the time the coach-house was constructed in 1851 (Grguric 2007:212). That the internally outward-splaying embrasures in the walls were for ventilation is highly unlikely, given the presence of ventilation bricks and a window. As one of its functions at least, this building appears to have been designed as a defensible refuge for those around the homestead in the event of an attack. The presence of a fireplace in the room with the apertures, as well as a loft, would make this building very well-adapted as a refuge. The hearth could have been used for warmth and for cooking, and the loft, only accessible via a ladder and trap-door, would provide a good fallback position or safe area for women and children. This building was also positioned in the centre of the homestead complex, retaining clear fields of fire and vision on the embrasured sides. This central positioning was possibly designed to allow it to be the same distance from either end of the homestead complex, so that wherever one was at the time of the threat, the refuge was not too far away.

10. The fortified homestead of the Australian frontier   201

Figure 10.7. Eastern aspect of the 'coach-house' at the site of Lizard Lodge, once a semi-remote farm, now in suburban Adelaide.

Two of the narrow vertical embrasures are visible. These splay out on the interior, allowing greater visibility and traversal of firearms, thereby greatly increasing the field of fire.

Source: Nic Grguric.

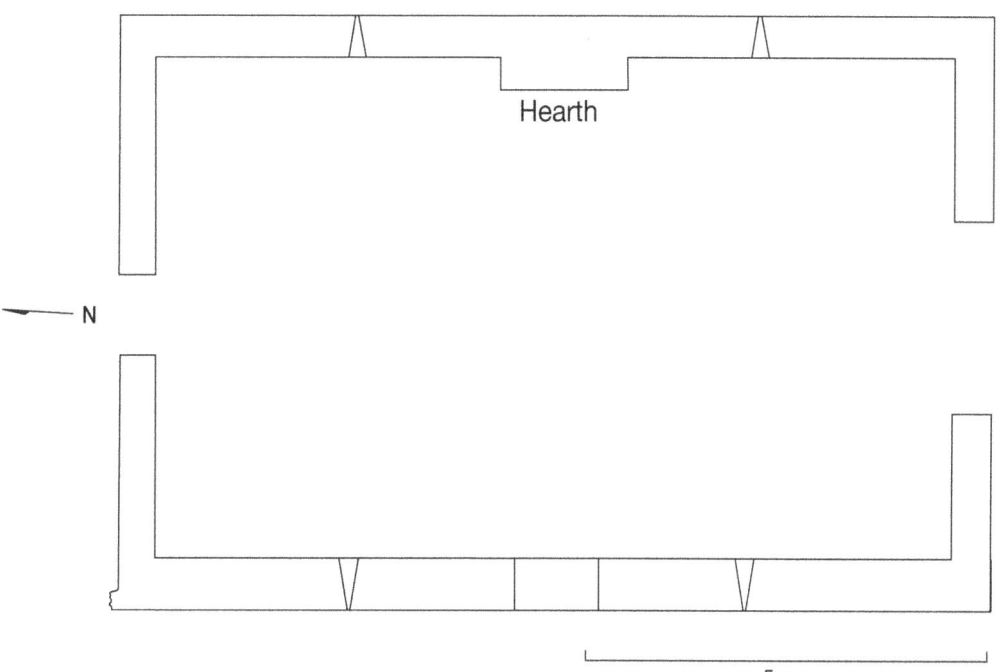

Figure 10.8. Plan of the 'coach-house' at the site of Lizard Lodge showing the position of the internally splayed embrasures in relation to the fireplace and conventional casement window.

Source: Nic Grguric; ANU CartoGIS (digitisation of plan).

Figure 10.9. Western elevation of 'the Old Fort' store building at the former site of Springvale Station, near Katherine, Northern Territory.

Showing the embrasures that pierce all sides of the upper level. Also note the absence of windows on the ground level.

Source: Nic Grguric.

The store at Springvale homestead was designed primarily for use as a store; however, at times, it has been popularly known as 'the Old Fort' or simply 'the Fort' (Allom 1980:1.0). It is evident that the embrasures doubled as ventilation apertures, since two of them would have been inaccessible for firing through; however, that it was designed to be functional as a defensive structure is evident from its overall secure design, with no windows in the ground floor, yet with accessible apertures that could function as embrasures around all four sides of the loft, and no windows. It seems most likely that the tactical role of the store was for it to be 'garrisoned' in order to defend its contents, in the event of an attack upon the homestead.

Springvale Station is not the only known site of an extant fortified store in Australia. Another, earlier example exists, known as 'Rainworth Fort' near Springsure in Queensland, built in 1862. Like that at Springvale, Rainworth Fort was built as a station store, with an upper storey whose walls were pierced on all sides with embrasures to serve as a defensive structure in the event of Aboriginal attack.

Firearms and fortified homesteads

Practical investigations into the capabilities of the typical firearms available to settlers on the Australian frontier indicated there was no evidence for an association between advances in firearms technology and changes to defensive architectural techniques (Grguric 2007:310–340). This is worth noting, though perhaps not surprising, even given the great advantage to firearms capability provided by the widespread adoption of breechloading firearms from the 1870s. Faster-firing and longer-ranged firearms did not render defensive architecture obsolete. This may have less to do with the capability of these firearms than with the nature of Aboriginal homestead attacks. The primary accounts that describe such attacks give the impression that the Aboriginal attackers were usually able to stealthily approach quite close to a building before the occupants were either aware of their presence or intention, thereby negating the increased accuracy of the later firearms at longer ranges.

The role of fortified homesteads—*now*

When the frontier had moved comfortably away from their location and the passage of time had consigned those desperate days to history, some of these fortified homesteads became items of historical interest and part of local lore. Stories were told that were sometimes recorded in local history books, specifically drawing attention to their having been fortified as a defence against Aboriginal attack. These stories constitute interpretations of the architecture just as much as purely material culture–based interpretations do. Likewise, such interpretations are sometimes disputed. A common method used by those who dispute the defensive interpretation of a particular frontier building is to omit of any mention of this interpretation, rather than putting forth their case why it was not so. Examples of this were found in literature dealing with two of the sites that served as case studies in the author's original research project: the coachhouse in Adelaide's southern suburbs (Bell 1997) and the dwelling and store at Springvale Station near Katherine in the Northern Territory (Forrest 1985).

By way of example, Peter Forrest's *Springvale's story* (1985) provides a prime example of the way local histories can create an exclusionary past by omitting mention of fortification and frontier conflict. This is the only published local history of the Springvale site and, as such, represents the definitive history of Springvale. This must be a deliberate omission, considering that 21 of the book's 73 pages deal with Alfred Giles's overland expedition to establish the station, Giles having been the builder of the structures in question. Giles's own account of the expedition describes several confrontations with Indigenous people, including several violent clashes that ended in fatalities (Giles 1870–1885:35–36, 39, 106). Forrest must have known about these incidents, since the manuscript in which they are found appears in his bibliography.

Turning to the homestead of Springvale itself, Forrest makes no mention whatsoever of the defensive function of the store building known as 'the Old Fort' (Allom 1980). Nor does he explain the function of the two round apertures built into the stonework on either side of the homestead's rear door, even though Giles's own son mentions them as having been built for defence (Giles n.d.:10). In doing so, Forrest contributes to the creation of a sanitised frontier where Aboriginal resistance has been painted out of the picture.

Haggis notes that:

> local history is not to be trusted because rural communities put a great deal of effort into covering up a past of violence and expropriation that was often uncomfortably recent in terms of family and community memory. (Haggis 2001:92)

Conversely, Foster, Hosking and Nettelbeck believe that this silence on frontier conflict is less true of local histories because they are 'the product of informed local history knowledge and completely at odds with the received wisdom of a twentieth century white historical silence' (Foster et al. 2001:9). While at first glance these two views appear opposed, both can actually be true within the context of one building, and both tie in to settler identity construction and social memory.

Figure 10.10. Interior (left) and exterior (right) of the circular embrasures either side of the rear door of Springvale homestead.

These are the features described by the builder's son, Harold Giles, who lived there in his childhood, as having been 'built in case of danger from blacks attacking' (Giles n.d.).

Source: Photograph by Nic Grguric.

Rather than omitting all mention of fortification and frontier conflict, those accounts that do highlight the defensive construction of frontier buildings usually frame it in such a way that it mythologises the settler. Many fortified frontier buildings have, through their associated stories, thus evolved in their meaning to become just as much monuments as statues. Monuments are meant to create consensus and stability and the durability of landscape and the monuments placed in it makes them effective symbols for the sustaining of values over long periods (Foote 1997:33). This is the role that fortified homesteads often play in contemporary settler society.

While in a way acknowledging a prior Aboriginal presence on the land, such stories of fortified homesteads serve to portray the settler as a victim of violent 'savages', intent on murdering the settler in his or her own home. In this light, the Aboriginal threat is portrayed as just one of a series of challenges the settler had to overcome in order to conquer and civilise the bush. Settler societies are notorious for developing such 'narratives of reversal' when it comes to dealing with frontier conflict, where Indigenous people are portrayed as the invaders and the settlers as the defenders (Curthoys 2003:193). The customisation of the frontier and Indigenous people by settler societies for their own ideological use has been discussed both in the United States, by archaeologist Patricia Rubertone, and in Australia, by historian Richard Broome, among others (Broome 1996:55; Rubertone 1994:34). Rubertone also demonstrated the important fact that archaeology has the potential to redress this situation, and thereby provide different interpretations of Indigenous history, and in particular Indigenous responses to colonialism that are often unrecorded in written sources (Rubertone 1994:32). Stories associated with fortified homesteads are typically framed in terms of the need for settlers to defend themselves against

Aboriginal attack, while no mention is made of the latter's motives for attack. 'Their [i.e. the Indigenous people's] history of the event has been overlooked, because it serves Euro-American [or Euro-Australian] needs to dehumanise [them] and justify conquest' (Shakel 2001:4). This one-sided portrayal of frontier conflict leads the average receiver to regard the aggressive actions of Aboriginal resistance as that of savages. To omit Aboriginal grievances but highlight their violent response has served an important role in contemporary settler identity construction, that of removing settler guilt. Furthermore, this reversal of roles, casting the Indigenous defender as aggressor and the invading colonist as defender, also serves the very important purpose of constructing a past that 'allocates the land as won through suffering, and therefore as theirs … the self-chosen white victim finds it extremely difficult to recognise what he or she has done to others' (Curthoys 2003:199). This is precisely what settler identity construction has traditionally been designed to do, since it serves to turn people's minds away from the dark truths of the foundations of their society and keep people proud of their whiteness and the community that it forged.

These sites tell us that, for both sides, the frontier was a place of open conflict and fear. Fear of Aboriginal attack may have caused the settlers to fortify their buildings, but this very specific fear of attack was only one aspect of the general atmosphere of fear that pervaded the lives of both sides. The particularly strong nature of the fear is reflected in the fact that it caused the builders to modify long-established vernacular construction techniques in order to help address it.

The existence of these civilian-built structures also speaks volumes about the lack of protection afforded to settlers by the government in the form of the police and military. The government was often either unwilling, unable or particularly poor at preventing frontier conflict, and the settlers evidently did not consider that they could rely on the government for protection. This message comes out very clearly in the following quote by squatter Dr Wilsone, where he complains of:

> the disgraceful manner we have been treated by the Governor of N.S. Wales & Protectors of the Blacks, a parcel of regular humbugs; in fact we are left totally unprotected, when we have paid so dearly to have been so by mounted police, & the consequence must rest on their heads, as we have all united to *defend* to the *utmost* our *properties* & woe betide the blasted race when they are caught injuring us. (Serle 1977:61, emphasis in original)

This shows that often the civilian settler really was the frontline agent of colonial invasion and, through being the one who settled on the land and then proceeded to fortify and defend it against its Traditional Owners, was the one who actually 'conquered' it. This should, however, by no means be taken as evidence that the British military in Australia did not take an active part in the frontier wars. John Connor's book *Australian frontier wars, 1788–1838* is specifically concerned with military actions carried out against Aboriginal resistance (Connor 2002).

Implications for protection and interpretation

Fortified homesteads are significant from a cultural heritage perspective in several ways. First, they are artefacts of the frontier conflict that occurred in their respective regions as a result of colonisation. They speak of the settlers' feelings of vulnerability, paranoia, fear and a 'siege mentality' in occupying someone else's land. They stand testament to the fact that Australia's colonial settlement often progressed in the face of determined Aboriginal resistance. They serve as indisputable physical reminders that the Australian frontier was most certainly not empty, terra nullius, or that Aboriginal people were just decimated by disease or somehow melted away before the advance of European settlement.

The cultural heritage of the Aboriginal communities in which these sites are located could also benefit from the sites' recognition and preservation as examples of defensive architecture. Similar to the way in which these sites are testaments to the settler's experience of the frontier, they are also memorials or monuments to the Aboriginal resistance.

Unfortunately, however, this perspective has not as yet managed to make its way into the popular mythology or public memory. Currently, the social memory constructing use of these sites is clearly dominated by non-Aboriginal, settler society. Only when all groups and sections of society can come to terms with both (or all) sides of their land's past, and accommodate the telling of more than one story, can that society be said to have reached maturity in terms of its identity.

However, with all of the above points, it is important that the actual interpretation and presentation of these sites be very carefully done. Poor interpretation and presentation could result in these sites reinforcing the old ideas of Aboriginal 'savagery' and the settler as 'victim'. Ideally, their interpretation would present these sites as representing the combined fears and circumstances of both Indigenous communities and settlers in a balanced and sensitive way.

From an architectural heritage standpoint, fortified homesteads are highly significant because they represent a hitherto almost totally omitted aspect of our built heritage—that is, a specifically frontier-influenced modification to Australia's vernacular architecture. Furthermore, compared to non-defensively built civilian structures, surviving examples of fortified homesteads are rare, owing to the majority most likely having been made of a perishable material such as timber. As a result, the need for their recognition and protection is heightened.

Conclusion

Borne out of a tragic lack of intercultural understanding and coupled with the unstoppable force of colonialism, conflict inevitably erupted wherever the frontier advanced across Australia. Aboriginal peoples who encountered the invaders mounted a guerrilla-style resistance in retaliation to the invaders for transgressing their laws, or to drive them from their Country altogether. The dwellings of the Europeans were attractive targets to Aboriginal warriors, as they contained many sought-after supplies such as food, tools and weapons. There were goods that the Aboriginal people demanded be shared with them in return for what the Europeans had taken: their food, water, land and, often, their women. The Europeans' concept of property, employment and racial superiority caused them to refuse to share, except on their terms only.

So well-known, and in many regions common, were Aboriginal attacks on frontier settlers' buildings that the long-established vernacular architectural styles were modified, if only minimally, in order to respond to the threat. The most common method was the incorporation of one or more embrasures in what would usually be blind walls, as well as in window shutters and doors, in order to provide a means of observing and directing fire upon and attacking Aboriginal warriors from a position of relative cover.

These buildings often passed into local settler society lore based on their defensive construction. Stories associated with them are framed so as to highlight the danger to the settlers and the challenges they overcame, namely 'aggressive' Aboriginal inhabitants, with no consideration of the causes of conflict. In other cases, these buildings' defensive function is actively denied or omitted, likewise serving current settler society's agenda of downplaying frontier conflict.

Rather than being anomalies, in some regions at least, fortified homesteads seem to have been the norm rather than the exception (Kerkhove 2015:8). This is, however, no longer the case, owing to the fact that the earliest frontier buildings were usually constructed in a temporary manner of a perishable material such as timber, and therefore few survive. It is argued here that it is important that surviving examples of fortified homesteads be protected owing to their rarity and their role as physical evidence of frontier conflict and Aboriginal resistance.

References

Allom, R. 1980. A report to the National Trust of Australia (Northern Territory) on the Old Fort, its potential for restoration and recommended action. National Trust, Adelaide.

Altman, J. 2011. A genealogy of 'demand sharing': From pure anthropology to public policy. In Y. Musharbash and M. Barber (eds), *Ethnography and the production of anthropological knowledge*, pp. 187–200. ANU E Press, Canberra. doi.org/10.22459/epak.03.2011.13.

Armstrong, R.E.M. 1980. *The Kalkadoons: A study of an Aboriginal tribe on the Queensland frontier*. William Brooks & Co. Pty Ltd, Brisbane.

Baillie, P. 1972. *Port Lincoln sketchbook*. Rigby Limited, Adelaide.

Baillie, P. 1978. *Port Lincoln and district: A pictorial history*. Lynton Publications, Blackwood.

Banks, J. 1970. *Kingston flashbacks (Part 1)*. Ladies Auxiliary of Kingston District Soldiers' Memorial Hospital, Kingston.

Barrowman, A. 1971. *Old days and old ways*. A.H. Barrowman, Robe.

Bell, P. 1997. Post-colonisation heritage study of Glenthorne CSIRO field station: Report to Janet Gould & Associates. Historical Research Pty Ltd, Adelaide, South Australia.

Blair St George, R. 1990. Bawns and beliefs: Architecture, commerce and conversion in early New England. *Winterthur Portfolio* 25(4): 241–287. doi.org/10.1086/496502.

Bonwick, J. 186–. Attack on a settler's hut [picture]. (PIC Drawer 7051 #T2448 NK1300) National Library of Australia. nla.gov.au/nla.obj-135224743.

Boyd, R. 1961. *Australia's home: Its origins, builders and occupiers*. Melbourne University Press, Carlton.

Broome, R. 1996. Historians, Aborigines and Australia: Writing the national past. In B. Attwood (ed.), *In the age of Mabo: History, Aborigines and Australia*, pp. 54–72. Allen & Unwin, Sydney.

Broome, R. 2005. *Aboriginal Victorians: A history since 1800*. Allen and Unwin, Crows Nest.

Burke, H., L.A. Wallis, B. Barker, M. Tutty, N. Cole et al. 2017. The homestead as fortress: Fact or Folklore? *Aboriginal History* 41:151–176. doi.org/10.22459/ah.41.2017.07.

Cannon, M. 1973. *Life in the country*. Australia in the Victorian Age 2. Thomas Nelson Ltd, Melbourne.

Cantlon, M. 1981. *Homesteads of Southern New South Wales 1830–1900*. Queensberry Hill Press, Carlton.

Clark, I. 1995. *Scars in the landscape: A register of massacre sites in western Victoria, 1803–1859*. Aboriginal Studies Press, Canberra.

Connor, J. 2002. *The Australian frontier wars, 1788–1838*. University of New South Wales Press, Sydney.

Conor, L. 2016. *Skin deep: Settler impressions of Aboriginal women*. UWA Publishing, Crawley.

Cox, P. and C. Lucas 1978. *Australian colonial architecture*. Lansdowne Editions, Melbourne.

Cox, P. and W. Stacey 1972. *The Australian homestead*. Lansdowne Editions, Melbourne.

Croft, J. 1965. *Murray Downs*. Mid-Murray Illustrated, Swan Hill.

Crosby, E. 1978. *Survey and excavation at Fort Dundas, Melville Island, Northern Territory, 1975.* The Australian Society for Historical Archaeology, Sydney.

Curthoys, A. 2003. Constructing national histories. In B. Attwood and S. Foster (eds), *Frontier conflict: The Australian experience*, pp. 185–200. National Museum of Australia, Canberra.

Denholm, D. 1979. *The colonial Australians.* Penguin Books Australia, Ringwood.

Dolling, A. 1981. *The history of Marion on the Sturt: The story of a changing landscape and its people.* Peacock Publications, Frewville.

Durack, M. 1997. *Kings in grass castles.* Bantam Books, Sydney.

Eyre, E. 1964 (1845). *Journals of expeditions of discovery into Central Australia and overland from Adelaide to King George's Sound in the years 1840–1841.* First published 1845. Libraries Board of South Australia, Adelaide.

Foote, K. 1997. *Shadowed ground: America's landscapes of violence and tragedy.* University of Texas Press, Austin.

Forrest, P. 1985. *Springvale's story: And early years at the Katherine.* Murranji Press, Darwin.

Foster, R., A. Nettelbeck and R. Hosking 2001. *Fatal collisions: The South Australian frontier and the violence of memory.* Wakefield Press, Kent Town.

Fysh, H. 1933. *Taming the north.* Angus and Robertson, Sydney.

Gardner, P. 1993. *Gippsland massacres: The destruction of the Kurnai Tribes 1800–1860.* Ngarak Press, Ensay.

Giles, A. 1870–1885. The first pastoral settlement in the Northern Territory. Manuscript. Private Record Group (PRG 1389/2). State Library of South Australia, Adelaide.

Giles, H. n.d. Memoirs of H.S. Giles (NTRS 298), Folder 1. Manuscript. Northern Territory Archives Service.

Grguric, N. 2007. Fortified homesteads: The architecture of fear in frontier South Australia and the Northern Territory, c. 1847–1885. Unpublished PhD thesis. Flinders University, Adelaide, South Australia.

Grguric, N. 2008. Fortified homesteads: The architecture of fear in frontier South Australia and the Northern Territory, ca. 1847–1885. *Journal of Conflict Archaeology* 4(1–2):59–85. doi.org/10.1163/157407808x382764.

Haggis, J. 2001. The social memory of a colonial frontier. *Australian Feminist Studies* 16(34):91–99. doi.org/10.1080/08164640120038944.

Halls, C. 1974. *Guns in Australia.* Paul Hamlyn, Sydney.

Holthouse, H. 1967. *River of gold: The story of the Palmer River gold rush.* Angus and Robertson, Sydney.

Kerkhove, R. 2015. Barriers and bastions: Fortified frontiers and white and black tactics. Unpublished paper presented at seminar 'Our shared history: Resistance and reconciliation', Central Queensland University, 11 June.

Lack, C. and H. Stafford 1964. *The rifle and the spear.* Fortitude Press, Brisbane.

McKernan, M. and M. Browne 1988. *Australia: Two centuries of war and peace.* Australian War Memorial, Sydney.

Mulvaney, D. 1989 *Encounters in place.* University of Queensland Press, Brisbane.

Norris, K. 1976. *Australia's heritage sketchbook*. Books For Pleasure, Sydney.

Pedersen, H. and B. Woorunmurra 1995. *Jandamarra and the Banuba Resistance*. Magabala Books, Broome.

Peterson, N. 1997. Demand sharing: Sociobiology and the pressure for generosity among foragers. In F. Merlan, J. Morton and A. Rumsey (eds), *Scholar and sceptic: Australian Aboriginal studies in honour of LR Hiatt*, pp. 171–190. Aboriginal Studies Press, Canberra.

Pike, G. 1978. *Queensland frontier*. Rigby, Hong Kong.

Pikusa, S. 1986. *The Adelaide house 1836–1901: The evolution of principal dwelling types*. Wakefield Press, Netley.

Police Commissioner 1848a. Letter (GRG 24/6/1848/1156). Correspondence files ('CSO' files) – Colonial, later Chief Secretary's Office. State Records of South Australia, Adelaide.

Police Commissioner 1848b. Letter (GRG 24/6/1848/424). Correspondence files ('CSO' files) – Colonial, later Chief Secretary's Office. State Records of South Australia, Adelaide.

Police Commissioner 1848c. Letter (GRG 24/6/1847/585). Correspondence files ('CSO' files) – Colonial, later Chief Secretary's Office. State Records of South Australia, Adelaide.

Reynolds, H. 1987. *Frontier*. Allen and Unwin, Sydney.

Reynolds, H. 2013. *Forgotten war*. NewSouth, Sydney.

Robinson, F. and B. York 1977. *The Black Resistance*. Widescope, Camberwell.

Roos, F. 1953. Ohio: Architectural cross-road. *The Journal of the Society of Architectural Historians* 12(2) (May): 3–8. doi.org/10.2307/987538.

Rubertone, P. 1994. Archaeology, colonialism and 17th-century Native America: Towards an alternative interpretation. In R. Layton (ed.), *Conflict in the archaeology of living traditions*, pp. 33–45. Routledge, London.

Ryan, L. 1996. *The Aboriginal Tasmanians*. Allen and Unwin, St Leonards, NSW.

Serle, G. 1977. Manuscripts: Excerpts from the letters of Dr. David Henry Wilsone, squatter, 1839–1841. *La Trobe Library Journal* 5(19):53–62.

Shakel, P. 2001. *Myth, memory, and the making of the American landscape*. University Press of Florida, Gainesville.

Smolicz, R.A. and W.W. Sharp 1983. *Australia's early dwellings and churches*. Angus and Robertson Publishers, London.

Taylor, P. 1988. *Station life in Australia, pioneers and pastoralists*. Allen and Unwin, Sydney.

Winer, M. 2001. Landscapes, fear and land loss on the nineteenth-century South African colonial frontier. In B. Bender and M. Winer (eds), *Contested landscapes: Movement, exile and place*, pp. 257–272. Berg, Oxford. doi.org/10.4324/9781003085089-20.

11

Archives, oral traditions and archaeology: Dissonant narratives concerning punitive expeditions on Malakula Island, Vanuatu

Stuart Bedford

Introduction

Violent clashes across the islands of the New Hebrides/Nouvelles-Hébrides (Vanuatu since 1980) (Figure 11.1) between Europeans and indigenous populations date from the very first contacts. As was the case for the wider Pacific, clashes related to a multitude of different reasons and motives and were matched by an equally diverse range of reactions and outcomes (e.g. Adams 1984; Douglas 1980; Muckle 2012; Nicole 2011). However, as European empires began to encroach and carve up the wider Pacific in the nineteenth century and their citizens began to settle and proselytise, these clashes became more frequent and increasingly lethal, with a regular naval presence and associated punitive expeditions being initiated in the south-west Pacific from the 1850s. From the 1870s, these expeditions became more frequent and retributive, with a grander scale of military operation in association with more lethal weaponry. It has been argued that these changes were related to the decreasing influence of humanitarianism in society at large from the mid-nineteenth century and it began to be replaced by concerns related more to the primacy of British prestige and reputation, which was served, at least in the south-west Pacific, through demonstrations of naval power (Adams 1984:42–44; Samson 1998:130–147). Other influential factors were also at play. One of these was the increasingly rigid racial stereotyping and the demonising of certain regions, and even specific islands, that had an increasing influence on decisions made by naval commanders and colonial authorities (Bach 1986:47; Samson 1998:7–23).

Naval enforcement, retribution and summary 'justice' constituted standard procedure in the New Hebrides from 1858 and continued for 60 years, with a final naval exercise in 1918 marking the end of major military punitive expeditions (Adams 1984; Bedford 2017; Thompson 1981). Many of the islands of the archipelago experienced some form of punitive expedition at least once, but a number of islands proved to be particularly tenacious in resisting colonial intrusion, mounting effective opposition for generations. Malakula, in the north, was first subject to punitive military expeditions in 1884 but they continued across various areas of the island until 1918 (Bedford 2017). Here the focus is on the 1916 expedition undertaken on the north-east of Malakula by British, French and Australian military personnel, along with auxiliary forces from

New Guinea, New Caledonia and Efate Island in the central New Hebrides. It was three months in the planning, involved two naval ships and more than 120 heavily armed men who converged on the shore on 3 November. The planned week-long campaign in the interior to destroy a number of villages was a fiasco as it was ambushed and suffered many losses. Subsequently, there were varying claims as to its success or failure and even questions as to whether the correct villages were targeted. Reservations as to the rationality and effectiveness of the government policy of punitive expeditions generally also began to be raised. There are a number of published accounts of the 1916 conflict, but they are almost exclusively based on the official New Hebrides government record. Here, archival records, oral traditions and physical remains relating to various incidents surrounding the 1916 fighting are combined in an attempt to develop a more balanced, unabridged narrative of the whole episode. Ultimately, the research highlights the value of an interdisciplinary approach, but also the complexities involved in determining, in any conflict situation, a detailed and accurate account.

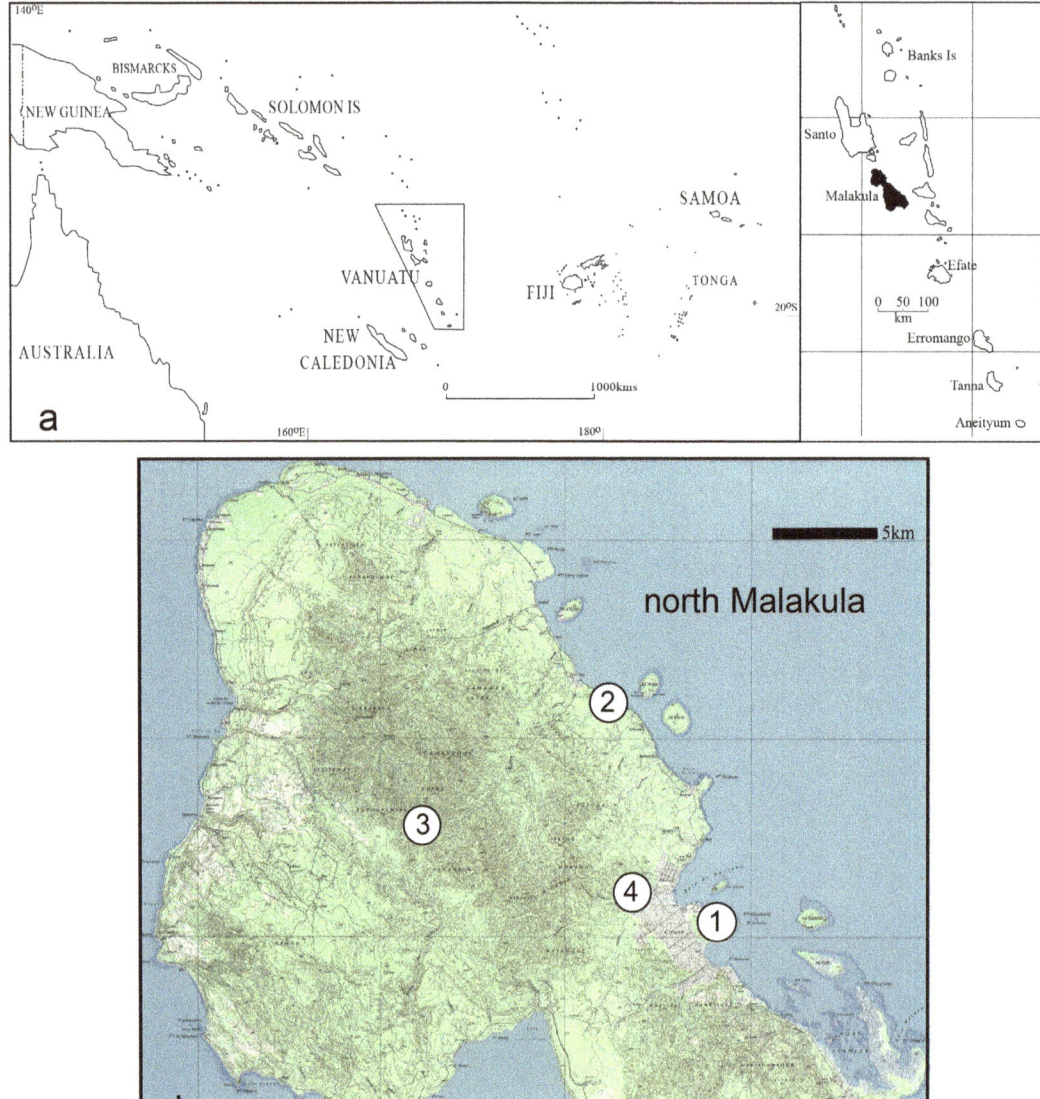

Figure 11.1. A. Southwest Pacific and Vanuatu inset; B. Northern Malakula showing locations of 1. Bridges Store, Tautu; 2. Sanwer beach, landing location; 3. Bartanar village; 4. Mae village.
Source: Stuart Bedford.

Dividing the Pacific

The eighteenth and nineteenth centuries witnessed a burst of exploratory expeditions across the Pacific sponsored by various European powers. The discovery of new lands and peoples fascinated the ruling and educated elite, but the potential for the extension of empires and accumulation of territory and resources was a major incentive. By the mid-nineteenth century, the latter had become the principal driver of European involvement in the South Pacific, with primarily the British, French and Germans in competition.

The New Hebrides archipelago remained in a state of limbo in terms of formal colonisation until the beginning of the twentieth century, when the French–British Condominium was established in 1906. However, Europeans and other foreigners, with a whole range of different backgrounds and motivations, began arriving on its shores from at least the 1840s. Settlement began in the south, on Tanna and Aneityum, primarily associated with Christian missions and trading and whaling stations. Sandalwood was a major attraction (Shineberg 1967), but arrowroot, copra, coffee and cotton were also early cash crops. From the 1860s, similar settlement began further north on the island of Efate, and then in the 1870s settlers began establishing themselves on Malakula and other islands in the north. Labour recruiting from the late 1860s greatly extended European contact across the entire archipelago (Corris 1970; Docker 1970).

The settlers and missionaries in the New Hebrides were primarily British and French nationals and so it was these two nations that became increasingly involved in the affairs of the archipelago (Scarr 1967:176–217). The respective navies policed the New Hebrides from the 1850s, ostensibly to protect their respective nationals but also to supposedly protect the rights of the indigenous population (Adams 1984; Samson 1998). Despite increasing petitions and enthusiasm from their various colonies (New Caledonia, Australia (Thompson 1980) and New Zealand), neither Britain nor France could agree on outright annexation of the New Hebrides. Rather, they formally agreed in 1878 to recognise their joint spheres of influence while maintaining the archipelago's independence. This arrangement became further formalised in 1887 when the British and French Joint Naval Commission was established. Its role was essentially to police the New Hebrides, protecting their respective nationals and shutting out other colonial powers. Annual naval patrols included joint on-ship meetings, which reviewed disputes as they arose, deciding on what sort of punishment should be dispensed among New Hebridean communities. This often involved the mounting of joint punitive expeditions, as the Naval Commission had neither judicial powers nor facilities suitable for incarceration. The Joint Naval Commission continued even after the establishment of Condominium Government in 1906, as the government had few resources of its own and only a small local police force, said in 1910 to comprise a total of 80 Islanders, mostly Ifira Islanders from Efate and Kanak from New Caledonia (Jacomb 1914). Colonial authorities, initially based only in the capital at Port Vila on Efate, relied primarily on traders, settlers and missionaries for information about what was happening on other islands. Naturally, such individuals were pursuing their own wide range of agendas, and government officials in Port Vila had to sift through a range of often competing correspondence to make decisions from afar that, in the case of the British, were then ultimately forwarded to the Western Pacific High Commissioner based in Fiji, who made final decisions and recommendations to naval commanders after conferring with London. From 1906 these decisions also had to be discussed and agreed on by the French Resident Commissioner, and French government officials in New Caledonia and France.

Competing for Malakula

The island of Malakula, located in the north of the Vanuatu archipelago, is the second largest (2000 km^2) of the group, comprising a large main island and concentrations of small islands in the north-east, south and south-east. Fertile coastal flats run from the north all the way down the east coast to the southern end of island. The centre of the island and particularly the south are mountainous and valleyed regions. Malakula was the first island in Melanesia visited by Cook in 1774, where he described it (Port Sandwich) as having an excellent harbour. However, European contact was relatively limited up until the 1860s. Labour trafficking brought increased interaction from the 1870s, with Malakula becoming an increasingly favoured destination. The island remained a primary source of labour on plantations within the archipelago even after the official end of the labour trade to Queensland in 1906 (Adams 1986; Cawsey 1998; Docker 1970; Shineberg 1999). Traders began to establish themselves on the island from the 1870s and land speculation was rampant from the early 1880s, with tens of thousands of hectares being secured through a range of dubious means (Bedford et al. 2017; Van Trease 1987). Much of the wide accessible coastal flats of the east coast had been claimed by the end of the nineteenth century. Presbyterian and Catholic missionaries began arriving on the east coast of the island in the late 1880s.

Increasing European intrusion inevitably led to conflict. Labour trafficking was initially the major point of friction, as any form of surveillance was minimal with authorities generally only becoming involved after the reporting of incidents that had interrupted European operations. The investigations and associated decisions regarding punishment initially appeared to be relatively restrained on Malakula. However, with greater European intrusion and visions of greater economic potential to be gained through further ascendancy on the island, primarily through land alienation, the level of conflict intensified significantly. Imperial competition between British and French interests was also in play. Further handicapping government perceptions and ultimately any decisions was a lack of reliable independent information generated from Malakula. There was no government representative on Malakula until 1913, when the French District Agent was established in the far south. Both British and French authorities relied heavily on European residents and missionaries for local intelligence.

Punitive expeditions on Malakula

The first major punitive expeditions recorded on Malakula were carried out in 1884, independently by French and British naval ships on the north-west and north-east of the island (Bedford 2017; Bedford et al. 2017). They were retributive attacks associated with the killing of labour traffickers and a trader, respectively. Collective guilt was apportioned and retribution, primarily the burning of villages and destruction of crops and animals, was undertaken. Following these initial expeditions there were regular clashes in different parts of Malakula over many decades. The first Joint Naval Commission retaliatory expedition combining British and French forces was in Port Sandwich in the south-east of the island in 1891. Six villages on the northern side of the harbour were destroyed and the associated communities were banned from returning to their traditional lands (Bedford 2017; Bedford et al. 2017).

Following the creation of the Condominium Government in 1906, punitive expeditions became more vengeful and forceful, in attempts to enforce colonial authority and its new regulations. Further complicating the duties of naval commanders from this time was the direction of the Condominium Convention that the Joint Naval Commission should now also intervene directly in indigenous disputes. From this period, explosives were routinely employed to destroy standing wooden drums and stone ceremonial structures, along with a new lethal weapon, the Maxim machine gun—using .303 calibre bullets that could be fired at 600 rounds per minute—which was standard issue and mainly used to clear intended routes. The wider demonisation of Malakulans also increased from this period. Allegations of their savagery, cannibalistic practices and warlike disposition are made in most publications and reports of the late nineteenth and early twentieth centuries, including regularly in accounts in newspaper reports (e.g. Grimshaw 1907:222; Mawson 1905:415; Rannie 1912:133). During a period of heightened tension and competition for economic resources and social control, this increasingly negative public rhetoric began to influence the colonial and imperial governments and naval authority decisions on how to deal with perceived transgressions.

The early punitive expeditions on the north-east of the island had involved attacks on coastal communities, which were relatively straightforward logistically: villages bombarded from the ship and troops landed to complete the destruction of villages and gardens. However, by the time of the establishment of the Condominium Government in 1906, conflict was being generated with tribal groups located well into the mountainous interior. Increased tensions with tribes in the interior of north-east Malakula date from June 1907. Captain Gaunt, commanding the HMS *Cambrian*, was ordered to investigate a dispute between two villages, located in the interior of the north-east of the island. Gaunt sent messages ordering the respective villages of Lalip and Bootoomar to meet to discuss the incident. The order was ignored by the latter, which resulted in the mounting of a punitive expedition involving 80 men from the *Cambrian*. However, the plan went awry early on as the recruited guides appeared to be either unaware of the location of the village or deliberately misleading. The expedition got into an early gunfight in open gardens and suffered a casualty. A Maxim gun was used to clear the area and save the situation. Some of the party then moved on in search of the village, again using the Maxim for track clearance, but after a further two hours among mountainous terrain and no sign of the village, the decision was made to return to camp (Stahlknecht 1907:27). Gaunt was unimpressed by such naval involvement and strategy and suggested that if this was to be future policy then 30–40 men of 'any hill tribe in India' should be supplied to the Resident Commissioner for dealing with such situations on Malakula (Gaunt 1907:44). Other subsequent commanders were to recommend or request contingents of Fijians, Pathans or Buka Islanders.

Serious tensions flared once again in the north-east in 1914. In the interior village of Putermwomo, on 22 February 1914, seven indigenous mission teachers were attacked during an invited visit, resulting in five of them being killed. A punitive expedition was mounted in July 1914 by a Joint Naval force involving 96 men: British, British Native Police, French and French Native Police (Maré Islanders, from New Caledonia) from HMS *Torch* and the French gunship the *Kersaint*. The British Resident Commissioner's yacht the HMSY *Euphrosyne* was also involved, used to transport an advance party of men from the *Torch* to the small islands off the north-east coast to impound canoes and prevent communication with the interior villages. However, despite having overwhelming superiority in men and weaponry the expedition achieved very little. Malakulans were prepared to sustain some level of destruction of property as they had done repeatedly elsewhere. They abandoned their villages, simply disappearing into the surrounding wild cane where they could take shots at the dispersed expeditionary force spread out along the mountain trails. The futile nature of the mission was summarised by the British Commander in his report: 'It cannot be said that the object of the expedition had been obtained' since no prisoners were taken, 'only pigs and yams of the village were destroyed', and several casualties were sustained (Ward 1914).

The expedition of 1916

Despite repeated concerns expressed by naval commanders over many years, and particularly in relation to the 1914 expedition, an almost identical and major expedition was mounted in a similar area two years later in November 1916. The punitive expedition of 1916 is one of the few actually mentioned in a number of published texts, often with the facts confused, but always emphasising both the casualties inflicted on the Joint Naval forces and the futility of the whole exercise (Guiart 1952:208–209, 1986:12–13; Harrisson 1937:405–406). This was a remarkable example of imperial obstinance and overreach, particularly considering the stretched military resources at the time. It appears also that little consideration was given to previous experiences in the region. The expedition was sparked by the killing of an Australian trader, Bridges, at Tautu on the north-east coast, along with five children in July 1916. However, it seems very likely that other factors were equally influential. The island continued to be perceived as persistently troublesome and there was also perhaps an element of retribution in association with the failed campaign in 1914 that may have played a role.

The Condominium Government remained handicapped in terms of reliable independent information in the area. In the case of the 1916 killings, and in many earlier incidents in the north of Malakula, they relied heavily on missionaries and Ewan Corlette, an Australian settler who had arrived in north-east Malakula in 1903 soon after having served in the Boer War. He knew the area well and had participated in punitive expeditions on the island since 1906. Tragically, Corlette's son was one of the children killed at Tautu in 1916 as he had been staying with Bridges. The killings occurred on 10 July: Corlette was informed on the 11th and arrived at the scene at 4.30 pm that day. The bodies had already been buried, but he wrote a lengthy, detailed and graphic description of the scene and his interpretation of the sequence of events in a letter dated 12 July and marked as received by the Resident Commissioner in Port Vila on 27 July. The same letter was translated for the French Resident Commissioner and extracts from it had already appeared in regional newspapers by August (Anon. 1916a). Corlette initially suggested 12 men from the bush had been involved who were from the village of Tiragi (Tiragh), claiming (incorrectly) that it was the same village that had been involved in the 1914 killings of local missionary teachers (Corlette 1916a). In a subsequent letter of 8 September, the information was slightly amended, adding further detail but in some respects less clarity on who had carried out the killings:

> Although a fairly numerous party of Bushmen went to Tautu only three were concerned in actual killing, the others keeping watch. They all belonged to Tiragi but I am not convinced that there were not some Melandraus men with them. (Corlette 1916b)

He also recommended 'a strong expedition, equipped to stay in the bush some time, to teach the natives a salutary lesson' (Corlette 1916b). Motivations for the killings were highly speculative in all reports and mostly put down to facilitating the robbing of the store. However, a report in a New Caledonian newspaper may have been closer to at least providing some background and history that led up to the killings and it also connects at some level to oral traditions. It indicated that Bridges had been warned on many occasions of malicious intent on the part of some locals due to the fact that a man employed by him had died while in his service (Anon. 1916b:15).

Commissioner King had already heard of the killings on 19 July, before Corlette's letter had arrived at the Residency in Port Vila. He left that night on the *Euphrosyne* to investigate and had the news confirmed when he arrived at Southwest Bay, Malakula, the next day. He then went to Port Stanley and met up with Corlette. In a letter to the High Commissioner in Fiji, King outlined the detail of the killings as recounted by Corlette and gave the same almost verbatim recommendations for a punitive expedition (King 1916a). The recommendations were soon acted upon. The French ship *Kersaint* was again assigned, with around 30 fighting men, mostly Kanaks from New Caledonia who made up the French component of the New Hebrides police. The sourcing of a British ship, however, to join the French was much more challenging. Correspondence between the Resident Commissioner and the Admiralty in London initially emphasised the need for a British ship rather than an Australian one, due to the generally anti-French sentiment held in Australia regarding the New Hebrides (PRO 1916). However, due to overstretched resources, the British ultimately had to seek support from the newly formed Australian Navy. Admiralty telegrams to Sydney led to further telegrams from Sydney to Rabaul, where the recently commandeered German ship, the *Komet*, renamed HMAS *Una*, was assigned the task of joining the French in the attack on Malakula. This expedition marked the first involvement of the Australian Navy and personnel (Figure 11.2) in the New Hebrides, and also included a contingent of 10 Papuans. The expedition was planned as a major campaign to finally pacify this area of Malakula. The village of Bartanar specifically was to be targeted then used as a base to destroy other neighbouring villages. Being aware of the rugged terrain, an expedition of a full week was planned, which involved significant logistical hurdles. Legal hurdles also had to be dealt with. The expedition was to be led overall by Commodore Jackson of the *Una* and he was duly made a temporary Deputy Commissioner for the Western Pacific on 16 October, as was standard procedure to cover legal concerns (Bickham Escott 1916).

Figure 11.2. Australian troops who had been engaged in the Malakula campaign of 1916.
Source: Australian War Memorial, P00792.001.

The *Kersaint* and *Una* met in October 1916 at Havannah Harbour on the west coast of Efate where a suitable area for training in the bush was selected. The training was carried out for a week. The ships then headed up to north-east Malakula on 31 October, arriving in the morning of 1 November. The first task was to blockade the small islands of the north-east so that logistical support could not be provided to villages in the interior. The *Euphrosyne*, with the Resident Commissioner on board, again played its part. It was to meet with Corlette, secure his participation and find guides and bearers. Once they were recruited, preparations for the week-long campaign were finalised.

It began on 3 November with the expeditionary force being landed on the beach at Sanwer opposite Wala Island (Figure 11.1b:2) at dawn and heading off with eight days provisions to the village of Bartanar. In an attempt to divert attention from expeditionary activities, the *Kersaint* was sent at the same time to bombard the west coast of the island (Jackson 1916).

The punitive party reached the outskirts of the village on the evening of the same day, but they decided on an early morning attack. This occurred at 6.00 am the next day with the Papuans leading the charge, although as it was spread among dense bush and rugged terrain, attack was extremely difficult. The village already appeared to be largely empty. In the fighting four men in the village were reported killed but it appears to have been quickly abandoned. Some satisfaction was gained with the immediate burning of the village and killing of pigs. The punitive force had sustained no casualties at this point, but their return to the main camp that had been set up the night before marked the beginning of a humiliating and terrifying retreat. In a repeat of the 1914 expedition the punitive forces appear to have been lured all the way into the interior so that they could then be attacked as they returned along the narrow tracks to their camp and ultimately back down to the beach. Soon after commencing their return the column came under heavy fire from the front and flanks and casualties were sustained. Fighting continued all the way to the main camp with the Malakulans having the advantage of being concealed in the wild cane only yards from the track and being able fire at will. The attacks increased with the column being sniped at from all sides and its progress slowed by the increasing number of casualties. The sniping finally stopped once the column moved beyond the wild cane into open bush and they reached their camp by 2.30 pm. Initially it was decided that they would camp the night, although due to the casualties sustained Jackson had already decided to abandon the expedition. Once a local guide suggested that other villages might now join the attack, the night's rest was also cancelled, and a night march was planned. They packed up and left the camp at 8.00 pm, leaving behind much of their food supplies. They advanced in single file that stretched over half a mile in length, reaching safer territory by 12.30 am. A halt was called due to darkness with the column recommencing its retreat at 4.30 am. The shore was reached at 2.00 pm on 5 November and all boarded the ships. As a parting gesture, shelling of the general area of the village by the *Kersaint* was carried out on the morning of 8 November (Jackson 1916).

Figure 11.3. Memorial plaque to eight native policemen who had fallen for France on Malakula since 1914. The plaque was bulldozed during roadworks in south Malakula, Vanuatu Cultural Centre, 2015.

Source: Stuart Bedford.

Though the campaign was a complete fiasco, two British reports—the summary account of Jackson, and a letter from Merton King, the Resident Commissioner to the High Commissioner in Fiji—both tried to cast it in positive light. Jackson suggested that the successful attack on and destruction of the village, which had not previously been visited by white men, 'should produce a good moral effect'. He further deemed the loss of a British seaman and eight native policemen (Figure 11.3) as not excessive, considering the eight hours of fighting the column had endured in the wild cane (Jackson 1916). King largely concurred with Jackson, although perhaps deflecting some blame, he added he thought it unlikely that other tribes would have joined the fighting (King 1916b). Others were less congratulatory. Corlette added his thoughts in two letters to the Resident

Commissioner, outlining the futile nature of the expedition and arguing that another should be organised forthwith. The letters highlight the difficulties for colonial authorities in reaching any considered decisions or subsequent assessments in relation to such situations. Corlette, who was very familiar with the region, had provided the initial detailed intelligence and had participated in the expedition, stated in a letter on 29 December that:

> I am convinced that very little harm was done to the natives beyond burning their houses. Other facts I do know from reliable sources are that the village we went to was not that which the murderer's belonged and that they are still defiant and unconquered. (Corlette 1916c)

In a later letter of June 1917, urging further action, he states:

> I have nothing too definite to report concerning the result of the punitive expedition but had heard rumours that confirm my own conviction as to its futility. It is now said that none of the shells fired by the French warship burst, which is a direct contradiction of the earlier rumours. (Corlette 1917)

However, despite this plea the punitive expedition of 1916 marked the last major colonial military action in the north-east area of Malakula.

Contemporary indigenous narratives

Apart from regular sensationalist newspaper reports, published accounts of the many punitive expeditions in the New Hebrides are relatively few. They are primarily gleaned from European historical resources and are largely restricted to the earliest clashes on Tanna (Adams 1984) and the 1916 Malakula expedition (Guiart 1952:208–209, see Bedford 2017). There is a large archival record housed across the globe relating to this colonial-period violence, in English, French and German, which awaits detailed analysis and wider publicity. However, what is really missing to date is the voices or accounts of the descendants of those groups who clashed with the imperial and colonial forces. Attempts to explicitly connect with the physical remains of these events in Vanuatu have also been absent to date.

An opportunity to redress these aspects developed out of an Australian Research Council project (FT120100716) to record stone ceremonial structures (*nasara*) (Deacon 1934; Layard 1942) across the Malakula landscape (Bedford et al. 2017). The recording of associated stories with many of the sites was a key component of the project and, having been made aware of the numerous punitive raids in various areas, attempts were made to seek out those sites specifically, along with the communities that were directly connected and descendants of those who had been impacted. With the passing of time, more than 100 years in most cases, coupled with disruption through extensive depopulation and land alienation, it is not surprising that in many cases details and dates of various punitive conflicts had begun to fade or had been conflated or substantially augmented. In almost all cases though, at least among the older generations, some memories were retained and most of those were commonly recorded in song (all stories and songs relating to conflict with imperial and colonial forces were recorded and are now held by the Film and Sound Archive Unit at the Vanuatu Cultural Centre). The 1916 conflict stood out in many respects in that it appeared to remain very vivid in the memory of the Tiragh tribe, the majority of which has been long based at the mission-established village of Mae, very distant from traditional lands (Figure 11.1b:4). Its relatively recent date may have contributed, with apparently many of the combatants still alive in the 1960s and into the 1970s, and who may well have been eager to recount, at least from their perspective, a victory against all odds.

The Vanuatu Cultural Centre fieldworker from Mae village, Massing Tamendal, was key to unlocking an indigenous perspective to the 1916 conflict. Vanuatu Cultural Centre Fieldworkers (*filwokas*) are volunteer representatives spread throughout the country who promote and preserve custom and culture. I was aware of the connections of Mae villagers with Bartanar and the 1916 fighting and an opportunity arose while on other fieldwork in 2014 to ask Massing whether he was aware of these events. Immediately he responded in the positive, saying that: 'yes indeed it was us who killed Bridges and fought the white men'. In September 2016, almost 100 years after the punitive expedition, we retraced events and visited associated sites with an enthusiastic group of young and old from Mae village. We started at Tautu on the coast, where Bridges' trading station had been based. It was here that a local version of the lead-up to the killing of Bridges and the children emerged. It was recounted that some time before the killings a group of Tiragh men had sought paid work from Bridges. The task assigned was the digging of a large well, located near the store, through the hard uplifted reef (the remains of the c. 3 m diameter uncompleted well can still be seen today). The men toiled for some days before returning to their village, but as they had not completed the work, they returned without any remuneration. This apparently enraged their chief, who instructed them to return to Bridges and seek some form of payment. No further detail could be provided as to what transpired at the store with Bridges and what ultimately led to the killings, although the incident is recorded in customary song.

Figure 11.4. Remnant standing stones, Bartanar nasara, north Malakula, 2016.
Source: Stuart Bedford.

On completion of the coastal visit we headed to Bartanar in the interior. After some kilometres on the back of a truck and then almost four hours walking, we reached the former village and associated *nasara*, defined by a series of standing stones (Figure 11.4). Most of the people in the group had never visited the site; even the older men of the group seemed initially confused as to its location, having not visited the site since their youth. It was impressive in its apparent isolation and elevation (Figure 11.1b:3), the strategic location and terrain immediately highlighting the challenges faced by any invading party. There was very limited knowledge in relation to the actual fighting at the site, apart from the fact that it did occur, and that houses were burnt, pigs killed and gardens spoiled. It was claimed that there had been no casualties. Nearby, we visited a number of other *nasara* sites associated with former villages that were said to have participated in the fighting of 1916. The Tiragh are a tribal entity that once encompassed many villages in the area rather than any single settlement and many of the neighbouring villages had familial and customary ties to Bartanar that obligated those communities to join in the combat. A large pit feature was also visited (Figure 11.5), and this was identified as having been the result of naval shelling. All confirmed that no damage had been inflicted by the shelling but chunks of iron had been later salvaged from the pit and subsequently used as very effective heat retainers in earth ovens. Although not definitively associated with the 1916 campaign, during separate surveys in interior areas nearby, sections of naval shells that had been collected and curated were identified (Figure 11.6).

Figure 11.5. Large impression said to be due to the result of naval shelling. Massing Tamendal (far left) and Chief Liten (second from right), 2016.
Source: Stuart Bedford.

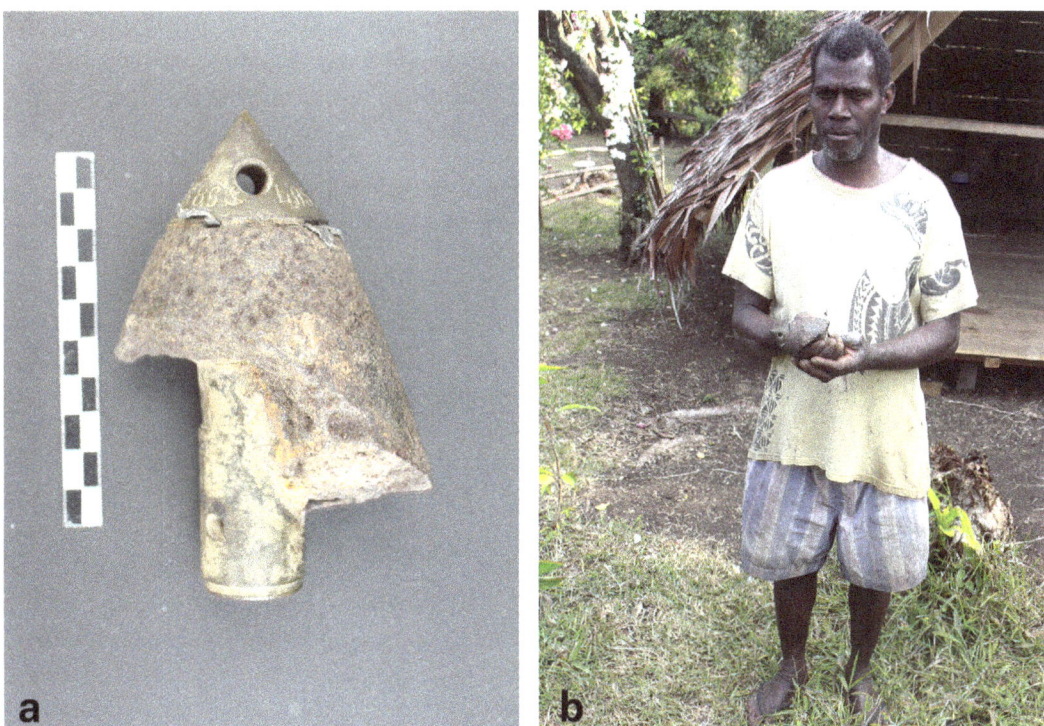

Figure 11.6. A. Fragment of 4-inch naval shell (inscribed on the nose: 1.05.No4.M.83164.7.158.6♲); B. Same shell fragment held by André Ralle, Peterpu village, north Malakula, 2015.
Source: Stuart Bedford.

Discussion

Attempts to understand the influences, decisions, strategies, events and personalities that were involved in the November 1916 clash on Malakula, using a range of sources, has clarified a number of aspects but has also uncovered, among those same sources, some level of dissonance. It would be surprising if it hadn't, considering the nature of the historical information and the time depth and disruption that has occurred among local communities since 1916. It was confirmed that men from Bartanar had been involved in the killing of Bridges and the children and that Bartanar had been subsequently the focus of a punitive expedition. Men from other villages were also involved in the fighting. Naval shells had been fired and apparently did explode in some cases. Both sides claimed some level of satisfaction: descendants of those from Bartanar said that no lives had been lost; while colonial and naval authorities accepted losses as inevitable, but thought that appropriate punishment had been administered. In constructing a post-conflict narrative all parties were no doubt playing to their respective wider audiences in order to justify their actions and assert their moral authority.

Colonial strategy in 1916 followed a well-worn pattern of assembling overwhelming numbers of armed men with superior weaponry to destroy settlements and gardens of entire communities. There was always an assumed level of strategic and technological superiority among Europeans, but it was often effectively nullified by the terrain and Malakulan tactics. Settlements could be quickly abandoned and fighters could lay in wait and attack as opportunities arose. While many facets of this conflict will forever remain in the realm of speculation, archaeology has potentially a key role to play in elucidating further detail of colonial-period conflicts such as these at a whole series of levels from a neutral perspective. The archaeological component of this study was superficial, involving only surface survey, but if excavation and geophysical investigations were undertaken across the wider area they would greatly enhance understanding of this conflict landscape.

Colonial violence is an integral component of the fabric of almost all Pacific Island nations and in some areas aspects of these clashes have been addressed in various detail by historians over the past 40 years (e.g. Belich 1986; Douglas 1980; Hempenstall 1978; Keesing and Corris 1980; Muckle 2012; Nicole 2011; Sack 2001). However, while conflict archaeology is a global trend (Scott and McFeaters 2011), it has yet to be engaged to any great extent in the Pacific.

Even in New Zealand, a nation forged through colonial violence, where pioneering excavations associated with the Land Wars were undertaken as early as the late 1970s, the research focus remains insipid (Prickett 1992, 2016). The need for greatly increased archaeological input into the New Zealand Wars has been emphasised by Professor James Belich, the pre-eminent historian of the subject (Crawford and McGibbon 2018:13). In Vanuatu, colonial-period violence remains strikingly under-researched by all academic disciplines. General histories relate a standard tale from the arrival of the early European explorers, sandalwood and labour traders, missionaries, resident traders and the Condominium Government through to the lead-up and struggle for independence in the 1970s. Serious indigenous opposition to colonial encroachment and associated colonial reactions in the nineteenth and early twentieth centuries are largely absent. This period of sustained opposition, which took many forms and occurred across much of the archipelago, remains largely excluded from contemporary historical narratives and public consciousness in Vanuatu today. Such histories can be complex, disturbing and often sensitive, but increasing the focus on colonial-period violence in the Pacific has the potential to contribute to a more balanced understanding of the legacy of colonialism in the region. More importantly for present-day communities, it may go some way toward resolving contemporary struggles over land, resources and identity across the region (Bedford et al. 2017; Flexner et al. 2016; Spriggs 1997:286–291).

Acknowledgements

Massing Tamendal, resident of Mae village and fieldworker for the Vanuatu Cultural Centre, was instrumental in facilitating the visit to Bartanar and the recording of oral traditions related to the conflict. Chief Eloi Liten of Dakel village guided us to other surrounding village sites associated with people who had also participated in the fighting of 1916. He also hosted our substantial group at Dakel village. I thank Stephen Innes and colleagues at Special Collections, University of Auckland Library, for their help and permission to conduct research among the Western Pacific High Commission records and to reference and reproduce information from various files. An Australian Research Council Future Fellowship (FT120100716) funded archival research and fieldwork on Malakula.

References

Adams, R. 1984. *In the land of strangers. A century of European contact with Tanna, 1774–1874*. Pacific Research Monograph No. 9. The Australian National University, Canberra.

Adams, R. 1986. Indentured labour and the development of plantations in Vanuatu: 1867–1922. *Journal de la Société des Océanistes* 42:41–63. doi.org/10.3406/jso.1986.2822.

Anon. 1916a. Island tragedy. Killed by Cannibals. Trader and children. *Sydney Morning Herald*, 22 August.

Anon. 1916b. Massacre d'une famille anglaise. Aux Nouvelles-Hebrides. *Le Bulletin du Commerce*, August.

Bach, J. 1986. *The Australia station: A history of the Royal Navy in the South West Pacific, 1821–1913*. NSW University Press, Sydney.

Bedford, S. 2017. 'A good moral effect?': Local opposition and colonial persistence in Malakula, New Hebrides, 1875–1918. *Journal of Colonialism and Colonial History* 18(1). doi.org/10.1353/cch.2017.0003.

Bedford, S., M. Abong, R. Shing and F. Valentin 2017. From first encounters to sustained engagement and alienation: European and ni-Vanuatu contact from 1774 to 1915, Port Sandwich, Malakula, Vanuatu, Southwest Pacific. In M. Cruz Berrocal and C.-h. Tsang (eds), *Historical archaeology of early modern Colonialism in Asia-Pacific*, pp. 92–112. Volume 1. University Press of Florida, Gainesville. doi.org/10.5744/florida/9780813054759.003.0005.

Belich, J. 1986. *The New Zealand Wars and the Victorian interpretation of racial conflict*. Auckland University Press, Auckland.

Bickham Escott, E. 1916. Letter from High Commissioner Bickham Escott to Commodore Jackson appointing him as temporary Deputy Commissioner for the Western Pacific (WPHC 2693/16). AU Microfilm 78–326. Records of the Western Pacific High Commission. Special Collections, University of Auckland.

Cawsey, K. 1998. *The making of a rebel: Captain Donald Macleod of the New Hebrides*. Institute of Pacific Studies, Suva.

Corlette, E. 1916a. Letter from Ewan Corlette to Resident Commissioner Merton King, 12 July 1916. New Hebrides British Service (NHBS 32/16). Records of the Western Pacific High Commission. Special Collections, University of Auckland.

Corlette, E. 1916b. Letter from Ewan Corlette to Resident Commissioner Merton King, 8 September 1916. New Hebrides British Service (NHBS 32/16). Records of the Western Pacific High Commission. Special Collections, University of Auckland.

Corlette, E. 1916c. Letter from Ewan Corlette to Resident Commissioner Merton King, 29 December 1916. New Hebrides British Service (NHBS 32/16). Records of the Western Pacific High Commission. Special Collections, University of Auckland.

Corlette, E. 1917. Letter from Ewan Corlette to Resident Commissioner Merton King, 19 June 1917. New Hebrides British Service (NHBS 32/16). Records of the Western Pacific High Commission. Special Collections, University of Auckland.

Corris, P. 1970. Pacific Island labour migrants in Queensland. *Journal of Pacific History* 5:43–64. doi.org/10.1080/00223347008572164.

Crawford, J. and I. McGibbon 2018. Introduction. In J. Crawford and I. McGibbon (eds), *Tutu Te Puehu: New perspectives on the New Zealand Wars*, pp. 11–14. Steele Roberts Aotearoa, Wellington.

Deacon, B. 1934. *Malekula: A vanishing people in the New Hebrides*. Routledge and Sons, London.

Docker, E. 1970. *The Blackbirders: The recruiting of South Seas labour for Queensland, 1863–1907*. Angus and Robertson, Sydney.

Douglas, B. 1980. Conflict and alliance in a colonial context: Case studies in New Caledonia, 1853–1870. *Journal of Pacific History* 15(1):21–51. doi.org/10.1080/00223348008572386.

Flexner, J., M. Spriggs, S. Bedford and M. Abong 2016. Beginning historical archaeology in Vanuatu: Recent projects on the archaeology of Spanish, French, and Anglophone Colonialism. In S. Montón-Subías, M. Berrocal and A. Martínez (eds), *Archaeologies of early modern Spanish Colonialism*, pp. 205–222. Springer International, Switzerland. doi.org/10.1007/978-3-319-21885-4_9.

Gaunt, E. 1907. Gaunt to Commander-in-Chief, 6 July 1907 (WPHC 8/II 3026869/28). Royal Navy Australia Station, New Hebrides Report. Records of the Western Pacific High Commission. Special Collections, University of Auckland.

Grimshaw, B. 1907. *From Fiji to the Cannibal Islands*. Eveleigh Nash, London.

Guiart, J. 1952. L'organisation sociale et politique du Nord Malekula. *Journal de la Société des Océanistes* 8:208–209. doi.org/10.3406/jso.1952.1740.

Guiart, J. 1986. La conquête et le déclin: Les plantations, cadre des relations sociales et économiques au Vanuatu (ex Nouvelles-Hébrides). *Journal de la Société des Océanistes* 82–83:7–40. doi.org/10.3406/jso.1986.2821.

Harrisson, T. 1937. *Savage civilisation*. Victor Gollancz, London.

Hempenstall, P. 1978. *Pacific Islanders under German Rule: A study in the meaning of colonial resistance*. Australian National University Press, Canberra. doi.org/10.26530/oapen_612753.

Jackson, J. 1916. Report to the Secretary of the Admiralty on the punitive expedition to Malekula (WPHC 3307/16). AU Microfilm 78–326. New Hebrides British Service, Records of the Western Pacific High Commission. Special Collections, University of Auckland.

Jacomb, E. 1914. *France and England in the New Hebrides: The Anglo-French condominium*. G. Robertson, Melbourne.

Keesing, R. and P. Corris 1980. *Lightning meets the west wind: The Malaita massacre*. Oxford University Press, Melbourne.

King, M. 1916a. Letter from Resident Commissioner King, New Hebrides, to High Commissioner Bickham Escott, 28 July 1916. Malakula Punitive Expedition, New Hebrides, 1914–1916. Admiralty Records, 8387/225. Public Records Office, London.

King, M. 1916b. Resident Commissioner King, New Hebrides, to High Commissioner Bickham Escott, 20 November 1916, Forwards, with comments, Commander Jackson's report on the punitive expedition to Malekula (WPHC 3307/16). AU Microfilm 78–326. New Hebrides British Service, Records of the Western Pacific High Commission. Special Collections, University of Auckland.

Layard, J. 1942. *The stone men of Malakula: The small island of Vao*. Chatto and Windus, London.

Mawson, D. 1905. The geology of the New Hebrides. *Proceedings of the Linnean Society of New South Wales* 3:400–485. doi.org/10.5962/bhl.part.12911.

Muckle, A. 2012. *Spectres of violence in a Colonial context: New Caledonia 1917*. University of Hawai'i Press, Honolulu.

Nicole, R. 2011. *Disturbing history: Resistance in early colonial Fiji*. University of Hawai'i Press, Honolulu.

Prickett, N. 1992. The archaeology of the New Zealand Wars. *Australasian Historical Archaeology* 10:3–14.

Prickett, N. 2016. *Fortifications of the New Zealand Wars*. New Zealand Department of Conservation Te Papa Atawahi, Wellington.

PRO 1916. Malakula Punitive Expedition, New Hebrides, 1914–1916. Admiralty Records, 8387/225. Public Records Office, London.

Rannie, D. 1912. *My adventures among South Sea Cannibals*. Seeley, Service & Co., London.

Sack, P. 2001. *Phantom history, the rule of law and the colonial state: The case of German New Guinea*. The Australian National University, Canberra.

Samson, J. 1998. *Imperial benevolence: Making British authority in the Pacific Islands*. University of Hawai'i Press, Honolulu. doi.org/10.1515/9780824862947.

Scarr, D. 1967. *Fragments of empire: A history of the Western Pacific High Commission 1877–1914*. Australian National University Press, Canberra.

Scott, D. and A. McFeaters 2011. The archaeology of historic battlefields: A history and theoretical development in conflict archaeology. *Journal of Archaeological Research* 19(1):103–132. doi.org/10.1007/s10814-010-9044-8.

Shineberg, D. 1967. *They came for sandalwood: A study of the sandalwood trade in the South-West Pacific 1830–1865*. Melbourne University Press, Melbourne.

Shineburg, D. 1999. *The people trade: Pacific Island laborers and New Caledonia, 1865–1930*. University of Hawai'i Press, Honolulu. doi.org/10.1515/9780824864910.

Spriggs, M. 1997. *The Island Melanesians*. Blackwell, Oxford.

Stahlknecht, 1907. Lieutenant Stahlknecht to Captain Gaunt, 1 July 1907 (WPHC 8/II 3026869/28). Royal Navy Australia Station, New Hebrides Report. Records of the Western Pacific High Commission. Special Collections, University of Auckland.

Thompson, R. 1980. *Australian imperialism in the Pacific: The expansionist era 1820–1920*. Melbourne University Press, Melbourne.

Thompson, R. 1981. Natives and settlers on the New Hebrides frontier 1870–1900. *Pacific Studies* 5(1):1–18.

Van Trease, H. 1987. *The politics of land in Vanuatu*. University of the South Pacific Press, Suva.

Ward, J. 1914. Report on the expedition to Putermwomo, Malekula Island. HMS Torch at sea, 6 July 1914 (WPHC 1891/14) New Hebrides British Service, Records of the Western Pacific High Commission. Special Collections, University of Auckland.

12

Invisible women at war in the West: An archaeology of the Australian Women's Army Service camp, Walliabup (Bibra Lake), Western Australia, c. 1943–1945

Sven Ouzman, Jillian Barteaux, Christine Cooper and the UWA Archaeology Fieldschool Class of 2017

Introduction

Imagine travelling from Tasmania and eastern Australia across the Nullarbor Plain, crammed into the back of an open army truck, during the height of summer, to a World War II bush camp where you perform a plethora of essential duties, only for history then to do its best to forget you.

This daunting scenario captures something of the lived experience of the women of the Australian Women's Army Service (AWAS), an under-researched component of Australia's World War II efforts (but see Beveridge 1988; Tucker 1991). Half-forgotten examples like the AWAS are nonetheless instructive in pointing the way to identifying and making known the specific and partial ways in which we remember large, global events like wars (cf. Symonds 2019). For example, wars often deploy tactics like deliberate concealment for operational or political reasons (cf. Burke et al. 2020). The benefit of archaeology is that it is often capable of 'ground-truthing' events known or hinted at through historical and oral sources, by finding the everyday 'small things forgotten' (cf. Deetz 1977) that are essential to a more comprehensive and democratic retelling of the past. Until as recently as a few decades ago, events like world wars, dating to within the last 100 years or so, were not considered suitable for archaeological study because archaeology had not then fully understood its own development and ambit—and because these events were seen as too recent and painful to permit objective study (cf. Baker 1988; Pollard and Banks 2005)—although John Carman says such studies are 'combined ideally with the testimony of those involved—[to give] archaeologists the opportunity to "turn the dead silence into an eloquent statement of experience"'(Carman 1997:2; see Carman 2013 on the value of studying conflict). We now have a well-developed subdiscipline of contemporary archaeology (Graves-Brown et al. 2013), yet there are still under-studied areas. World War II is one such area, typically much less of a focus than the archaeology of World War I—especially in Australia, with relatively few sites on Australian soil either studied or accorded heritage site status. This imbalance is largely because 'battlefield archaeology' remains the most prominent field of study in conflict archaeology (e.g. Beck et al. 2002) and most Australian world war sites never saw actual conflict; these sites are predominantly abroad (e.g. Gallipoli and Kokoda).

This chapter contributes to the under-reported archaeology of recent conflict on at least three fronts. First, it is about World War II (but see Clark 2018 for a growing archaeological scholarship). Second, it is not a 'battlefield archaeology' (cf. Sutherland 2017) but about a site far behind the frontlines that never saw any 'action'. Finally, it is about women.

Even so, our report details the results of an eight-day University of Western Australia fieldschool in 2017, showing we had great difficulty in 'finding' clear evidence that a site at Bibra Lake, approximately 20 km south-south-west of Perth, was an army camp, never mind gendering any of its places or artefacts. We explore the utility of archaeology, combined with archival sources and oral histories, in identifying sites of war such as camps, as well as the lived experiences of army personnel, especially women and other subaltern groups. We begin by supplying the background, context and 'facts' of our work, before moving to a more conceptual treatment of the archaeologies of war and women, concluding with thoughts on war and its memorialisation and role in present-day Australia.

Background: A campground then and now

An Aboriginal home and hearth

The place Noongar/Nyungar people call 'Walliabup', which may mean 'place of tears' on account of funerary rites held there (Lyon 1833:64–65), is also known as 'Bibra Lake', located approximately 20 km south-south-west of Perth in Western Australia (Figure 12.1). This area is characterised by 19 lakes and wetlands and has been a landscape of Aboriginal occupation and endeavour for thousands of years, with multiple camping, food-gathering, trade and ceremonial sites listed on the Western Australian Department of Planning, Lands and Heritage's Aboriginal Heritage Inquiry System (Department of Planning, Lands and Heritage 2020–2021). In 1973 Sylvia Hallam (1987) documented over 2000 quartz and other stone tools and stone tool fragments going back at least c. 5000 years, as well as historic artefacts such as reworked glass and clay pipes, which show a continuing occupation and attachment. This work was followed up and extended by Hook and Dortch (2017), who found more non-local quartz, chert and granite artefacts, and also charcoal. Their work was collaborative and Traditional Owners suggested these finds—usually located on higher-lying areas—matched their received knowledge of people camping on higher ground.

The reworked glass shows that this area was a 'contact zone' between Aboriginal people and non-Aboriginal invaders/settlers after the 1829 CE establishment of the Swan River Colony (Bracknell and Collard 2012:85–87). Aboriginal people continued to camp and live in this area until at least the 1980s (Bracknell and Collard 2012:88; testimony of Henry Ford) when the construction of the 'Adventure World' water park in 1982 served to force most remaining people out. This did not extinguish the recent, contested nature of this landscape, with the most recent iteration being the 2016–2017 Liberal State Government's unsuccessful plans to extend the Roe 8 Highway through this site (Chambers and Jennings 2017). Indeed, the fieldschool that produced the data for this article was to help provide empirical details of the area's heritage footprint, used to best manage and ameliorate development. The Roe 8 extension was stopped with the change in state government in 2017 but was reactivated in the 2021 state elections. Walliabup continues to remain important to Nyungar-Whadjuk people's maintenance of identity, being and health (Polglaze 1986).

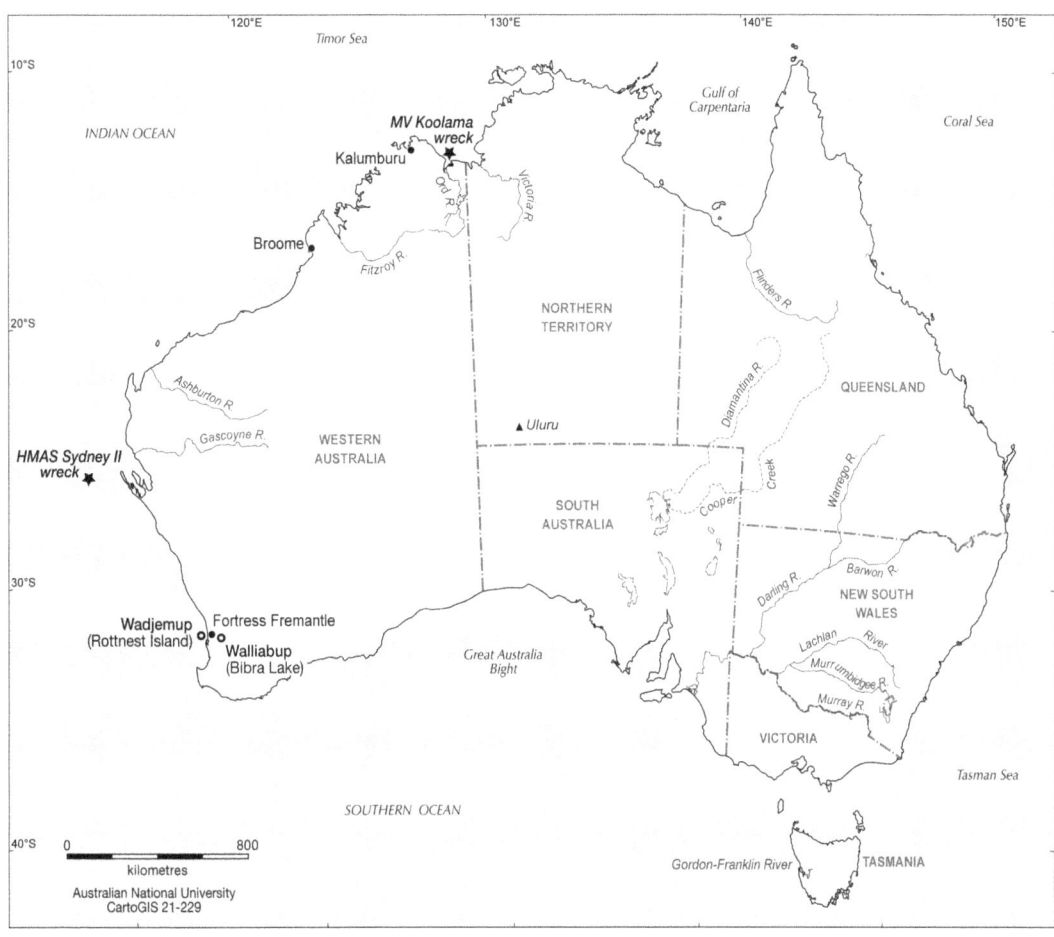

Figure 12.1. Location of World War II sites mentioned in text including Walliabup (Bibra Lake).
Source: Rentia Ouzman and ANU CartoGIS.

The character of the landscape has thus both remained the same—a campground for Aboriginal and army personnel—but also changed, from a place of meeting to a landscape of colonial occupation, war and neoliberal exclusion. It is on this more recent history that we focus, reporting on the often ambiguous and ephemeral archaeological evidence, in tandem with similarly ambiguous archival and oral evidence, in order to better understand the nature of World War II and women's participation in it. We now turn to the militarised history of Walliabup.

An army camp: But which one?

For over 70 years Walliabup's World War II history was almost forgotten, barely surviving in local memory. For example, one of us (Christine Cooper) heard the testimony of a friend from nearby Coolbelup who mentioned seeing searchlights in the sky as small child during World War II. The Bibra Lakes Residents Association, led by Christine Cooper, felt this almost-forgotten military history of Walliabup needed to be told. A major question to resolve was whether there was ever an AWAS camp at Bibra Lake, or if it was being confused with the 116th Light Anti-Aircraft Regiment's camp and headquarters, the 66th Searchlight Battery—or some combination of these (see also Tucker 1991). Indeed, we also had to consider whether there was ever an army camp at this location. Local memories and histories were incomplete and often contradictory, as is often the case decades after an event, especially something as momentous as a world war (Moshenka 2006), where subsequent memorialisations often skew our understanding of events. Indeed, much of the Walliabup war information 'out there' is contained on websites and in non-traditional—and non-refereed—electronic formats. But there was general agreement that whatever heritage was present at the site needed to be investigated so that the City of Cockburn—who in 2015 added the site to the Local Government Inventory as a heritage site (City of Cockburn 2017)—could better manage its heritage inventory. Initially they engaged the University of Western Australia's Society of Exploration Geophysicists Student Chapter in 2015 to conduct a geomagnetic survey that produced some promising but inconclusive results of sub-surface anomalies. A citizen science metal detector survey was also commissioned, which showed several areas of interest across a c. 50 000 m^2 area, with each sub-surface 'target' flagged. In 2016 the Residents Association engaged Terra Rosa Consulting for a one-day survey that noted in situ concrete features and associated construction material such as bricks and asbestos sheets, with occasional finds of glassware, ceramics and metal artefacts in the surrounding bushland (Terra Rosa Consulting 2016). The Residents Association then approached University of Western Australia (UWA) Archaeology in 2016 for more substantive work and in 2017 an eight-day fieldschool was held on site, combining survey, mapping and excavation, with a watching brief for any Aboriginal artefacts, and which produced a student-authored final report (ARCY3002 2017).

After the bushland to the east of Bibra Lake and North Lake was reconnoitred twice, we felt that Lot 65, Hope Road, Bibra Lake (Figure 12.1) was the most likely location for an army camp based on previous survey results and above-surface features and artefacts. The land is owned by the City of Cockburn, who were very accommodating of the fieldschool and provided all required permits. The South West Aboriginal Land and Sea Council was consulted, and cultural as well as occupational health and safety regulations were put in place. As a component of normal archaeological practice, the ARCY3002 Fieldschool students conducted a literature survey of the area, focusing on any AWAS mentions, so that areas of potential interest could be identified—especially given there are at least three candidates for an army camp in this area.

The Australian Women's Army Service (AWAS)

The AWAS was created on 13 August 1941 with the brief:

> to release men from certain military duties for service with fighting units. The service recruited women between the ages of 18 and 45 and they served in a variety of roles including clerks, typists, cooks and drivers. (Heywood 2009; see also Beveridge 1988; Desmond 1988; Oliff 1981; Tucker 1991)

Initially, approximately 1600 women joined the service, and their number peaked at 24 206 in 1945 (with 679 receiving rank—mostly lieutenant, with a single, remarkable colonel), before demobilisation in June 1947, with all camps closed. It is unlikely that an AWAS camp would be situated isolated far from any other camps, as theirs was a service brief, so it is probable that they would have been twinned or subsumed into one or both of the following camps.

The 116th Light Anti-Aircraft Regiment (116th LAA)

Records indicate Lot 65 was also the probable home to the 116th LAA, which was formed in 1942 from the remnants of the disbanded 2nd, 3rd and 116th LAA batteries (Sharp 2002). Our evidence for this derives from the regiment's Intelligence Summary documents (or 'War Diary', which was kept by all camps and is today lodged at the Australian War Memorial in Canberra). For the period 1 January – 31 October 1943, the first clear mention of the 116th LAA at 'Bibra Lake' dates to 9 January 1943 (Australian War Memorial 1943a). Prior to this, the 116th LAA was based at a naval base nearer Fremantle, which was about 11 km to the north-west. The full entry reads:

> RHQ 116 Aust L A A Regt moved from NAVAL BASE (Map ref; 758258) no established at BIBRA LAKE (map ref; 811315). Move completed by 09:00 hours.

Helpfully, a phone number is listed as 'BIBRA LAKE 1'. Camouflage is said to be 'good' and tellingly 'material borrowed from local inhabitants has provided many comforts and conveniences for the men'. This move was likely prompted by fears Fremantle was a known military nexus vulnerable to attack, and distributing key material and personnel to new, unknown locations was a strategic decision to reduce risk and improve defences for what was then a very fearful and nervous populace. We have not found any mention of an 'AWAS' camp in these Intelligence Summaries, although these are voluminous and somewhat costly to obtain. Most likely, there was technically never an 'AWAS camp', as the AWAS personnel were absorbed into camps like the 116th LAA and/or 66th Searchlight Battery to perform service roles.

The 66th Searchlight Battery (66th SL Bty)

The other possible entity encamped at or near Lot 65 was the 66th Searchlight Battery. Originally the 66th Anti-Aircraft Company, the 66th SL Bty was another amalgam, this time formed in 1941 out of the 55th Anti-Aircraft Company (Australian War Memorial 1943b). We know the 55th was located on 'North Lake Road' (Bibra Lake) by 1942 (Tucker 1991:64). They were likely twinned with the 116th LAA camp—the idea being that the battery's searchlights would illuminate airborne targets that the 116th LAA would then shoot down, although no such action was ever seen at this site or, indeed, Perth during World War II (though there are reports of Japanese reconnaissance planes from time to time). We know the 66th SL Bty requested AWAS personnel in September 1942 and a year later, AWAS personnel comprised half their non-commissioned personnel (see also Athena 1943 for a contemporary news article on women 'manning' the searchlights). Eileen Tucker, then Eileen Reilly, who was part of the AWAS from 8 April 1942 until 9 May 1946, provides a firsthand account in her book *We answered the call* (1991). Written almost 50 years after the war, Tucker devotes several pages to the AWAS who were 'attached to the 66 S/L battery and camped at Bibra Lake south of Perth' (1991:78; see also subsequent pages for an engaging series of descriptions of life in the bush including snakes, bushfires and never actually seeing the nearby Bibra Lake). The 66th SL Bty's Intelligence Summaries suggest they were operational by April 1943 at several locations around Perth (Como, Kings Park, Mosman Park and Swanbourne), but no Location Statements mention 'Bibra Lake' specifically. Eileen Tucker mentions a Bibra Lake camp of between 100 and 200 people and provides a large group photograph captioned '66 AA Battery, Bibra Lake' (Tucker 1991:99). This attribution is, however, contested by military historian Graham McKenzie-Smith, who holds that Bibra Lake was too small and limited in infrastructure to be either a searchlight battery or AWAS camp and was more likely home to around 50 personnel from the 116th LAA with five or six AWAS support staff (see Higgins 2015). The 116th LAA is known to have been at this site, but only for less than six months in the first half of 1943, representing a possible overlapping occupation with the 66th SL Bty.

No maps are known to exist of the site/camp from this time, although one of the Intelligence Summaries, written by the 116th LAA's commanding officer Lieutenant-Colonel Henley ?Burton (his surname is only partially legible in the Intelligence Summaries), makes mention of an attached rough sketch of an 'administration block and general layout' (Australian War Memorial 1943a: letter dated 9 January, sketch not found). Oral histories, one or two generations removed, from City of Cockburn residents do suggest an AWAS presence. For example, Ruby (nee Tranter) Hone is reported as being an AWAS member at the Bibra Lake Barracks, where she transported linemen in trucks to Jandakot, Bibra Lakes and Cable Beach near Leighton (Dunn 2015). During fieldwork we also received several anecdotal accounts of a camp in the area. Our post-fieldwork research did, however, locate a *Sunday Times* auction notice from 16 September 1945 (Figure 12.2) and another such notice in *The Daily News* from October 1945. The *Sunday Times* notice describes auction Lot 7 as: 'Searchlight Station 10. BIBRA LAKE, COR. OF WARWICK [Warwick road was later renamed Hope Road] AND DIXON ROADS', listing several buildings (kitchen, mess and recreation room [£75], latrines, ablutions and engine shed [£12] 'built over [the] bore' with two 2000-gallon water tanks). Materials listed for sale include asbestos, barbed wire fencing, concrete slabs, cisterns, galvanised iron 'skillion' roofing, piping and timber framing. This auction, authorised by the Commonwealth Disposal Commission, concludes 'this is an exceptional opportunity to secure building material now *in short supply*— FOR REMOVAL' (italics added). There was thus substantial infrastructure on what is today Lot 65. The auction notice is clear this is a searchlight station, which would imply a nearby anti-aircraft presence—and service personnel like the AWAS. We now turn to the archaeology of the site to see if we can better identify the use to which Lot 65's structures and artefacts were put to.

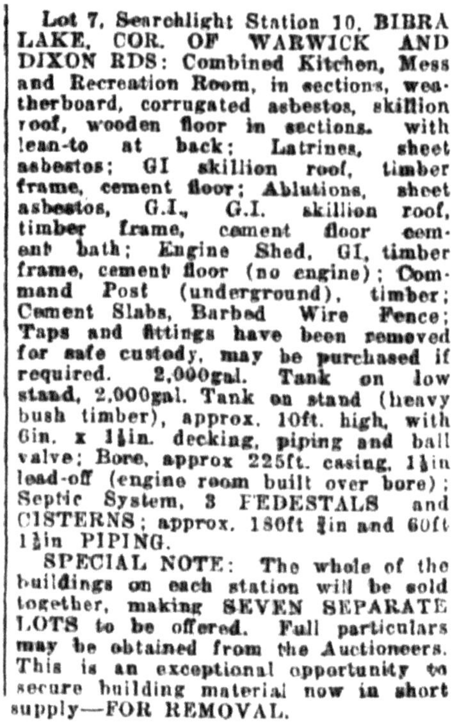

Lot 7, Searchlight Station 10, BIBRA LAKE, COR. OF WARWICK AND DIXON RDS: Combined Kitchen, Mess and Recreation Room, in sections, weatherboard, corrugated asbestos, skillion roof, wooden floor in sections, with lean-to at back; Latrines, sheet asbestos; GI skillion roof, timber frame, cement floor; Ablutions, sheet asbestos, G.I., G.I. skillion roof, timber frame, cement floor cement bath; Engine Shed, GI timber frame, cement floor (no engine); Command Post (underground), timber; Cement Slabs, Barbed Wire Fence; Taps and fittings have been removed for safe custody, may be purchased if required. 2,000gal. Tank on low stand, 2,000gal. Tank on stand (heavy bush timber), approx. 10ft. high, with 6in. x 1¼in. decking, piping and ball valve; Bore, approx 225ft. casing, 1¼in lead-off (engine room built over bore); Septic System, 3 PEDESTALS and CISTERNS; approx. 180ft ¾in and 60ft 1¼in PIPING.
SPECIAL NOTE: The whole of the buildings on each station will be sold together, making SEVEN SEPARATE LOTS to be offered. Full particulars may be obtained from the Auctioneers. This is an exceptional opportunity to secure building material now in short supply—FOR REMOVAL.

Figure 12.2. *Sunday Times* auction notice 'Lot 7, Searchlight Station 10', 16 September 1945.

Source: *Sunday Times* (1945). trove.nla.gov.au/newspaper/article/59338865.

An AWAS archaeology?

Primed by these various, sometimes conflicting and partial, sources of information, we set out to see what Lot 65's archaeology could offer—if anything. Between 18 and 24 April 2017, 16 third-year students and two UWA Archaeology staff (SO and JB), assisted by Christine Cooper and local residents, conducted transect survey of a c. 72 800 m^2 area of Lot 65, Hope Road (Figure 12.3). The terrain is a coastal upland swamp, with banksia and eucalypt woodland, and wetland *Melaleuca* trees and associated flora, parts of which were converted to extensive market gardens from c. 1890–World War II (Drake and Kenneally 1998). We came across regular scatters of everyday artefacts, such as twentieth- and twenty-first-century bottles, ceramic and metal plates, other metal objects and building rubble. This area only received municipal rubbish removal in the 1970s and is used for illegal dumping so it was very hard to associate any of this material unequivocally with an army camp, which would have used many material culture items indistinguishable from those used by the general population. We could, however, predict a material culture signature in terms of these artefacts' quantity, frequency and context. In the south of our survey area, closer to Hope Road, we noticed extensive compacted limestone paths and larger compacted hardstands, three partial toilets in a concreted row, a septic tank and a concrete pad with metal-piped hole. Immediately north-east of these finds is a large, disturbed

c. 3.5 x 4.0 m square of earth surrounding a depressed interior space that local residents call the 'bunker' and may be what the auction notice refers to as 'command post (underground)' (see Figure 12.3).

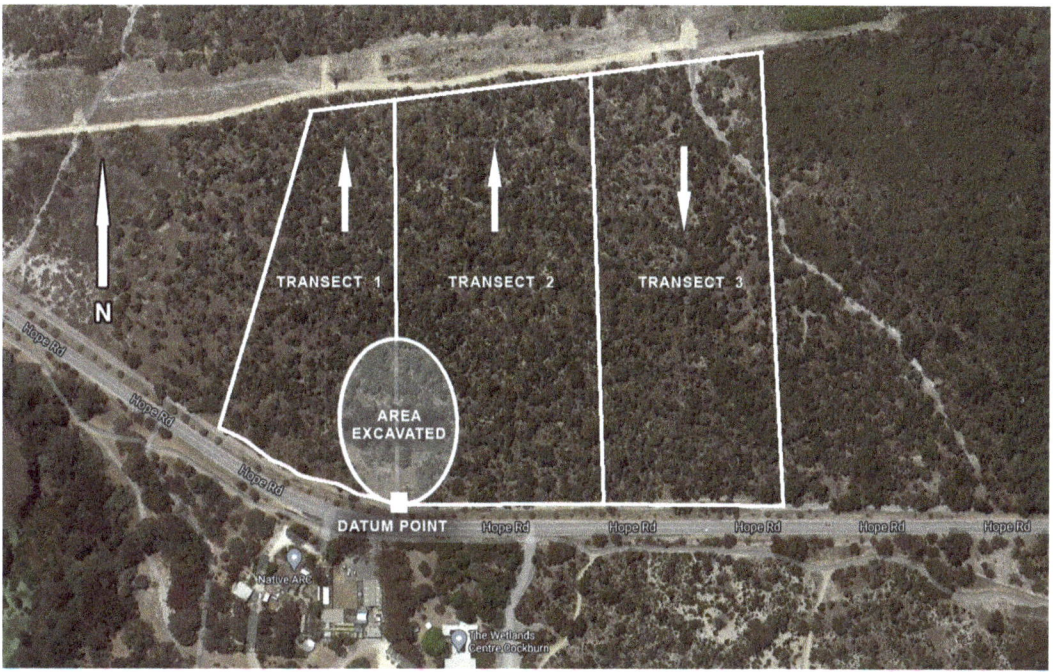

Figure 12.3. Area surveyed and excavated by 2017 UWA Archaeology Fieldschool.
Source: Rentia Ouzman.

Methods

Our site map (Figure 12.4), derived from 84 total station points, shows substantial limestone paths and hardstanding, with nearby concrete and brick ablution structures, consistent with a medium-term housing of people such as an army camp. The evidence of three toilets, which would not be adequate for a large quantity of people, might support McKenzie-Smith's argument for a smaller, 116th LAA site. However, 'latrines' are mentioned in the auction notice and it may be that the porcelain toilets were for commissioned officers only and the ranks used the usual 'long drops', which would have been accommodated in tents and prefabricated asbestos buildings; but we did not notice any changes in vegetation that might support this theory. We decided to excavate an area of pathway that had what was either collapsed brick walling or bricks used as paving stones, in a 4 x 1 m trench (Figure 12.6) and then also the toilet block in a 2 x 2 m trench, with a later 2 x 1 m trench added to the west (Figure 12.7). Excavation was undertaken in 5 cm spits owing to a lack of discernible stratigraphy (which would be unexpected at any short-duration site). Measurements of pH and soil colour were taken, along with bulk soil samples. Nested sieves (5 mm and 3 mm) were used and at the end of the excavation, sondages were sunk into each trench to a depth of approximately 1 m through largely undifferentiated sand to test for any Aboriginal artefacts, but with no success. In the final two days of the fieldschool, the concrete pad south-east of the toilet excavation was excavated. This concrete pad may have been an ablution block or washhouse. Test pitting was also undertaken towards the end of the fieldschool in c. 24 of the locations where previous metal detector survey had suggested sub-surface anomalies. These test pits were excavated in 25 x 25 cm squares. For division of labour, students were assigned to a trench and rotated duties such as path mapping and public engagement, as the excavation was advertised and visits by the public encouraged. Indeed, over 60 members of the public visited us—Aboriginal and non-Aboriginal—in addition to protesters from the nearby Roe 8 campaign. In some cases, people shared tantalising memories of war and other times of Walliabup/Bibra Lake.

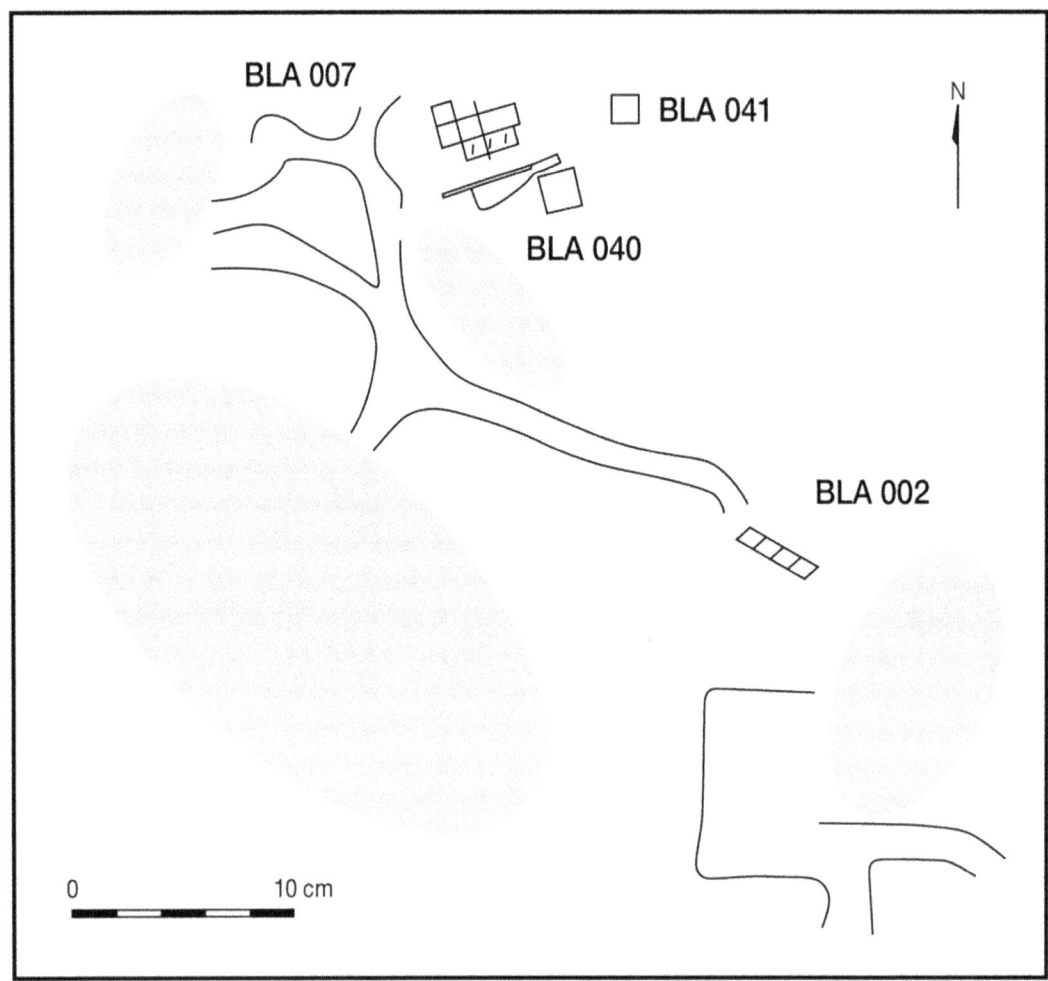

Figure 12.4. Site map of excavated areas, pathways (indicated by black lines) and compacted areas (grey ovals).
Source: Danielle Kelly, Rentia Ouzman and ANU CartoGIS.

Finds and features

Perhaps counterintuitively for an army camp—or at least for a substantial habitation area as suggested by the features reported on below (pathway, toilet/ablution block, laundry/shower, septic tank and borehole)—we found very few artefacts not linked to the construction of these features. These few artefacts are largely undiagnostic in both material and form (Table 12.1 and Figure 12.5). In addition to the expected finds of glass (bottles, windowpanes and a possible light bulb), ceramic (mostly plates and cups), metal (nails, wire, barbed wire, large and small bolts, two D-sized batteries), wood (jarrah construction timbers) and brick (with diagnostic examples from the Cardup factory), we also found many asbestos fragments, porcelain toilet bowl fragments and also brown stoneware sewage pipe sections. Other finds included a large chunk of anthracite, a possible bakelite clothing button, burned bone, a heavy-duty flat piece of fibre or card, charcoal, a small bottle stopper fragment made of stoneware (14 mm diameter), a strip of lead, and a possible toothpaste tube. We now turn to a discussion of each of the five features we investigated, as well as our test pitting program, to place these finds in context.

Table 12.1. Summary artefact table from excavations at Walliabup (Bibra Lake).

Material	Artefact type	Area(s) found	Notes
Asbestos	Fragments of asbestos wall and roofing	BLA 007 A1, B1 and B3 all in XUs [XU = excavation units] BLA 041 (Septic tank)	Approx. 50–100 small pieces found in BLA007—not cleaned. Seven large pieces found in BLA041—two painted greenish colour (possible camouflage).
Bakelite	Small bakelite clothing button	BLA 002 A2 XU2	Beige-coloured clothing button with two holes. Diameter 11.1 mm.
Ceramic (porcelain)	Broken fragments of three toilet bowls	BLA 007 B1-4 in all XUs, A1	Approx. 300–350 pieces of white broken toilet bowl.
Ceramic (stoneware pipe)	Broken fragments of stoneware pipe	BLA 007 B1-4 in all XUs BLA 041 (Septic tank)	Approx. 30–50 pieces of brown stoneware pipe; some pieces with engraved maker's marks.
Charcoal	Small pieces of charcoal, including that of the native Zamia palm	BLA 002 A1-4 BLA 007 B1-4, C4 Test pits (BLA 013, -021, -042)	Samples retained from most areas—significant amount discarded; presumed large burning event.
Concrete/stone/gravel	Fragments of concrete, gravel/concrete/limestone	BLA 002 A1-2 BLA 007 B1-3, C4 Test Pits (BLA 013, -016, -042, -045)	Small fragments found in abundance—samples retained from most areas, significant amount discarded.
Glass (bottle)	Small, brown, rectangular glass bottle	BLA 041 (Septic tank)	142.7 mm (height) x 57.3 mm (base diameter), 'F3 864 D' (on bottom).
Glass (fragments)	Fragments of varying colours	BLA 002 A1-3 Test pits (BLA 016, -018, -021)	Glass fragments, mostly small, ranging from brown to colourless. Predominately found on surface levels.
Glass (jar)	Average-sized brown glass jar	BLA 041 (Septic tank)	'F20 H37 E 5' (on bottom) Hemingray Co. Factory 37; preserve or jam jar; 110.7 mm (height) x 75 mm (base diameter) x 65 mm (opening diameter).
Metal (assorted)	Barbed wire, battery, bolts, bottle cap, lead off-cuts	BLA 007 B2 BLA 040 (Shower block) Test pits (BLA 013, -016, -042)	Various types of metal pertaining to different uses; most corroded and/or broken.
Metal (fragments)	Fragmented sheet metal	BLA 002 A2 and A4 BLA 007 A1 and B3 BLA 040 (Shower block)	Small pieces significantly corroded, easily broken.
Metal (nails)	Asbestos clout nails and wood nails	BLA 002 A2 and A4 BLA 007 A1, B1-3, C4 BLA 040 (Shower block) BLA 042 (Test pit)	19 nails with varying levels of corrosion, depending on location; predominately found in association with walls. Average 26 x 7 mm.
Wood	Human-modified wood	BLA 002 A2 BLA 007 B4 Test pits (BLA 021, -042)	Nine pieces of dark red/brown wood of varying sizes.

Source: ARCY3002 class and Sven Ouzman.

Figure 12.5. Selected finds from excavations at Walliabup (Bibra Lake).
Clockwise from top left: barbed wire, bottle, Cardup brick, ?military button.
Source: Sven Ouzman.

BLA 002 (pathway or road)

Almost no artefacts were recovered from this putative pathway or road (Figure 12.6 for plan and section diagrams). In total, we had <20 artefacts in the form of glass fragments, a heavily corroded circular 10 cm diameter metal object, a brick with 'Cardup B+H Press' stamped into the frog (depressed area of the brick), plastic fragments, fibreboard, porcelain fragments and the head of a nail. Yet despite this paucity of artefacts, one of our most diagnostic artefacts came from BLA 002 in the form of a khaki-coloured plastic (possibly bakelite) button that was possibly from a military uniform (Figure 12.5). While the finds were few, the pathways were substantial and required tonnes of crushed limestone; probably for narrow roads for army trucks, and/or paths to a parade ground (see the larger ovoid hardstanding areas shown in Figure 12.4). pH readings varied from neutral to alkaline.

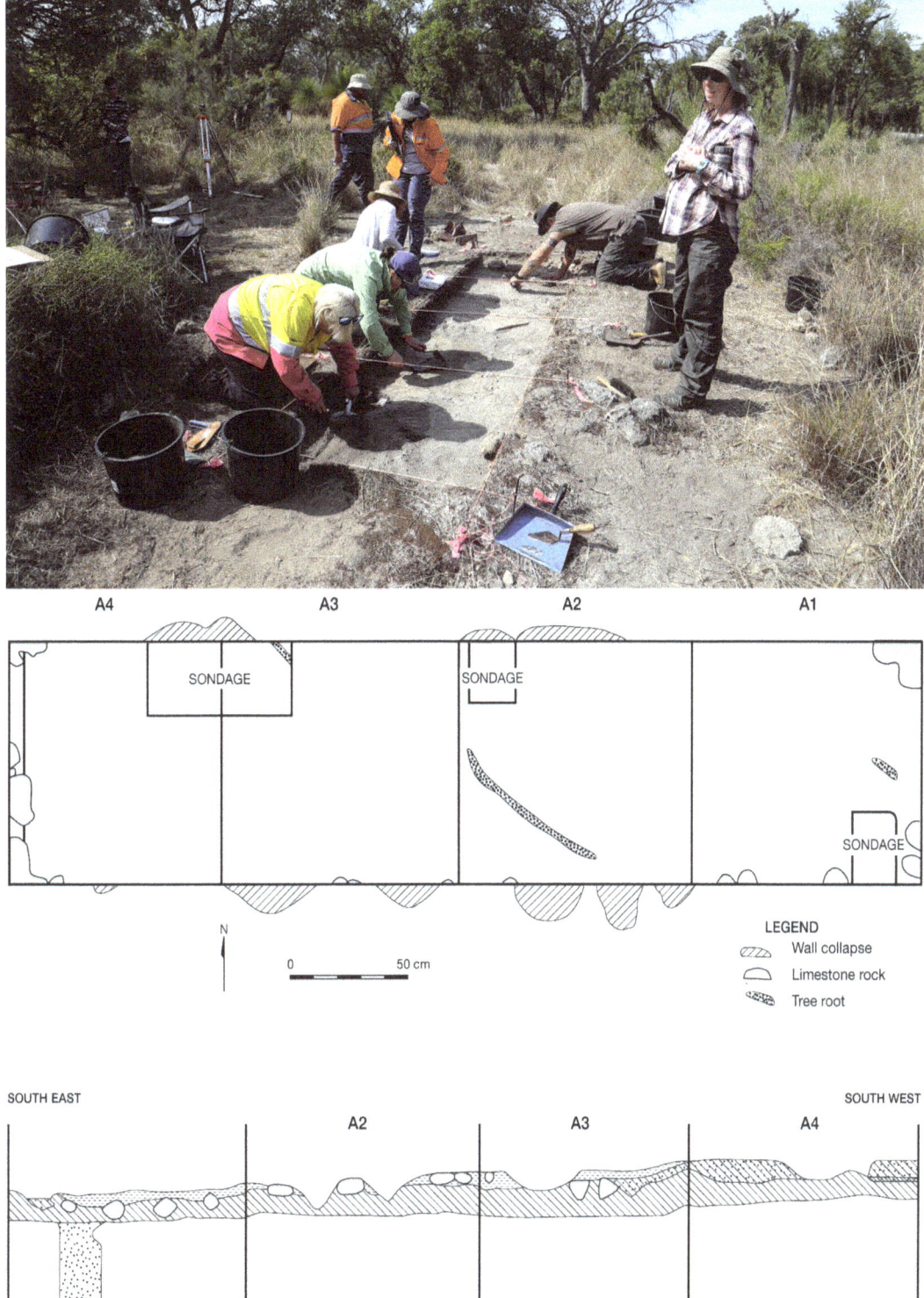

Figure 12.6. General aspect, plan and section of BLA 002 (pathway) excavation.
Source: Sven Ouzman (photo); ARCY3002 class (drawings); ANU CartoGIS (digitisation of plan and section).

BLA 007 (toilet block)

Approximately 65 m north-west of the pathway excavation, we made a 2 x 1 m concrete base our focus (Figure 12.7). It had three raised sections supporting porcelain toilet bases, each in front of a vertical brown clay sewage pipe. Many pieces of sewage pipe were lying on the surface to the south within 2 m from the toilet block. Four approximately 40 x 40 cm concrete paving slabs were found approximately 75 cm in front (north) of the toilets, with concreted brick wall coursing plus repurposed concrete chunks forming a wall/structure to the north-west. A second 2 x 1 m trench was opened to investigate this feature, which may have been a room that had been inexpertly added or modified at some point; possibly to add a toilet/changing area. Artefacts recovered included clouting nails, flat asbestos fragments, porcelain fragments, a posthole, concrete slabs, sewage pipe sections and a piece of anthracite. pH readings varied from 6 to 7.

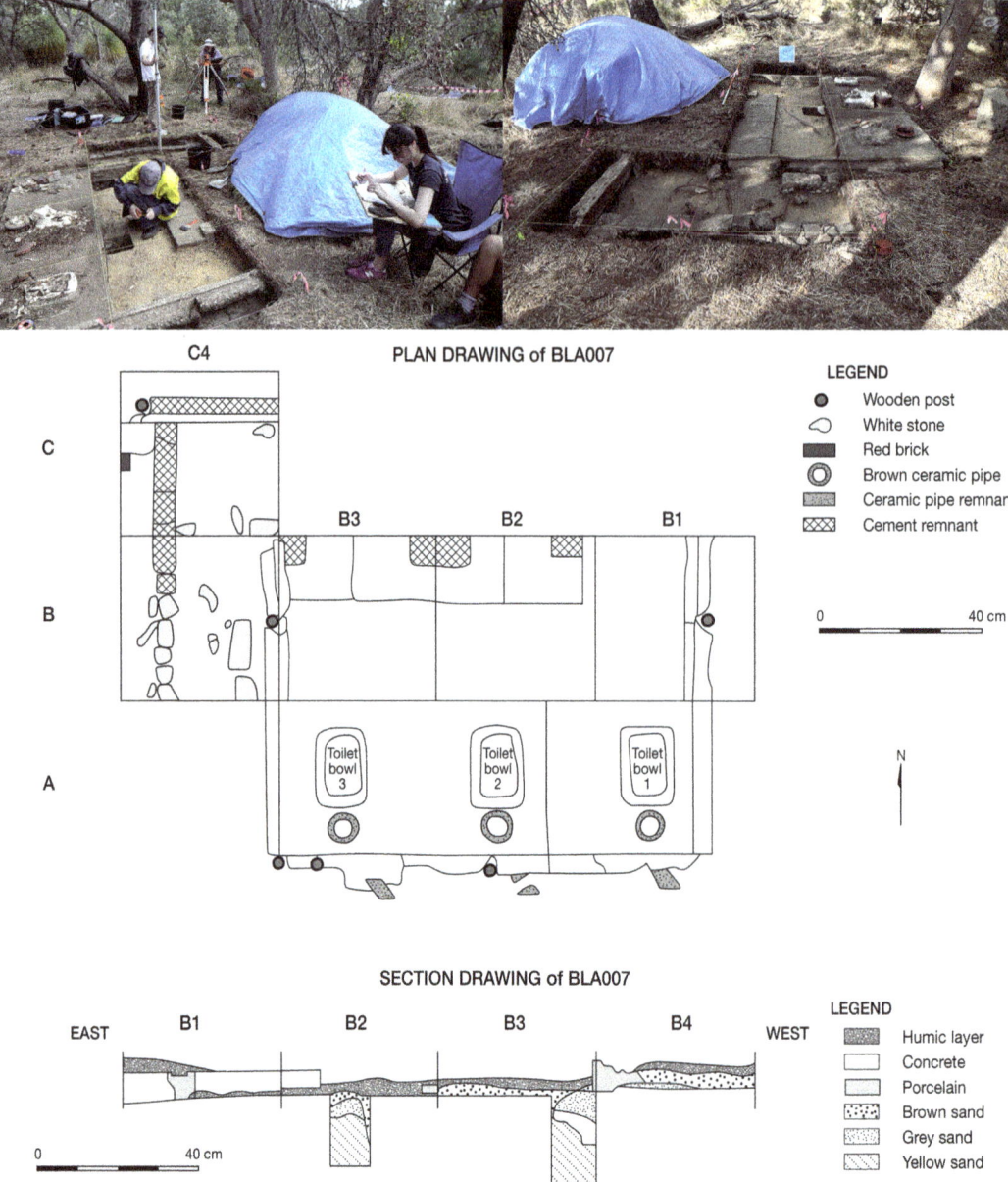

Figure 12.7. General aspect, plan and section of BLA 007 (toilet block) excavation. Blue tarpaulin protecting large grass tree (*Xanthorrhoea* sp.).

Source: Sven Ouzman (photos); ARCY3002 class (drawings); ANU CartoGIS (digitisation of plan and section).

BLA 040 (laundry or ablution block)

Located c. 3 m south (behind) of the toilet block, this substantial structure (Figure 12.8) had a concrete drainage channel and series of paving slabs leading up to it and a larger 25 cm deep concrete trough associated with it. Interestingly, the lowest (and only) brick coursing directly on the concrete pad evinced torque breakage, supporting the auction notice's contention that building material was scarce (cf. Figure 12.2). The site appeared cleaned—with some vigour. Indeed, almost all above-ground materials were removed—even if they had been nailed/bolted/concreted in place, providing some evidence of post-war scarcity and hardship. This structure also had short (c. 12 cm) metal rods protruding from the lowest concrete coursing—of the kind often used to support asbestos walling in shower blocks or laundries. Indeed, tens of fragments of asbestos were recovered from the surface and near surface and placed in Ziploc bags and buckets of water to ensure safety of excavators. Finds included one complete and two partial D-sized batteries, a corroded metal button (possibly brass, and 14 mm in diameter), a metal bottle cap, two metal bolts (91 mm and 131 mm long, 13 mm diameter), 12 metal fragments, six round nails (27–56 mm long), five bricks marked 'CARDUP EXPRESS' and glass bottles, including two with the markings 'F3 864 D' and 'F20 H37 E 5' on their bases. Out of interest, a few metres east of this feature is a substantial tree with marked diagonal scarring on three sides of its base, which we interpret as the tree being used as a holdfast for a cable that stabilised a water tank, which would have been needed for the toilets and possible laundry. pH readings were 7 in the slab area and 6 in the drainage/trough area.

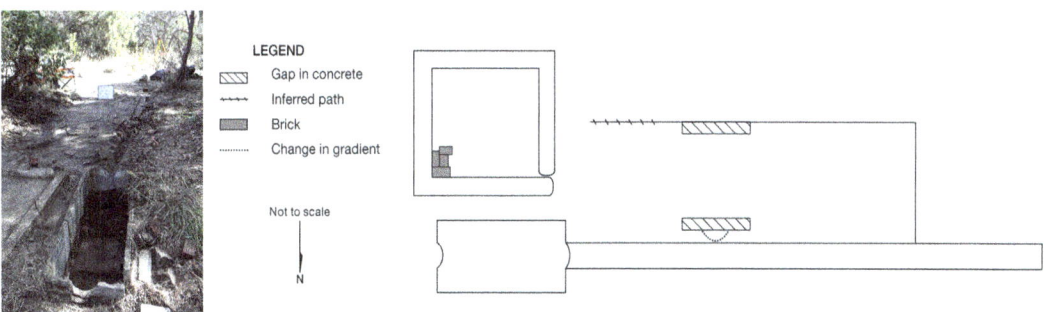

Figure 12.8. General aspect and plan of BLA 040 (?laundry) clearance.
Note concrete water channel and trough and remnant metal rods.
Source: Sven Ouzman (photos); ARCY3002 Class (drawings); ANU CartoGIS (digitisation of plan).

BLA 041 (septic tank)

Approximately 4 m south-east of the toilet block was a 2.0 x 1.5 m concrete slab in two parts covering a 1.5 m deep brick and concrete septic tank (Figure 12.9). Approximately 680 litres of water was bailed out and a long-necked tortoise was removed (the tortoise was taken to the nearby Native Ark), revealing a collection of over 50 artefacts. These included intact glassware of all descriptions, jarrah timber planks with a dark green enamel paint, asbestos fragments, 14 bricks, clay sewer pipe sections/fragments and toilet porcelain fragments.

Figure 12.9. BLA 041 (septic tank) and finds.
Source: Sven Ouzman.

BLA (concrete pad and borehole)

No artefacts bar chunks of concrete and some rusted metal sheeting were recovered from surface clearing, but the pad had clear footings, inset wooden sleepers/supports, and a vertical metal pipe (Figure 12.10). We interpret this as the site of the 2000-gallon water tank listed in the auction notice (Figure 12.2), which may have required a diesel pump, likely mounted on wooden supports to mitigate vibrations.

Figure 12.10. Concrete pad, inset wooden supports and borehole.
Source: Sven Ouzman.

Shovel test pitting

Our final set of activities focused on metal detector–identified areas of interest. We found little material—mostly metal fragments in the form of barbed wire and nails, with some glass fragments and large quantities of scattered charcoal (the bushland burns regularly). The glass fragments ranged from the very thin (probable light bulbs) to very thick (probable truck lights or similar; different from bottle bases). The so-called 'bunker' depression had barbed wire but no other finds on the surface and we did not excavate this feature because it would take more time than we had available.

Making sense of the artefactual evidence

No single artefact or feature unequivocally resolves the issue of which one or combination of the three army units were camped here—if any. Indeed, most of the artefacts are what one could expect from a school (the original school is only a few hundred metres away), agricultural business or similar institution. Some artefacts are tantalising. The green 'camouflage' paint on the jarrah timbers from the septic tank; the quasi-military button from the pathway excavations, and the ubiquitous barbed wire finds would not be out of place in a military camp—but neither would they be unique to it. Turning to dating, many artefacts are from the right time period. For example, Cardup bricks with the markings we found were made between 1926 and 1942, when production halted because of World War II, only to resume again in 1954 with a different set of markings (Cardup then closed in 2012 and reopened in 2018 as Austral Bricks) (Department of Planning, Lands and Heritage 2000; Western Australian Museum n.d.; for brick dating see Stuart 2005). One glass bottle from the septic tank has tentatively been identified as a preserve or jam jar (Figure 12.5), possibly from the Hemingray Company, who were better known for making glass insulators (Whitten 2015). The considerable effort put into the pathways—with limestone that would have been brought from the coast on trucks and extensive paths/roads made—suggests an order, structure and availability of labour beyond the means of a farm, school or similar. Indeed, when writing about the Attadale camp of the 55th Searchlight Battery, Tucker reports that 'the battery was a special tented area with gravelled paths between tent lines' (1991:65). The recurrent asbestos finds suggest extensive use of prefabricated structures, which also suggest an institutional rather than a domestic use. But while there is no individual, definitive martial material or artefact, we also need to consider these artefacts and structures in volume and in aggregate. What other use would explain this spatial layout, dearth of artefacts and substantial infrastructure? A military use and subsequent auction is certainly more likely than almost any other scenario. Indeed, it is unusual to have such an investment in infrastructure which is then almost completely removed. The short period of occupation plus military emphasis on cleanliness may also help explain the dearth of artefacts. Finally, the information from the auction notice about the near-complete removal of the SL Bty's artefacts and features raises the question of how we deal with the systematic absence of evidence where the majority of a site is sold off and used at multiple other sites for non-war purposes.

Beyond the finds and features and back to nature for the (eco)facts

We did, however come across one off-site artefact type that (almost) provides definitive evidence of an AWAS presence. This is in the form of two photographs that Private Margaret May Robertson (Royal Australian Signal Corps) took on 1 January 1944 that show AWAS personnel posing in front of a fallen jarrah tree (*Eucalyptus marginata*) with a distinctive bend in it (Figure 12.11).

Thanks to jarrah's legendary resistance to termites, we were able to re-locate this tree, definitively establishing an AWAS presence on the site. Of course, this presence could have been a visit by AWAS personnel and not a permanent camp, but photos from the same collection show tents, substantial structures and a rather disconcerting image of a man with a large knife at the quartermaster's store (Figure 12.12; see also Tucker 1991:99 for male and female personnel at '66 AA Battery Bibra Lake').

Figure 12.11. Photographs of AWAS personnel at distinctive jarrah tree, Walliabup (Bibra Lake), 1 January 1944.
Bottom photograph of fieldschool participants on the same tree, 73 years later.
Source: (Top) Private Margaret May Robertson, provided by her daughter Kaye McNally. (Bottom) Sven Ouzman.

Figure 12.12. Photographs of AWAS personnel, Walliabup (Bibra Lake).
Source: Private Margaret May Robertson, provided by her daughter Kaye McNally.

Discussion: The archaeology of war and of women at war

These photographs provide valuable glimpses of daily life as well as details of material culture, uniforms and terrain. The photographs are, however, posed and belie the very real anxiety the people of Perth experienced during war. Though never a major combat arena, for a considerable time people in Western Australia thought it might be, resulting in an extensive defensive military infrastructure that ran from the north-west's telegraph, observation and radar stations, radar outposts, airfields and ammunitions dumps, to Fortress Fremantle, and to regional and southern Western Australia (cf. Bowman 2016). Actions such as the 1941 sinking of Australia's HMAS *Sydney II* (only rediscovered in 2008) by the German ship *Kormoran*, the eventual 1942 sinking of the MV *Koolama* in Wydham, the 1942 and 1943 Japanese air attacks on Broome and Kalumburu, plus two Western Australian emergencies in 1942 and 1944 for a forecast sea invasion of the coast and especially Fremantle Port (see Cairns 2011), created a very uncertain and anxious atmosphere. A similar situation is documented in Martin Wimmer's (2014) study of air raid shelters and associated structures in Adelaide, South Australia, where there was a similar fear of imminent aerial bombardment and invasion by sea. This widespread atmosphere of terror and preparation is hard to properly understand almost 80 years later dealing with inert archival and archaeological sources. Recorded oral testimonies provide some of this texture, though with more bias. Rather like Hannah Arendt's characterisation of evil as 'banal', a great deal of the archaeology of war is similarly quotidian to the point of being hard to distinguish from the material culture of the wider society at the time.

Archaeological 'ground-truthing' of military sites, especially short-lived ones, can be surprisingly equivocal, as our experience at Walliabup (Bibra Lake) shows. But multi-stranded archaeological investigation is sorely needed because we want a democratic discipline able to remember both the places history is forgetting and, especially, the people that populated these places. While all sources have their bias—from non-diagnostic artefacts, to biased archives to evolving oral testimonies—archaeology's strengths at dealing with multiple sources of evidence creates a mutually enabling and constraining web of evidence and argument that also helps humanise this past. At Walliabup (Bibra Lake) this humanising still has some way to go. For example, we struggle to gender places and artefacts, especially within the context of 'total institutions' such as the military. In addition, scholarship tends to be masculinist (see Garton 1998 for overview). So far, our contribution to understanding how 200 or more women, many of them far from home in an unfamiliar place, experienced the war, is modest (see Seitsonen et al. 2017 for work on the dislocation of military personnel). Basic information such as knowing where these women were stationed requires considerable effort to glean. Indeed, our reading of the Intelligence Summaries suggests Walliabup (Bibra Lake) may have been a temporary situation and even training location for many AWAS personnel, who were then redeployed to places like Wadjemup (Rottnest Island) as part of their considerable naval defences. The AWAS identity was also largely subsumed into that of the 66th Searchlight Battery and/or 116th Light Anti-Aircraft regiment.

These are serious challenges, as it is not just women who are under-represented in the master narratives of war. There are Indigenous people (e.g. Saunders 1995), children and immigrants to consider. For example, at Bibra Lake, Chinese market gardeners—and probably people of other ethnicities—enjoyed regular trade with the camp for fresh produce. We have one account where one such gardener's life was saved by AWAS personnel when he was caught alight during a bushfire (Tucker 1991:79). Also, Bibra Lake was home to many Italian immigrants, who were rounded up and sent to internment camps on Wadjemup (Rottnest Island) and elsewhere. Further, subaltern histories of LGBTIQ or differently abled people and the like could also be an important area for study, and incipient work in this regard has begun (e.g. Barrett 2007; Davila and Epstein 2020).

Conclusion: The role of past colonial wars in a post-colonising society

The AWAS 'signature' at Walliabup (Bibra Lake) has not been resolved by archaeology, but by primary off-site artefacts in the form of the auction notice and photographs from the time, as well as first-person testimony from Eileen Tucker. Had we worked in different areas—such as to the west where there are more roads and metal scatters, we may, for example, have located the camp midden, which would contain diagnostic artefacts. Or we could have worked south of Hope Road, where we have unsubstantiated reports of prefabricated living quarters for army personnel. Our frequent finds of asbestos support the statement that 'pre-fab huts were erected' at Walliabup (Bibra Lake) (Tucker 1991:65). It is almost certain where we worked was where the 66th Searchlight Battery was stationed, with AWAS support personnel. This does not mean archaeological fieldwork—which is costly and can be destructive—is of no use. Collating and synthesising information, while being able to calibrate spatial and temporal contexts from individual personnel to the wider arena of the world war, helps craft a more coherent, fact-rich and socially responsive narrative. At times, archaeology may be the only way to recover certain kinds of evidence. At the very least, archaeology provides another strand of evidence that allows for a convincing 'cabling' of evidence (cf. Wylie 2002). Also, the very activity of fieldwork is socially productive and engaging. Our activities, initiated by the Bibra Lakes Residents Association's invitation, literally brought people together (Figure 12.13). Dozens of visitors, local newspaper articles (e.g. Luff 2017), public talks and word-of-mouth created a 'public archaeology' (cf. Moshenka 2017). Importantly, our activities made people regard their backyard, so to speak, in a new light—and engage with an almost-forgotten history. This engagement has included independent public and municipal archival research and oral testimony work. For example, there is the very competent 'Bibra Lake AWAS Camp' Wikipedia entry (Wikipedia 2015–ongoing) and the Cockburn Libraries (2015) entry and work on the camp. The publication of books by AWAS personnel (Beveridge 1988; Desmond 1988; Oliff 1981; Tucker 1991) and increasing mentions via the web and social media (see also ARCY3002 2017) provide the much-needed detail and texture of lived experiences. Our work contributes to a still small-but-growing set of case studies on histories of war that are important to local communities (e.g. Burke et al. 2011), rather than being proclaimed as important by distant authoritative metanarratives.

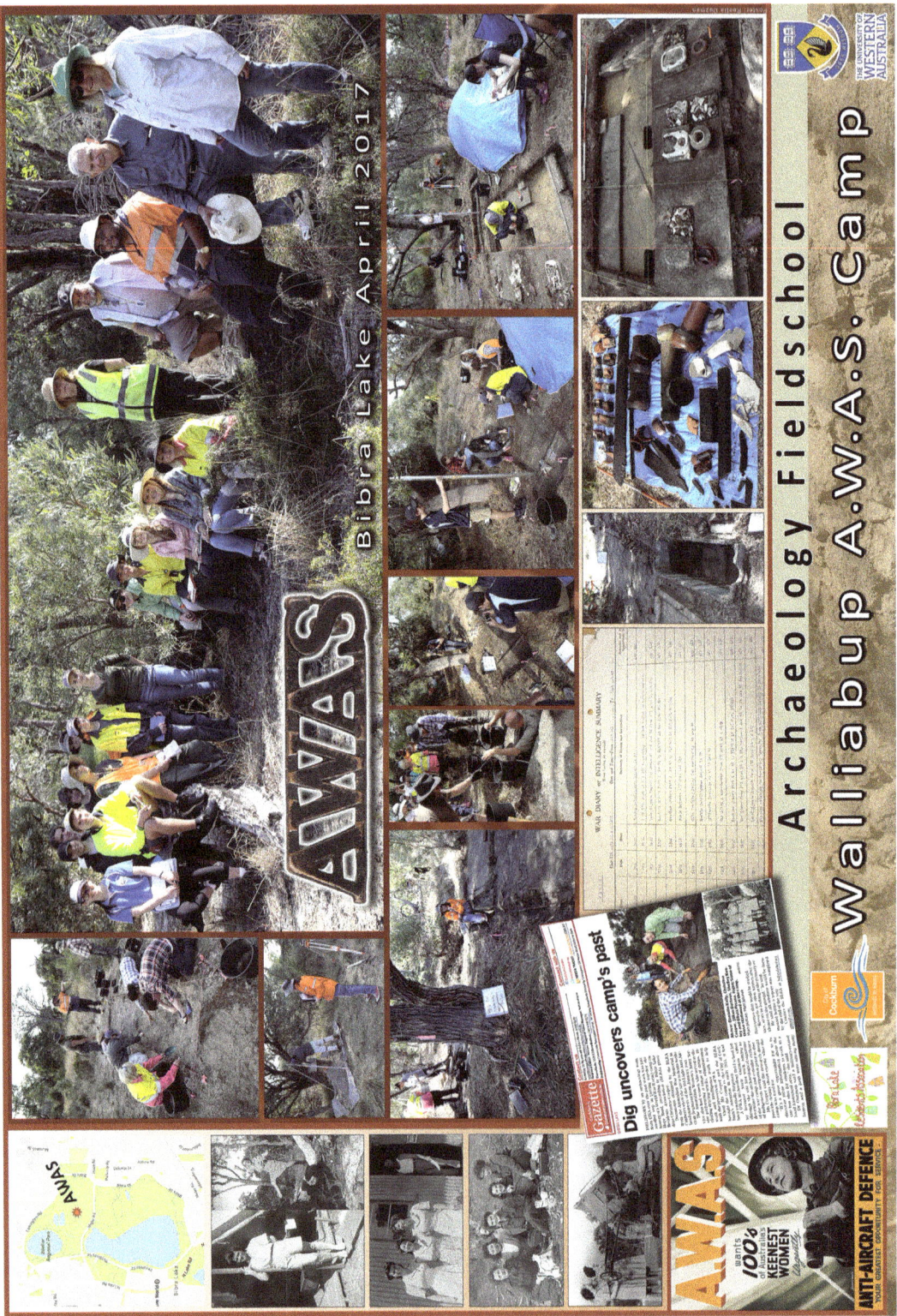

Figure 12.13. Community poster of 2017 AWAS archaeology fieldschool.
Source: Sven Ouzman.

War archaeology is, however, often painful, with remembrances of death, violence, loss and subjugation to foreign powers (Moshenka 2006). But it can also be useful. Meskell and Scheermeyer (2008; see also Symonds 2019) write about archaeology and heritage as 'therapy'. Archaeology's often slow, methodical way of understanding the past helps people come to terms with difficult or occluded pasts in a slow, managed way. In Australia we have many unresolved issues of history, race, gender and war—with the militarisation of the present through distorted versions of national events like Anzac Day and the associated 'Anzackery' a prime example (Stephens 2015; see also Ouzman 2021). A war is, after all, a failure of humanity and communication, and results typically from the actions of a few powerful interests who do not bear the brunt of their decisions. Australia's participation in World War II is as much a colonial legacy as an action to fight against unjust and hostile actions. Scale is a key discriminant here as it is easy to lose sight of individual contributions and experiences of people who did have agency, but not in conditions of their choosing. The women of Walliabup (Bibra Lake) are no longer as invisible as they were, though much more work needs to be done to rehumanise their lives and contributions. But the outlook is positive and there is evidence of a more human, less jingoistic remembrance of this past at the Walliabup (Bibra Lake) site. In 2019, an inspection of the site to make sure our post-excavation rehabilitation was still in order came across a touching tribute to the women and men and others who had lived here in the latter half of World War II. This tribute took the form of a small wreath and private message of thanks that had been placed in a banksia tree at the toilet block site; showing that 'small things' are not always forgotten or, at the very least, can be re-remembered.

Acknowledgements

We acknowledge this work and chapter were undertaken on Whadjuk Nyungar land. We thank the City of Cockburn, Azelia Ley Museum, Bibra Lakes Residents Association and South West Aboriginal Land and Sea Council for their support of this project. We also thank the Cockburn Wetlands Centre and Native Ark for logistical support. We thank the UWA Archaeology Fieldschool class of 2017—Sophie Antulov, Victoria Bird, Alexander Burcham, Meg Drummond-Wilson, Jonty Franklin, Nicole Gan, Jessica Green, Emily Grey, Shelley Keeley, Danielle Kelly, Duane Kelly, Gary Nicol, Olivia Pisan, Fiona Reid, Matthew Tetlaw and Sarah-Jane Waters—for their physical and intellectual labour and acknowledge them as collective co-authors. We thank Rentia Ouzman and Jennifer Sheehan from the ANU College of Asia & the Pacific, CartoGIS Services at The Australian National University for the digitisation of the sections, site plans and maps. We thank Beth Battrick for her meticulous copyediting. We thank Mirani Litster and Geoffrey Clark for their initiative in making this volume a reality, and for their kind and constructive comments on this chapter.

References

ARCY3002 2017. Bibra lake archaeology: Results from the 2017 ARCY3002 Field Methods undergraduate fieldschool at a possible AWS site, Bibra Lake. Unpublished collaborative student report. University of Western Australia, Perth.

Athena 1943. Front line girls: Work of the A.W.A.S. manning the searchlights. *The Northern Times*, 14 May. trove.nla.gov.au/newspaper/article/75135291.

Australian War Memorial 1943a. Unit war diaries, 1939–45 war. 116 Australian Light Anti-Aircraft Regiment (AIF), January–September 1943 (AWM52 4/11/11/6). AWM 2019.366.1548-1555. Australian War Memorial, Canberra.

Australian War Memorial 1943b. Unit war diaries, 1939–45 war. 55 Australian Composite Anti-Aircraft Regiment, Royal Australian Regiment (Lower Establishment) October–December 1943 (AWM52 4/13/10/1). Australian War Memorial, Canberra.

Baker, F. 1988. History that hurts: Excavating 1933–1945. *Archaeological Review from Cambridge* 7(1):93–109.

Barrett, M. 2007. Subalterns at war. *Interventions* 9(3):451–474.

Beck, C., M. William Gray Johnson and J. Schofield (eds) 2002. *Matériel culture: The archaeology of 20th century conflict.* Routledge, London.

Beveridge, J. 1988. *AWAS: Women making history.* Boolarong Publications, Chevron Island.

Bowman, C. 2016. Forgotten Australian radar sites rediscovered. *War History Online*, 11 May. www.warhistoryonline.com/war-articles/forgotten-australian-radar-station-sites-rediscovered.html.

Bracknell, C. and I.L. Collard 2012. Beeliar Boodjar: An introduction to Aboriginal history in the City of Cockburn, Western Australia. *Australian Aboriginal Studies* 2012(1):86–91.

Burke, H., A. Gorman, K. Mayes and D. Renshaw. 2011. The heritage uncertainty principle: Excavating air raid shelters from the Second World War. In O. Katsiyuki and A. Matsuda (eds), *New perspectives in global public archaeology*, pp. 139–154. Springer, New York. doi.org/10.1007/978-1-4614-0341-8_11.

Burke, H., B. Barker, L. Wallis, S. Craig and M. Combo. 2020. Betwixt and between: Trauma, survival and the Aboriginal Troopers of the Queensland Native Mounted Police. *Journal of Genocide Research* 22(3):317–333. doi.org/10.1080/14623528.2020.1735147.

Cairns, L. 2011. *Secret fleets: Fremantle's World War II submarine base.* Western Australian Museum, Welshpool, Western Australia.

Carman, J. 1997. Giving archaeology a moral voice. In J. Carman (ed.), *Material harm: Archaeological studies of war and violence*, pp. 220–239. Cruithne Press, Glasgow.

Carman, J. 2013. *Archaeologies of conflict.* Bloomsbury, New York.

Chambers, J. and P. Jennings. 2017. Roe 8: Perth's environmental flashpoint in the WA election. *The Conversation*, 9 March. theconversation.com/roe-8-perths-environmental-flashpoint-in-the-wa-election-74155.

City of Cockburn 2017. WWII army camp, Bibra Lake (site). Local Government Inventory. 17 February. www.cockburn.wa.gov.au/getattachment/029e0f9c-f21b-428d-9a9b-66ca20550e75/ECM_5576126_v1_Bibra-Lake-WWII-Army-Camp-pdf.aspx.

Clark, B.J. 2018. Artifacts, contested histories, and other archaeological hotspots. *Historical Archaeology* 52:544–552. doi.org/10.1007/s41636-018-0128-5.

Cockburn Libraries 2015. Bibra Lake AWAS camp. 28 September. www.cockburnlibraries.com.au/blog/cockburn-history-bibra-lake-awas-camp/.

Davila, D. and E. Epstein 2020. Contemporary and pre–World War II Queer communities: An interdisciplinary inquiry via multimodal texts. *English Journal* 110(1):72–79.

Deetz, J. 1977. *In small things forgotten: The archaeology of early American life.* Anchor Press, New England.

Department of Planning, Lands and Heritage 2000. Brick kilns. inHerit database. inherit.stateheritage.wa.gov.au/Public/Inventory/PrintSingleRecord/f3df98af-3255-4924-8ffc-8852ae0b19bd. Accessed 12 November 2020.

Department of Planning, Lands and Heritage 2020–2021. Aboriginal Heritage Inquiry System. www.dplh.wa.gov.au/ahis. Accessed 12 November 2020.

Desmond, M. (ed.) 1988. *Backing up the boys: The Australian Women's Army Service and Albury army area.* The Club, Bandiana, Victoria.

Drake, C. and S. Kenneally 1998. *Recollections of the Beeliar Wetlands: Recollections of long-time local residents. City of Cockburn,* Cockburn, Perth.

Dunn, P. 2015. Bibra Lake army camp, Bibra Lake, WA, in Australia during WWII. *Australia at war.* www.ozatwar.com/ausarmy/bibralakearmycamp.htm. Accessed 2 February 2021.

Garton, S. 1998. War and masculinity in twentieth century Australia. *Journal of Australian Studies* 22(56):86–95. doi.org/10.1080/14443059809387363.

Graves-Brown, P., R. Harrison and A. Piccini (eds) 2013. *The Oxford handbook of the archaeology of the contemporary world.* Oxford University Press, Oxford. doi.org/10.1093/oxfordhb/9780199602001.013.010.

Hallam, S. 1987. Coastal does not equal littoral. *Australian Archaeology* 25:10–29. doi.org/10.1080/03122417.1987.12093122.

Heywood, A. 2009. Australian Women's Army Service (AWAS) (1941–1947). *The Australian Women's Register.* 12 June. www.womenaustralia.info/biogs/IMP0149b.htm.

Higgins, J. 2015. The ruins of Bibra Lake's history. *Perth Freight Link Info Blog*, 18 September. perthfreightlink.blogspot.com/2015/09/the-ruins-of-bibra-lakes-history.html.

Hook, F. and J. Dortch. 2017. Archaeology in the age of alternative facts: Archaeological investigations and Roe 8. In A. Gaynor, P. Newman and P. Jennings (eds), *Never again: Reflections on environmental responsibility after Roe 8*, pp. 107–117. UWA Publishing, Perth.

Luff, B. 2017. UWA dig uncovers World War II camp on Hope Road in Bibra Lake. *Cockburn Gazette*, 24 April. www.perthnow.com.au/community-news/cockburn-gazette/uwa-dig-uncovers-world-war-ii-camp-on-hope-road-in-bibra-lake-c-808284.

Lyon, R.M. 1833. A glance at the manners, and language of the Aboriginal inhabitants of Western Australia: With a short vocabulary. *Perth Gazette and Western Australian Journal*, 20 April.

Meskell, L. and C. Scheermeyer, 2008. Heritage as therapy: Set pieces from the New South Africa. *Journal of Material Culture* 13(2):153–157. doi.org/10.1177/1359183508090899.

Moshenska, G. 2006. Scales of memory in the archaeology of the Second World War. *Papers from the Institute of Archaeology* 17:58–68. doi.org/10.5334/pia.269.

Moshenska, G. (ed.) 2017. *Key concepts in public archaeology.* UCL Press, London.

Oliff, L. 1981. *Women in khaki.* Olli Publishing Company, Sydney.

Ouzman, S. 2021. Archaeologies of Austral: Australian identities from the Pleistocene to the Anthropocene. *Journal of Australian Studies* 45(2). doi.org/10.1080/14443058.2021.1910857.

Polglaze, R. 1986. The Aboriginal significance of Coolbellup/Walliabup wetlands (North Lake and Bibra Lake). Unpublished manuscript, Perth. Accessible from Azelia Ley Museum.

Pollard, T. and I. Banks 2005. Why a journal of conflict archaeology and why now? *Journal of Conflict Archaeology* 1(1):iii–vii. doi.org/10.1163/157407705774929024.

Saunders, K. 1995. Inequalities of sacrifice: Aboriginal and Torres Strait Islander labour in northern Australia during the Second World War. *Labour History* 69:131–148. doi.org/10.2307/27516395.

Seitsonen, O., H. Vesa-Pekka, K. Nordqvist, A. Herva and S. Seitsonen 2017. A military camp in the middle of nowhere: Mobilities, dislocation and the archaeology of a Second World War German military base in Finnish Lapland. *Journal of Conflict Archaeology* 12(1):3–28. doi.org/10.1080/15740773.2017.1389496.

Sharp, J.L. 2002. *Short histories of the 116th and 2/3rd Light Anti-aircraft Regiments*. Australian War Memorial, Canberra.

Stephens, D. 2015. Anzac and Anzackery: Speech to Kogarah Historical Society, 14 May. *Honest History*, 9 June. honesthistory.net.au/wp/anzac-and-anzackery-kogarah-speech/.

Stuart, I. 2005. The analysis of bricks from archaeological sites in Australia. *Australasian Historical Archaeology* 23:79–88.

Sutherland, T. 2017. *Battlefield archaeology: A guide to the archaeology of conflict*. Bradford University Practical Guide Series 8. Bradford University, Bradford.

Symonds, J. 2019. Difficult pasts and haunted presents: Contemporary archaeology and conflict in an age of global uncertainty. *Acta Universitatis Lodziensis. Folia Archaeologica* 34:5–21. doi.org/10.18778/0208-6034.34.01.

Terra Rosa Consulting. 2016. Results of a historical and archaeological investigation of a World War II AWAS army camp located at Bibra Lake W.A. Unpublished report. Perth.

Tucker, E. 1991. *We answered the call: AWAS of Western Australia and their mates*. E. Tucker, Cloverdale.

Western Australian Museum n.d. Shipwreck databases. www.museum.wa.gov.au/maritime-archaeology-db/artefacts-debug?page=56&order=field_site_area_code_value&sort=asc&ancods=&id=&field_registration_number_value=&name=&filename. Accessed 5 November 2020.

Whitten, D. 2015. Hemingray glass company. *Glass bottle marks*. glassbottlemarks.com/hemingray/. Accessed 3 September 2017.

Wikipedia 2015–ongoing. Bibra Lake AWAS camp. en.wikipedia.org/wiki/Bibra_Lake_AWAS_Camp. Accessed 25 January 2021.

Wimmer, M. 2014. Gimme shelter: Archaeology and the social history of structural defence in Adelaide 1941–1943. Unpublished PhD thesis. Flinders University, Adelaide.

Wylie, A. 2002. *Thinking from things: Essays in the philosophy of archaeology*. University of California Press, Berkley.

13

Painting war: The end of contact rock art in Arnhem Land

Daryl Wesley and Jessica Viney

Introduction

World War II represented a seismic shift in mid-twentieth-century history in the Northern Territory, Australia. Military activity leading up to and during World War II intensified in the region, given the role northern Australia had as a platform to conduct operations in the South West Pacific Area (SWPA) (Grey 1999; Powell 1982). The global conflict had profound impacts on Indigenous communities across northern Australia, however the archaeological signature of these impacts is limited (Riseman 2007, 2010, 2012a, 2012b; Saunders 1995; Trudgen 2000).

At least three major contact-period occupation nodes have been identified in the archaeology of the Wellington Range—Djulirri, Malarrak and Maliwawa (Figure 13.1) (May et al. 2010; Taçon et al. 2010, 2012; Wesley et al. 2012; Wesley, Litster, Moffat et al. 2018; Welsey, Litster, O'Connor et al. 2018). At two of these three nodes, rock art motifs related to World War II have been recorded—a warship at the Djulirri rock-shelter and an aircraft at Maliwawa. Of all the recorded depictions of non-Indigenous ships, boats and aircraft in the rock art record of Arnhem Land there are few motifs that can be identified with as high a level of certainty as a modern-era military warship and aircraft (Barrett 1946; Burningham 1994, 2000; Chaloupka 1988, 1993, 1996; Clarke 2000a; Clarke and Frederick 2006, 2008, 2011; Cole 1980; Edwards 1979; Gunn 1988; Gunn et al. 2012; May et al. 2010; Mountford 1956; Roberts 2004; Taçon et al. 2010, 2012; Turner 1973; Wesley et al. 2012). The depictions in the Wellington Range provide a platform to discuss some of the earliest Indigenous records of encounters between the Commonwealth of Australia's Royal Australian Navy (RAN) and Royal Australian Airforce (RAAF) (Taçon 2018). As there are limited records of Indigenous engagement with naval shipping and aviation in the Northern Territory that identify specific encounters between Indigenous people of the Wellington Range region, these motifs demonstrate the significance arising from cross-cultural engagement between Aboriginal communities in north-western Arnhem Land and the operations of wartime ships and aircraft (Clarke and Frederick 2006, 2008; Porr and Bell 2012).

Differentiating the timing of the paintings is also significant for our understanding of the continuity of Indigenous traditional knowledge and customs in north-western Arnhem Land. These rock art images provide tangible evidence for interaction between the coastal Indigenous communities of western Arnhem Land and operations arising from World War II beyond written historical records and documentation, and also provide the basis for discussing the diminishing representation of introduced imagery in Arnhem Land rock art production during and after World War II.

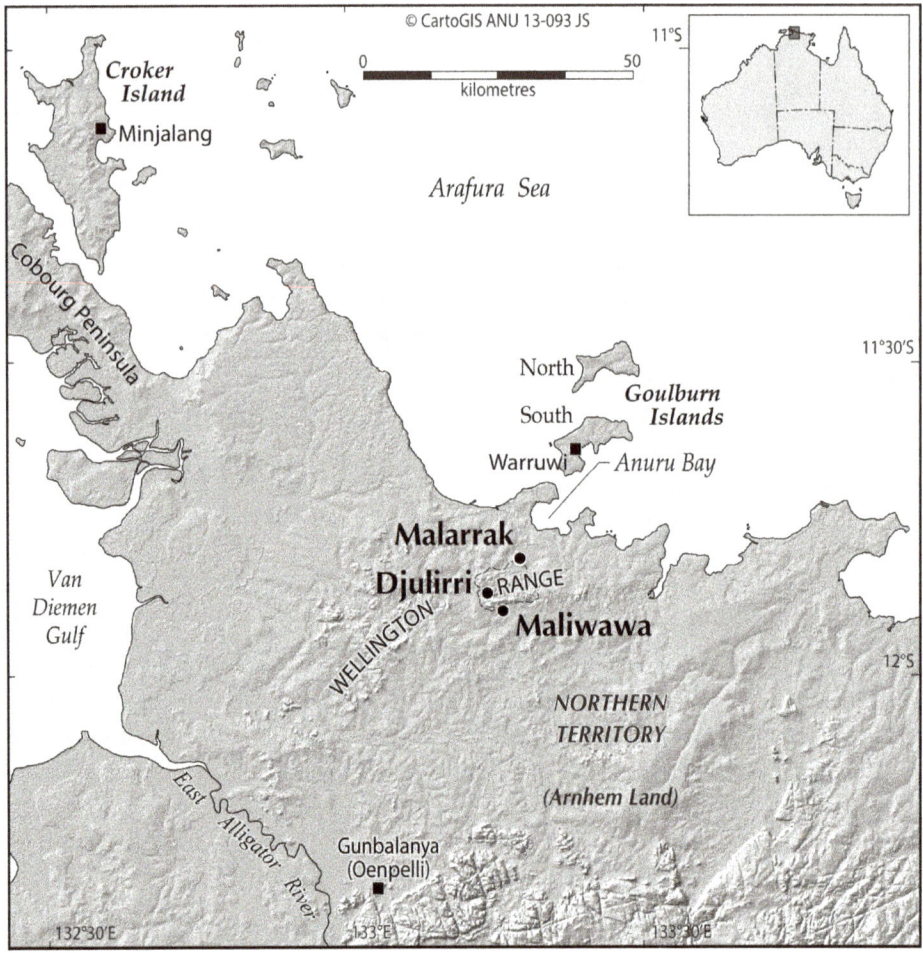

Figure 13.1. Location of the study area.
Source: ANU CartoGIS.

Figure 13.2. Rock art panel from Djulirri, Arnhem Land, illustrating the maritime imagery recorded by Indigenous artists.
Source: Daryl Wesley.

World War II and Indigenous engagement in western Arnhem Land

Allied military units located along the north Australian coastline required a constant supply of provisions, fuel and equipment during World War II. Darwin was a focal point of military build-up for all three services from 1939 with periods of intense Allied army, navy and air force activity across the Northern Territory (Rayner 2001). Various ships and aircraft were used to supply remote coastal RAAF radar installations on Bathurst and Melville Islands, North Goulburn Island and Marchinbar Island; with numerous squadrons of bomber and fighter aircraft operating out of airfields located at Milingimbi and Gove and seaplane bases on the Tiwi Islands and Groote Eylandt. These forward operation bases provided opportunities for direct engagement between service personnel and local Indigenous populations, especially those located near existing mission settlements of Warruwi, Milingimbi, Yirrkala and Angurugu.

Most research about Indigenous engagement during World War II concerns the wartime roles of Indigenous servicemen and women during this conflict (Ball 1991; Hall 1997). The reality for most Indigenous north Australians was not active service, but largely support roles through the provision of labour (Hall 1980, 1997; Saunders 1995). In the past, the narrative of Indigenous Australian interactions with the Australian military has been considered from European perspectives, but more recently there has been a significant increase in literature discussing other roles of Indigenous participation in World War II (e.g. Hall 1997; Riseman 2007, 2010, 2012a, 2012b; Saunders 1995; Trudgen 2000). Saunders (1995) and Riseman (2007, 2010, 2012a, 2012b) both provide excellent accounts of the roles, participation and the conditions that Aboriginal and Torres Strait Islander people endured during World War II across northern Australia. The service role of Indigenous people in the Northern Territory is mostly documented through their participation in surveillance activities with the mobile troops of the North Australian Observer Unit (NAOU) and the Northern Territory Special Surveillance Unit (NTSRU) (Gray 2006; Riseman 2007, 2010, 2012a, 2012b). Indigenous communities in eastern Arnhem Land were known to play a significant role in the NTSRU during World War II (Riseman 2007, 2010, 2012a, 2012b). Closer to the Wellington Range, Indigenous labour from the Goulburn Island Mission contributed significantly to the operation of the RAAF 309RS radar station on North Goulburn Island from May 1943 to February 1945 (Adcock 1999:12; Nottle 2007:106; Vahtrick 2007:113). The 309RS was mostly serviced with personnel transfers and supplies by small coastal ships and aircraft, most notably RAAF Avro Ansons (Alford 2011:171; Nottle 2007:106; Vahtrick 2007:113).

World War II resulted in a dichotomy in Indigenous mobility, with the centralisation of Aboriginal populations into internment camps at one end of the scale and, on the other, with many families maintaining a highly mobile, traditional existence on Country to avoid internment and the threat of Japanese invasion. Administration of the north was taken over by the Australian military during World War II and mass civilian evacuations followed the bombing of Darwin in February 1942. Many Aboriginal people were forcibly moved off Country to live in large, regulated settlements between Darwin and Larrimah (Layton and Williams 1980:110; Ritchie and Bauman 1991:25). At the outbreak of war in 1939 the Government set about looking for a suitable 'holding place for incorrigibles and other natives requiring repatriation' (Foley 1982:11). After the bombing of Darwin in 1942, the Commonwealth Department of Native Affairs marshalled as many Aboriginal people as possible, interning them in control camps at Adelaide River, Pine Creek, Katherine, Koolpinyah and Mataranka for the duration of the war to be prisoners in their own land (Hall 1980:80). By 1943, 140 people were camped at Adelaide River and a further 1157 at Mataranka (Keen 1980:54; Layton and Williams 1980:114; Ritchie and Bauman 1991:25). During the war, the Australian Army insisted that Aboriginal people be confined to these camps to ensure their safety, prevent Aboriginal people assisting the Japanese, ease rationing and prevent contact with troops (Foley 1982:22; Hall 1980:80). From these camps up to 724 Aboriginal men and women provided a labour force for wartime capital works and day-to-day camp labour at many military installations, farms, gardens and canteens (Hall 1980:80–81; Keen 1980:54; Layton and Williams 1980:115; Ritchie and Bauman 1991:25–26).

The war years also had a notable detrimental impact on the customary practices and ceremonial systems of Aboriginal groups, as traditional movement was heavily restricted and consequently the continuity of ceremonial activity became virtually impossible (Ritchie 1980:12). Wartime rationing and other restrictions also meant life at mission settlements in Arnhem Land was difficult. In order to avoid interment in military camps and the hardship of mission life, many Indigenous families moved out to be on their Country, living off traditional economies, resulting in a very high level of mobility (R. Petherick, pers. comm. 1996). While many Aboriginal people returned to their Country or pastoral stations at the close of war, some Aboriginal families remained at these military settlements (Keen 1980:54; Layton and Williams 1980:115; Ritchie and Bauman 1991:25–26). Historical evidence of Indigenous mobility and life in Arnhem Land during World War II is relatively scant and archaeology provides an avenue to explore the impact of the war on Indigenous populations. Despite the significant Indigenous involvement in various activities of World War II and exposure to the enormous diversity of warships, military aircraft and other war materiel involved, it is a conundrum that there is a distinct lack of introduced imagery associated with this period in the contact rock art assemblages of western Arnhem Land.

The warship painting at Djulirri

Djulirri is a large rock-shelter complex and the main shelter contains approximately 1300 rock art paintings, of which 29 are paintings of transportation, consisting of Macassan ($n = 2$) and European ships and boats ($n = 25$) and a single depiction each of a wagon and biplane (May et al. 2010; Taçon 2018; Taçon et al. 2010, 2012). The images of the Indonesian praus have been radiocarbon dated to a period starting from c. 1650 CE indicating an extended period of Indigenous interaction with foreign maritime activities (Taçon et al. 2010). Identification of the types of shipping vessels is a familiar constituent of wartime history and maritime archaeology (Dellino-Musgrave 2006; Green 1990; McCarthy 2001; Staniforth and Nash 2008). Using similar methods that were developed for the identification of shipwrecks, as used in maritime archaeology, it is possible to identify ship types represented in the rock art (Burningham 1994, 2000; Wesley et al. 2012). The rock art painting of the warship depicts the port side view of the naval vessel (Figure 13.3). It has been illustrated with an outline and solid infill technique with white, grey and black pigments. The white and grey illustrates the deliberate use of two pigment tones, illustrating a waterline and a distinctive keel shape. It has two masts with lines connecting the masts and a forward stay to the bow (Figure 13.3). The detail of the lines is typical of a modern naval radio array. There are two guns depicted, fore and aft. A single funnel is shown. A bridge is located forward on top of the superstructure above the deck. The bow and stern are steep and not curving like many other ship paintings in the site (Figure 13.3).

Figure 13.3. Line drawing and photograph of Djulirri ship.
Source: Daryl Wesley and Virginia das Neves.

Significantly, there were many naval ships operating in Northern Territory coastal waters during this period (Rayner 2001). RAN corvette ships like the HMAS *Castlemaine*, HMAS *Cootamundra*, HMAS *Latrobe* and armed motor launches escorted cargo ships to provide protection against Japanese air force attack (Alford 2011). However, the shape and configuration of these other ships do not match the profile of the ship motif at Djulirri, which closely resembles that of HMAS *Moresby* (May et al. 2013). The colour scheme, fore and aft masts, radio array, guns without turrets (as they are not distinguished from the upper structure), the very low bow and stern to the waterline and distinctive rectangular depiction of the superstructure are all features that closely mirror the design of the HMAS *Moresby*. When compared with photographs there are similarities in the layout of the masts, rigging and superstructure. In contrast to other warships of the interwar and wartime periods, very few ships with twin mast configurations were operating and fewer still in Northern Territory waters. The depiction of the forward and rear guns suggests that this is a representation of the HMAS *Moresby* in a re-armed configuration for World War II escort duty.

Figure 13.4. HMAS *Moresby* c. 1933, Bowen Queensland.
Source: Joseph William Bell, State Library of Queensland (John Oxley Library). Copyright expired.

The HMAS *Moresby* was tasked with undertaking coastal surveys and improving nautical charts along the Arnhem Land coast. HMAS *Moresby*, formerly HMS *Silvio*, was put into service with the RAN in 1925 (Bastock 1975:100). The *Moresby* is shown in Figure 13.4 as having both fore and aft masts, which was an unusual feature for modern warships (Bastock 1975:100). The shape of the ship is also unusual: it was built by the British in World War I as an anti-submarine escort and therefore had a distinctive profile. The bow and stern looked very similar, to confuse U-boats as to which way the ship was heading (Bastock 1975; O'Connell 1994). The *Moresby* was converted for use in a surveying role between 1926 and 1929. O'Connell (1994:6) describes its conversion in 1925, writing that both bow and stern of the

> Moresby seem to have emerged to be again identical. The guns were removed. A long wide boat deck was superimposed at the bridge wheelhouse level and a suite suited to the needs of a captain of such a vessel added aft of the 'dummy' bridge.

The presence and absence of major armaments for peacetime duty is critical for chronological identification of the Djulirri rock art motif.

Recommissioned in 1935, the *Moresby* was sent to Darwin to survey the Clarence Strait in Northern Territory waters (Bastock 1975:100; O'Connell 1994:6). At the outbreak of World War II, HMAS *Moresby* was re-armed for patrolling the east coast of Australia and convoy escort duties in 1941 (Bastock 1975:100). After 1941, the *Moresby* made numerous appearances in Darwin during the war years, operating in the South West Pacific Area (SWPA) on convoy escort duty. This period of service after 1941, when the HMAS *Moresby* was re-armed, becomes a significant factor for identifying the Djulirri motif. In 1935, during coastal charting service in the north, when encounters between the HMAS *Moresby* and Indigenous people in Queensland and the Northern Territory first occurred, the *Moresby* was missing the forward and rear guns. The *Northern Standard* reported in 1935 that the Aboriginal crew, aboard the *Moresby* while the ship was conducting survey work, complained of their working conditions, undertaking the majority of 'heavier and dirtier' tasks, as well as their low wages. The article goes on to say that the Aboriginal crew had 'warned other boys not to accept employment should the vessel return to Darwin waters for survey work' (*Northern Standard* 1935:9). Furthermore, support for the ship motif relating to Indigenous contact during its wartime service can be found in a 1944 photograph from the Australian War Memorial. Figure 13.5 shows the crew from the HMAS *Moresby* interacting with local Tiwi Island Traditional Owners as guides on a shooting party near the Snake Bay flying boat base on Melville Island.

Figure 13.5. HMAS *Moresby* shooting party on Melville Island.
Source: Australian War Memorial (P02305-019).

The aircraft painting at Maliwawa

The Maliwawa complex is formed by three major rock-shelters with a series of smaller rock art panels interspersed around a small sandstone outlier of the Wellington Range (Wesley, Litster, O'Connor et al. 2018). The main gallery of the Maliwawa art site contains 542 paintings, beeswax figures, stencils, drawings, a print and an engraving (Taçon et al. 2012:432). A painting of an aircraft is depicted in a perspective manner, like some of the ships on the Djulirri panel (Figure 13.2). The motif has been painted using an outline and solid infill method, with further line infill to create details of feature within the painting (Figure 13.6). The outline and line infill are painted in black pigment with a combination of red and yellow pigment infill. The motif has well-defined aircraft characteristics which illustrate the fuselage, monoplane wings, a vertical stabiliser (rudder), possible horizontal stabiliser (elevator), cockpit and fuselage windows and a RAAF roundel on the fuselage behind the main wing. In consultation with the Australian War Memorial's curator of aircraft, this aircraft was identified as the Avro Anson, operated by the RAAF during World War II (John White, pers. comm. 2011). The RAAF were operating squadrons with Avro Anson aircraft in the Northern Territory from 1938 to 1945.

Figure 13.6. Rock art motif and D-stretch image of the aircraft from Maliwawa.
Source: Daryl Wesley.

Figure 13.7. RAAF Avro Anson circa 1940 in flight.
Source: Australian War Memorial (P128002). Copyright expired, public domain.

The Avro Anson was a twin-engine aircraft designed as a light bomber. The RAAF began to acquire the British built planes (Figure 13.7) in 1936 and later went on to operate 1028 of them in Australia (RAAF Museum 2009). RAAF Avro Anson squadrons began to arrive in Darwin in 1938 as part of the Northern Territory coastal defence build-up, firstly on long-distance flying tests, and then posted on a permanent basis in 1939 (Alford 2011; *Northern Standard* 1938:4). With the outbreak of World War II, the Avro Anson squadrons were tasked with aerial survey and photography of the Northern Territory coastline and had begun regular patrols of the Arnhem Land coast by December 1939 (Alford 2011:14; *Northern Standard* 1939:4). Early in the Pacific War, the Avro Anson was found to be a poor performer as a bomber or attack aircraft and was then relegated to supply and transport duties in the Northern Territory through World War II (Alford 2011:171–173). Avro Anson aircraft were used by the No. 6 Communications Unit (notably commanded by Flight Lieutenant Clyde C Fenton, the renowned Northern Territory Flying Doctor, well known to Indigenous communities) to transport and supply remote RAAF stations during World War II (Alford 2011:171–173). The 309 Radar Station (309RS) based on North Goulburn Island from 1943 to 1945 was regularly supplied, via the South Goulburn Island Mission airstrip, by a variety of RAAF aircraft including the Avro Anson (Nottle 2007:106; Vahtrick 2007:113).

These aircraft were marked with the traditional red, white and blue roundels. After the Allies engaged in combat with Japanese air forces from December 1941, the RAAF ordered the removal of the red centre from the roundel owing to numerous 'friendly fire' incidents during the Malayan campaigns in June 1942—the Allied aircraft's roundels were easily confused with the Japanese Rising Sun air force symbol (Dunn 2003). All RAAF aircraft from June 1942 to 1945 were marked with blue and white identification roundels painted on the wings and fuselage (Cochrane and Elliot 1998:13). This is a significant temporal identifier for depictions of RAAF aircraft in the Northern Territory during World War II. The roundel on the aircraft motif at Maliwawa is significant, as it is depicted in the tricolour style with a red circle in the centre. Given that the tricolour roundel (red, white and blue) was replaced by the bicolour roundel (blue and white) in August 1942 (Dunn 2003), the painter witnessed this aircraft between late 1938 and August 1942. Therefore, this motif could not have been painted before 1938. The painting is very likely to reflect the artists' wartime experience of observing the aircraft between 1938 and 1942 and suggests that this motif was painted at Maliwawa during the wartime period.

End of contact imagery in rock art

The western Arnhem Land sandstone plateau holds an enormous body of Indigenous rock art spanning from the Pleistocene through to the recent past, recognised as one of the greatest rock art precincts in the world (Chaloupka 1993; Flood 1997; Layton 1992; Morwood 2002). The introduced imagery of Macassan and European material culture greatly assists in developing an almost decadal chronology for western Arnhem Land contact rock art. Methods to classify the ships painted in rock art have been established where studies can reliably identify the type and class of the ship; however, only a few are identified by name (Burningham 1994, 2000; May et al. 2013; O'Connor and Arrow 2008; Roberts 2004; Taçon et al. 2010; Wesley et al. 2012). Despite these methodological difficulties, Arnhem Land rock art researchers have attempted to identify historical individuals (e.g. the explorer Leichhardt), named ships and aircraft depicted in rock art paintings (Chaloupka 1993; Gunn et al. 2012; May et al. 2010, 2013; Roberts 2004; Roberts and Parker 2003). The distortions of time that are generally referred to as a problem for ethnographic analogy are far less problematic when dealing with a warship motif with a date unlikely to be older than 1945, when the HMAS *Moresby* was reaching the end of its service life. Aircraft also prove to be excellent chronological markers owing to rapid changes in design and technology. Because the aircraft motif painted at Maliwawa can be dated to a very specific period between 1939 and 1942, the artwork would have probably been painted in response to early wartime experiences of Indigenous people residing in the region or at the nearby South Goulburn Island Mission of Warruwi.

Porr and Bell (2012) challenge the primacy of Western scientific and literary academic methodologies in the study of Aboriginal rock art. They state that Indigenous ways of knowing need to be utilised seriously in a critical re-evaluation of the Western scientific endeavour (Porr and Bell 2012:15). Hodder (1998:65) would argue that the painting of the warship and aircraft motifs are part of an intellectual body of knowledge and work that should be differentiated from that of practical consciousness or habitus. Equally, Layton (1998:71) argues that in Aboriginal society creative retelling is inherent in the structure of Aboriginal cognition. Layton (1992:73) contends that Indigenous communities are trying to make sense of wholly new experiences to which they were subject during the colonial period, which is revealed through their creative endeavours. Baker (2005:17) challenges historical orthodoxies in the examination of the history of Arnhem Land in relation to Aboriginal mission history where 'invasion narratives speak of the chaos associated with un-negotiated crossing of boundaries, trespass, intrusion, death, disruption, dislocation and destruction of local culture'. Baker (2005:17) identifies that concepts of negotiation and consent vary greatly during the mission occupation of Arnhem Land throughout the early twentieth century. There are many examples of Indigenous groups owning their version of the historical narrative of negotiation with outsiders entering Arnhem Land (Baker 2005). Therefore, the rock art at Djulirri and Maliwawa are very likely to be an important layer of this Indigenous ownership of a post-colonial narrative and experience.

The twentieth-century ships that share the same rock art panel as the warship motif at Djulirri represent specific points in time when European contact experiences were still being represented through a traditional idiom (Layton 1998:73). In eastern Arnhem Land, contemporary Indigenous artistic practices continue to include imagery from the precolonial period, representing Macassan culture contact, which has been incorporated into Yolngu history and dreaming (McIntosh 1996, 2006, 2009; Morphy 1991; Sutton 1988). Layton (1998:76) states that:

> it can be argued that there is both a strong, conservative strand in traditional Aboriginal society, which has enabled the impact of colonialism to be withstood, and for traditional rights to land to be asserted in a traditional idiom, and also a creative strand which repeatedly generates new variants of cultural practices and, more rarely, transforms the cultural structure itself.

Relationships that developed through long periods of culture contact—as with the Macassans—manage to penetrate through cultural structures and have lasting incorporation into traditional narratives, language and mythology (McIntosh 1996, 2006, 2009; Morphy 1991; Ryan 1990; Wiseman 1996); whereas culture contact with Europeans and experiences of World War II may generate a new variant of cultural practice such as painting European ships and aircraft, but emerge for a very limited period in Indigenous rock art production in western Arnhem Land.

World War II imagery is notably lacking in both the rock art record and the contemporary artistic traditions of Arnhem Land, despite the proliferation of personnel, ships, vehicles and aircraft in the Northern Territory. Gunn et al. (2012:63) establish a well-defined record of customary designs during the post-contact Indigenous rock art produced from 1845 to 1940. These motifs consist of polychrome x-ray paintings and designs that dominate Nawarla Gabarnmang (Gunn et al. 2012:63). The introduced contact image of a horse at Nawarla Gabarnmang is found underneath many layers of customary zoomorphic x-ray imagery painted within a 95-year time span (Gunn et al. 2012:61). Therefore, the Indigenous rock art painting experience demonstrated by Gunn et al. (2012) at Nawarla Gabarnmang illustrates the primacy of customary motifs and designs in Indigenous rock art production. In the case of wider western Arnhem Land, introduced contact imagery, such as European ships, people, boats, animals and guns are seldom represented in post–World War II traditional Indigenous art production (McLean 2011; Ryan 1990; Sutton 1988; Taylor 1999). Bardayal 'Lofty' Nadjamerrek identified three rock-shelter sites where he painted customary imagery in the years immediately following World War II, when he was travelling between the Maranboy tin mine and Gunbalanya (Peter Cooke, pers. comm. 2017). Brandl (1982:31, 69, 124–125) documented experiences working with Mandarg and Jacky Bunggarnial in 1969, where both had produced rock art paintings using customary anthropomorphic imagery, a crocodile design and a rainbow serpent in Cadell River rock-shelters. Chaloupka (1993:241) also describes the postwar activities of artists such as Nayombolmi, Djimongurr and Djorlom, who painted various traditional anthropomorphic and zoomorphic rock art motifs within different areas of Arnhem Land. These are all examples that illustrate the primacy of cultural structures represented by traditional motifs and cultural designs in the Indigenous art production of western Arnhem Land.

Contrasting this, history and oral history attest to the immense impact of World War II on Indigenous society in northern Australia (Hall 1980, 1997; Riseman 2007, 2010, 2012a, 2012b; Saunders 1995; Trudgen 2000). These experiences were varied and differed significantly from any that Indigenous communities had encountered before, or after, in terms of the size and scale of personnel and material culture. Therefore, the absence of these experiences in rock art is at odds with how Indigenous people had previously expressed their cross-cultural experiences with abundant contact rock art imagery. This cannot be explained via an absence of occupation of western Arnhem Land either. Indigenous occupation and mobility in Arnhem Land substantially increased during the war years as many Aboriginal families lived on Country to avoid internment. We propose that by the 1940s, there had been a fundamental shift in Indigenous perceptions of Europeans and material culture as the 'other'. Therefore, ships, aircraft, vehicles and material culture had started to become part of the larger normative Indigenous experience. Material culture such as ships, aircraft, trucks, bicycles, firearms, carts and cars, which have all been noted in the rock art record of western Arnhem Land, had now become part of the normative social and economic life of Indigenous society. As a result, this repertoire of introduced imagery significantly diminished in Indigenous artistic production within rock-shelters in Arnhem Land post–World War II.

Conclusion

Despite the increase in naval shipping and aircraft across the Northern Territory coastline during World War II, this period of conflict is represented in the Indigenous rock art record in the Wellington Range by only a single ship at Djulirri and an aircraft at Maliwawa. The World War II chronological timeline provides a significant platform to discuss the implications of transformations in cross-cultural interactions for local Aboriginal people operating in a much larger maritime seascape and landscape than their local estates and territories prior to Macassan and European contact (Clarke 2000a, 2000b; Clarke and Frederick 2006, 2008, 2011; Porr and Bell 2012). Importantly, it marks the decline of contact rock art in the region and heralds a period of marked change in rock art production, reflecting the manner in which engagement with Europeans had become part of the 'normative' experience in Indigenous society in western Arnhem Land by the 1940s.

Acknowledgements

This research was funded by an Australian Research Council Linkage grant (LP0882985), and was supported by a Discovery Early Career Researcher Award to Daryl Wesley (DE170101447). First, the authors would like to acknowledge Traditional Owners Ronald Lamilami and his family for their permission and support to undertake the fieldwork and use the information for this chapter. The authors would like to acknowledge the assistance with the identification of maritime features by Jennifer McKinnon and Jason Raupp. Fieldwork was conducted in collaboration with Paul Taçon and Sally K May and the Picturing Change project. Fieldwork was facilitated by Ian White, the Northern Land Council and the Jabiru Regional Office. Additional assistance in the field was kindly provided by Cameco Australia, Office of the Supervising Scientist, the Northern Territory Department of Natural Resources, Environment and the Arts, and the Bushfires Council of the Northern Territory. Aircraft identification was aided by John White (former curator of aircraft, Australian War Memorial) and Michael Pearson assisted with identifying the naval warship. Permission to reproduce Figures 13.4, 13.5 and 13.7 was obtained from the Australian War Memorial. The final chapter has benefited from comments and suggestions made by Sally Brockwell and Mirani Litster.

References

Adcock, N. 1999. *A history of 309 radar station.* Neville Adcock, Drumoyne.

Alford, B. 2011. *Darwin's air war, 1942–1945: An illustrated history.* Aviation History Society of the Northern Territory, Darwin.

Baker, G. 2005. Crossing boundaries: Negotiated space and the construction of narratives of missionary incursion. *Journal of Northern Territory History* 16:17–28.

Ball, D. 1991. *Aborigines in the defence of Australia.* Australian National University Press, Canberra.

Barrett, C. 1946. *Coast of adventure: Untamed northern Australia.* Robertson and Mullens, Melbourne.

Bastock, J. 1975. *Australia's ships of war.* Angus and Robertson Publishers, Sydney.

Brandl, E.J. 1982. *Australian Aboriginal paintings in Western and Central Arnhem Land: Temporal sequences and elements of style in Cadell River and Deaf Adder Creek Art.* Australian Institute of Aboriginal Studies, Canberra.

Burningham, N. 1994. Aboriginal nautical art: A record of the Macassans and the pearling industry in the Northern Territory. *The Great Circle* 16:139–151.

Burningham, N. 2000. Sublime but not ridiculous: Observations on the technical analysis of ships of first contact represented in various genre of art. *Bulletin of the Australasian Institute for Maritime Archaeology* 24:63–70.

Chaloupka, G. 1988. Groote Eylandt Archipelago rock art survey 1988. An unpublished report to the Heritage Branch, Conservation Commission of the Northern Territory. NT Government, Darwin.

Chaloupka, G. 1993. *Journey in Time: The 50,000-year story of the Australian rock art of Arnhem Land.* Reed Books Australia, Sydney.

Chaloupka, G. 1996. Praus in Marege: Makassan subjects in Aboriginal rock art of Arnhem Land Northern Territory, Australia. *Anthropologie* 2:131–142.

Clarke, A. 2000a. Time, tradition and transformations: The negotiation of cross-cultural engagements on Groote Eylandt, northern Australia. In R. Torrence and A. Clarke (eds), *The archaeology of difference: Negotiating cross cultural engagements in Oceania*, pp. 1–31. Routledge, London.

Clarke, A. 2000b. The moormans trowsers: Macassan and Aboriginal interactions and the changing fabric of Indigenous social life. In S. O'Connor and P. Veth (eds), *East of the Wallace Line: Studies of past and present maritime cultures of the Indo-Pacific region*, pp. 315–335. AA Balkeman, Rotterdam.

Clarke, A. and U. Frederick 2006. Closing the distance: Interpreting cross-cultural engagements through Indigenous rock art. In I. Lilley (ed.), *Archaeology in Oceania: Australia and the Pacific Islands*, pp. 116–133. Blackwell Publishing, Oxford. doi.org/10.1002/9780470773475.ch6.

Clarke, A. and U. Frederick 2008. The mark of marvellous ideas: Groote Eylandt rock art and the performance of cross-cultural ideas. In P. Veth, P. Sutton and M. Neale (eds), *Strangers on the shore: Early coastal contacts in Australia*, pp. 148–164. National Museum of Australia, Canberra.

Clarke, A. and U. Frederick 2011. Making a sea change: Rock art, archaeology and the enduring legacy of Frederick McCarthy's research on Groote Eylandt. In M. Thomas and M. Neale (eds), *Exploring the legacy of the 1948 American-Australian scientific expedition to Arnhem Land*, pp. 135–155. ANU E Press, Canberra. doi.org/10.22459/elale.06.2011.07.

Cochrane, J. and S. Elliott 1998. *Military aircraft insignia of the world.* Airlife Publishing, Shrewsbury.

Cole, K. 1980. *Seafarers of the Groote archipelago: Aborigines and mariners of the islands off Eastern Arnhem Land.* Keith Cole Publications, Bendigo.

Dellino-Musgrave, V. 2006. *Maritime archaeology and social relations: British action in the southern hemisphere.* Springer Series in Underwater Archaeology 28. Springer, New York.

Dunn, P. 2003. A case of mistaken Identity during WW2. *Australia at war.* www.ozatwar.com/friendlyfire/mistakenidentity.htm. Accessed 10 February 2013.

Edwards, R. 1979. *Australian Aboriginal art: The art of the Alligator Rivers Region, Northern Territory.* Australian Institute of Aboriginal Studies, Canberra.

Flood, J. 1997. *Rock art of the Dreamtime: Images of ancient Australia.* Angus & Robertson, Sydney.

Foley, M. 1982. History of the Cox Peninsula. Unpublished manuscript. Held in the Northern Territory Collection, Northern Territory Library (NTC 994.295 FOL).

Gray, G. 2006. Stanner's war: WEH Stanner, the Pacific War and its Aftermath. *Journal of Pacific History* 41(2):145–163. doi.org/10.1080/00223340600826045.

Green, J. 1990. *Maritime archaeology: A technical handbook*. Academic Press, London.

Grey, J. 1999. *A military history of Australia*. Cambridge University Press, Melbourne.

Gunn, R.G. 1988. Rock Art in Kudjumarndi and Kukalak Areas—Western Arnhem Land. Unpublished Report to the Northern Land Council.

Gunn, R.G., R. Whear and L. Douglas 2012. Dating the present at Nawarla Gabarnmang: Time and function in the art of a major Jawoyn rock art and occupation site in western Arnhem Land. *Australian Archaeology* 75:55–65. doi.org/10.1080/03122417.2012.11681950.

Hall, R. 1980. Aborigines, the army and the second World War in Northern Australia. *Aboriginal History* 4(1/2):72–95. doi.org/10.22459/ah.04.2011.05.

Hall, R. 1997. *The black diggers: Aborigines and Torres Strait Islanders in the second World War*. Aboriginal Studies Press, Canberra.

Hodder, I. 1998. Creative thought: A long-term perspective. In S. Mithen (ed.), *Creativity in human evolution and prehistory*, pp. 44–56. Routledge, London.

Keen, I. 1980. Alligator Rivers Stage II Land Claim. Unpublished report to the Northern Land Council.

Layton, R. 1992. *Australian rock art: A new synthesis*. Cambridge University Press, Cambridge.

Layton, R. 1998. Creative thought in traditional Aboriginal society. In S. Mithen (ed.), *Creativity in human evolution and prehistory*, pp. 78–89. Routledge, London. doi.org/10.4324/9780203978627-11.

Layton, R. and N. Williams 1980. The Finniss River land claim: A claim on unalienated Crown Land in the Adelaide River-Batchelor-Wagait Reserve Area of the Northern Territory. Unpublished report to the Northern Land Council.

May, S.K., P.S.C. Taçon, D. Wesley and M. Travers 2010. Painting history: Indigenous observations and depictions of the 'other' in northwestern Arnhem Land, Australia. *Australian Archaeology* 70:29–37. doi.org/10.1080/03122417.2010.11689384.

May, S.K., P.S.C. Taçon, D. Wesley and M. Pearson 2013. Painted ships on a painted Arnhem Land landscape. *The Great Circle* 35(2):83–102.

McCarthy, M. 2001. *Iron and steamship archaeology: Success and failure on the SS Xantho*. Plenum Publishers, New York. doi.org/10.1007/b109955.

McIntosh, I.S. 1996. Islam and Australia's Aborigines? A perspective from north-east Arnhem Land. *Journal of Religious History* 20(1):53–77. doi.org/10.1111/j.1467-9809.1996.tb00692.x.

McIntosh, I.S. 2006. A treaty with the Macassans? Burrumarra and the Dholtji ideal. *The Asia Pacific Journal of Anthropology* 7(2):153–172. doi.org/10.1080/14442210600763181.

McIntosh, I.S. 2009. Pre-Macassans at Dholtji? Exploring one of north-east Arnhem Land's great conundrums. In P. Veth, P. Sutton and M. Neale (eds), *Strangers on the shore: Early coastal contacts in Australia*, pp. 165–180. National Museum of Australia, Canberra.

McLean, I. 2011. *How Aborigines invented the idea of contemporary art*. Institute of Modern Art and Power Publications, Sydney.

Morphy, H. 1991. *Ancestral connections: Art and an Aboriginal system of knowledge.* University of Chicago Press, Chicago.

Morwood, M.J. 2002. *Visions from the past: The archaeology of Australian rock art.* Allen and Unwin, Crow's Nest.

Mountford, C.P. 1956. *Art, myth and symbolism: Records of the American-Australian scientific expedition to Arnhem Land.* Melbourne University Press, Melbourne.

Northern Standard 1935. Work on the 'Moresby'. 23 August. nla.gov.au/nla.news-article49426342.

Northern Standard 1938. Cabinet speeds up defence. 22 November. nla.gov.au/nla.news-article49451673.

Northern Standard 1939. Aerial Reconnaissance. 5 May. nla.gov.au/nla.news-article49455328.

Nottle, A.G. 2007. A grass fire on North Goulburn Island (309RS). In E. Simmonds and N. Smith (eds), *Radar yarns: Being memories and stories collected from personnel who served in RAAF ground based radar in World War II or a potpourri of people, places, problems and pleasantries,* p. 106. Radar Returns, Hampton.

O'Connell, J. 1994. *HMAS Moresby 1925–1946.* Naval Historical Society of Australia Monograph No. 38. Naval Historical Society of Australia, Garden Island.

O'Connor, S. and S. Arrow 2008. Boat images in the rock art of northern Australia with particular reference to the Kimberley, Western Australia. In G. Clark, F. Leach and S. O'Connor (eds), *Islands of inquiry: Colonisation, seafaring and the archaeology of maritime landscapes,* pp. 397–409. ANU E Press, Canberra. doi.org/10.22459/ta29.06.2008.25.

Porr, M. and H.R. Bell 2012. 'Rock-art', 'animism' and two-way thinking: Towards a complementary epistemology in the understanding of material culture and 'rock-art' of hunting and gathering people. *Journal of Archaeological Method and Theory* 19(1):161–205. doi.org/10.1007/s10816-011-9105-4.

Powell, A. 1982. *Far country: A short history of the Northern Territory.* Melbourne University Press, Melbourne.

RAAF Museum 2009. A4 Avro Anson. Viewed 15 June 2021. www.airforce.gov.au/sites/default/files/minisite/static/7522/RAAFmuseum/research/aircraft/series2/A4.htm.

Rayner, R.J. 2001. *Darwin and Northern Territory Force.* Rudder Press, Illawarra.

Riseman, N.J. 2007. Defending whose country? Yolngu and the Northern Territory special reconnaissance unit in the Second World War. *Limina: A Journal of Historical and Cultural Studies* 13:80–91.

Riseman, N.J. 2010. Contesting white knowledge: Yolngu stories from World War II. *Oral History Review* 37(2):170–190. doi.org/10.1093/ohr/ohq051.

Riseman, N.J. 2012a. Rectifying 'the Great Australian Silence'? Creative representations of Australian Indigenous Second World War service. *Australian Aboriginal Studies* 1:35–48.

Riseman, N.J. 2012b. *Defending whose country? Indigenous soldiers in the Pacific War.* University of Nebraska Press, Lincoln. doi.org/10.2307/j.ctt1ddr6qd.

Ritchie, D. and T. Bauman 1991. Limilngan-Wulna (Lower Adelaide and Mary Rivers) Land Claim: Senior Anthropologists' Report 1. Unpublished report to the Northern Land Council.

Roberts, D.A. 2004. Nautical themes in the Aboriginal rock paintings of Mount Borradaile, western Arnhem Land. *The Great Circle* 26(1):19–50.

Roberts, D.A. and A. Parker 2003. *Ancient ochres: The Aboriginal rock paintings of Mount Borradaile.* J.B. Books, Marleston.

Ryan, J. 1990. *Spirit in land: Bark paintings from Arnhem Land in the National Gallery of Victoria.* National Gallery of Victoria, Melbourne.

Saunders, K. 1995. Inequalities of sacrifice: Aboriginal and Torres Strait Islander labour in northern Australia during the Second World War. *Labour History* 69:131–148. doi.org/10.2307/27516395.

Staniforth, M. and M. Nash (eds) 2008. *Maritime archaeology: Australian approaches.* Springer Series in Underwater Archaeology. Springer, New York. doi.org/10.1007/b136782.

Sutton, P. 1988. Responding to Aboriginal Art. In P. Sutton (ed.), *Dreamings: The art of Aboriginal Australia*, pp. 33–58. Viking, New York.

Taçon, P.S.C. 2018. From rock art to contemporary art: Indigenous depictions of trains, planes and automobiles. *Australian Archaeology* 84(3):281–293. doi.org/10.1080/03122417.2018.1543095.

Taçon, P.S.C., S.K. May, S. Fallon, M. Travers, D. Wesley and R. Lamilami 2010. A minimum age for early depictions of southeast Asian praus in the rock art of Arnhem Land, Northern Territory. *Australian Archaeology* 71:1–10. doi.org/10.1080/03122417.2010.11689379.

Taçon, P.S.C., J. Ross, A. Paterson and S.K. May 2012. Picturing change and changing pictures: Contact period rock art of Australia. In J. McDonald and P. Veth (eds), *A companion to rock art*, pp. 420–436. Wiley-Blackwell, West Sussex. doi.org/10.1002/9781118253892.ch24.

Taylor, L. 1999. Rainbows in the water: Western Arnhem Land, Northern Territory. In L. Taylor (ed.), *Painting the land story*, pp. 33–52. National Museum of Australia, Canberra.

Trudgen, R. 2000. *Why warriors lie down and die: Towards an understanding of why the Aboriginal people of Arnhem Land face the greatest crisis in health and education since European contact.* DoctorZed Publishing, Darwin.

Turner, D.H. 1973. The rock art of Bickerton Island in comparative perspective. *Oceania* 43 (4):286–325. doi.org/10.1002/j.1834-4461.1973.tb01225.x.

Vahtrick, C. 2007. South Goulburn Island Mission. In E. Simmonds and N. Smith (eds), *Radar yarns: Being memories and stories collected from personnel who served in RAAF ground based radar in World War II or a potpourri of people, places, problems and pleasantries*, pp. 113–114. Radar Returns, Hampton.

Wesley, D., J. McKinnon and J. Raupp 2012. Sails set in stone: A technological analysis of non-indigenous watercraft rock art paintings in North Western Arnhem Land. *Journal of Maritime Archaeology* 7(2):245–269. doi.org/10.1007/s11457-012-9103-z.

Wesley, D., M. Litster, I. Moffat and S. O'Connor 2018. Indigenous built structures and anthropogenic impacts on the stratigraphy of Northern Australian rockshelters: Insights from Malarrak 1, north western Arnhem Land. *Australian Archaeology* 84(1):3–18. doi.org/10.1080/03122417.2018.1436238.

Wesley, D., M. Litster, S. O'Connor, E. Grono, J. Theys et al. 2018. The archaeology of Maliwawa: 25,000 years of occupation in the Wellington Range, Arnhem Land. *Australian Archaeology* 84(2):108–128. doi.org/10.1080/03122417.2018.1521237.

Wiseman, J. 1996. *Thomson time, Arnhem Land in the 1930s: A photographic essay.* Museum of Victoria, Melbourne.

Contributors

Atholl Anderson – The Ngai Tahu Research Centre/Ka Waimaero, University of Canterbury, PB 4800 Christchurch 8140, New Zealand

Jillian Barteaux – Archaeology, University of Western Australia, M257, Stirling Highway, Crawley 6009, Western Australia

Stuart Bedford – Archaeology and Natural History, School of Culture, History and Language, College of Asia and the Pacific, The Australian National University, ACT 2600, Australia; and the Max Planck Institute for the Science of Human History, 07745 Jena, Germany

David Burley – Department of Archaeology, Simon Fraser University, Burnaby, BC V5A 1S6, Canada

Geoffrey Clark – Archaeology and Natural History, School of Culture, History and Language, College of Asia and the Pacific, The Australian National University, ACT 2600, Australia

Christine Cooper – Bibra Lake Residents Association, Western Australia

Boyd Dixon – Cardno-GS and SEARCH Inc., 425 Chalan San Antonio Rd, PMB 1004, Tamuning, Guam 96913

Nic Grguric – Independent scholar

Andrea Jalandoni – Place, Evolution and Rock Art Heritage Unit, Griffith Centre for Social and Cultural Research, Australian Research Centre of Human Evolution, Environmental Futures Research Institute, Griffith University, Gold Coast, Queensland, Australia

Maria Kottermair – Griffith Centre for Social and Cultural Research, Griffith University, Gold Coast, Queensland, Australia

Jolie Liston – Micronesian Heritage Consulting LLC, Hagåtña, Guam 96932

Mirani Litster – Archaeology and Natural History, School of Culture, History and Language, College of Asia and the Pacific, The Australian National University, ACT 2600; the Centre for Creative and Cultural Research, University of Canberra, ACT 2617; and the College of Arts, Society and Education, James Cook University, Queensland 4870, Australia

Vincent Marolleau – Université de la Polynésie française, Centre International de Recherche Archéologique en Polynésie (CIRAP), Campus d'Outumaoro, B.P. 6570-98702 Faa'a, Tahiti, Polynésie Française

Helene Martinsson-Wallin – Department of Archaeology and Ancient History, Uppsala University, Campus Gotland, Cramérgatan 3, 62267 Visby, Sweden

Malia Melekiola – Lapaha Village, Tongatapu, Kingdom of Tonga

Guillaume Molle – School of Archaeology and Anthropology, College of Arts and Social Sciences, The Australian National University, ACT 2600, Australia

Sven Ouzman – Archaeology, University of Western Australia, M257, Stirling Highway, Crawley 6009, Western Australia

Colin Pardoe – Archaeology and Natural History, School of Culture, History and Language, College of Asia and the Pacific, The Australian National University, ACT 2600, Australia

Phillip Parton – Archaeology and Natural History, School of Culture, History and Language, College of Asia and the Pacific, The Australian National University, Canberra, ACT 2600, Australia

Christian Reepmeyer – College of Arts, Society and Education, Centre for Tropical Environmental and Sustainability Studies, James Cook University, Cairns, Queensland, 4870, Australia; and Archaeology and Natural History, School of Culture, History and Language, College of Asia and the Pacific, The Australian National University, Canberra, ACT 2600, Australia

The UWA Archaeology Fieldschool Class of 2017 – Department of Archaeology, University of Western Australia, M257, Stirling Highway, Crawley 6009, Western Australia

Jessica Viney – Independent scholar

Daryl Wesley – Archaeology, College of Humanities, Arts and Social Science, Flinders University, Bedford Park, SA 5042, Australia

www.ingramcontent.com/pod-product-compliance
Lightning Source LLC
Chambersburg PA
CBHW061124010526
44114CB00029B/3000